In the early hours of 1 September 1983 a Korean Airlines Boeing 747 was shot down by a Soviet fighter and plunged into the Sea of Japan with the loss of all its 269 passengers and crew. Reactions around the world were of horror and indignation, and the second Cold War passed into a yet more frigid phase. The Reagan Administration energetically propagated the view that KAL 007 had somehow drifted fatally off course as a result of an unforeseen human or technical error – a view which was, at the time, widely accepted. As time has gone by, however, doubts have grown as to whether this explanation could possibly be true. If not, the credibility of the Reagan Administration's entire Cold War stance is in doubt – which is why the mystery of KAL 007 remains as live and critical an issue as when it was first shot down.

The Oxford political scientist, R. W. Johnson, has studied the case in unprecedented depth, and in this compelling and disturbing book he sets the story in its international and political context, and makes sense, for the first time, of the often bizarre theories which have grown up around the tragedy. At last, with this book, it is possible to reach a final verdict on the mystery of KAL 007.

This book is dedicated to the innocent victims
who died aboard KAL 007 and to the friends and relatives
who grieve for them.

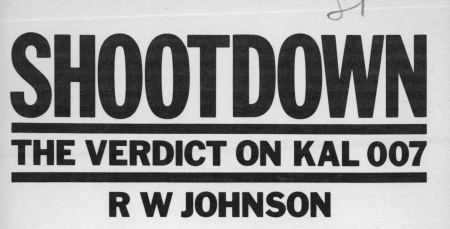

# SHOOTDOWN

## THE VERDICT ON KAL 007

### R W JOHNSON

UNWIN PAPERBACKS
London          Sydney

First published in Great Britain 1986 by
Chatto & Windus Ltd, 40 William IV Street,
London WC2N 4DF
First published in paperback by Unwin® Paperbacks, an imprint of
Unwin Hyman Limited, in 1987

UNWIN HYMAN LIMITED
Denmark House, 37–39 Queen Elizabeth Street,
London SE1 2QB
and
40 Museum Street, London WC1A 1LU

Allen & Unwin Australia Pty Ltd
8 Napier Street, North Sydney, NSW2060, Australia

Unwin Paperbacks with the Port Nicholson Press,
60 Cambridge Terrace, Wellington, New Zealand

British Library Cataloguing in Publication Data

Johnson, R.W. (Richard William)
    Shootdown: the verdict on KAL 007. —
    (Counterpoint).
1. Korean Air Lines Incident, 1983
I. Title
957'.7      E183.S65

ISBN 0–04–327105–7

Printed in Great Britain by
Cox & Wyman Ltd, Reading

# Contents

# Illustrations

# Maps and Figures

# Abbreviations and Acronyms used in the text

| | |
|---|---|
| ABM | Anti-Ballistic Missile |
| ACDA | Arms Control and Disarmament Agency (US) |
| ADIZ | Aerospace Defence Identification Zone |
| AID | Agency for International Development (US) |
| ANC | Air Navigation Commission (ICAO) |
| ASAT | Anti-Satellite (weapon) |
| ASDF | Air Self-Defence Force (Japan) |
| ASW | Anti-Submarine Warfare |
| AWACS | Airborne Warning and Command System |
| | |
| BAM | Baikal–Amur Railway (USSR) |
| | |
| CIA | Central Intelligence Agency (US) |
| COCOM | Co-ordinating Committee on Export Controls |
| COMINT | Communications Intelligence |
| CRITIC | Critical Intelligence (message) |
| CRITICOM | Critical Intelligence Communications |
| | |
| ECM | Electronic Counter Measures |
| ECCM | Electronic Counter-Counter Measures |
| EDT | Eastern Daylight Time (US and Canada) |
| ELINT | Electronic Intelligence |
| EW | Electronic Warfare |
| | |
| FAA | Federal Aviation Administration (US) |
| FAO | Food and Agriculture Organisation |
| FBI | Federal Bureau of Investigation (US) |
| FSS | Flight Service Station |
| | |
| GLASS | Ground Launched Anti-Ship (missile) |
| GMT | Greenwich Mean Time |
| | |
| HF | High Frequency |
| | |
| IATA | International Air Transport Association |
| ICAO | International Civil Aviation Organisation |

| | |
|---|---|
| ICBM | Inter-Continental Ballistic Missile |
| IFALPA | International Federation of Airline Pilots' Association |
| IFF | Identify Friend or Foe (message) |
| IFSS | International Flight Service Station |
| ILO | International Labour Organisation |
| INF | Intermediate Nuclear Force (talks) |
| INS | Inertial Navigation System |
| ITT | International Telephone and Telegraph Corporation |
| KAL | Korean Air Lines (now Korean Air) |
| KCIA | Korean Central Intelligence Organisation (S. Korea) |
| KGB | Komitet Gosudarstvennoy Bezopasnosti (Committee for State Security) (USSR) |
| MHZ | Megaherz |
| MIRV | Multiple Independently Targeted Re-entry Vehicle |
| MSA | Maritime Safety Agency (Japan) |
| MX | Missile Experimental ('The Peacekeeper') (US) |
| NASA | National Aeronautics and Space Administration (US) |
| NATO | North Atlantic Treaty Organisation |
| NICPAC | National Conservative Political Action Committee (US) |
| NORAD | North American Defense (agency) |
| NSA | National Security Agency (US) |
| NSC | National Security Council (US) |
| NSPG | National Security Planning Group (US) |
| NTSB | National Transportation Safety Board (US) |
| OSS | Office of Strategic Services (US) |
| OTH | Over-The-Horizon (radar) |
| PVO | Voiska Protivovozdushnoi Oborony (Soviet Air Defence Force) (USSR) |
| RCAG | Remote Control Air–Ground (radio) |
| ROCC | Regional Operations Command Centre (USAF) |
| SAC | Strategic Air Command (US) |
| SALT | Strategic Arms Limitation Talks |
| SAM | Surface-to-Air Missile |
| SCC | Standing Consultative Commission (US–USSR) |
| SDA | Self-Defence Agency (Japan) |
| SDI | Strategic Defense Initiative ('Star Wars') (US) |

| | |
|---|---|
| SEC | Securities and Exchange Commission (US) |
| SIGINT | Signals Intelligence |
| SLAR | Sideways-Looking Airborne Radar |
| SOSUS | Sound Surveillance System |
| SPINTCOM | Special Intelligence Communications |
| START | Strategic Arms Reduction Talks |
| TACAMO | Take Charge and Move Out (i.e. provision of survivable communications with submerged ballistic missile submarines in case of nuclear war) (US) |
| TELINT | Telemetry Intelligence |
| USAF | United States Air Force |
| USIA | United States Information Agency |
| VDS | Variable Depth Sonar |
| VDU | Visual Display Unit |
| VHF | Very High Frequency |
| VOA | Voice of America |
| VOR | VHF Omni Range (radio beacon) |
| WGF | Western Goals Foundation |

# Foreword

I became interested in the tragedy of KAL 007 in the weeks following its shooting down. Like most people I was horrified at the terrible loss of life and appalled that a civilian airliner had been shot down as a military act: this was no 'ordinary' air disaster. Like many another air traveller, I also felt a more selfish *frisson* of 'There but for the grace of god . . .'. But I was, again like many others, both mystified that the tragedy could ever have taken place and fascinated at its immense political repercussions. I have followed the trail for almost two years since then and this book is the result.

At an early stage I became acutely dissatisfied with the 'official' explanations of the event offered by the Reagan Administration, which seemed to beg too many questions. At the least, it seemed to me, proper consideration had to be given to a variety of other explanations, including the possibility that KAL 007 was, as the Soviet Union alleged (and still maintains today), involved in some form of surveillance mission. In December 1983 I wrote an article for the *Guardian* in which I attempted to explore the hypothesis that KAL 007 might indeed have had some such role and tried to imagine how the Russians might have reacted to and interpreted the flight. This article produced a considerable reaction, both in Britain and elsewhere. A number of conservatives, on both sides of the Atlantic, angrily denounced me on the simple matter of principle that it was unthinkable that the US Administration could ever have morally stooped so low as to endanger a large number of civilian lives as part of a surveillance project. Even to think such thoughts aloud was, they averred, a form of treason in the Cold War. Unfortunately, such critics generally felt it was sufficient to keep to the high ground of principle and were unwilling to confront the many arguments of detail which are the very essence of the matter. This is simply no good. Anyone is welcome to choose their own principles, but the KAL 007 case is, *par excellence*, one where one has to examine such matters as the plane's loading weight, airline procedures, US surveillance capabilities, the surrounding political and strategic circumstances, and so on.

A second type of reaction was the left-wing mirror image of the first. Some of this was simply pro-Soviet. (The Russians, without seeking, let alone acquiring, my permission – indeed, over my angry *post-facto* protest –

reprinted a carefully edited version of the *Guardian* article in the *Soviet Literary Gazette*, omitting all remarks critical of the USSR.) I was immediately invited to join the Anglo–Soviet Friendship Society and to address sundry pro-Soviet or left-wing groups on the 'true facts' of the KAL 007 case. All such invitations I declined, pointing out that what I had set out was merely a hypothesis: it was evident enough that those kind enough to make such invitations also had principles which had caused them to jump to conclusions in just the same way that their conservative counterparts had done. Moreover, I wished to avoid as far as possible the accusation of political bias (in the end an impossible task, of course). And I am, in any case, not a joiner – I am not a member of any political party or group. I was happy to stay that way.

The principal reason why I felt I had to write this book was that two hundred and sixty-nine people, including babies and small children, died in the tragedy of KAL 007. These people, their grieving relatives and friends, and indeed the world at large, deserve nothing less than a full and thorough investigation into the circumstances of that tragedy. To date this has not taken place: all we have had is a rushed, small-scale inquiry by a politically-constrained international organisation, ICAO (the International Civil Aviation Organisation), which was unable to examine even such key documents as the Japanese radar recordings of KAL 007's last minutes, and whose findings, not surprisingly, left the whole matter hanging in the air. This is not good enough. It is, I feel, important to lay out all the evidence that exists to date so that the world can make up its own mind. I feel that it is important for KAL too that all the evidence should be looked at. I make no suggestion in the book that KAL might have directed 007 to fly off course – there is no evidence for that – but the airline is unlikely to win friends by seeking to suppress honest and wide-ranging investigations of other possibilities. I stand ready to alter my ideas further in the light of the further information which a proper, full and thorough investigation might reveal. I have gone as far as I can on the basis of the evidence that currently exists publicly, but it is quite clear that there is more to be known. The greatest success that this book could know would be for that full and proper investigation to take place.

The quest for further information about the whole affair had the effect of bringing me into contact with a great variety of people – airline pilots, aviation officials, technical specialists, journalists and politicians. I have benefited very greatly from these contacts and enjoyed them. It is both a sadness to me and perhaps in the nature of the subject that I am unable to name all those to whom I owe a debt. Happily, though, I can pay tribute to both Fred and Jon Halliday for their crucial early encouragement; to Murray Sayle, who spent several hours pressing me properly and hard about weaknesses in my argument – a session which had a crucial effect on all I wrote; and to Philip J. Klass, who initiated a long and fruitful correspondence with me. I was also grateful for the help given at various points by Wilhelm Bittorf, John Gittins, Haruki Wada, John Keppel, Michael Klare, the late George Martin, David Pearson, Kunihiko Miyoshi, Gideon Remez, Anthony Sampson, Graham Sheppard and Arthur Stockwin. Anne Summers, though involved in an even bigger writing project of her own, gave me all the love and support any writer needs. My son, Dicken – undoubtedly the world's greatest twelve-year-old aviation expert – was an indefatigable and invaluable helper.

The person to whom I owe most, though, is Bob Allardyce. I first met Bob through our mutual concern with the KAL 007 tragedy – of the many Americans who have pursued the mysteries of this affair, Bob is surely the doyen, and it has been a rare privilege to have him as a friend. Not only has Bob brought to bear his many years of flying and technical experience, but he was endlessly generous, both with his time and information. His unselfishness, good humour, and unflinching honesty have placed me for ever in his debt. I am also deeply indebted to Bob's wife, Barbara, who displayed exemplary patience faced by the disturbance of my long transatlantic phone calls and my often complicated arrangements to meet Bob. I am, too, grateful to the generosity of Bob's associate, Jim Gollin.

I was also deeply touched by the many, many people who wrote to me, volunteering information. Mostly particularly I think of the many fine Americans and Canadians who wrote repeatedly to me, evincing their own concern with the tragedy, sending me clippings and tape cassettes, sometimes visiting me in Oxford. I marvelled, as any Englishman must do, at their generosity, their forthright sense of involved citizenship in public affairs, and their sheer openness. Whatever critical notes about American politicians may be sounded in this book, I am second to none in my admiration for these great distinguishing hallmarks of North American society.

I have not sought or enjoyed any access to the Soviet side of this affair. In part this was simply because their press is so much less useful and because it was evident from the slim pickings gained by others who sought access to Soviet sources that there was not a lot of point in trying. But I was also undoubtedly guilty of the normal cowardice which suggests that a reputation for objectivity in the West means one has to avoid reliance on Soviet sources.

It will be apparent that following the KAL 007 affair has involved ploughing through and attempting to understand a vast mass of technical data in many different areas. At the end I felt satisfied that I had mastered what I needed to know – though often thanks only to the greater technical expertise of others. Any mistakes which may remain are, of course, my fault and not theirs.

Finally, it should be noted that the technically correct designation of the plane was KE 007, but I have used the more common 'KAL 007' throughout.

R. W. Johnson
Magdalen College, Oxford
September 1985

# ONE

# The Last Flight of KAL 007

In the early hours of the morning of 1 September 1983 a South Korean 747 jumbo jet, KAL flight 007, was shot down by a Soviet SU-15 ('Flagon') fighter just as the plane was leaving Russian airspace over Sakhalin Island. All the 747's passengers and crew – 269 people in all – were killed. It was the fifth worst air disaster in history, but the circumstances surrounding the plane's destruction also made the tragedy a major turning point in world politics. The already chilly climate of Cold War politics suddenly froze almost solid amidst a welter of furious recrimination, the Americans charging the Russians with deliberate mass murder of innocent civilians and the Russians accusing the US of having deliberately put those lives at risk by sending KAL 007 on an espionage mission. For a while it seemed that the whole structure of international intercourse, which had survived the worst that the 1947–53 Cold War could do, might not survive this time. International air traffic between East and West was interrupted by a series of officially sponsored boycotts and the Soviet Foreign Minister was refused landing rights to attend the UN. The notion that the US should kick the UN out of America – and thus deal it a blow from which it was unlikely to recover – was given support by the American President himself. The arms race between the great powers switched smartly upwards into a yet higher gear. Such moves to break even the most elementary contacts between East and West would presumably be among the last moves in the final weeks of escalation towards nuclear war. This symbolism was deliberate and it was lost on no one.

The world came back from the brink but nothing would bring back those 269 lives. The vision of the innocents in the apocalypse their deaths afforded lingers powerfully and continues to affect the tenor of the Second Cold War. Any sign of a thaw is often greeted in the West with cries that 'we can't forget the Korean airliner', while any negative Soviet move will be said to be all that one could expect of the barbarians who shot down KAL 007. The Russians, whose role as final executioner – witting or unwitting – is not in doubt, have seemed eager from time to time to resume business as usual with all bygones forgotten. But all Russians, Communists or not, are resentfully aware that their characterisation as barbarian brutes has a history of centuries, not decades, in the West. It is the cry which, they feel, has unfairly pursued them down the ages – an ethnic rather than a political slur. So they too cannot forget and have repeatedly returned to what is, in effect, their plea of extenuating circumstances – that they could not know the plane was an airliner and that it was anyway on a surveillance mission.

But the tragedy also refuses to fade because the mystery remains: what *was* KAL 007 doing deep within Soviet airspace? Despite the passage of time and exhaustive investigation, this question has not been conclusively answered, and even many of the basic facts are in dispute. Inevitably, these disputes have become heavily overlaid with the usual wild slanging of the Cold War. Those who raise questions which discomfort one side or the other will quickly find themselves accused of being the conscious agents of a Soviet or CIA disinformation campaign. All this threatens to make the case of KAL 007 into an aerial *Marie Celeste*.

Several possible explanations have been put forward. The most 'obvious' is that the aircraft flew off course as a result of navigational error: either because its Inertial Navigation System (INS) was wrongly programmed; or because it was flying on its magnetic compass alone without realising it. To be plausible either of these explanations would also have to be accompanied by the presumption, as the International Civil Aviation Organisation (ICAO) put it, of 'a considerable degree of lack of alertness and attentiveness on the part of the entire flight crew'.[1] This version of events was, in effect, adopted by the Reagan Administration, with the further gloss that the USSR had shot down the plane despite knowing it was a civilian airliner or as a result of a culpably inadequate attempt to verify that it was.

Such explanations have been rejected by a variety of schools of thought, having in common only their refusal to believe that KAL 007 was off course by accident. The American far Right takes the view that the plane was deliberately lured off course by the Russians – perhaps by a KGB agent inserting a false program in the flight computer, more likely by the use of an electronic ray which disabled 007's navigation equipment. The Soviet intent, they aver, was to murder the head of the John Birch Society, the US Congressman Larry McDonald, who was a passenger on board 007.[2] Less elaborately, some suggest that 007 was deliberately cutting a corner off its scheduled route in order to save fuel. Others argue that the USSR is essentially telling the truth when it claims that the plane was part of a CIA-backed surveillance probe. Finally some have argued that irrespective of whether 007 was off course deliberately or by accident, the US had the means to know that this was so and culpably failed to inform the plane or the USSR that this was so.

This book will attempt to assess all these theories, weighing both the evidence and the probability of each in turn, but readers will, inevitably, have to decide for themselves what they finally believe. But the book is also concerned to examine how and why the tragedy had the impact that it did. This is not a question of small moment. History reveals numerous examples of wars which have stemmed from 'arranged' incidents and political manipulation of their meaning: the Ems telegram triggered the Franco–Prussian war; the *Lusitania* sinking and the Zimmerman telegram were crucial to American entry into the First World War; the arranged incident of the Tonkin Gulf provided *casus belli* for the Americans in Vietnam. Given the far greater reach and immediacy of the modern media, the danger now exists that escalation towards nuclear war could derive from nothing more substantial than a manipulated incident and the stampeding of mass opinion through an all-out media campaign. The arms race of the 1980s and the heightened Cold War tensions which are both its cause and result thus place a particularly heavy responsibility on the great powers. Not only is it incumbent on them to avoid the risk of major incidents (and in the case of KAL 007 certainly one and possibly both the superpowers were taking fearful risks), but also an equal importance attaches to the way they react publicly, in front of the media, should such an incident occur. Again, as one studies reactions to the tragedy of KAL 007 it is difficult not to conclude that several of the leading actors behaved with a questionable regard for their responsibilities.

First, however, let us summarise the main facts of the flight of KAL 007.

The plane started its flight from John F. Kennedy airport, New York, on 31 August at 11.05 pm New York time (i.e. 04.05 hours GMT, which this account will use henceforth). At 11.30 GMT it completed the first leg of its journey, touching down at Anchorage airport, Alaska. The plane was not scheduled to take off on its final leg to Seoul until 12.20 and so passengers intending to continue their flight were given the option of disembarking to stroll around the airport's shops (Anchorage's largest shopping centre). Those who did so were soon joined by the passengers of another Korean jumbo, KAL 015, which had arrived from Los Angeles and was to make the Seoul run almost simultaneously with KAL 007.

Among KAL 015's passengers were the US Senators Jesse Helms and Steve Symms and Congressman Carroll Hubbard, all on their way to South Korea to take part in the thirtieth anniversary celebrations of the US–South Korean Mutual Defence Treaty. Undoubtedly they would have been glad to see their fellow conservative, Larry McDonald, on his way to the same jamboree, but McDonald had remained asleep aboard KAL 007 and they did not know he was there. It was not surprising that McDonald was tired, for he had had a wretched trip since leaving his Georgia constituency. His flight from Atlanta had been diverted from New York to Baltimore due to bad weather and when he finally got to New York it was to find the Kennedy air terminal half-flooded. By the time he got his luggage back he found that the KAL flight he had booked on had already left. Only after the normal miserable wait in the airport lounge had he been found a seat on KAL 007.[3]

The KAL crew which had flown 007 from New York signed off at Anchorage, their captain, Choy Tack Yong, reporting that his number two VHF radio had been noisy on the way up. Airport mechanics checked this and reported it to be in good working order. A defect in the number two compass was left to be repaired in Seoul – after all, the plane still had its other compass and four other heading reference systems in excellent order.[4] This was hardly surprising – KAL 007 was still well within its designed service life and had had a complete overhaul only three weeks before.[5] Command of the aircraft was now assumed by a fresh crew, headed by Captain Chun Byung-in.

## KAL – airline extraordinary

Just as Captain Chun was a remarkable pilot, so KAL was a remarkable airline. Originally KAL had been a tiny, state-owned airline concerned only with domestic flights – in 1969 it had eight planes and only one of those was a jet. In that year the South Korean government decided to hand the line over to private management and selected the Hanjin Group for the task. Hanjin was run by the Choong brothers, Cho Choong Koon ('Harry' Cho) and Cho Choong Kun, legendary as exceptionally hard-driving buccaneers even in a country where that is the preferred business style. Harry, the elder, had set up Hanjin as a trucking outfit and made his first real killing during the Korean War, hauling drinking water for US troops. Thereafter the Hanjin group retained a close relationship with the US and South Korean military in many of its ventures. The group also displayed a notably bold entrepreneurial style: thus Steve Lohr of the *New York Times* reported that when Hanjin operated as contract hauliers to the US Army in Vietnam, 'Hanjin trucks, it is said, would deliver ammunition to areas where other hauliers were reluctant to go.' The Choongs brought great entrepreneurial style to KAL. To cite Lohr again: 'Korean Air Lines ... has a mixed reputation among aviation officials, industry executives and pilots. But all seem to agree that the Korean flag-carrier is "extremely aggressive" in its quest for rapid growth ... According to some airline officials and pilots, the corporate inclination toward aggressiveness is seen in the flying practices of Korean Air Lines pilots.' But the Choongs brought unparalleled success to KAL. Between 1969 and 1982 KAL revenue multiplied 180-fold as the carrier became a major international line with a large, modern jet fleet. This all-out growth was achieved by rock-bottom fares (KAL did not join IATA or accept its price structure): many of KAL 007's passengers were Tokyo-bound but given that Japan Air Lines' ticket for the New York–Tokyo run was $1800 and KAL's was $938, it was well worth going to Seoul and doubling back. But if KAL's passengers were happy, its competitors were not. 'Competitors complain,' reported Lohr, 'that KAL offers rebates to travel agents, which they call a shady practice and do not match.' Harry Cho dismissed such charges as 'invalid' and claimed that 'There is a lot of talk against us by others who have dirt on their pants yet criticize us for not being clean.'[6] Certainly some of the allegations made against KAL are unusual in the airlines business. In 1983, for example, KAL and two other South Korean companies were alleged to have bought sixty US Hawk anti-aircraft missiles and sold them on to Iran, despite a State Department ban on such 'third-party transfers'.[7]

The cornerstone of KAL's success was, though, a 'sweetheart' deal between the South Korean and US governments which allowed KAL to charge whatever fares it chose for trans-Pacific flights,[8] even though this inevitably meant undercutting American carriers on the same routes. Within the trade, as Major-General Richard Rohmer points out in his book, *Massacre 007*, KAL earned criticism for being 'aggressive' – Rohmer alleges the practice of 'jumping the line' by KAL pilots, which involved their deliberately giving false position reports to their ground controllers.[9] Anthony Sampson in his book, *Empires of the Sky*, alludes to KAL's 'semi-military pride: it recruited its pilots from the Korean air force – with a reputation for daring rather than steadiness – and to forestall hijacking some of its cabin crew regularly carried guns'.[10]

More serious were the charges that KAL's growth was based on a debt mountain – by 1982 it owed $1.1 billion, equal to its whole annual revenue – and that the airline had a close relationship with the South Korean CIA (KCIA) and the military. KAL was not only in the business of assembling military aircraft,[11] but most KAL pilots were former Korean fighter pilots with high security clearance. Moreover, the American journalist, Fred Kaplan, cited a former CIA officer stationed in South Korea as saying, 'Anything that the Korean government wanted done that involved international movement involved KAL . . .'.[12]

Not surprisingly, KAL's pilots had a Clint Eastwood profile. As one American pilot put it, 'As individuals, some of the Koreans are tough, hard-edged characters. That is the reason they have had a reputation with some people for being kind of macho pilots, guys with more guts than brains.'[13]

## 007: the crew and the plane

Even among this élite cadre, however, Captain Chun stood out. As an airforce fighter pilot he was known as an exceptionally tough, bold and aggressive character; strong-willed, uncompromising and willing to take risks.[14] Such qualities had made him something of an ace – he was a flight-formation leader and took part in a number of military air shows.[15] He was not a man to trifle with. Although he had been a KAL pilot since 1972, he remained lean and fighting fit – he held a black belt in Tae Kwon Do, the Korean martial art.[16] But Chun was no ordinary daredevil. He was highly experienced with over 10,600 flying hours (6618 on 747s) and was so thoroughly conversant with modern aviation electronics that he was known among other KAL pilots as 'the human computer'. He had been flying the Anchorage–Seoul run for five years, had received a citation for his accident-free record in 1982,[17] and only six weeks before this, his last flight, had again received grades of 'excellent' for flight navigation procedures and as a pilot overall.[18] This rare combination of qualities had early on brought him to the attention of the South Korean authorities, particularly since there was no question about his political reliability: he had been nominated as the Korean president's personal pilot just after the president had survived several assassination attempts in 1981.[19] No ordinary KAL pilot had political connections like these, and the South Korean ambassador to the US was happy to count Chun as a friend.[20] (The Ambassador, Lew Byong Hion, was one of Korea's most senior soldiers – a former Chairman of the Korean Joint Chiefs of Staff and for six years in charge of 'Anti-Infiltration Operations' – i.e. rooting out internal subversion.)[21] A final point about Captain Chun worthy of note is that he had already once previously encountered Soviet fighters while flying the Alaska–Seoul run (in undisclosed circumstances).[22]

Chun's copilot, Son Dong-Hui, was also a cut above most ordinary pilots. A graduate of the Korean Air Force academy, he had nearly twenty years' military experience. On leaving the KAF as a Lieutenant-Colonel he was paid the rare compliment of being recruited to fly for the Korean Ministry of Transport. He had nearly 9000 flying hours to his credit, including 3411 on 747s. The flight engineer, Kim Eui-Dong, had served in the Korean Marine Aviation Corps, had passed a proficiency check only a month before, and had over 4000 flying hours to his credit, 2614 of them in 747s. It was an exceptional team. In addition a fresh crew of twenty stewards and stewardesses joined the plane, giving a total crew of twenty-three. This was rather extraordinary: the normal 747 flies with a crew of sixteen to eighteen. In addition to that, however, another six KAL crew joined the plane, 'deadheading' (flying as passengers) to Seoul. Remarkably, all six were either pilots or flight engineers.[23] All told, this meant that KAL 007 was carrying six pilots and three flight engineers plus twenty other crew.

This unusually large crew was not, however, matched by a full complement of passengers. A 747 can, with the maximum seat configuration, take up to 500 passengers, but more normally the figure is around 350. KAL 007 had just 240 passengers and was thus flying about one-third empty. Despite this – and a little oddly – a paying cargo item of 1800 pounds was scrubbed shortly before the flight. (This can be seen on the Flight Release Sheet, reproduced in Appendix, under the 'payload' section, where the figure 1800 is crossed through.)

This was as nothing, though, compared to the oddities about 007's fuel.[24] The data on the plane's load, speed, the probable wind conditions, temperature and so on, had all been fed into a computer which had chattered out its calculations. These may be seen on the flight plan, reproduced in Appendix. About a third of the way down the page the computer (which omits the last two zeros from its calculations, which are thus all in hundreds of pounds weight of aviation fuel) had made allowance for the basic trip fuel, for an extra forty minutes' fuel in case of in-flight diversions, a further thirty minutes' fuel for holding, and a general contingency 10 per cent reserve on top of that. In total this had produced the final (FOB) figure of 2558 – that is, 255,800 pounds of fuel. Most pilots accept such data unquestioningly, but on this occasion – as can be clearly seen on the computerised flight plan – Captain Chun simply crossed through all these figures and made his own peculiar arrangements about fuel.

These arrangements can be seen on the Flight Release Sheet and the Weight and Balance Manifest (reproduced on p. 300 and p. 301 respectively). On the Flight Release Sheet – on which Captain Chun promised to conduct his flight in accordance with civil aviation law and KAL's operations manual – Chun wrote that he had loaded 253,700 pounds of Ramp Fuel, though with 2000 pounds needed for taxiing, this left gross fuel at takeoff (the column entitled GATO) at 251,700 pounds – a whole 4100 pounds less than the computer had indicated would be required.

This would have been extraordinary enough, but the Weight and Balance Manifest showed that actually Captain Chun loaded 263,700 pounds of fuel (plus another 2000 pounds for taxiing) (see columns 18 and 20 on the Manifest). Disregarding the taxi fuel in both cases, this means that Chun had actually loaded 10,000 pounds (five tonnes) more fuel than he had said he had done on the Flight Release Sheet and 7900 pounds more than even the initial computerised figure.

To play around with the fuel supply like this – and to make an inaccurate record of the amount of fuel one is actually taking – is highly exceptional. Moreover, if Captain Chun had, for some reason, wanted extra fuel, he should have entered it under the 'Extra' column on his papers – but this column was left deceptively blank. Fuel is an expensive item and to carry unnecessary extra fuel (thus increasing the plane's weight and increasing its fuel consumption) is deplored by airlines. It is extremely difficult to reconcile this behaviour with Captain Chun's reputation for meticulous observation of detail and procedure.

## The flight

007 was scheduled to take off at 12.20, with a flying time of eight hours 20 minutes to Seoul down the air route known as Romeo 20. Romeo 20 is one of the five major air lanes running across the north Pacific from Anchorage to Seoul. Since it is the one that most closely hugs the Soviet coast and is thus shorter, it is greatly preferred by airlines – and is one of the busiest routes in the world.

On this occasion the headwinds along Romeo 20 were predicted to be less severe than usual, and this was expected to shorten 007's flight by 27 minutes. Accordingly, takeoff was put back by 30 minutes to 12.50 – though 007 did not actually take off until 13.00 exactly.

Before that, however, Captain Chun and his officers went through the normal prescribed flight routine of programming the Inertial Navigation System (INS) for the flight. The INS is a miracle of modern electronics, consisting of three computers (so the system can survive not one but two computer malfunctions) linked to an exceptionally sensitive gyroscopic system. The plane's present position, its destination and the waypoints *en route* to it are all fed in. (A waypoint is a reporting point: over the sea such points are purely geographical coordinates and do not correspond to any natural 'signpost'.) The INS can then not merely navigate the plane with astonishing exactitude (less than one mile's variance in a 5000-mile flight) but will read off (and correct for) the plane's speed (within one knot), altitude, wing angle, outside wind speed and so on. Standard international procedure, followed by KAL, is for the flight engineer to insert the coordinates – in this case, runway position, the waypoints of Bethel, NABIE, NEEVA, NIPPI, NOKKA and NOHO. At NOHO, to the south of Japan, the final waypoints to Seoul would be inserted. To ensure against any possibility of 'finger error' airlines typically reduce such routes as Romeo 20 which KAL 007 would be following to preprogrammed cassettes. This is what was done on this occasion, with a prepacked flight plan supplied by a Continental Airlines subsidiary. But the final check is then made, with the flight engineer reading off the program from his INS while the pilot and copilot sit behind him, monitoring his check on the other two INS. (After the tragedy the prepacked plan supplied by Continental was checked and found to be accurate in all respects,[25] so the possibilities of 'finger error' on this occasion were minimal.)

There is no doubt that modern technology has revolutionised civil air safety. The number of passenger fatalities per 100 million passenger miles flown has fallen from 4.6 in 1938 to 0.34 in 1970 to 0.006 in 1978 – an improvement of over 74,000 per cent.[26] And the triple INS represents a considerable advance on what was available in 1978. It is regarded by airline pilots as virtually infallible.

The INS is, nonetheless, backed up by a variety of other aids, including the en route VHF Omni Range radio beacon (VOR). As it happened the Anchorage VOR had been closed down for maintenance operations when KAL 007 took off. Captain Chun was informed of this an hour before takeoff. It was not a major problem – it would merely mean that he would need to check his position against the next VOR at Bethel, 346 miles away – and that VOR was working. In fact KAL 007 began to deviate to the north of Romeo 20 almost immediately. As it passed the nondirectional radio beacon on Cairn Mountain (halfway to Bethel) Anchorage ground control noted on its radar that 007 was six miles north of track. Anchorage did not bother to notify 007 of this – it was a minor deviation which 007 would easily be able to correct by using the Bethel VOR and its INS. Well before that, however, 007 slipped out of range of the Anchorage radar.

Fifty minutes out of Anchorage, KAL 007 radioed back routinely to say that it was passing Bethel. Anchorage had no means of checking this but, as the records of the US military radar station at King Salmon show, the plane was actually 12 miles to the north of Bethel.

007's deviation at Bethel is crucial in several respects. Although, as we shall see, the plane seems to have altered course several times thereafter, even the course it was flying at Bethel would have taken it deep inside Soviet territory – into those areas on Captain Chun's navigation map marked with the blue-lined injunction: 'Warning: Aircraft infringing upon Non-Free Flying Territory may be fired on without warning.' It was quite impossible for 007 to be in this position at Bethel if it was operating according to normal procedures: the INS would have brought 007 exactly over Bethel and the autopilot locked on to Bethel VOR would have done the same. Had the INS and autopilot not been functioning, passage over the Bethel waypoint would have provided Captain Chun with the compulsory occasion to check his instruments and see that this

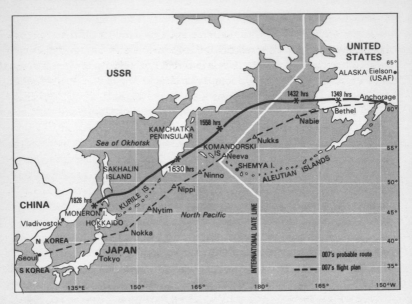

1 007's probable route, and the Romeo 20 route which 007 was supposed to follow, with its waypoints marked. NUKKS, NINNO and NYTIM are non-compulsory reporting waypoints: the route cuts the international dateline near NEEVA. *Source*: Robert W. Allardyce and James Gollin, 'The Final Moments of KAL 007', *Berkshire Eagle*, 23 May 1985; Eugene Kozicharow, 'FAA Studies Upgraded Pacific Navaids', *Aviation Week and Space Technology*, 19 September 1983.

was so. Moreover, Captain Chun knew that with the Anchorage VOR not working he had to be certain to check his course with most particular care at the Bethel VOR. Had he been flying Romeo 20 correctly his INS would have ensured that any deviation at this point could have been measured in feet: as it was he was 12 miles off course. Moreover, even 007's ordinary magnetic compass (independent of all the other systems and mounted inside the cockpit) would have shown the deviation quite clearly (and as the flight proceeded, would have shown it more and more clearly). Thus, to believe that 007 was off course by accident at Bethel one has to believe that Captain Chun and his fellow officers were guilty of the most extraordinary negligence and inattention. (Captain Chun's widow, Mrs Kim Ok Hee, found such a contention incredible: 'You would not find a more painstaking person than my husband. With him everything had to be in the right place.')[27]

The possible explanations as to why 007 was off course at Bethel are thus extremely limited.

*Either*

1. Both the INS and autopilot were uncoupled *and* 007's crew failed to notice this *and* they failed to notice the amber warning light which this would produce on the autopilot. *In addition* the crew would have had to fail to notice the reading on their magnetic compass *and* the fact that their weather radar, set in ground-mapping mode, was showing a different part of the Alaskan coastline than that which they should have been crossing.

*Or*

2. The wrong route had been deliberately programmed into the INS back at Anchorage, with the intention of flying 007 over Soviet territory. This could not have been done without the connivance of the crew, especially since they would then have known they were sending back a false position report at Bethel.

*Or*

3. There had been a programming error in the INS back at Anchorage *and* the autopilot locked onto Bethel VOR was not functioning to correct this *and* the crew failed to notice the same instruments as in (1) above or carry out the checks they were required to make.

There is no fourth alternative.

KAL 007 was not on its own. KAL 015 had been scheduled to take off 20 minutes after it, also on Romeo 20. In fact 015 unaccountably departed from schedule and left Anchorage only 14 minutes later.[28] Moreover, 015 seems to have been in something of a hurry, for at its first waypoint, NABIE, it was between six and eight minutes ahead of schedule. Robert Allardyce, a veteran US pilot, has reconstructed 015's flight and concluded that 015 must have been flying at unusually high Mach numbers ('red-lining') to catch up so fast.[29] Given that the departure of both 007 and 015 had been delayed so that they should not arrive at Seoul before 6 am local time, this untoward turn of speed was rather odd. (Unfortunately, we do not have access to 015's digital flight-data recorder, which would reveal exactly at what speeds it was flying.) KAL 007, on the other hand, appears, at least, to have taken the first part of its flight in something of a dawdle. As ICAO's Air Navigation Commission put it, 007 'reported passing NABIE two minutes behind its estimated time and passing NEEVA five minutes behind its revised estimated time (nine minutes behind its original estimated time)'.[30] The net result of these contrary movements was that KAL 015 came close to catching up with 007, so that the two planes were flying almost in parallel for a good part of the time.

The importance of this was twofold. As 007 diverged further and further from its proper course, it fell out of VHF range of Anchorage but always remained within VHF range of 015 and was thus able to use 015 as its major relay post back to ground control. (This form of relay is common enough aviation practice.) This led, however, to a major oddity, for 007 reported back truthfully enough on the wind conditions it was meeting and these conditions were notably different from those 015 met. It is strange that 015, which frequently had the job of relaying 007's wind reports back to Anchorage, did not remark on this discrepancy – particularly given that 015, if 007's location coordinates were to be believed, was soon backing up only a few minutes behind 007's path. (In fact, of course, 007 was diverging increasingly north of 015's path – which is what explains the different wind reports.)

007 was due to pass the first waypoint, NABIE, at about 14.30 when, compulsorily, it had to report its position to Anchorage. It was most unlike the supremely scrupulous Captain Chun to fall short on such an obligatory procedure, but fall short he did: 007 made no report at 14.30. Accordingly Anchorage tried twice, at 14.32 and 14.34, to call 007 but received only unintelligible squawks in reply. To miss reporting a waypoint by even two minutes is an extremely serious matter – indeed, to do so automatically starts procedures which build towards a search and rescue operation. Accordingly, Anchorage tried another means of reaching 007. Anchorage maintains remote control air–ground (RCAG) facilities at Kenai, Bethel, St Paul and Shemya, and through these it can also maintain direct, two-way radiocommunication with planes under its control. So at 14.32 Anchorage used the St Paul RCAG to try to contact 007. These efforts, too, failed.

The situation was now potentially very serious. Anchorage ground control had yet a third way open to it, though. All its attempted communications with 007 were on VHF radio. But HF radio could be tried as well. So Anchorage ground control called the separate Anchorage flight service station/international flight service station (FSS/IFSS), which handles all HF radio, and asked the FSS/IFSS to contact 007 for him, and if it managed to do that, to tell 007 to get in touch immediately with Anchorage ground control on VHF. However, just at this point KAL 015 called up Anchorage ground control and said it was relaying 007's waypoint report from NABIE. At this, ground control called up FSS/IFSS and cancelled its earlier request. The emergency seemed to be over – but everything depended on what KAL 015 *said* about 007. It was only at 14.44 – 14 minutes late – that 007 called up the FSS/IFSS and gave its own report for NABIE. This was all very well, but it still meant that there had been no direct contact between 007 and Anchorage ground control, so FSS/IFSS advised 007 to make its next report to ground control direct on VHF. Similarly, ground control asked KAL 015 to tell 007 the same thing: specifically, 007 must use a VHF channel to report its own position at the next waypoint, NEEVA. In fact, 007, despite these requests, never complied.

By these circuitous means Anchorage ground control had thus finally managed to get two indirect reports on 007's position at NABIE. Both of them were false, for 007 had never been at NABIE at all. If one assumes 007 had continued in a straight line from Bethel (turns of any sort would take a great deal more explaining), then it must have been around 100 miles north of NABIE. To ask how Captain Chun could thus misreport his position at NABIE is to pose all the same questions as when he had misreported at Bethel, together with the extra query as to how he could have maintained an incorrect course through a checking operation designed precisely to correct such errors.

But there was another point about NABIE too. Pilots flying along Romeo 20 know that when they are passing over NABIE they come within range of the US military radars and radio beacons on St Paul's Island and these they use as an extra check on their position. But 007 was flying too far west of NABIE to pick up the St Paul's signals. Even if Captain Chun had somehow missed all the other indications that he was off course, this alone should have been enough to alert him. Similarly, Romeo 20 brings airliners within range of the US military radars and VOR on Shemya Island, providing another regular checkpoint.[31] All the same questions arising at the earlier points of decision have to be posed yet again here.

For all this time 007 would have been easily visible to US military radar, first from King Salmon, then from Cape Newenham (and for 40 minutes on both of them, overlapping). In addition, of course, the US radars at Shemya and elsewhere had the capabilities to follow 007 throughout its flight. But at around 15.51 007 also came within range of Soviet radar. If, for any reason, US radars had not been tracking 007, then the Soviet pick-up would have had the effect of lighting up the blue light on 007's transponder panel.

The passengers inside the cabin would, no doubt, have been quite unaware of the terrible danger they were now heading straight towards. Some would have been watching the in-flight movie, *Man, Woman, and Child* (a tearjerker about a man discovering late in married life that he had fathered a child in a previous affair), the rest, no doubt, trying to catch some sleep before arriving in South Korea, 'the land of morning calm'.

007 had, via KAL 015, estimated that it would reach NEEVA, the next waypoint, at 15.53. As we have seen, 007 was under firm instructions to contact Anchorage ground control directly this time. In fact 007 made no contact at all. After the customary further two minutes had passed, one would have expected Anchorage to charge into action, as had happened at NABIE.

Strangely, this time Anchorage did nothing. More minutes ticked by and ground control still did nothing – did not even contact the FSS/IFSS in order to try to reach 007. It was only at 16.00:39 that the ground controller called up not 007 but 015 – and then 015 volunteered a position report for 007 at NEEVA which, it said, 007 had passed on to it for relay. (This was rather odd, too: if 007 had made such a request, why had 015 not called Anchorage and passed it on? Why wait for Anchorage to call?) It was only at 16.03:55 that 007 itself called up – a whole 10 minutes after it was supposed to have compulsorily reported a waypoint – and it did not call Anchorage ground control, but the FSS/IFSS instead. Even so, it merely transmitted its call sign three times, with no message, and then went off the air. That is, even when 007 did make radio contact, it made no attempt to report.

Anchorage had accepted KAL 015's report of 007's position at NEEVA. But, again, this was a false report – 007 had been some 150 miles north of NEEVA. All the questions raised before have again to be posed about this false NEEVA report, though this time with an added twist, for 007 now had another way of knowing where it was – its weather radar which, when turned to ground-mapping mode, would have shown in colour graphics the contours of Kamchatka, whose nearest point was only some 110 miles distant. The weather radars carried by 007 (and it had two of them) had a range of over 200 miles and a 180-degree visibility angle. Presuming that these were turned on, as KAL procedure instructs, 007 may, at about the same time, have picked up the blip of a USAF RC-135 (an electronic surveillance plane) passing in front of it.

Again, if 007's flight deviation was accidental it would have been easy to shrug off the presence of the RC-135 – US surveillance activity in the area was intense and thus normal. If, on the other hand, 007 was deliberately off course this too would have been a moment of some excitement: if 007 was attempting to cheat the rules to save fuel it would have had its eyes peeled for other planes; if its purpose was more sinister it is difficult not to believe that this was part of a planned rendezvous. This was certainly how the Russians, watching on their radars below, interpreted the manoeuvre.

The Russians might also have been confused by 007's speed. Airliners normally travel at a constant ('economy cruising') speed, but 007 seems not to have done so. Although it (like KAL 015) had a speed of Mach 0.84 designated on its flight plan, in fact, as we have seen, it went far more slowly than this at first, losing nine minutes (a very large amount) between reported NABIE and NEEVA. Then, however, it speeded up considerably, catching up two minutes on schedule by the next reported waypoint. According to Robert Allardyce, the veteran pilot and navigator who has made a close analysis of both 007's and 015's speeds, KAL 015 was simultaneously travelling at speeds of Mach 0.9 – far in excess of normal 747 speeds and enough to set the Mach buzzer going in the plane's cabin cockpit.[32] 015 neither asked nor secured permission from Anchorage ground control to depart so radically from its flight plan. There was no record of Anchorage hearing 015's Mach buzzer during its communications with the plane, so it seems possible that the buzzer had been switched off.[33] The Russians no doubt puzzled over these varying speeds, but their attention would have been increasingly drawn to the converging paths of 007 and the RC-135 which, like 007, was moving steadily towards the Kamchatka coast.

As Pearson persuasively argues,[34] 007's meeting with the RC-135 must have taken place north of the Komandorski Islands. This is where 007 would have flown to if it had maintained a straight line Great Circle course from Bethel on. It certainly couldn't have been south of those islands, for then 007 would have missed Kamchatka and Sakhalin altogether and the tragedy would not have occurred. Nor could this meeting have taken place over the Komandorski (Commander) Islands, which belong to the Russians, for the Russians would certainly have shouted loudly about such a violation of their airspace. Certainly, the Russians themselves claim to have plotted KAL 007 and the RC-135 to the north and east of the Komandorskis and it seems certain that they were telling the truth about this, at least.

This in turn means that the Russians have to be right in their claim that 007 made a change of course at about this time. In the tape transcripts later released by the US, Soviet pilots can be heard repeatedly checking that 'the target' (007) is on a course of 240 degrees. But that course would not have brought 007 to a position north of the Komandorskis – setting out from Bethel 007 seems to have been on a course of about 252 degrees. *Ergo*, there must have been a change of course, and this change must have occurred around the time that 007 flew closest to the RC-135. (Had 007 continued on the Great Circle course from Bethel it would have shaded only the southernmost tip of Sakhalin.) In terms of the surveillance-mission hypothesis, of course, one of the purposes of the RC-135 'rendezvous' would have been precisely to effect this sort of course alteration. But even without committing oneself to that hypothesis, one has to face the awkward fact of this change of course. This could hardly have been other than a conscious act by 007's pilot and such a change could only have been taken after careful consideration of the plane's location before and after the change. In fact the 240-degree course now taken by 007 saw it adopt a path almost exactly parallel to Romeo 20.

There are several further oddities as regards 007's altitude. On leaving

Anchorage 007 had informed ground control that it was climbing to 31,000 feet, and at 13.50 007 had confirmed that it was at that altitude. At 14.35 KAL 015 confirmed that 007 was still at 31,000 feet, but at 14.44 007 called Anchorage FSS/IFSS to request permission to climb to 33,000 feet. Oddly, although this request was passed on to Anchorage ground control, ground control simply ignored it for 82 minutes. Then, at 16.06, ground control called up KAL 015 and asked if 007 still wanted to climb to 33,000 feet. KAL 015 said that 007 had already passed on a request to it for such an ascent. This too was odd – why hadn't 015 called Anchorage to pass on the request, instead of waiting until Anchorage called it? This time Anchorage gave immediate permission for the ascent, and within a few seconds KAL 015 was back on the line to Anchorage confirming that 007 was now climbing to 33,000 feet. Thus, according to the official record, 007 approached Kamchatka at 31,000 feet and then ascended to 33,000 feet shortly after coming within range of Soviet radar.

The Russians, however, say that their radar tracked both 007 and the RC-135 at 26,000 feet and that 007 entered their airspace still at that height. It is impossible to reconcile these two accounts. It is also difficult to see what motive the Russians could have for lying about this: they were, after all, determined to intercept the intruder and would hardly have gained anything by disseminating a false altitude report. On the other hand, it seems certain that the Russians would have been listening in to these conversations between 007, 015 and Anchorage, and their suspicions regarding the intruder would hardly have been lessened by the discovery that it was sending out altitude reports which did not tally with what their own radars were showing. According to the Russians 007 did climb while over Kamchatka, though only to 29,500 feet, the height at which, the Russians say, it was flying when it left Kamchatka airspace.

The Russians maintain around their territory a 60-mile Aerospace Defence Identification Zone (ADIZ). Standard procedure is for every aircraft entering this zone to be identified and reported to the National Command Post of the Soviet Air Defence Force at Kalinin, near Moscow, before the plane actually infringes on Soviet territory itself.[35] There is little doubt that this would have been the procedure followed on this occasion, particularly since recent measures had been taken to tighten both Soviet law and practice in regard to frontier protection.[36] In addition, however, the Russians had reportedly planned that very night to launch their new PL-5 missile towards their Kamchatka testing ground and would have been doubly watchful of the predictable and heavy US surveillance attention such a test would attract.

All of which serves only to deepen the mystery of why KAL 007's flight did not come to a summary end over Kamchatka. According to the Russians, they first picked up 007 on their radar at 15.51, watched its radar blip merge with that of the RC-135 at 16.01 and stay merged until 16.11, when one of the blips moved off towards mainland Alaska and the other headed towards Kamchatka. At about 16.20 007 entered the Soviet ADIZ.

The Russians claim that their ground control stations attempted to contact 007 – presumably from this point on – but failed to get any response. This is strange, for 007, having maintained a long radio silence, now broke it, calling the Anchorage FSS/IFSS at 16.23 to make a brief radio check. No doubt this transmission was heard by the Soviet ground controllers below. At that stage – with 007 in fact just 50 miles short of the Kamchatka coastline – 007 was due to pass out of Anchorage's control and be handed over to ground control at Narita airport (Tokyo). At 16.12 Anchorage had contacted Narita and made the handing-on arrangements. This was a considerable euphemism, though, for 007 had not really been under any sort of direct control by the Anchorage ground controllers for a very long time. Indeed the last time that Anchorage ground control had had a direct radio contact of its own with 007 was at 13.50, when 007 had (falsely) reported passing over Bethel. So Anchorage ground control was handing over a plane with whom it had not in fact talked for two hours 22 minutes.

At 16.30 007 crossed the Kamchatka coast. If the Soviet defensive system had been working properly, one would have expected their fighters to have intercepted 007 at this point at the very latest – though really, had they been on their toes, they should have made such an interception somewhere near the edge of the 60-mile ADIZ. But neither of these things happened. Indeed, when four Soviet MIG-23s and SU-15s scrambled to meet the intruder it was already 16.37[37] – by which time 007 was some 50 miles inland. This was a remarkably late Soviet reaction.

The Russians claimed that their fighters did locate 007 over Kamchatka. Indeed, on 10 September Soviet TV produced a Kamchatka fighter pilot who described how he went through all the standard international interception procedures to secure an intruder's identification and compliance – all with no response. 007 was, he averred, flying without lights: 'the aircraft was entirely dark. Even on the side of the dark area of the sky, there were no signs of any illumination.'[38] This (unnamed) pilot filled out his account in an interview with the Red Army paper, *Krasnaya Zvezda* (Red Star), of 13 September. 007's pilot, he said, 'knew his onions very well ... You know how he manoeuvred after spotting me? He began wildly varying his course, altitude and speed. He saw me perfectly well.'[39]

This is all very odd – for 007 proceeded on its way, leaving Kamchatka at 17.08. The Soviet version must then be (though they do not say) that they deliberately let the intruder go. But their standing orders would have compelled them to shoot down any intruder who failed to respond. If, for any reason, the fighters had failed to do this, then the SAM-2 batteries at Petropavlovsk would have been ordered to do so: indeed, Pearson reports that the batteries were ordered to fire but were unable to obtain a solid radar lock on 007.[40] If the Russian explanation is correct, we are being invited to believe either that their pilots disobeyed their orders to shoot down unidentified intruders or that Soviet ground control decided for some reason that this particular intruder could be allowed to escape. Yet the Russians emphatically refuse the notion that they let the plane escape because it was only an airliner, for they assert that they never identified it as such, not even much later. (And it is most unlikely that they would have let it escape even had they identified it as such.)

An alternative explanation is that the Soviet fighters never made contact with 007 and that the story that 007 was showing no lights is a cover for the fact that the plane was never sighted at all. Two reasons have been advanced why this might have been so: that 007 was part of a surveillance probe and that US electronic countermeasures were being used to disable Soviet radar;[41] or simply that the Soviet defence was caught slow-footed and napping. Either way, 007 certainly made no reference to any of the Soviet activity going on below and around it, and at 17.08:38 – one minute after leaving Kamchatka airspace – 007 was calling up Tokyo ground control to report that it had just passed waypoint NIPPI. Again, this was another checking operation that failed – for 007 was then 180 miles north of NIPPI.

It is worth remarking on the pattern of 007's radio calls in this period. As we have seen, the plane had in practice avoided all direct contact with Anchorage ground control ever since Bethel, ignoring repeated instructions to re-establish a direct VHF contact. (007 was actually out of VHF range of course – an extra clue to the pilot that he was not on course.) Then, just prior to crossing into Kamchatka airspace, 007 had radioed Anchorage FSS/IFSS. 007 then observed radio silence all the way across Kamchatka, to burst into life (on a working VHF radio) to talk six times to Tokyo between 17.08 and 17.10. These transmissions, too, must have been picked up by the Russians below. Thereafter 007 maintained radio silence for a considerable period, so the Russians got no more radio clues as 007 began to move towards Sakhalin.

007 now headed out across the Sea of Okhotsk. Given the way the plane had – for whatever reason – eluded the Soviet grasp during 38 minutes in

Kamchatka airspace, the question was whether it might not do the same in the 11 minutes it would spend in the airspace over Sakhalin. On the other hand, the Russians must by this time have been thoroughly alerted – whatever their initial state – and would be ready and waiting. But the Russians had no way of knowing that the intruder would continue on a straight line: it might well have turned south and headed out of the hornet's nest. To cater for this possibility Soviet fighters were scrambled from a Soviet base on Paramuschiv Island (in the Kuriles) to cover that exit route.[42] In addition, though, there are strong indications that communications between Kamchatka and Sakhalin were not all they might have been that night. US intelligence officials believe that Kamchatka radar failed to 'hand over' 007 to their Sakhalin colleagues, who may not even have known that 'their' intruder was the same plane that had just crossed Kamchatka.[43]

But the Soviet fighters faced another difficulty, too, which was that as 007 approached Sakhalin it left its previous straight-line course and began to describe a northward arc actually taking it deeper into Soviet airspace – quite the opposite of what they might have expected an errant airliner to do. This course change was taken by the Russians to be a form of evasive action and thus further evidence that 007 was on a surveillance mission. For no doubt similar considerations in reverse, all the official maps initially used by the Reagan Administration effectively denied the course alteration by showing 007 on a straight-line flight over Sakhalin – and these were the maps used by the Western press in general.

There is, though, no doubt at all that 007 changed course at this point. ICAO compared the radar reports provided by the Russians on the one hand and the Japanese military radar at Wakkanai on the other. Both reported 007 making a distinct curve in its flight path, though the Russian curve was steeper than that shown by the Japanese. ICAO had various technical explanations for this discrepancy, but the essential point that 007 did change course is uncontested.[44] Again, this throws up obvious questions – for such a course change could only have been deliberate. What is certain is that this manoeuvre threw the Soviet defences into some confusion. This seems clear enough from the transcripts of the Soviet fighters' conversations later released by the US.

The Soviet fighters scrambled at 17.42 but the transcripts pick up their conversation only at 17.56 as they headed out of Soviet airspace in an attempt to intercept 007 at the edge of the ADIZ. It is worth noting that although the Russians claim that 007 was flying at 29,500 feet when it left Kamchatka, they do not provide any altitude for the plane as it approached Sakhalin, contenting themselves with the more general statement that in the vicinity of Sakhalin 'the aeroplane made frequent manoeuvres, changing its heading, altitude and airspeed'.[45]

There is some evidence at least that 007 did increase its speed at this point. Allardyce's analysis of 007's flight speeds shows that while early on the plane had gone far slower than it should, as it moved into Sakhalin airspace it speeded up very markedly, so that it was doing around Mach 0.9 – far in excess of its flight plan's Mach 0.84 and enough to set its Mach buzzer going.[46] Such acceleration could only have been conscious and it would have certainly have burned up some of the extra fuel 007 had taken on board at Anchorage. The evidence for altitude changes by 007 at this point is, though, of exclusively Soviet provenance.

The Soviet fighters waiting for 007 on its approach towards the Sakhalin coastline had been scrambled from Dolinsk PVO (Air Defence Force) base, just north of the Korsakov naval base. They were led by Major Vassily Kasmin in an SU-15. When Major Kasmin sighted 007 at 18.05 (still some way from the Sakhalin coast) he several times reported back to his ground controller that he was taking up position behind the intruder on a heading of 240 degrees and at a height of 8000 metres (26,250 feet). Probably Major Kasmin was also following interception procedures which required him to fly somewhat lower than the intruder, so this suggests an altitude of perhaps 27,000 feet for 007. The 240-degree heading was, of course, the same as that which 007 had switched to after its course change west of Kamchatka, so it would seem that the airliner had maintained a straight-line course since then. Nonetheless, 007 seems to have been flying some 6000 feet lower than it had earlier reported to its ground control: again, there seems no reason for the Russians to lie about this – they had to get the altitude right to make a correct interception.

007 seems to have commenced its turn just under two minutes after Major Kasmin's SU-15 took up position behind it. Suddenly Kasmin was on the radio to his controller: 'Roger. Repeat heading . . . To the left surely. Not to the right.' Then, a few seconds later, Kasmin announced that he was altering course to 260 degrees (a swerve to the north) to keep 007 in sight. After a further minute he confirmed to his ground controller: 'Affirmative, it has turned . . . The target is 80 degrees to my left.' Then, half a minute later, Kasmin confirmed that he was back behind 'the target' on a course of 240 degrees – that is, 007 had made a turn south and then reassumed its old directional heading – yet another alteration of course. Naturally enough, the Russians interpreted these course changes, occurring immediately after they had located 007, as deliberate attempts at evasion. Indeed, it is so difficult to fit these yet further changes of course into an 'accidental' explanation of 007's

flight that it is not easy to see what other interpretation than the Russians' *could* be accorded them.

The transcript of the Soviet fighters' conversations also make it clear that the Russians were experiencing acute problems with their radar. The fighters – Kasmin's SU-15 and two MIG-23s – were guided by three ground-control stations, Karnaval, Deputat and Trikotazh. Despite that they did not report sighting 007 until 18.05 – and then visually ('Am observing'). Only at 18.12 do we get the double report: 'Am observing it visually and see it on the screen.' At 18.17 one of the MIG-23s reports, 'Deputat is observing me'; an odd comment, suggesting that Deputat had had difficulties until then in following its own fighter, let alone 'the target'. The MIG then asks of the SU-15, 'Deputat is enquiring. Do you see the target or not?' – and then adds that 'Karnaval does not observe'. A few minutes later the MIG again asks of his ground controller, 'Do you see me?' (i.e. on radar). Pearson has suggested that these evident radar difficulties are consistent only with the deployment of jamming and electronic countermeasures against the Soviets' radar by the US,[47] but sheer incompetence and technical failure are also possibilities. What does seem quite likely is that the Soviet fighters located 007 in the end as much by luck, skill and eyesight as by radar.

Thereafter, the Russians claim, their fighters went through the full normal procedures of light-flashing, wing-waggling and attempted radio contact – all with no response from 007. 'The target' was, they aver, flying without strobe, navigation or cabin lights on.

007 had maintained radio silence with Tokyo (Narita) ground control for over an hour at this point. Just as it was entering Sakhalin airspace and the Soviet fighters closed on its tail (at 18.13:05 Major Kasmin finally reported, 'I see it. I'm locked onto target') 007 broke radio silence, at 18.15 exactly. This must have seemed extremely suspicious to the Russians monitoring 007's radio conversation below: immediately their fighter managed to get a lock on the 'target', the target burst into life – thus illustrating that he had a working radio, even if their attempts to call him up weren't working. 007 certainly made no mention of the fighters on his tail and instead merely requested permission to make an altitude change. Tokyo told 007 to wait a few moments, while it checked if the requested ascent from 33,000 to 35,000 feet was in order.

At 18.16 007 entered Soviet airspace. The fighters sitting on the plane's tail now knew that they had only 10 minutes in which to force the plane down or, failing that, shoot it down. If it was to come to a shoot-down, no doubt the decision would be left to the last possible moment, just before the intruder exited from Soviet airspace. These must have been 10 minutes of electric and growing tension for the Soviet pilots.

Major Kasmin, who took the lead throughout, was later interviewed on Soviet TV and gave his own account of these moments. 007, he said, was flying 'almost over our base. I approached this plane and flashed onboard lights. Naturally, there is a large crew on such a plane and they had to see the flashing onboard lights. Second, I sent four rounds of tracer shells right by his nose. They can be seen at night for many kilometres, and this was right next to him. I also wagged my wings. You can also see those wagging onboard lights.'[48] (The four tracer shells contained 120 individual tracer cartridges, the Russians said.)

The fact that 007 did not respond even to the tracers is very hard indeed to explain. As Senator John Glenn, himself an experienced former fighter pilot, said, 'If they were all tracers, it's inconceivable that he [007] would have missed all those tracers going by.'[49] This led some Reagan Administration spokesmen later on to suggest that Kasmin must have fired cannon shells, not tracers, and was merely lying after the event. No evidence was offered for this contention which does not, in any case, remove the whole problem: cannon shells would have been less visible but would still have made a great noise which 007 would have been bound to hear. (In a 747 cockpit one can easily hear the engine noise of nearby passing planes, let alone shell bursts.)

It is even possible that there may have been witnesses to this part of the engagement – the Japanese crew of the fishing boat, *Chidori Maru No. 58*, then about 19 miles off Moneron Island. The crew reported that at 'about three o'clock in the morning' (18.00 GMT) they heard two or three booms overhead and a midair flash.[50] If their recollection of the time was correct then this was too early to have been the actual shoot-down. But if they could see and hear such bangs and flashes six miles below, it is harder than ever to explain why 007 did not hear, see and respond to the tracers or cannon shells.

It was immediately after this that 007 carried out a remarkable manoeuvre. Just as Major Kasmin in his SU-15 (code number 805) was complaining to his controller that 'The target isn't responding to the call', 007 received permission from Tokyo to ascend from 33,000 to 35,000 feet. What happened next is best illustrated by juxtaposing the twin conversations of 007 to Tokyo with Kasmin's (in 805) to his controller:

| Time | 007/Tokyo conversation | SU-15 (805) to base |
|---|---|---|
| 1820.10 | *TOKYO:*<br>Korean Air Zero Zero Seven<br>clearance. Tokyo ATC<br>clears Korean Air Zero<br>Zero Seven climb and<br>maintain flight level three<br>five zero. | |
| 1820.12 | | Answering. |
| 1820.17 | | I answered. |
| 1820.20 | *007:* Roger Korean Air Zero<br>Zero Seven climb maintain<br>three five zero leaving<br>three three zero this time. | |
| 1820.22 | | Must get closer to it. |
| 1820.30 | *TOKYO:* Tokyo roger. | I'm turning lock-on off<br>and I'm approaching the<br>target. |
| 1820.49 | | I have broken off lock-on.<br>. . . exactly, I have<br>executed. |
| 1821.24 | | Yes, I'm approaching the<br>target, I'm going in<br>closer. |
| 1821.35 | | The target's light is<br>blinking. I have already<br>approached the target to a<br>distance of about two<br>kilometres. |
| 1821.40 | | The target is at 10,000<br>metres. |
| 1821.55 | | What are instructions? |
| 1822.02 | | The target is decreasing<br>speed. |
| 1822.17 | | I'm going round it. I'm<br>already moving in front<br>of the target. |
| 1822.23 | | I have increased speed. |
| 1822.29 | | No. It is decreasing<br>speed. |

| 1822.42 | | It should have been earlier. How can I chase it? I'm already abeam of the target. |
| 1822.55 | | Now I have to fall back a bit from the target. |
| 1823.05 | *007:* Tokyo Radio. Korean Air Zero Zero Seven level three five zero. | Say again. |
| 1823.08 | *TOKYO:* Korean Air Zero Zero Seven. Tokyo roger. | |
| 1823.10 | | The target's altitude is 10,000 metres. |
| 1823.18 | | From me it is located 70 degrees to the left. |
| 1823.37 | | I'm dropping back. Now I will try rockets. |

The full significance of this becomes apparent if one realises that Soviet ground control was undoubtedly monitoring 007's conversation with Tokyo, presumably with a slight lag as a translation was obtained. Thus they must have heard that 007 was about to ascend to 35,000 feet and communicated this to Kasmin (805). This clearly did not correspond to what Kasmin was observing: he calls back that 'The target is at 10,000 metres' (32,800 feet) – which means that 007 had climbed nearly 6000 feet since 18.11 when Kasmin gave his altitude as 8000 metres. Kasmin then reports that 007 has actually done something quite different than his reports to Tokyo suggest, for he has lost speed and caused Kasmin's SU-15 to overshoot. But then 007 confirms to Tokyo that he has actually reached 35,000 feet ('level three five zero' – the last two noughts are customarily omitted). This is relayed to Kasmin, who can't believe his ears ('Say again') and, to reassure his no doubt confused ground control, gives further details of 007's position ('From me it is located 70 degrees to the left').

Immediately after the shoot-down, the Japanese admitted that this crucial part of 007's flight was something of a mystery to them, for their radar at Wakkanai showed that 007 never did climb to 35,000 feet.[51] Only in May 1985, however, were the full facts revealed to the Japanese Diet.[52] The radar recordings show that 007 was, in fact, deceiving – indeed, lying to – his ground controller about this claimed ascent, and even about his original altitude. When Major Kasmin's SU-15 closed on 007 the airliner was at

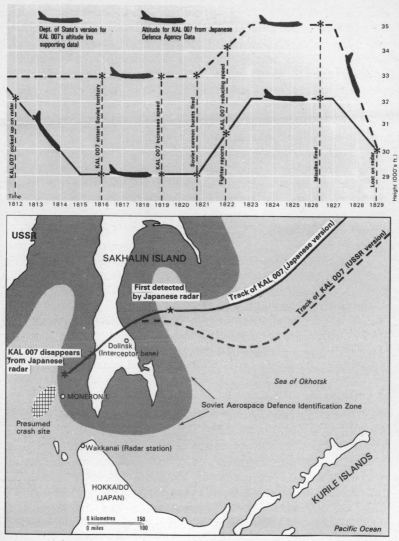

2(a) Japanese Self-Defence Agency altitude data compared to the State Department version of 007's altitude changes in the last moments of its flight. 007 told its ground controller that it was ascending from 33,000 to 35,000 ft.

2(b) The two versions of 007's turn over Sakhalin. The thin line depicts 007's course as viewed by the Japanese radar station at Wakkanai, the thick line its course as reported by Soviet radar. 007 made no mention of a turn to its ground controller: despite the differences in the two tracks, the all-important fact is that both authorities concur that there was a turn. *Sources*: D. Pearson, 'The Facts of 007', *New York Review of Books*, 26 September 1985; Duncan Campbell, 'What Really Happened to KE007?', *New Statesman*, 26 April 1985; Clarence A. Robinson Jr., 'US Says Soviet Knew Korean Air Lines 747 was Commercial Flight', *Aviation Week and Space Technology*, 12 September 1983.

32,000 feet, not 33,000 feet. Then 007, having announced his impending climb, actually did the reverse, losing speed and *diving down* to 29,000 feet. At this altitude 007 reaccelerated and, just as Major Kasmin fired his tracers past the plane, 007 began to climb again to 32,000 feet. It seems impossible to avoid the conclusion that Captain Chun had seen the Soviet fighter on his tail (and its tracer bursts); decided not to tell Tokyo ground control about it; and determined instead to try evasive tactics to throw the fighter off his tail.

For the Russians (who were running out of time and airspace) this manoeuvre seems to have been the last straw – 007 was behaving as if it was in an aerial dogfight, feinting a climb and then doing the opposite. (No doubt they would have been even more suspicious if they had known that Captain Chun, at the controls of 007, was an experienced fighter pilot and aerobatics ace.) Major Kasmin gave his own account of these moments in an interview with *Krasnaya Zvezda* (13 September 1983). 007's pilot, he claimed, lowered all the 747's flaps, enabling it to reduce speed so that Kasmin's SU-15 would overshoot and be forced to make a turn and reapproach, thus giving 007 time to escape. 'But I did not fall for that trick,' said Kasmin and, realising this, 007's pilot had retracted his flaps and gained speed again. One of Kasmin's colleagues in one of the MIG-23s added that 007's pilot 'knew his onions very well', for he had manoeuvred and changed course the moment he was spotted. Such tactics, the newspaper added, were typically practised by RC-135 pilots operating off the Soviet Siberian coast. 'The military call it a feint. The novelty was only in the fact that it now was a passenger plane, moreover a plane belonging to a foreign airline, that was used as the soloist, go-getter, kamikaze, if you like.'[53]

Kasmin's response was lethal and immediate: 'Now I will try rockets.' At that moment 007's fate was sealed. At 18.26 and 20 seconds Major Kasmin reported, 'I have executed launch,' and, two seconds later, 'The target is destroyed.' This latter statement was, as it turned out, premature. Kasmin must have fired his rockets, seen a tremendous explosion take place on 'the target' and assumed that that was the end of that. (There is a considerable, unexplained – and, indeed, irresoluble – conflict over this moment. The Russians stated quite flatly that 'the flight was terminated in Soviet airspace over USSR territory – above the Pravda housing project in the southwest part of Sakhalin Island – on 1 September 1983 at 06.24 Sakhalin time',[54] that is, at 18.24 GMT. The time given on the US-provided tapes of 18.26:20 is not only noticeably different, but would clearly have placed 007 further on in its flight, somewhere in Soviet airspace beyond the Sakhalin coastline. If the time given by the Russians is correct, the radio transmissions apparently made by 007 after 18.24 become even more impossible to understand.)

The SU-15 is equipped with two Anab AA-3 air-to-air missiles, one heat-seeking, one radar-guided. Each is a 600-pound projectile, crammed with high explosive, which travels at Mach 2.5.[55] Major Kasmin fired both missiles, but it seems likely that only one hit 007: the impact of two such missiles would probably have caused a much quicker end than seems to have occurred. For, 38 seconds after the plane had been hit 007 called up Tokyo again – giving only the standard call signal, not a Mayday distress signal. Ten seconds later came 007's last, fragmentary message: 'Radio . . . Korean Air Zero Zero Seven . . . All engines . . . Rapid decompression . . . descending to one zero . . . Delta . . .' This transmission lasted 18 seconds[56] – so 007 was still on the air a remarkable 56 seconds after it had been hit.

Exactly what happened next is a matter of some dispute. The Japanese Self-Defence Agency claimed that 007 fell rapidly, disappearing off the Wakkanai radar screen at 18.29. The US, which maintains a separate radar facility at Wakkanai, but claims to rely for its information on the Japanese facility in this case, insisted that 007 made a far slower descent. According to this version of events – which soon became accepted as the correct version – the Wakkanai radar saw the large blip it had been following (without knowing it was 007) descend to 16,400 feet at 18.30 and to 1000 feet at 18.38, at which altitude it fell below the radar net and disappeared off the screen.[57] At the time it was hit 007 had been some 365 miles off course[58] and perhaps as little as one minute's flight from international airspace.

The conflict between the 18.29 and 18.38 crash times is not easily resolved: it would certainly have been far happier for the passengers and crew if the former time were correct and, as we shall see,[59] there is some reason to believe it may be. Nonetheless, it seems sensible as long as this point remains unresolved, to follow the 'official' US version. What happened, then, after 007 was hit?

We know that the initial missile impact was not fatal, for First Officer Son Dong-hui was, according to the ICAO transcript,[60] able to call Tokyo 38 seconds later without even mentioning an attack, wait a few seconds for Tokyo to reply and then shout that rapid decompression was taking place and that, following standard emergency procedure, 007 was descending to 10,000 feet as quickly as possible. The rapid decompression mentioned by First Officer Son could only mean that there was a hole in the fuselage – which would also have caused a drop in temperature (outside it was minus 50°C)[61] and oxygen loss. But the hole can't have been a big one, for then all the passengers and crew would have been irresistibly sucked out and flung into the freezing blackness. Clearly this did not happen for Son was still on the radio 56 seconds later. This in turn means that no missile could have hit the fuselage (for it would have blown a huge hole there if it had). So the plane was clearly hit on one of its wings and probably by only one missile. If two missiles had both hit a single wing it would probably have been torn right off and 007 would have spiralled down in far less than 12½ minutes. If two separate wings had been hit the effect would probably have been much the same. All this suggests that the radar-guided Anab missed for some reason but that the heat-seeking Anab hit: it would have gone straight into one of the engines, causing a large explosion and flinging pieces of it with immense force in all directions. Some of these pieces would have torn holes in the fuselage skin – the shrapnel effect would probably have made a number of small holes.

A few of the passengers may have been lucky enough to have been killed outright by the metal fragments tearing through the plane. Those who were still asleep would have been awoken by an immense shock wave and a terrifying crash. The oxygen would have been rapidly sucked out of the plane and the onrush of thin, freezing air would have produced both a thick mist and a stupendous drop in temperature. In these conditions, with people screaming and probably thrown around the cabin, many – most notably the babies and smaller children – would have failed to get their oxygen masks on. There were twenty-eight children under the age of fifteen on 007. Those who did not suffer rapid asphyxiation would have begun, quite rapidly, to freeze to death. Unfortunately, though, some would have got oxygen masks on and the residual warmth of the cabin (plus their sleeping blankets) and the plane's rapid descent into more breathable air would have meant that some – perhaps many – of the 269 people aboard would have survived to live through another 12 minutes of utter terror before meeting their deaths.

The explosion of the engine would have sent jet fuel pouring over red hot metal, but at 32,000 feet the air would have been too thin to allow combustion. At about 16,000 feet the thicker and warmer air might have caused ignition to take place (though none of the wreckage ultimately recovered showed any trace of fire damage). But if the US version is correct, 007 did not blow up – if this had happened, or even if a wing had sheared off, it would not have remained a single large blip on the Wakkanai radar. Indeed, it seems clear that Captain Chun and his fellow officers (who would certainly have got their oxygen masks on) were still in some measure of control of 007 – though doubtless it would have been a desperate struggle. For, if the reported Wakkanai radar readings are correct, 007 descended 15,600 feet in the first four minutes after missile impact: a descent rate of 3900 feet a minute. But it then took a further eight minutes to reach 1000 feet – so in this latter stage the plane had levelled out, losing height at less than 2000 feet a minute. This would clearly imply that someone was at the controls: if there hadn't been, the reverse would have happened and the plane would have put itself into a steepening dive. Moreover, the us experts who reported on the Wakkanai radar tape say that 007 came down in a series of widening spirals[62] – probably an attempt to lose forward speed.

Captain Chun was, in a word, deploying all his redoubtable fighter-ace skills – and to some effect. He would have known that perhaps his best chance now was to level out and lose enough speed to attempt a belly landing on the sea's surface. With luck the 747 would stay afloat long enough to scramble at least some of its complement into escape dinghies. But all this leaves another mystery: why, in these 12½ minutes, did not Chun or one of his co-officers radio a Mayday message? They would have known that this was the key to a rapid air–sea rescue, on which 269 lives might rest. And we know that 007's radio was still working after the missile impact. If the radio had not been knocked out by the initial impact or in the first 56 seconds after it, it is difficult to see why it should have ceased to work after that. Some doubt exists, too, whether a belly landing was the only alternative: 747s can fly quite considerable distances on only one engine. 007 was clearly flyable and may have had up to three engines working – but the extent of the damage may have given Captain Chun little choice.

Overhead the Soviet fighters were still circling. They had broken off straight after the attack and immediately begun questioning their ground control about how far it was back to base and giving repeated checks on their own rapidly reducing fuel gauges. Clearly, they wanted to get back home fast. But – after a crucial one and a half minutes' delay – Soviet ground control decided it wanted confirmation of the kill. Perhaps this was because their radar was still having difficulty picking up 007 and they just wanted to be sure; perhaps the Russians, too, could see what we are told Wakkanai saw – the controlled descent, the single large blip, denoting a plane still all in one piece. But above all, of course, the Russians must have been picking up 007 apparently broadcasting on its radio a full 56 seconds after the missile impact – and become seriously alarmed that the intruder was, after all, getting away. So while the su-15 was ordered back to base right away, the two mig-23s were ordered to fly down and see what had happened to 007 – no doubt to finish it off with more missiles if necessary. The Soviet ground controller must have been puzzled by hearing the last snatches of 007's radio conversation, and particularly by the absence of the mandatory Mayday call. How to reconcile this with Kasmin's 'The target is destroyed'? So Major Kasmin was now called up and asked a question to which he replied, 'I launched both.' Clearly, the question has been, 'Did you fire both missiles?' – as if the plane's continued flight threw into doubt whether it could really have been hit by both missiles. Meanwhile, the MIGs reported no sight of 007 anywhere.

If the US version of the 18.38 crash-down time is to be believed, then the MIGs failed badly in their quest, for somewhere beneath them 007 must still have been rushing downwards. The scene inside the plane must have been utterly terrifying – people falling and sliding, children screaming and an icy, knifelike wind shrieking into the plane as it fell and fell through an age of blackness. It would be more pleasant to believe that death came quickly at a great height, but if the US version is correct those inside 007 – including 28 children under the age of fifteen – had to endure a long 12½ minutes of utter horror. One cannot read, let alone write, about such scenes without experiencing the strongest and most elemental emotions.

The plane, we are told, went off the Wakkanai radar at 1000 feet. If it was still falling at 2000 feet a minute, it had another 30 seconds to impact. If Captain Chun had wholly succeeded with his manoeuvre he would have put the plane down level at 90 knots or less. Perhaps he even achieved it but the 747's great under-wing engines, protruding awkwardly under the plane and hitting the water first, would probably have caused the plane to jackknife down into the depths. But it seems more likely that the plane hit the surface at too steep an angle or still going far too fast, the resulting impact breaking the plane into pieces. The sad remains of the headless torso of a child were brought up in a fishing net off Shiretoko peninsula (eastern Hokkaido) on 8 September.[63] Such dreadful injuries – the tearing off of the arms, legs, and head – suggest an immense explosion and, mercifully, an instantaneous death for all aboard. Indeed, the problem with evidence like this is that it throws grave doubt on the whole notion of a gradual descent, suggesting instead a huge midair explosion.

At 18.38:37 one of the MIGs made its last search report: 'I don't see anything in this area. I just looked.' The fighters gave up and sped back home. No doubt Major Kasmin and his fellow pilots have since relived these moments through many long days and nights.

Many questions remain about the last flight of KAL 007 but none is of more importance than how the plane came to be off course. In this respect, there is one potentially key piece of evidence which has not, to date, received sufficient attention. It lies in the papers Captain Chun left behind at Anchorage. The ICAO *Final Report* faithfully reproduces 007's computerised flight plan, reproduced in Appendix, and Captain Chun's notations are scribbled in longhand alongside various stages of the route.[64] At the top he wrote 'ETP 1501 NM' and under that '3HR 22Min'. ETP stands for Equal Time Point – i.e. an *en route* staging point – an oddity, for there is no such point 1501 nautical miles (NM) along Romeo 20. What is striking is that 1501 nautical miles along the route that 007 actually took brings one exactly to the edge of Soviet airspace. In fact 007 was to cross the Kamchatka coastline three hours and 30 minutes after takeoff – but by then the plane had fallen nine minutes behind schedule in terms of its reported position; but for that 007 would have entered on its path across Soviet territory almost exactly three hours and 22 minutes from takeoff.

The flight-plan schedule lists all the waypoints along Romeo 20, together with the times at which 007 was due to arrive at them. The time to reach NEEVA is listed as two hours and 50 minutes. Under that Captain Chun scribbled '+32'. This again produces the three hours and 22 minutes figure. In the space below NEEVA Captain Chun made a heavy V-shaped mark, inside which he wrote '250 NM'. This too is highly suggestive, for it was, of course, after falsely reporting NEEVA that 007 actually crossed Kamchatka. If one retraces the actual flight path of 007 across Kamchatka one finds that the plane was inside Soviet airspace for approximately 250 nautical miles.

The heaviest mark made by Captain Chun is a thick arrow pointing at waypoint NOKKA, and he has also circled the time at which that waypoint was to be reached and written, inside a circle, '1826'. There is a certain poignancy to this, for it was at 18.26 that 007 was shot down – just as the plane should have been readying itself to report waypoint NOKKA (though, of course, 007 was nowhere near the real waypoint NOKKA). Had 007 actually got to its notional waypoint NOKKA, it would have meant that it had eluded the Soviet fighters and was home free in international airspace. It looks for all the world as though Captain Chun was using his flight-plan paper to work out amendments to that plan to take into account the path that 007 actually took. If so, this might help explain Chun's failure to respond to the increasingly aggressive signals of the Soviet fighters in the last moments before the shoot-down. Having circled '1826' Chun may have felt that once 007 had reached that time point it was safe – and but for the final swerve over Sakhalin 007 would indeed have reached international airspace at that time. A priori, at least, these scribbles on the flight plan give an impression of deliberateness and premeditation which sit awkwardly with any 'accidental' explanation.

Although many questions about the last flight of KAL 007 remain in dispute, there was never any doubt about the danger the plane and its occupants was in once it deviated off course – for it was then flying over perhaps the most dangerous part of the world's surface. It is to the question of why the northwest Pacific plays so tense and pivotal a role in superpower conflict that we must now turn.

1 Captain Chun Byong-in, the pilot of KAL 007, in the front row of a KAL group photograph (front row, left). His status among KAL pilots is clearly reflected by his position next to the KAL President, Mr Cho Choong-Hoon ('Harry') Cho. (*Camera Press*)

**RC-135:**
Wing span: 145 ft. 9 in.
Length overall: 152 ft. 11in.
Length of fuselage: 145 ft. 6 in.
Height overall: 42 ft. 5in.

**Boeing 747-200**
Wing span: 195 ft. 8 in.
Length overall: 231 ft. 4 in.
Length of fuselage: 225 ft. 2 in.
Height overall: 63 ft. 5 in.

2 A scale comparison of the RC-135 and a KAL 747 jumbo similar to the shot-down 007. Unfortunately, appreciation of scale is a matter of distance and visibility conditions. (*The Associated Press*)

3 A Sukhoi SU-15 'Flagon' of the type piloted by Major Kasmin. (*The Associated Press*)

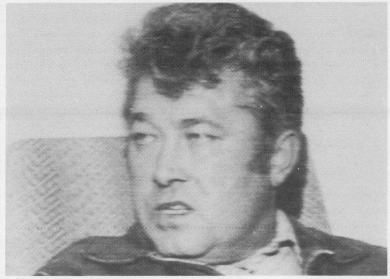

4  Major Kasmin interviewed (anonymously) on Soviet TV after the shootdown. (*The Press Association*)

5  Anxious relatives of KAL 007's passengers being addressed by the KAL Vice-President, Mr Cho Choong-kun (younger brother of 'Harry' Cho), at Kimpo Airport, Seoul. (*The Associated Press*)

6 President and Mrs Reagan appear for the first presidential announcement on 'what can only be called the Korean Airline Massacre'. (*The Associated Press*)

7 Men near the heart of the storm over KAL 007.

(a) William P. Clark, National Security Advisor.

(b) Larry Speakes, the White House Press Secretary. 'You don't tell us how to stage the news and we don't tell you how to cover it.'

(c) Ed Meese, White House Counsellor at the time of the shoot-down. Meese and Clark, the two leading members of President Reagan's 'California mafia', were the first two men to have to deal with news of the shoot-down.

(d) Assistant Secretary of State Richard Burt together with his wife, Gahl Hodges (a White House Social Secretary). Burt provided the media with the authoritative official version of how news of the shoot-down arrived in Washington.

(e) William Casey, Director of the CIA.

(*Camera Press*)

8 Mrs Jeane Kirkpatrick, US Representative at the UN, with the tape of the Soviet fighters' conversations. The tape was claimed to present the definitive truth about the shoot-down – but the transcript of it provided by Mrs Kirkpatrick was soon discovered to be misleading in important respects. (*The Associated Press*)

9 The dramatic scene in the UN Security Council when the visual mock-up of the incident created by the USIA Director, Charles Z. Wick, was shown. Mrs Kirkpatrick on the left, glasses in hand. Soviet Ambassador Troyanovsky, who had earlier objected to the (unprecedented) placement of the visual monitor, keeps his back resolutely turned to the screen. (*The Associated Press*)

10 Demonstrators from the National Conservative Political Action Committee gather near the White House. The far right frequently depicted the tragedy as an assassination attempt on Larry McDonald. (*The Associated Press*)

11 Mrs Kathryn McDonald, widow of Congressman McDonald, addresses the congregation of the Rev Jerry Falwell's Baptist Church on the KAL 007 tragedy. (*The Associated Press*)

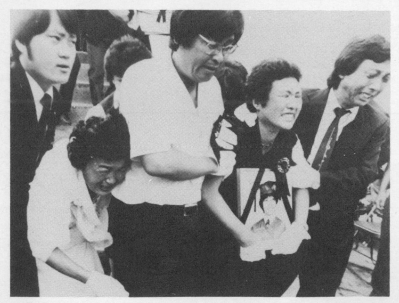

12 The family of one of the Korean victims of the tragedy (in graduation photograph) bent double in grief at the special altar to the victims erected at Kimpo Airport, Seoul. (*Camera Press*)

13 A section of the crowd at the 100,000 strong rally held in Seoul to protest against the shoot-down. At the rally's highpoint a Soviet pilot was burnt in effigy. (*Camera Press*)

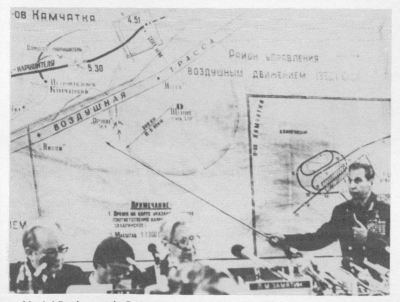

14 Marshal Ogarkov puts the Soviet case at his Moscow press conference. KAL 007's track is shown in black on the large map, with a turn shortly before Kamchatka. The tip of Ogarkov's pointer rests just under a P-3C Orion surveillance plane claimed to be in the vicinity. The smaller map immediately behind Ogarkov shows the Soviet depiction of KAL 007's rendezvous with the RC-135. (*The Associated Press*)

15  Wreckage from KAL 007 under examination at Wakkanai police station. (*The Associated Press*)

16  A Japanese official hails a Soviet vessel in the search area near Moneron Island, asking for news. In fact co-operation between the rival search flotillas was nil. (*Camera Press*)

# TWO

# East Asia: Great Power Politics at the End of the World

The last flight of KAL 007 took place over one of the coldest and most remote regions on earth. The East Asia edge – the giant littoral which runs from the shores of Alaska to Indo-China – has long been considered, both literally and figuratively, as the end of the world. Sakhalin was so remote from European Russia that it was only in 1849 that the Czar learned that it was an island, not a peninsula.[1] Japan remained sunk in feudal sleep until the visits of Commodore Perry and Admiral Putyatin in 1853. Even in 1867 the Czar could quite casually dispose of Alaska to the USA for $7 million and even that price – two cents an acre – was regarded as so exorbitant in Washington that the Russians had to bribe a number of American newspapers and Congressmen to ensure the deal went through.[2]

For a long time the region – lacking any great powers of its own – was quite nakedly up for grabs. In 1853 the Czar had to beat off an Anglo-French attempt upon Kamchatka and the French went on to take the whole of Indo-China. But the greatest prize was the pillage of China. As Lord Rosebery pointed out: 'There we have a sick man worth many Turkeys, of more value to us than all the Armenians that ever walked the earth; as a commercial inheritance priceless, beyond all the ivory and peacocks that ever came out of Africa.'[3] It made the American Wild West seem like a small-scale exercise in orderly and peaceful progress. The emergence of Japan as a great power merely added another energetic party to this free-for-all.

The result was a century of incessant wars. The great powers bullied the crippled giant of China into one concession after another in a running series of conflicts. Japan's victory over China in 1894–95 was followed by an even greater one over Russia in 1904–05. Japan's bloody annexation of Korea in 1910 was followed by her move in force into China in 1915. Between 1918 and 1925 the US and Japan carried out a large-scale invasion of Siberia[4] – a prelude to the Japanese invasion of Manchuria in 1931, another Russo-Japanese war in 1937–39, and finally Japan's great sweep across the Pacific in 1941–42 – an adventure which came to a brutal halt in the nuclear fireballs over Hiroshima and Nagasaki in 1945.

Japan's bid to expel all other powers from the region merely had the effect in the end of accelerating the movement of Soviet and American power into the area. During the Second World War Stalin even went so far as to offer the Americans a series of bases on Kamchatka and Komsomolsk–Nikolayevsk from which the USAF could bomb Japan – though with the curious stipulation that the Americans would have to wear Soviet uniforms. The Americans had happily assembled their men and measured them for such uniforms before the war's end brought all such plans to a halt.[5] Without this the Cold War might have begun with the interesting complication of a string of USAF bases on Soviet territory itself. As it was, the war left the superpowers in a direct confrontation across the Sea of Japan. US power, expanding westwards across the Pacific, had finally culminated in the US occupation of Japan itself. Russia's own advance eastwards, already signalled by the building of the Trans-Siberian railway, simultaneously culminated in their recapture of southern Sakhalin from the Japanese and their seizure of the Kurile Islands.

The advance of the superpowers did not put an end to the region's wars but it gave them a different character. The collapse of Japan left a forest fire of Communist insurgencies in its wake – in China, Korea, Malaya, the Philippines and all the countries of Indo-China. One of these insurgencies culminated in the world's greatest revolution – in China; while in Indo-China it launched a still continuing series of wars in which the French, the US, the Chinese and now the Indo-Chinese themselves have wrought a dreadful carnage. In 1950–53 Korea witnessed the largest direct conflict between East and West the world has yet seen. The region has, indeed, continued to be the cockpit of savage frontier violence, though on a gigantic canvas with all the most modern horrors of military technology deployed. This is still the only region in the world where nuclear weapons have been used in war (and their use was threatened again over Korea and again, later, over Formosa) and no region has seen such massive use of napalm, chemical defoliants and electronic warfare. Here, too, the only armed clash between the two Communist superpowers took place (along the Amur and Ussuri rivers). Disputes remain endemic here: the two Koreas remain locked in a state of cold (and sometimes hot) war; Japan disputes Russian possession of the Kuriles; China disputes its borders both with the USSR and Vietnam and faces a bitter resistance to its claims on Taiwan; Korean animosity towards Japan remains intense – the list is almost endless.

This bitter topography of human conflict is matched by an equally violent physical environment. The archipelago of the Sea of Japan – which includes both some of the densest and most sparsely populated settlements in the world – is prone to earthquake and volcanic action. Sakhalin, although it is at the same latitude as Germany, enjoys an arctic climate thanks to the Kurile current: the temperature is below freezing for over half the year. Kamchatka – like Sakhalin a land of forests, tundra, mountains, fog and freezing high winds – is even colder, with the seas around it frozen solid for most of the year. Little wonder that the exploitation of the area's mineral wealth was for long dependent on prison labour which, both under the Czars and Stalin, was quite normally worked to death. As Chekhov put it in his *Sakhalin Diaries*, 'I have seen Ceylon, which is paradise, and Sakhalin, which is hell.' In recent years the Russians have launched a prodigious effort to begin the exploitation of Siberia's economic wealth and to link their East Asian provinces more tightly into the USSR, most notably through the construction of the mighty 2000-mile Baikal–Amur (BAM) railway. It seems safe to say, however, that Sakhalin and Kamchatka will be among the last regions of the USSR to be transformed by this effort.

To most people the region remains a byword for obscurity: perhaps the only fact about Sakhalin known in the West is that Yul Brynner was born there. Nonetheless, the region has latterly become one of the major pivots of the world's political and military balance. Across the narrow seas of the Japanese archipelago the world's four greatest powers – the US, the USSR, China and Japan – face one another in tense confrontation. Nowhere else on the earth's surface is this the case. Great nuclear armadas of air and sea face one another here, separated by just a few minutes' flying time. Strategically, East Asia is no longer just an obscure and freezing last frontier – it is a potential flashpoint which dwarfs Berlin in significance. This is now perhaps the most likely region of the world in which a third world war could begin.

## The strategic balance

According to Admiral Robert Long, the Commander-in-Chief of US forces in the Pacific, 'in the last decade, the most dramatic military action that has occurred anywhere in the world has been the Soviet military build-up in the Pacific.'[6] There is some substance to such a view. The number of Soviet ground-force divisions in the USSR's far eastern regions increased from eighteen in 1965 to forty-seven by 1982, comprising nearly half a million men. These are, though, almost exclusively concentrated along the Chinese frontier, with only one division on Kamchatka and two on Sakhalin.[7] In roughly the same period Soviet airforce strength in the Far East increased sixfold, so that by 1979 the USSR had some 2400 combat aircraft in the region, comprising 800 fighters, 350 bombers, 1200 strike aircraft and sundry other transport craft.[8] These include all the most modern combat aircraft types, most notably ten of the new TU-22M Backfire bombers.[9]

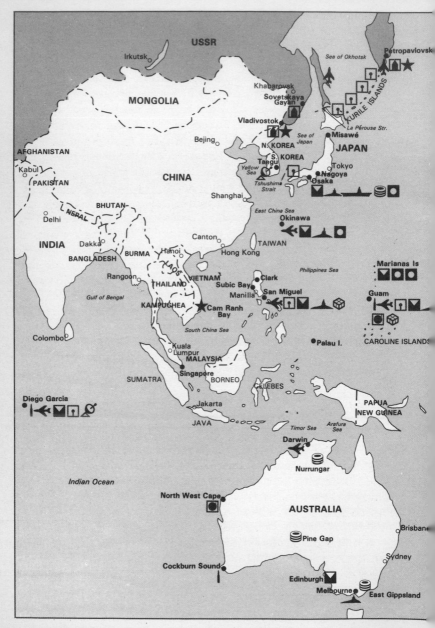

3 The Strategic Context of the KAL 007 Flight. *Source*: adapted from Michael Klare, 'Les Tensions dans la Pacifique du Nord-Ouest', *Le Monde Diplomatique*, October 1983.

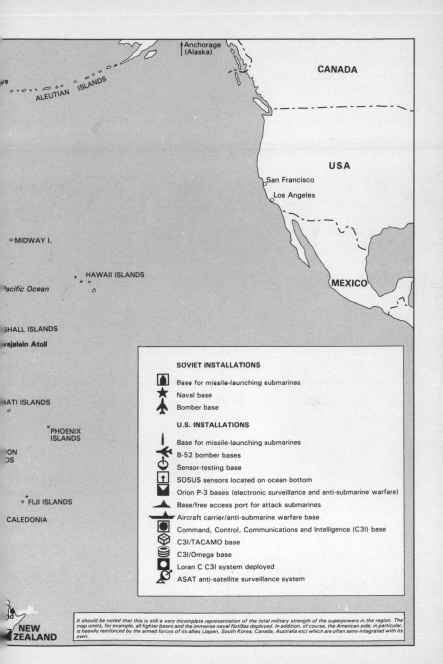

Anchorage
(Alaska)

ALEUTIAN ISLANDS

va

CANADA

USA

San Francisco

Los Angeles

MIDWAY I.

HAWAII ISLANDS

Pacific Ocean

MEXICO

SHALL ISLANDS

vajalein Atoll

ATI ISLANDS

PHOENIX
ISLANDS

ON
OS

FIJI ISLANDS

CALEDONIA

NEW
ZEALAND

**SOVIET INSTALLATIONS**

Base for missile-launching submarines

Naval base

Bomber base

**U.S. INSTALLATIONS**

Base for missile-launching submarines

B-52 bomber bases

Sensor-testing base

SOSUS sensors located on ocean bottom

Orion P-3 bases (electronic surveillance and anti-submarine warfare)

Base/free access port for attack submarines

Aircraft carrier/anti-submarine warfare base

Command, Control, Communications and Intelligence (C3I) base

C3I/TACAMO base

C3I/Omega base

Loran C C3I system deployed

ASAT anti-satellite surveillance system

*It should be noted that this is still a very incomplete representation of the total military strength of the superpowers in the region. The map omits, for example, all fighter bases and the immense naval flotillas deployed. In addition, of course, the American side, in particular, is heavily reinforced by the armed forces of its allies (Japan, South Korea, Canada, Australia etc) which are often semi-integrated with its own.*

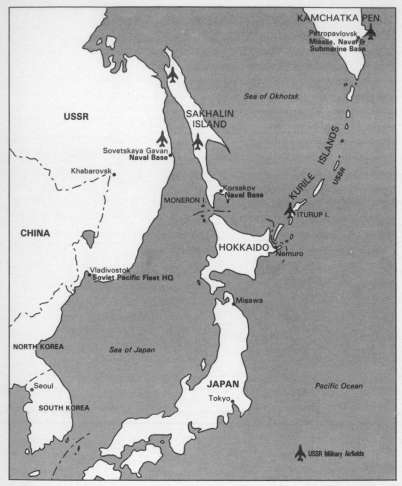

4 Soviet military facilities in the path of 007's flight – which took it almost directly over both the Petropavlovsk and Korsakov bases. *Source*: *Newsweek*, 12 September 1983.

The most striking development in recent years has, however, been the build-up of the Soviet Pacific Fleet into the largest of the USSR's four fleets. By 1982 it comprised 352 surface ships, 105 submarines and about 400 naval aircraft, with the most notable recent addition being the 40,000-ton aircraft carrier, *Minsk*.[10] To its traditional home port of Vladivostok, the Soviet fleet has added major naval bases at Petropavlovsk (Kamchatka) and at Sovyet-skaya Gavan (opposite Sakhalin). Other military outposts – essentially comprising fighter bases and the troops required to defend them – are to be found on Sakhalin, Kamchatka and Iturup, one of the Kurile chain. Although the appearance of the large amphibious landing craft, *Ivan Rogov*, in the waters of the Sea of Okhotsk created a certain stir in western naval circles,[11] the most significant development of recent years has undoubtedly been the deployment from Petropavlosk of 24 modern missile-carrying submarines. In particular the nuclear-powered Delta-class submarine added a new dimension to Soviet capabilities. The Delta II packed 16 SS-N-8 missiles[12] and the Delta III even more, all with a near-5000-mile range which brought most targets within the continental US well within its reach, even if the missiles were launched from within the Sea of Okhotsk. In practice, such craft could be expected to lurk in the great trenches off Japan, the Kuriles, Kamchatka or the Aleutians – or even right up against the US West Coast. The Deltas thus constitute almost half of the USSR's sea-borne nuclear deterrent force. Even the Deltas were eclipsed, however, by the even bigger Typhoon-class submarines of 25,000 tons – the world's largest submersible craft, each carrying 80 nuclear warheads – which began to deploy from Petropavlovsk in September 1983. The USSR had offered to halt the Typhoon deployment if agreement were reached not to deploy cruise and Pershing II missiles in western Europe. When cruise and Pershing went ahead, so did the Typhoon.

Despite all this, it is clear that the US retains a quite overwhelming strategic advantage in the area, for all that it is the USSR's back garden. Partly this is just because the Soviet position is riddled with vulnerabilities. The overwhelming majority of the ships in the Soviet Pacific Fleet are small and old, suitable only for coastguard duty. In large modern ships the US has a clear supremacy even in numerical terms.[13] Almost all the Soviet ground forces are focused on the Chinese threat: the forces the USSR maintains on Kamchatka, Iturup and Sakhalin would be quite inadequate to repel a determined amphibious assault. All the Soviet military bases in the region are many thousands of miles away from the Soviet heartland, making reinforcement in men and equipment difficult. Vladivostok depends utterly on the single Trans-Siberian railway line which, for most of its length, runs within easy artillery range of the Chinese border and which could be cut at a moment's notice by the USAF.

Petropavlosk and Iturup do not even have a rail link and have to be supplied by air or sea. They are thus even more vulnerable.[14] Moreover, the USSR, though ringed by hostile bases and forces in the Aleutians, Guam, Japan and South Korea, has no real ally in the area. Its fleet enjoys port facilities at Da Nang and Cam Ranh in Vietnam, but these are not major bases and they are far away. It has no bases of any sort in North Korea (which is attempting to balance delicately between China and the USSR) and the North Korean Air Force now relies on such obsolete planes that it is dismissed by the USAF as a derisory quantity.[15] Above all, most of the Soviet Pacific Fleet, whether operating from Sakhalin, Vladivostok or Sovyetskaya Gavan, can only gain entry to the Pacific through two narrow straits, Tsushima (between South Korea and Japan) or La Pérouse (between Sakhalin and the Japanese isle of Hokkaido). It is a relatively simple matter to interdict passage through those straits for any power that wants to.

Against this highly vulnerable Soviet position is ranged an immensely stronger American force. The US maintains major air and naval bases at Shemya and Adak in the Aleutians, a naval base at Yokohama and Kadena air base on Okinawa, air bases at Osan, Kunsan and Taegu (South Korea), and further such bases at Yokota and Misawa in Japan. In all these cases US forces are backed by the considerable forces of Japan and South Korea, both of which are equipped with the same ultramodern US aircraft, most notably the F-16 fighter–bomber for which the Russians have no equivalent. Beyond that US forces are well within range from the gigantic air and naval bases at Subic and Clark in the Philippines and from Guam in the Marianas. Guam houses a considerable force of B-52 bombers, and also a large force of US nuclear-powered submarines armed with Polaris, Poseidon and, soon, Trident missiles.

To all this must be added the gigantic force of the US Seventh Fleet which patrols the western Pacific. Its battle groups are headed by four enormous aircraft carriers (each more than twice as big as the sole Russian carrier). If need be, the Seventh Fleet could be reinforced by the US Third Fleet, with its three further carriers, which cruises generally in the eastern Pacific. All told, this would bring American air strength to some 780 planes, a high proportion of which can carry nuclear weapons, and most of which are considered technically superior to their Soviet counterparts.[16]

There seems little doubt that this mighty array of force not only far outmatches the Soviet forces opposite it but could, in case of war, deliver a knockout blow against the USSR even if US forces elsewhere in the world had been disabled. Officially, at least, the US purpose is more modest: to bottle up the Soviet Pacific Fleet and supporting forces inside the Sea of Japan and to be in a position to cut off and destroy its bases at short notice. Such, at least, was the traditional US strategy. The advent of the Reagan Administration has, however, set in motion a series of developments which collectively suggest that a far more radical – and risky – strategy has been taking shape.

## The Reagan build-up

Ronald Reagan entered office in 1981 committed to an arms build-up without precedent in history. Already under President Carter early promises to trim the arms budget had been put into full reverse and spending sharply increased. Thus Reagan came to power with a defence budget for 1982 already set at $183 billion – one whole quarter of the federal budget. Unbothered by this, Reagan immediately set forth plans which would double defence spending over his first term to $324 billion – one whole third of the federal budget.[17] Justification for such a programme was sought in a series of inflated claims of rocketing Soviet military expenditure. In November 1983 the CIA admitted that such claims were nonsense: between 1966 and 1976 Soviet defence expenditure had grown at 4 to 5 per cent per annum but since 1976 had slowed down to a steady 2 per cent per annum.[18] Such embarrassing figures were simply ignored: indeed, by 1984 Reagan had laid down a programme which envisaged a further doubling of defence expenditure over his second term to a total of $1.9 trillion.[19] No country in the history of the world had hitherto spent such sums on arms even in wartime. Such spending in peacetime only made sense as preparation for a major war – though many doubted, of course, that it made much sense at all.

In the controversies over US defence spending unleashed by this prodigious leap in the arms race, the high ground was inevitably occupied by the most glamorous new weapons – the MX missile, the F-18 fighter, the B-1B bomber, the M-1 tank – and by the emplacement of the new cruise and Pershing II missiles. Less noticed but just as significant was the immense further build-up in US naval power, much of which was to be used to strengthen even more the ring of steel around East Asia.

Reagan's new Navy Secretary, John Lehman, announced early on that the Administration's aim was to achieve 'a frank maritime superiority over any other power or group of powers'.[20] To this end the number of the US Navy's ships would be increased from 479 in 1981 to 610 by 1988, this mighty force to be grouped round 15 carrier groups – the carriers themselves to be of the giant *Nimitz* (90,000 ton) class.[21] Thus afforced, the US would be able to conduct at least three simultaneous wars around the world at any given time.

In the northwest Pacific the fruits of such a policy were quickly seen in major fleet reinforcements, most notably the new fourth carrier, the nuclear-powered *Carl Vinson*, and the *New Jersey*, now entirely refitted as the world's largest battleship (each of its shells is the size of a small car, devastating an area of half a square mile on impact). In 1983 the dispatch was announced of a further 36 F-16s to South Korea and the emplacement of a further 48 F-16s on Misawa (Japan).[22] At the same time South Korea was defined as a 'first line of defence', thus putting it on the same footing as Western Europe, and its status as a 'zone of significant interest' upgraded to that of a 'zone of vital interest'.[23] Japanese and US forces were ordered to go onto a permanent alert, patrolling twenty-four hours out of twenty-four, around the various straits out of the Sea of Japan.[24] Similarly, in early 1983 plans were leaked about the impending emplacement in South Korea of a new GLASS system of ground-launched antiship cruise missiles.[25] In October 1983 the US Defence Department issued a report calling for the emplacement of further GLASS systems at Sasebo and Misawa (Japan).[26] The Japanese, the report argued, should be encouraged to buy such systems which would not only cover the whole of the Sea of Japan but would enable them to strike at targets deep within the USSR. If Japanese sensitivity about nuclear weapons remained a problem, the report continued, it would be possible to arm the GLASS missiles with conventional warheads.[27] The resulting uproar led the Japanese Self Defence Agency to deny all such plans and to dismiss the report as merely part of Boeing's campaign to sell more cruise missiles, but the effect of this was somewhat attenuated the next day when the Commander-in-Chief of the US Pacific Fleet confirmed that as from June 1984 antiship cruise missiles would be deployed throughout the Pacific.[28] In practice, of course, the official Japanese ban on the stationing of nuclear weapons in Japan has been flouted quite openly for years. Not only do US ships armed with such weapons routinely call at Japanese ports, but harbour guides at Yokohama will quite openly point out to tourists the sheds where cruise missiles are housed.[29]

The attempt to overcome Japan's anti-nuclear sensibility and generally to push Japan into far higher levels of defence spending was, of course, one of Washington's chief diplomatic objectives. The advent of the Nakasone Administration in Tokyo, with its far tougher and more assertive defence posture, suggested at least a limited success for such a policy. At the same time, of course, the continuing pursuit of Sino–American détente, with clear suggestions of future military cooperation between the two powers,[30] meant that the USSR was now hemmed in between three hostile great powers in East Asia. Beyond this a whole series of other developments strengthened the US posture in the region. In 1983 the US delivered $900 million of military aid to the Marcos regime in the Philippines in return for an agreement guaranteeing the US complete freedom of action (i.e. full nuclear deployment) from its Subic and Clark bases there.[31] In July 1983 the US secured the right to use the Palaos Islands in Micronesia for the transit of nuclear materials.[32] A new ASAT (anti-satellite) radar facility was announced for construction at Taegu (South Korea) to add to the existing facilities at Guam and Kwajalein (Marshalls).[33] The new TACAMO aircraft, with a seven-kilometre-long radar antenna, was introduced, thus ensuring the continuity of communications and intelligence even if the existing facilities at San Miguel (Philippines), Yosami (Japan) and Northwest Cape (Australia) were to be knocked out.[34] New B-52G bombers, equipped with cruise missiles, replaced the older B-52DS at Guam.[35] The Rapid Deployment Force, in which the Diego Garcia base plays a pivotal role, was brought up from a strength of 100,000 men to 400,000.[36] There is no end to this build-up in sight.

The big question posed by all this was, what was it for? Well before the Reagan build-up, after all, US superiority was hardly in doubt. *Newsweek* reported, while Carter was still in office, that 'ship for ship, American analysts say, the Soviets do not measure up to the US Navy. "In a conflict with the United States," said one naval expert, "the Soviet Navy would lead a short, exciting life."'[37] Similarly, Harold Brown, President Carter's Defence Secretary, was of the opinion that the alliance between the US, China and Japan 'must be the real nightmare for the Soviets, for the modest cooperation [between them] achieved in the years 1975–80 has modified the balance of forces to the Soviets' detriment to a degree which exceeds to a significant degree their substantial military effort in this region at the end of the 1960s and during the 1970s'.[38] Moreover, the urgency which the US attached to getting the Japanese to take over the US Navy's traditional role of bottling the Soviet fleet up in the Sea of Japan suggested that the US was considering a new role for its own forces.

Caspar Weinberger, Reagan's Defence Secretary, gave a powerful clue to the answer as early as May 1981 when he enunciated the Administration's new strategic doctrine of 'horizontal escalation': if the USSR were to attack US interests at one of its weak points 'we must be ready to launch counteroffensives in other regions and exploit the aggressor's weaknesses wherever we find them.'[39] This alarming doctrine would thus mean that if the USSR – or a 'Soviet surrogate', say, Syria – was thought to be behind a development in, say, the Middle East, which was taken to threaten US interests, then the US might respond by launching an attack either on the USSR or one of its clients in a quite different part of the world. This was pretty much what happened in late 1983 when Syrian pressure on Lebanon was immediately followed by the

US invasion of Grenada. Certainly, the traditional US view is that the Caribbean is the obvious zone for such a 'horizontal' response – it is close at hand, where the US has an overwhelming strategic advantage, and Nicaragua and Cuba make tempting targets.

Clearly, one of the more alarming features of such a strategy is the Reagan Administration's highly elastic notion of what constitutes a 'Soviet surrogate': a sudden move by a highly unpredictable radical state such as Libya might be taken as *casus belli* for a major US offensive somewhere else. But even more alarming is the notion that the Soviet Far East may have been designated as such a target region. This idea has been floated by the former Pentagon official and defence analyst, William Kennedy, who pointed out in March 1983 that the northwest Pacific was an ideal candidate for such action: 'That is the only place on earth where geography would permit the US to marshal superior forces at points crucial to Soviet interests and objectives while making it difficult or impossible for the Soviets to respond in kind.'[40] Kennedy went on, indeed, to suggest that the US should quite formally adopt a 'North Pacific strategy', including the use of amphibious assault troops against Kamchatka–Sakhalin. Nothing, he argued – plausibly enough – would more strongly dissuade the USSR from Third World adventures than if it realised that the US riposte might be an attack on Soviet territory itself. Given the huge US advantage within the region in conventional forces, there would be no need, after all, to use nuclear weapons – and the Russians, having promised they will never make first use of nuclear weapons, would be on the spot. (That the Russians, finding their bases impacted by conventional high explosives, might mistake these for nuclear weapons and react accordingly, is, of course, only one of the many high-wire risks attached to such a strategy.)

Despite this, it seems clear that such thinking has entered the mind of the Reagan Administration and that, by a whole series of actions and gestures, it has been 'sending a message' to the Russians that bad behaviour on their part engenders a direct threat to the Soviet Far East. Even if such action is never taken, its threat would constitute a potent, indeed terrifying, pressure on Soviet freedom of manoeuvre right round the world. Would the USSR dare, for example, to reinforce Nicaragua or Cuba against a US invasion if it believed that this would lead to the US grabbing the bases on Kamchatka which they so nearly got in 1945?

Clearly, the open enunciation of such a strategy by the US would lead to uproar in the UN and the desertion of a number of American allies under the pressure of local public opinion. So while the US has publicly inveighed only about the emplacement of 108 SS-20s in the Soviet Far East, the 'message' it has been sending the USSR has been delivered with the minimum publicity in the West. The first signal was the Norpac Flexops '82 (North Pacific Flexible Operations) carried out in September 1982, which involved two whole carrier groups in operations off Kamchatka. As Klare reports, 'Although it received scant attention in the Western press, this exercise produced so much concern in Moscow that Backfire bombers were sent out to shadow the US fleet and an intelligence satellite was moved into position overhead.'[41] This was followed in April 1983 by Fleetex '83 in which three whole carrier battle groups, with 23,000 men and 300 aircraft, carried out exercises in the same area. 'It was,' said the Commander-in-Chief, Admiral Long, 'the largest fleet exercise conducted by the Pacific Fleet since World War II.'[42] In terms of firepower it was, very easily, the greatest armada ever assembled anywhere, particularly since it was reinforced by a further four warships from Canada's Pacific Fleet.

The way Fleetex '83 was mounted revealed how keen the US was that the exercise should receive minimum attention in the West but maximum attention in Moscow. First the 90,000-ton nuclear-powered USS *Enterprise* ('Big E') appeared in the Sea of Japan in February 1983 to take part in Team Spirit '83, the annual exercises conducted by US and South Korean forces. It then sailed into the Japanese port of Sasebo amidst a blaze of publicity. On 25 March it sailed out, leaving everyone in Sasebo under the impression that it was heading back to the US – this was certainly what the sailors themselves believed. In fact it proceeded north and rendezvoused at an unknown point in the Aleutians with the two huge carriers, *Midway* and *Coral Sea*, accompanied, like the *Enterprise*, by their own mighty battle groups. The whole fleet then turned and moved down the Siberian coast, 'taunting' the Soviet garrisons there by sailing within a few minutes' flying time of Petropavlovsk. 'In classical naval theory,' the *Far Eastern Economic Review* reported, 'a demonstration of this kind shows your prospective opponent that he is outclassed off his own coastline and had better stick close to home if he knows what is good for him. Patrolling Soviet TU-95 Bear naval reconnaissance aircraft seem to have got the message . . . Curiously enough, no attention was paid to this mighty flexing of maritime muscles by the Japanese press . . .'[43] Without doubt, though, alarm bells must have been ringing loud and clear in the Soviet High Command. As Admiral Long said, 'It was a visible demonstration of the refocusing of the United States on the Pacific, particularly on the northern Pacific and northeast Asia.'[44]

In fact Fleetex '83 was only the beginning: it was followed in May–September 1983 by no fewer than nine further major military exercises by the US and its Pacific allies. There is little doubt – and certainly Moscow would have been left in no doubt – that these exercises went far beyond the traditional purpose of bottling the Soviet fleet up in the Sea of Japan: they were dress rehearsals in force for a major strike against and invasion of the Soviet Far East. The only thing that couldn't be practised off Kamchatka–Sakhalin was the amphibious landings themselves and so, on 9 June 1983, 30,000 US troops, together with a Japanese contingent, carried out a massive amphibious assault exercise at Blue Beach, Okinawa. To make the point quite clear Admiral Long announced that the Pacific region 'is, I believe, the one where a confrontation with the Soviet Union is most likely to take place'.[45]

These repeated exercises in the period immediately preceding the fateful flight of KAL 007 (and another large-scale US naval exercise was planned for 25 September–5 October)[46] must have kept the Soviet Far Eastern Defence Command on almost continuous alert, with their defence controllers and fighter pilots alike in a tense, even jittery state. This makes it difficult – though of course not impossible – to believe that Soviet errors in the handling of the 007 intrusion were due to mere sloppiness and incompetence. Certainly, all those involved on the Soviet side would have known that errors traceable to such causes were likely to result in heavy sanctions. Indeed, according to General George J. Keegan Jr, former head of USAF Intelligence, Soviet pilots who have failed to shoot down intruders in the past have actually been executed.[47] And, although it is seldom realised in the West, the manner in which US aerial surveillance of the USSR is conducted means that such intrusions are by no means a rare or academic possibility.

## The surveillance presence

In addition to the off–on pressures of US naval exercises, the Soviet Far Eastern defences must confront a massive and quite continuous US surveillance effort. Both sides deploy the full panoply of modern surveillance platforms to monitor the other, of course – ground listening posts, spy satellites, and reconnaissance ships and planes – but there is no doubt that the US surveillance effort is by far the more intrusive and active of the two. The Americans boast that for all that the Sea of Okhotsk is virtually a Soviet inland sea, no Soviet ship or plane can operate there without attracting the minute and immediate attention of US surveillance. Similarly, the US boasts that while its own nuclear-missile submarines have carried out 2000 sorties without the Russians detecting them, no single equivalent Soviet sortie has escaped US detection.[48]

In part the US advantage stems merely from the fact that its surveillance forces are more aggressively deployed in forward roles. But even this rests on the fact that, as William Claytor, US Navy Secretary under Carter, puts it, 'the qualitative advantage which we have over the Soviets both in equipment and personnel is terrifying'.[49] For nowhere is the large US lead in computers and advanced electronics so tellingly deployed as in the field of surveillance. The 1960s and 1970s saw the US develop an immensely sophisticated radar technology in which pulse-doppler radar was harnessed to rapid digital processing to provide an over-the-horizon (OTH) capability able to pick up and then factor out even such minor movements as those of falling leaves or sea spray. By the mid-1970s, aboard such aircraft as the E-3 Sentry, this had been coupled with computers capable of 1.25 million operations per second, providing the US with a surveillance ability deep into the Soviet hinterland. Even aboard such older craft as the E-2C Hawkeye nearly five tons of electronic gear provided the capacity to track over 600 targets simultaneously and control over forty airborne intercepts automatically.[50] The far greater carrying capacity of the RC-135 provided an even more formidable multi-sensor platform, while the SR-71 Blackbird, flying at 2100 mph at heights up to 90,000 feet, provides what is effectively an invulnerable reconnaissance capability. Above even such craft fly satellites with a quite astonishing high-resolution photographic capacity. US satellites are now able to photograph Soviet ships in such detail that even the rivets on the deck are visible from space, while on another occasion a photograph of one Soviet city could actually reveal a man reading a newspaper on a street corner with the headlines on his paper readable from space.[51] In some of these cases the USSR simply has no equivalent capability at all, in others only a considerably inferior capability.

The Soviet Far East is ringed with an extensive US network of electronic reconnaissance posts, with ground facilities in Japan, South Korea, Australia, Guam, Diego Garcia, the Philippines, the Aleutians, and in the Marshall and Marianas Islands. To these must be added extensive shipborne electronic reconnaissance equipment and a large fleet of spy planes – RC-135s, SR-71s, U-2s, EP-3As and EP-3Es. Above these circle not only photo-reconnaissance and communications satellites, but 'ferret' (electronic interception) satellites – Rhyolites, Big Birds and Keyholes.

With such awesome technology the US is able to deploy the whole range of electronic warfare (EW) techniques, ranging from the use of electronic countermeasures (ECM) to baffle and confuse Soviet radars and sensors, to electronic counter-countermeasures (ECCM) negating their ability to reply in like mode; and to practise the several varieties of electronic intelligence (ELINT). These encompass the interception of signals (SIGINT), communications (COMINT) and telemetry (TELINT). (Telemetry refers to the emission of electronic signals by missiles in flight, giving the missile's speed, altitude, course, etc.)

All of these systems relate their information back to the headquarters of the biggest American intelligence agency, the National Security Agency (NSA), at Fort Meade, Maryland – halfway between Washington and Baltimore. With so many intelligence platforms round the world sucking up a huge quantity of communications and shooting them back to Fort Meade via satellites, there is inevitable delay in the decoding and integration of all this information. In some cases, this will simply not do, so the NSA maintains two ultrasecret communications networks, SPINTCOM (special intelligence communications) and CRITICOM (critical intelligence communications). If an intelligence receiver sends a CRITIC message then it will be flashed via Fort Meade to the White House for the immediate attention of the President and his top advisers. This network has hugely accelerated the flow of vital information to the President[52] (or, more exactly and usually, his National Security Adviser). Whereas it took eighteen hours for news of the *Mayaguez* incident to reach Gerald Ford's White House in 1975, when US Navy F-14s shot down two Libyan MIGs in 1981 the information took less than 60 seconds to flow from the F-14 cockpits over the Mediterranean to the White House.[53] In general the NSA aims to get all CRITIC messages onto the President's desk within two minutes of an event's occurrence. Thus the capability exists for the White House to be almost instantaneously informed of – and, indeed, to assume battlefield control over – developments on the other side of the world. In fact, of course, the President himself is seldom likely to be immediately available to assume such a role (President Reagan was not even woken by his advisers to hear about the Libyan MIGs), so the network places an awesome power in the hands of whoever happens to be in control of US foreign policy at the time. Except during the period when Henry Kissinger was Secretary of State, this has generally meant the President's National Security Adviser and his staff.

The intercept platforms which cruise off Soviet East Asia can expect to obtain a great variety of militarily useful intelligence. Apart from the raw data in the signals and communications they pick up, they will amass information on the nature and abilities of the Soviet command structure, its radar and other electronic facilities, where the gaps in the defensive system are – the USAF's bomber lanes in case of war – and so on. Naturally, the more radar and communications systems are activated, the more data will be picked up. This fact, together with the large US superiority in the surveillance and ECM fields, has led the US to practise continuous and deliberate intrusions into Soviet airspace. Intruder planes fly sufficiently far in to activate the Soviet defensive and communications system; these signals are hungrily sucked up by intercept platforms, and the intruder beats a hasty retreat before the Soviet missile or fighter forces can bring it down.[54]

The US has played this game of 'chicken' with Soviet air defences all round the world for over thirty years now, but quite particular attention has been paid to the region round the Sea of Japan. A *New York Times* report based on interviews with US intelligence officials in the wake of the KAL 007 incident pointed out:

The US, hoping to ascertain the extent of Soviet defences in the region, deliberately planned flights there to elicit a Soviet response from the 1950s . . . experts said that this week's incident came against the backdrop of an aggressive American effort to develop technical intelligence penetration of the Sea of Okhotsk over more than thirty years and after more than a score of such incidents, many of them recorded in considerable detail.[55]

Indeed, this practice has led Bamford to comment that in effect the NSA has been 'engaged in a secret and bloody air war with the Soviet Union'. Bamford details a number of incidents going back to 1953, in which US surveillance planes have been attacked while on missions over and around the Kamchat-ka–Sakhalin region, on several occasions resulting in the loss of the planes and their crews.[56] According to *Time*, US reconnaissance planes involved in this 'tickling' around the borders of the USSR have had more than 900 SAM missiles shot at them, but have always managed to escape.[57] This suggests an advanced US defensive capability against SAMs: the real trouble is Soviet fighters – all the known shoot-downs have occurred as a result of fighter interception. One result is that US intelligence is particularly highly geared to the takeoff of Soviet fighters. General George Keegan, the retired head of USAF Intelligence, boasts indeed that 'We're all alerted, so that if the Soviets launch a fighter to intercept, we may be aware of this in one to three minutes and can issue a warning in time for that ["tickling"] aircraft to turn away'.[58]

It is important to realise that the very fact of these deliberate intrusions into Soviet airspace has remained shrouded in secrecy. When a USAF EC-130 was shot down over Soviet Armenia in 1959, the State Department released a transcript of the MIG pilots in conversation as they shot it down, but carefully concealed from Congress and the public the fact that the plane had been flying a spy mission 'carrying electronic specialists and special equipment for receiving at close range the signals of Soviet radar transmitters'.[59] Senator Hubert Humphrey was only one of many Congressional liberals to join in the chorus of bitter attacks on the USSR for this 'unprovoked' act. The NSA Director, John Samford, used the Agency's public-address system to instruct all NSA employees not to discuss the incident: a ten-year jail sentence faced them if they did.[60]

This veil of secrecy was partially lifted in May 1960 when a U-2 spy plane was shot down over the USSR. President Eisenhower first denied any such incident and then had to admit he had been lying when the Russians produced the U-2 pilot, Gary Powers. Until then few had even known that an aircraft such as the U-2 existed and there was no mention of the fact that this was at least the thirty-fourth such incident in the secret Soviet–American air war since the early 1950s.[61] Given the legendary openness of American society and the general assumption that nothing can remain secret there for long, it is worth pointing out how successful the effort at secrecy has been. Thus, when the SR-71 was chosen to replace the U-2 both Lockheed and the USAF managed to achieve total secrecy throughout the period of the plane's design, building and flight-test programme.[62] Similarly, the electronic capabilities of US surveillance planes have remained almost wholly secret.

The next breach of secrecy did not come until 1969 when an EC-121 was shot down by North Korean MIGs over the Sea of Japan, with the loss of all thirty-one men aboard. President Nixon could not restrain himself from blurting out to a press conference that the US had been able to recreate both the North Korean and Russian radar patterns exactly so that they could read off their screens what their opponents were seeing. The NSA was furious. 'I died when I heard it,' said one official. 'This was my business. I just fell out of my chair – I literally did.' The USSR and other countries all immediately changed all their frequencies, codes and net structures – though after a few months these too had been broken.[63]

We know little in detail about US surveillance and border penetrations over East Asia since 1969, but it seems a safe bet that activity since then will have increased, not decreased. At the time of the 1969 incident US surveillance flights in the Sea of Japan had been averaging sixty a month – and this pattern was resumed only three days after the incident.[64] Given the long endurance times of reconnaissance planes, an average of two flights a day means that at least one plane is likely to be on station for twelve hours out of any 24-hour period. With the immense military build-up around the coast of Soviet East Asia since 1969 and the almost continuous large-scale naval exercises there in 1983, it seems likely that aerial surveillance was being conducted virtually around the clock. Certainly, the USSR has repeatedly complained of surveillance intrusions into its airspace here, while the North Koreans made protests over SR-71 intrusions into its airspace at a rate of over three a month throughout 1982–83.[65] During daylight hours, of course, the unparalleled abilities of photo-reconnaissance and infra-red satellites could take much of the strain. But these are less useful at night and can easily be blocked by cloud cover. So the night belongs to the ELINT satellite and, far below, to the mysterious and supersophisticated night prowlers of the USAF.

This then was the regional and military context within which the last flight of KAL 007 took place. It would be difficult to devise a more dangerous scenario. It was not surprising that the Russians, seeing a large plane far off civilian routes and deep in Soviet airspace, should believe it to be a spyplane of some sort, especially given its erratic behaviour and its failure to respond to interceptor signals. Nor, if they caught such a plane, was there very much doubt about what its likely fate would be.

# THREE

# The Political Context:
# Arms Control in the Balance

It is important to realise that the tragedy of KAL 007 not only took place within a specific military and regional context, but against the background of a finely balanced political situation – a situation which the tragedy was to transform. In essence, the Cold War between the superpowers, which had heated up steadily and fast since the advent of the Reagan Administration, had entered a promising lull by the summer months of 1983. It had begun to seem just possible that the two governments, for all their hostile rhetoric and reciprocal prejudices, might after all be able to restabilise the situation. The KAL 007 tragedy was to put paid to such hopes and tip the relations between the two superpowers down into a new and frightening spiral.

## The Reagan arms build-up in trouble

In the first two years of the Reagan Administration a succession of dramatic victories in Congress had seen the military build-up press ahead further and faster than many had believed possible. The political climate had, however, changed considerably in the wake of the 1982 midterm elections, which had seen the Democrats make striking gains. Suddenly, the President again seemed politically vulnerable. His critics were emboldened and increasing attention began to fasten on the two sets of arms-control talks – the Intermediate Nuclear Force (INF) negotiations and the Strategic Arms Reduction Talks (START). In neither case was any progress visible, but the President now came under increasing pressure, both from his European allies and domestically, not to allow them to fail through anything which could be presented as American intransigence. Either, if they failed, the responsibility for failure had to be clearly pinned on the Russians, or – preferably – they should result in some form of agreement which could be brandished to great electoral effect in both Europe and the US. The problem had been enormously heightened by President Reagan's surprise announcement of 23 March 1983 of the new Strategic Defense Initiative (SDI or, as it instantly became known, Star Wars). It seemed clear that the SDI, if it went ahead, would be a clear infringement of the 1972 ABM Treaty – indeed, it would effectively mean tearing that treaty up. It was difficult to see how the Administration could evade the charge of an aggressive escalation of the arms race and thus the responsibility for a breakdown in the arms-control process if it came.

Arms control was, indeed, the true Achilles' heel of the Reagan Administration. A number of the leading hawks within the Administration – most notably Richard Perle, the Assistant Defence Secretary – were frank opponents of arms control or, indeed, any constraints at all on a maximal US arms build-up. The prejudices of these superhawks were partly shared by many other Reaganauts, and were bolstered by the strong support of an influential group of far-Right Senators, most notably Jesse Helms, organised as the Steering Committee within the Senate. On the other hand it was quite clear that such wholesale opposition to arms control was not generally politically saleable. Not only was there no majority for such views amongst the US electorate, but it was quite clear that even European conservatives were quite alarmed by them. To insist on such views openly would be to split the NATO alliance completely. Accordingly, the Administration's stance had imperatively to be one of overall support for the arms-control process, but it was a stance dogged by the persistent splits within the Administration over the issue and the general reluctance of Administration members favourable to arms control to defend their position openly and risk being labelled as a 'détentenik'.[1]

These strains were perhaps most vividly present within the Administration's Arms Control and Disarmament Agency (ACDA). Almost immediately after Reagan came to power there had been a major clash between Lawrence Eagleburger, the Assistant Secretary of State for European Affairs, and the acting deputy director of ACDA, Michael Pillsbury. Pillsbury was a protegé of the right-wing Senate group and an out-and-out opponent of arms control. On discovering that Eagleburger was concerned to give the Europeans some reassurance that the US was indeed serious about arms control, Pillsbury attempted to pressure Eagleburger with the threat that he would use his Senate connections to oppose Eagleburger's confirmation in his post, unless he withdrew any favourable reference to arms control. Eagleburger called Pillsbury's bluff and the new director of ACDA, Eugene Rostow, got rid of Pillsbury as soon as he took office. But Pillsbury simply returned to work for the Steering Committee superhawks and waged a year-long vendetta against the State Department, ACDA, and anyone else who could be labelled a 'crypto-arms-controller'.[2] Over time this pressure told and in late 1982 the President fired Rostow and replaced him with Kenneth Adelman, formerly Jeane Kirkpatrick's deputy at the UN. Although Adelman had to survive

stormy confirmation hearings over his (and the President's) lack of knowledge of or commitment to arms control, the fact was that ACDA was now
headed by someone who was no friend to arms control. By July 1983 the
newsletter of the respected and nonpartisan Arms Control Association was
pointing out that ACDA had become 'a shambles' and a 'basket case'. Morale
was low, turnover high, and staff levels had shrunk to their lowest in a decade,
with 30 per cent of its top management positions now unfilled for two years.
Above all, the Association said, the Administration seemed to be wholly
unserious about arms control and far more concerned to build up arms first:
to it ACDA was just a nuisance.[3] The problem was, of course, that the hawks of
the Senate Steering Committee round Helms packed formidable clout – and
had powerful connections into the Pentagon and CIA, from whom they could
quite normally get secret inside information. This group was able to harass
and block many of Rostow's nominees to management posts and generally to
exert an enormous and baleful pressure over the Administration's arms-
control stance.

With the shift in the political climate of spring 1983, the far Right found
itself thrown onto the defensive. America's European allies, under pressure
from their own domestic opinion, had begun to lobby insistently for some
display of US flexibility and reasonableness ahead of the emplacement of
cruise and Pershing II missiles in Europe, due for autumn 1983 – and similar
sentiments were echoed in the US. With the 1984 Presidential election
already in sight, there was a clear 'danger' that the more moderate elements in
the Administration would push the President into concessions which the
Right could not stomach. At the same time, similar pressures were being felt
from the Europeans over Perle's attempt to railroad the NATO allies in the
COCOM (Co-ordinating Committee on Export Controls) into virtual economic warfare with the USSR. Here too the far Right found itself on the
defensive.

More alarming still to the hawks was the fact that Congressional opposition
to key weapons programmes was mounting. Thus the Administration's
proposal that $130 million should be spent on the production of the new
Bigeye nerve-gas bombs and shells had run into trouble even in the Republi-
can-controlled Senate. Opponents pointed out that the US had refrained
from making nerve-gas devices ever since President Nixon had agreed to halt
production of chemical weapons, and that President Ford had also signed the
1925 Geneva Protocol (which the US had always hitherto refused to sign)
banning first use of poison gas. To go ahead with Bigeye was clearly to break
an international treaty commitment. In June 1983 the proposal went down to
defeat in the House and in July, after much anguished debate, it only passed

in the Senate on the Vice-President's casting vote.[4] Its chances of repassing
in the House in the autumn were not rated high. Even more critical was the
rising opposition to the MX missile programme. In July a House vote on the
programme passed by only 220–207, a thirteen-vote majority. The last time it
had been debated by the House it had received a 53-vote majority. Support
was slipping away – and there were many crucial votes ahead. Congressman
Les Aspin, the leader of a crucial block of pro-MX Democrats, was openly
predicting that the programme would go down to defeat in the autumn unless
the Administration could come up by then with more flexible arms control
proposals in the Geneva negotiations.[5] Meanwhile, Congressional support
for the entire SDI programme seemed a great deal less than assured and there
was clearly some danger that it could be stillborn.

## The thaw of summer 1983

If Washington hawks felt themselves under growing pressure at home, they
were even more alarmed at the unmistakable signs of a growing thaw in
relations between the two superpowers – a thaw which might even bring back
the horror of détente. The pressures for such a thaw were enormous. Even
conservative Republicans in Congress were bound to feel increasingly
tempted by the thought of some form of arms-control agreement with the
Russians, as the 1984 elections neared – and the President was bound to feel
the same pressures. No one had forgotten the way in which Richard Nixon
had proudly exhibited the SALT I agreement before the electorate in 1972 –
and had been returned with a landslide. Such achievements were generally
regarded as providing a sort of proof of 'presidential stature' – any incumbent's greatest asset.[6] The conservative leaders of Britain and West Germany
– both facing elections too – added their pressures to these. Indeed,
Chancellor Kohl had visited Moscow in July 1983 and lost no time in
communicating to Reagan his belief that the Russians were willing to do a
deal – and his own fervent wish for such a deal.

The Russians, for their part – and despite their distaste for the Reagan
Administration – seemed willing to make the same calculation they had in
helping Nixon to win re-election in 1972. After all, if they could do a deal with
Reagan, he would probably be able to secure its ratification in the Senate –
something which Carter's Democratic Administration had signally failed to
do with SALT II. In any case, if the Russians tried to assist Reagan's
Democratic opponent to win, he would be under some pressure to show that
he was in no way beholden to the Russians. But above all, the Russians had to
face the dread prospect that Reagan might be re-elected without an arms-

control agreement. In that case they would face four years more of a President who hated them anyway, owed them nothing and, facing no further re-election pressures, could afford an implacable anti-Sovietism.

Such calculations almost certainly underlay the growing signs of Soviet flexibility on arms issues. When Reagan made a minor conciliatory move in the START talks in June 1983, the Russians immediately responded by expressing a willingness to drop its MIRV rocket levels lower than in any previous agreement and to permit a greater degree of on-site inspection. Even the White House acknowledged that this offer had 'some positive elements'.[7] Andropov followed this in August by reiterating his offer of a complete freeze in the nuclear arsenals of both superpowers, and also undertook that the USSR would unilaterally refuse to be the first to test-launch anti-satellite weapons. Moreover, whereas the Russians had always previously coupled talks on this question with an insistence that the US space shuttle had to be included in such a ban, Andropov now omitted all mention of the shuttle.[8] The US response was generally favourable and even the ultrahawkish US START negotiator, Edward Rowny,[9] agreed that the Russians had recently moved a considerable way towards accepting US positions in the talks and dropping some of their own demands.[10]

Perhaps even more dramatic was a clear Soviet willingness to help Reagan on the vexed question of grain purchases. After President Carter had embargoed US grain shipments to the USSR in 1980 (in response to the Soviet intervention in Afghanistan), American farmers had lost their 70 per cent share of this gigantic market – and known real distress as a result. In the 1980 campaign Reagan had promised to help the farmers out of this hole. To redeem this pledge what the Administration needed was a new, long-term grain pact with the highest possible guaranteed purchase level. The Russians, badly burned by the previous ban and determined never to put themselves in such a vulnerable position again, were expected to hang tough. Indeed, in 1982 they had agreed to buy only the 6 million tons they were committed to in terms of the old agreement, though the US tried hard to sell them four times as much.[11]

There was thus quite general amazement when, in late July 1983, the Russians sunnily agreed to a new five-year agreement with a 9-million-ton guaranteed purchase level. Reuters commented that Western diplomats 'said they were surprised the Soviet side had agreed so soon and that they had conceded to US demands for higher purchase levels . . . A diplomat said that by agreeing so quickly, the Russians "appear to be burying the hatchet . . . and showing they want to put political as well as economic relations on a new footing".'[12] US Secretary of State for Agriculture, John R. Block, who met with the Soviet deputy premier, Geidar Aliyev, while signing the formal agreement in Moscow in late August, spoke happily of 'a very constructive, useful and friendly discussion'.[13] Similarly, the US Secretary of State, George Shultz, began a round of numerous and friendly contacts with the Soviet Ambassador to the US, Anatoliy Dobrynin.[14]

There were many other straws in the wind too. In July the US and USSR concluded three years of negotiation with an agreement on human rights and a new proposal for European disarmament.[15] In August the US Deputy Secretary of State, Kenneth W. Dam, was accorded an uncensored interview on Soviet TV – the first time for years such a thing had been allowed to a high-ranking American politician.[16] The Russians suddenly announced that they would grant exit visas for fifteen Pentecostalist dissidents, and there were reports that similar leniency might be expected for other dissidents.[17] The Jaruzelski regime in Poland also released a number of political prisoners, appeared ready to lift martial law, and gave the go-ahead for the Pope's visit to Poland. Andropov also moved to conciliate one of America's major allies, Japan, promising that any SS-20 missiles removed from Europe would not be relocated in Asia. There was a noticeable 'warming trend' in Japanese–Soviet relations as the summer progressed, with renewed diplomatic conversations and the revival of the previously suspended Japan–Soviet film festival.[18] There could be no mistaking the general mood of thaw.

Almost all these moves had come from the Russians and pressure grew on the Reagan Administration to respond. In early August a US delegation held talks with the USSR about the establishment of a new hot line between the Pentagon and the Soviet Defence Ministry.[19] But more was clearly required and the moderates within the Reagan Administration pressed hard for the expression of a more substantive American goodwill. The crunch came in early August over the question of US restrictions on the sale of oil equipment to the USSR.[20] Such equipment had no military utility and previous US attempts to prevent such equipment reaching the Russians had provoked a major crisis with America's European partners in 1982. The Russians wanted the equipment for a huge oil exploration programme in the Barents Sea, comparable to the US development of the Alaskan North Slope. Theoretically, of course, the ban on trade with the USSR extended only to items of potential military use, but the true hawks in the Administration wanted nothing less than all-out economic warfare.

Now the issue arose of a large Soviet order for pipe-layers. The Caterpillar Tractor Company was desperate to fulfil the order – the firm was in the red and knew that its great Japanese rival, Komatsu, would happily fill the order if Caterpillar didn't. The Secretaries of State for Foreign Relations and

Commerce, George Shultz and Malcolm Baldridge, made an 'exceptionally hard' stand in favour of filling the order and, besides State and Commerce, rounded up the departments of Treasury, Trade, Energy and Budget to back them. For the first time the hawks were thrown onto the defensive. Caspar Weinberger, the Defence Secretary, sent a 'blistering' note to Reagan demanding a ban on supply, and enlisted the National Security Adviser, William Clark, in his cause. On most foreign and defence-related issues the Weinberger–Clark combination was invincible, but this time, after considerable Presidential dithering, they lost.

The lesson could hardly be lost on Washington's hawks: in the new climate of thaw the battle was turning against them. A skirmish over oil equipment was one thing, though. The real battle lay just ahead, amidst the mounting pressures for some real concessions on arms control. For the first time the hawks began to fear that this was a battle they might not win.

## Russian violations of SALT?

This left the Senate ultraconservatives and Pentagon hawks with one major card which they played for all it was worth: it was no good reaching arms-control agreements with the Russians because they were already cheating on SALT I and II. Any future arms-control agreement would represent a one-sided shackling of the US, if one had regard to the history of Soviet violations of arms treaties.

The allegation that the Russians had seriously violated SALT had long been an article of faith among Reaganite true believers. Perhaps the key figure was David Sullivan, an ex-CIA analyst and adviser to the right-wing Senate group, who had been made an acting counsellor to ACDA in 1981. As Talbott puts it,

Sullivan was, in his own eyes and many on the right, Washington's most knowledgeable and outspoken expert on Soviet cheating under SALT. He kept a constantly expanding list of alleged transgressions. In all instances, Sullivan's case for the prosecution rested on the presumption of guilt. He would interpret a questionable activity as an open-and-shut violation. He resolved ambiguities, both in Soviet behaviour and in the provisions of SALT, in favour of a judgement to convict.[21]

Sullivan's allegations provoked such a storm that it was decided to set up a major inquiry under James Timbie of various experts from the agencies (including the CIA) to resolve the matter. Their lengthy report concluded that Sullivan was wrong. There was no single case of the USSR being caught red-handed in a treaty violation. When the various allegations had been raised with the Russians they had either given adequate explanations or simply stopped whatever it was that was giving offence. The Timbie Report was a serious embarrassment to the Administration and so it was given a code-word classification higher than top secret and never issued as a report. With the report thus hidden from sight Sullivan was free to go on disseminating his views to Congressional committees and anyone else who would listen.[22] Naturally, the Senate superhawks listened hard and repeated the allegations at every opportunity. Nonetheless, the evidence was thin, to say the least. By May 1983 even Perle's superior, Fred Iklé, the Pentagon's Under Secretary for Policy – himself no mean hawk – felt able to announce 'We are not in conflict in what we are doing with the provisions of the SALT I and II agreements. The Soviets, based on our observations and verification, are likewise not in conflict with these provisions . . .'[23]

In the past the enemies of arms control had frequently been able to appeal to the President's own gut instincts. Indeed, Reagan's famous speech about détente being 'a one-way street' and the Russians feeling able to 'reserve unto themselves the right to commit any crime, to lie, to cheat' was tacked to the wall in David Sullivan's office as an almost biblical authority for his campaign about alleged Soviet violations.[24] But the President was a problem. He knew almost nothing about arms control or even the most basic facts about nuclear weapons – Iklé's statement had been prompted by the President's astonishing off-the-cuff claim that submarine-launched missiles were less dangerous because they could be recalled in midflight.[25] Similarly, Reagan had insisted that the SS-19 must surely be the Russians' biggest missile. When told that the SS-18 was the biggest, he had replied 'So, they've even switched the numbers on their missiles in order to confuse us!' It had to be pointed out to the President that the numbers involved were assigned to Soviet missiles by the Pentagon, not by the Russians themselves . . .[26] So there was no point in relying on the President. In any case, he was a politician who could be expected to bend with the wind and the arms-control wind was now blowing quite briskly. If the card of Soviet SALT violations was to be played with any real effect, there was a desperate need for some hard, new evidence.[27]

## The Krasnoyarsk violation?

It was exactly at this point that news emerged of a possible major Soviet violation of SALT I in the shape of a gigantic new radar being built at Abalakovo, near Krasnoyarsk, in central Siberia, which, it was claimed, might constitute a major violation of the ABM Treaty. This was exactly the sort of news that the Senate hawks of the Steering Committee had been looking for.

It is worth noting how the news of the Krasnoyarsk radar surfaced. On 20 June the US launched a secret KH-9 Big Bird satellite from Vandenberg Air

Force Base.[28] Big Bird – a 12-ton, 55-feet-long monster – can distinguish objects no more than eight inches long from a height of 90 miles.[29] Pretty certainly it was this satellite which spotted the Krasnoyarsk installation – it was about three weeks after its launch that analysts at the CIA's National Photographic Interpretation Center came across the radar.[30] It was a considerable shock. Not long before the US had received a similar shock on discovering a large new Soviet phased-array radar at Pechora already eighteen months under construction.[31] Now it was realised that the Krasnoyarsk facility had also been under construction for more than a year without being detected. Undoubtedly, these long delays in discovery represented something of a triumph for the Russian Maskirovka (concealment) programme, launched by Marshal Ogarkov, deploying a variety of camouflage, concealment and deception tactics to shield Soviet military installations from US photographic and, particularly, electronic surveillance.[32]

No doubt the news of the new radar would have flashed instantly to the White House, but no immediate announcement was made. Time for further analysis would be needed and, of course, going public with the news could well have dire effects on the delicately balanced arms-control talks. But a crucial leak came on 27 July 1983 in the syndicated column by Roland Evans and Robert Novak.[33] Evans and Novak have long had excellent contacts on the Congressional far Right, and it was from this milieu that their information seems to have come. Evans and Novak had the bare bones of the story: the satellite had spotted the radar earlier in July, they said, and its inland location could well make it a violation of SALT.

The Pentagon, CIA and White House said nothing in response to the Evans–Novak story. Instead, the chief word on the affair came from the Senate conservatives, who immediately began exerting maximum pressure on the White House, arguing the folly of trying to reach any new arms-control agreement with the Russians in light of this new 'proof' of their SALT violations. By 3 August, indeed, the White House felt it had to respond to these pressures by sending a special message to the Senators saying that the US had already raised the Krasnoyarsk issue with the Russians.[34] Thus what seems to have happened is that the news of the satellite sighting had flashed straight from Pentagon and CIA/NSC hardliners to the Senate hawks, and thence to Evans and Novak.

One consequence of this was that it was the hawks' interpretation of what Krasnoyarsk meant which was first in the field and quickly became the conventional wisdom – a wisdom which, as we shall see, was to be by no means uncontested by cooler heads in the intelligence community later on.

The case against the Krasnoyarsk radar ran as follows. The 1972 ABM

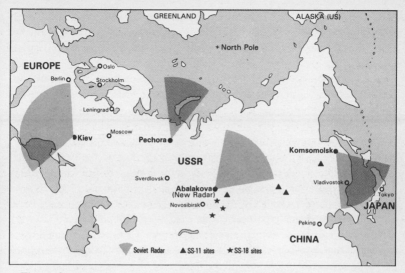

5 The new Soviet phased-array radar at Abalakova (Krasnoyarsk), discovered by US reconnaissance six weeks before 007's flight. This fixed position and long-range radar will stare out over the Kamchatka-Sakhalin coast, where 007's intrusion took place. The radar may be designed to plug gaps in the Soviet radar network – gaps whose existence the 007 intrusion would probably have revealed. *Source*: Philip J. Klass, 'US Scrutinizing New Soviet Radar', *Aviation Week and Space Technology*, 22 August 1983.

Treaty allowed the US and USSR each to defend a single site with battle-management radar and ABM missiles. The Russians chose to defend Moscow with a series of ABM radars, while the US chose to defend the Minuteman ICBM fields at Grand Forks, North Dakota – but later scrapped the scheme, believing that its ABM capability was unlikely to be really effective. The problem was that ABM battle-management radars were of the phased-array type – that is, large building-type structures which do not have movable antennae but rely instead on wave interactions among signals from a multitude of small antenna elements.[35] But phased-array radars themselves were not banned by the Treaty – their use for early warning of attack, space tracking and arms-control verification was quite legitimate. To try to ensure that phased-array radars were used only for these purposes, the Treaty directed that early warning phased-arrays could be built only on the coastal peripheries of the US and USSR and must face outward. They must also not be close to missile fields they could protect and, being on the coast, would themselves be vulnerable to attack. Phased-arrays used for space tracking or arms-control verification could, however, be built anywhere. (A significant problem was that some phased-arrays can serve several purposes – the US Pave Paws phased-arrays can be used both for early warning and space tracking.[36])

The Krasnoyarsk facility – still under construction when spotted and not expected to be completed until 1988[37] – raised suspicion because it was located deep within Soviet territory (see map 5) and the nearest periphery – the Mongolian border – was some 500 miles away. It was a huge structure – as big as a fifty-storey building – with its single face directed east across 6000 miles of Soviet territory towards the northern Pacific and the Bering Sea.[38] Moreover, not far to the south and southwest were fields of SS-18 ICBMS which, if Krasnoyarsk was an ABM battle-management radar, it might be designed to protect. Certainly, the notion that Krasnoyarsk *was* an ABM radar was henceforth taken as gospel by American right-wing politicians. Thus the right-wing Heritage Foundation's 1984 *Mandate for Leadership* stated categorically that Krasnoyarsk was 'a major ABM radar'.[39] Similar assertions became the common coin of Administration hard-liners – and many politicians far beyond their ranks. In its most extreme form it was suggested that Krasnoyarsk was just part of a network of Soviet radar violations of SALT in the Far East, linking up with a radar at Komsomolsk and another ABM radar on southern Kamchatka.[40]

In fact the case was, from the first, fairly palpable nonsense. Krasnoyarsk was hopelessly ill-fitted for ABM functions. A US missile attack on the USSR would send Minuteman and MX missiles looping over the North Pole. Krasnoyarsk failed completely to cover this 'ICBM attack corridor'. It was far too far to the east and its single fixed face looked out towards the Pacific, away from the North Pole. Moreover, there was no sign of any interceptor missiles near the radar site or even the infrastructure to support such facilities.[41] Such facts – though they must have been known to Pentagon analysts right away – did not emerge until more than two years later, however. In the meantime the right-wing view that it was an ABM radar was the only one to get a hearing and, for many, quickly became axiomatically true.

It is unlikely, though, that serious analysts ever really believed this view, but in that case, what was Krasnoyarsk designed for? It clearly wasn't an ordinary air-defence radar. It might (as the Russians claimed) simply be for space tracking. But it might also be an early-warning radar, focused against possible US air attack from the Pacific or the Trident missiles which would be launched from US submarines off the Soviet coast. While this would be less threatening, it would still constitute a serious violation of the 1972 Treaty. The problem about this, though, was that if the USSR really was placing a new early-warning radar in central Siberia, it would be sacrificing a precious six minutes of attack-warning time – and the radar would be incapable of handling the crucial engagement phase of a US attack.[42] Still, whether or not Krasnoyarsk was designed to play an early-warning role would depend to some extent on whether there were gaps in the USSR's north Pacific early-warning radar line. If there were, and if Krasnoyarsk could fill those gaps, this would be circumstantial evidence pointing towards an early-warning function for the Krasnoyarsk radar. The issue of such cheating could hardly be taken lightly – indeed the Russians were to make similar charges of treaty violations against the US for planning to build two Pave Paws early-warning radars in Georgia and Texas, and even some American experts were not confident that the charges might not be justified.[43] The willingness of both sides to cheat when they could was not in doubt.

With the Senate conservatives now on the warpath over the Krasnoyarsk issue – clearly with the aim of undermining the crucial autumn sessions of the INF and START talks – the White House was on the spot. The way in which the question of such possible SALT violations was supposed to be handled was through the US–Soviet Standing Consultative Commission in Geneva, whose setting up in 1972 had been a major achievement of the détente era. However, the SCC had finished its spring session in April and was not due to meet again until the autumn. This was too late in the day for the purposes of the Senate conservatives and thus for the White House. Accordingly, the White House sought to reassure the true believers of the Right by several moves. First, control of arms-control policy was taken away from both the Defence and State Departments (let alone the hapless ACDA) and placed instead under a Senior Arms Control Policy Group, headed by the President's National Security Adviser, William Clark, and including representatives of the CIA and the Joint Chiefs of Staff, plus Perle, Richard Burt, Eagleburger and Clark's deputy, Robert McFarlane.[44] This new group – which met for the first time on 19 July 1983 – was an extremely hard-line body: Clark believed in arms control as little as Perle did. Shultz, the Secretary of State, who took arms control seriously, was excluded altogether. Putting arms-control policy under a group like this was a considerable message to the Senate conservatives that they need not worry too much that any progress towards arms control might be achieved.

Secondly, Shultz formally brought up the question of the Krasnoyarsk facility with the Russians – and asked for a special meeting of the SCC in Geneva on 11 August to discuss it.[45] The Russians replied that the new radar would be wholly for space-tracking purposes (a view which British intelligence was to find 'plausible' given projections of manned Soviet space flights in the 1980s and 1990s).[46] Meanwhile, they were not disposed to have an emergency meeting of the SCC at only a few weeks' notice and suggested that if the US was worried about the facility, it could bring up its concerns in the normal way at the autumn SCC session – after all, the radar would not be completed for another five years, so there was no real rush.

On 3 August Senator James A. McClure, one of the most hawkish on the Krasnoyarsk issue, wrote to the President warning that 'the new Soviet ABM radar is the most flagrant Soviet SALT violation yet' and informing him that the Senate conservatives would ask Vice-President Bush to give a special closed session briefing on the issue to the whole Senate in the autumn.[47] On the same day President Reagan sent a special message on the issue to the Senate. While in 1982 Reagan had said there was a lack of 'hard and fast evidence' on Soviet violations, by March 1983 he had shifted under the pressure of the Senate conservatives to saying that there were 'increasingly serious grounds for questioning'[48] Soviet compliance with SALT (although this was before Krasnoyarsk was known about). Now he informed the Senators that the US had raised its fears about the new radar with the Russians but that 'the information they have provided to date does not satisfy our concerns'.[49]

This left matters in an uncomfortably indeterminate position, with the Senate hawks furiously unsatisfied and the White House unable to reassure this, its natural constituency. The Soviet refusal to advance the SCC meeting for a month, noted the *New York Times*, 'has caused debate in the White House, with some officials pressing for President Reagan to make another public statement about the alleged Soviet violations, while others prefer to handle the problem quietly until more can be learned about the disputed Soviet activities'.[50] President Reagan departed on holiday to his California ranch on 12 August with the matter still hanging awkwardly.

## August 1983: A fateful month?

The issue of the Krasnoyarsk radar was, it will be seen, no mere technical quibble. With support for the Administration's military programmes eroding steadily in Congress – and worse expected to come in the autumn – and with pressure growing on the White House to make concessions in the INF and START talks, it seemed possible that the Reagan Administration could reap the worst of all possible worlds if the Krasnoyarsk issue was not speedily resolved. It could well watch the MX, the nerve-gas programme and the SDI go down to defeat in Congress – and feel itself impelled towards concessions in the arms-control talks in an attempt to reassure opinion or bargain for these programmes (as Aspin had already suggested they would have to). If, after all that, it were to turn out that Krasnoyarsk really was an ABM radar or, more possibly, that it was an early-warning radar – a still serious violation; or even if the issue could not be resolved one way or another – then Reagan would find himself under bitter and reproachful attack from key conservative elements. This would be wholly unacceptable to the Administration. Psychologically it had adopted an approach of 'no enemies on the Right' and feared the reproach that in office it had become just another 'patsy for the Russians'. Moreover, the President needed a united conservative coalition as the re-election contest of 1984 loomed nearer. Potentially, a very great deal turned on the resolution of the Krasnoyarsk issue. Politically, of course, it would be most convenient if the radar could be proved to be a violation – for then the President could hope to get his military programmes through *and* feel justified in hanging tough on arms control.

But the timing was all wrong. The SCC was not due to meet until 30 September – and when it did, its sessions typically meandered through weeks or months. The Russians would be in no hurry, and the whole meeting would be utterly overshadowed by the arms-control talks anyway: if the US did hang tough there then the Russians would probably respond by procrastinating in the SCC, trying to force the US into some concession on arms control before revealing its hand definitively over Krasnoyarsk. Neither European nor domestic American opinion would easily understand a tough US position on arms control just because of an unresolved US worry about a radar – a radar was not a missile, after all. In any case, long before the SCC had finished its work a final decision would have to be implemented on the deployment of cruise and Pershing in Europe.

The KAL 007 tragedy took place against the background of this delicately balanced political situation. The impact of the tragedy was so great that all the outstanding issues facing the Administration were settled easily on the hard-liners' terms without any need for the Krasnoyarsk issue to be raised at all. But it is important to remember that, until the tragedy, the Krasnoyarsk issue was of paramount importance.

There is – it is important to say – no proof that the flight of 007 was connected with the Krasnoyarsk issue. But it is certainly a striking coincidence that just a month before its fateful flight the US had developed a very powerful motive for testing the Soviet radar network in Soviet East Asia – and there seems little doubt that 007 did exactly that. A prolonged and mysterious intrusion by an unidentified aircraft over several hours would have caused the Russians to turn on not just their coastal radars but, almost certainly, some of their radars further inland. From this the US would have obtained a picture of a large sector of the Soviet radar network in the entire region. This in turn would have revealed any gaps in that network – and allowed a judgement as to whether Krasnoyarsk was correctly situated to fill that gap. And after the event, according to Pentagon specialists, it emerged that there was just such a gap in the north Pacific coverage of the Soviet network – which Krasnoyarsk might indeed fill.[51] It is also worth noting that a secondary concern related to the (alleged) Soviet ABM radar on southern Kamchatka, and that 007 must have flown almost right over this facility.

There is another striking coincidence too. A considerable worry for either side was that, while carrying out permissible ABM tests under the 1972 Treaty, either side might decide to turn on its ordinary air-defence radars in an 'ABM mode'. Such concurrent usage of air-defence radars (which are permissible in any number, anywhere) would enable the side that did it to circumvent the ABM Treaty by giving their air-defence radars the capability to guide interceptor missiles against incoming missiles. So in 1978 both superpowers had agreed to ban such concurrent usage. In 1982, however, a fresh agreement had been reached: one could turn on one's air-defence radars during an ABM test if, for example, an unidentified aircraft intruding over one's territory was detected. That is, in precisely the situation which KAL 007 created. And since the Soviet ABM testing ground (i.e. for the permitted Moscow ABM site) is close to the Chinese border, it was possible that the 007 intrusion could have triggered precisely that concurrent usage. It is striking, too, that after the 007 tragedy US representatives suddenly announced – without any explanation – that the US was not prepared after all to sign the agreement reached in 1982.[52] This agreement had earlier been unsuccessfully opposed by the Office of the US Defence Secretary,[53] and it seems that the 007 tragedy enabled the Pentagon to win the day on this after all. It is also worth pointing out that a later US allegation was precisely that the USSR had made concurrent use of its air-defence radars.

Such considerations as these were certainly not in the minds of the anxious relatives of KAL 007's passengers as they waited in the arrival lounge at Kimpo International Airport, Seoul, for the badly overdue plane in the early morning of 1 September. However, not the least mysterious aspect of the whole tragedy was that just at this moment they were given false hopes that the aircraft might, after all, be perfectly safe. It is to this curious – and cruel – incident that we now turn.

# FOUR

# False Hopes

007's last message to Narita Air Traffic Control (Tokyo) at 18.27 GMT had spoken, alarmingly, of 'rapid decompression' and an unscheduled descent to 10,000 feet – sure signs of an emergency. Narita, though, said that the report was too garbled to understand. Nonetheless, they knew something was wrong, for the line to 007 had gone completely dead. Moreover, 007 had been due to report at that precise minute that it was passing the NOKKA compulsory reporting waypoint – and this it failed to do. Attempts to reach 007 by relaying messages through KAL 015 also failed. Moreover, 007 was due to come within range of Hakodate (civilian) radar at about 18.34 and this too failed to happen.[1] Thus within a very few minutes of the shoot-down Narita had reason to believe that something had gone very seriously wrong.

It is thus a little surprising that half an hour was allowed to elapse before Narita alerted other Japanese air-traffic control stations – and the Japanese military – that 007 was missing.[2] It might have been expected that the first move of the Japan Defence Agency would have been to check with their Wakkanai radar controllers (who had a longer range than Hakodate). If so, this would have produced speedy indication of 007's probable fate. But there is no mention of such a move and another half hour slipped by before Narita declared an alert over 007. Astonishingly, nobody made contact with KAL or with Kimpo International Airport (Seoul) where the relatives and friends of 007's passengers and crew were anxiously awaiting their arrival.

By this time – presumably as a result of a report from the Wakkanai radar – the notion occurred to Narita that 007 might have flown into Soviet airspace. Accordingly, at 20.30 GMT Narita phoned Khabarovsk air-control centre to ask if the Russians had any information about 007. Khabarovsk knew nothing immediately but promised to check. Narita still said nothing to KAL or Kimpo.

The scene at Kimpo had become increasingly tense. It was known that 007 had been only 40 minutes late taking off from Anchorage. It was difficult not to fear the worst, given that most of its route lay over icy waters. Rumours of a hijacking began to circulate. Finally, at 20.20 GMT Narita alerted KAL offices in Tokyo, Seoul and Anchorage of the situation. This delay of almost two hours has never been explained. By then the status of 007 had moved from 'uncertainty' through an 'alert' phase to 'distress'. During this nearly two-hour period Narita had been in contact over the affair with the Japanese military, Anchorage, Honolulu, the Russians, and sundry air-control centres in Japan and the US. The people who most needed to know – Seoul and KAL – were the very ones kept in the dark – and yet KAL maintains offices at Narita airport itself.

The effect at Kimpo was electric: the KAL office put out an alert in four minutes flat and 007 was declared 'missing'. The KAL Vice-President, Cho Choong Kun, quickly arrived at the airport to speak to the weeping relatives.[3] At 20.50 Khabarovsk came on the line to say they had no information about 007. By this stage the Japanese and US intelligence services were in constant communication with one another over the affair.[4] Again, one would have thought that this would have resulted in a speedy unearthing of the data from the Wakkanai radar and the huge US surveillance network in the area which would have allowed a speedy conclusion to be reached. Instead, hours dragged by with no further news. The distress of the passengers' relatives mounted as it was realised that 007 would by now have run out of fuel anyway.

Finally, at 01.00 GMT[5] (six and a half hours after the shoot-down) the South Korean Foreign Ministry received welcome news – speedily transmitted to KAL and the waiting relatives: 007 was safe. It had been forced down by the Russians and had landed on Sakhalin Island. Badly shaken but immensely relieved, the relatives went home. The same story was put out over the (government-controlled) Korean Broadcasting System[6] and also by the KAL spokesman in New York, Bonnie Villerico: although KAL could offer no explanation of how it had all happened, Ms Villerico said 'she had been told it was a forced landing. She said arrangements were being made to send another plane to the island to pick up the passengers and bring them to South Korea.'[7] Other reports went even further than this. According to *Aviation Week and Space Technology*, KAL said that another plane had actually been sent to Sakhalin (though there is no record of this, and certainly not of its landing there). The magazine also spoke of 'earlier reports that all the passengers appeared safe after the aircraft was forced to land'.[8] These reports, relayed by Associated Press, caused newspapers to lead their early editions in many parts of the world with this cruelly false story. For the passengers' relatives and friends the result was an extra and torturous refinement to the grief they were ultimately to face.

How could the South Korean Foreign Ministry have made such a terrible mistake? South Korea has only very modest electronic surveillance capabilities and had no pretensions itself to being able to determine if a plane had landed on Sakhalin. Nor had the information come from the Japanese or the Russians. South Korea, having no diplomatic relations with the USSR, uses the Japanese as intermediaries when necessary. So it fell to the Japanese Embassy in Moscow to make an early contact with the Soviet Foreign Ministry to enquire about 007's presence on Sakhalin. The Embassy was told no such plane had landed there.[9] In fact, as the *New York Times* reported, 'Korean Foreign Ministry officials cited the US CIA as their source for the report that the plane had been forced down on Sakhalin, but American officials in Seoul, Tokyo and Washington said they could not confirm or deny that report.'[10]

This did not mean that CIA spokesmen denied that the report of the false forced landing had come from the CIA: when the *New York Times* asked the CIA's official Washington spokesman, Dale Peterson, he merely said that he could not confirm or deny whether 007 was on Sakhalin.[11] The possibility remained quite open that such a report had emanated from somewhere within the Agency and that official spokesmen (as is not uncommon) had simply had no information either way about it. In fact the CIA did not at any later stage deny that it had been the source of this mistaken report.

There seems little doubt that the report did emanate from the CIA. The report was accepted as gospel not only by the South Korean Government and KAL but, as we shall see, by the US State Department. And yet it was virtually incredible: the last report to Tokyo ground control from 007 had spoken of 'rapid decompression' and hasty descent, and these words were shouted by copilot Son Dong-Hui, evidently in a state of high tension.[12] All this was a clear sign of a desperate emergency. The plane had then descended very fast and slipped off the radar – into the sea, it seemed clear. And the plane had been missing for five hours. It was a very, very tall order after that to believe that 007 was safe and sound on dry land. Nobody would have accepted such a report unless the source for it was thought to have very superior and reliable means for knowing the truth. Indeed, had anyone less than the CIA come up with such a report they would simply not have been believed.

The CIA never did confirm (or deny) that it had been the source of this report and were clearly embarrassed by the South Korean attribution. Nonetheless, the Seoul Foreign Ministry stood its ground when the *New York Times* took the matter up again on 8 September: the source was now given as the intelligence service of 'a friendly government'[13] – which could only mean the US (the Japanese indignantly denied it was them). So there seems little doubt that the fateful false report did come from someone within the CIA. If one does not accept this, the alternative is to believe that the Korean Foreign Ministry was deliberately lying. It is difficult to see what motive it could possibly have had for that. If the CIA were not the source, the Koreans were risking considerable American wrath by saying it was. This possibility can surely be discounted. After all, the Korean Foreign Ministry did not *have* to say anything at all – one would have expected such statements to be left to KAL or the Transportation Ministry. So if the Foreign Ministry was willing to take responsibility for what turned out to be such a damaging report, it must surely have done so only because it had received its information from what it regarded as a quite authoritative source; perhaps even because it was pushed into making such a statement. Everything points to the CIA.

This false report has also to be put alongside the extraordinary and potentially tragic delay in launching the search and rescue operation.[14] As we have seen, Narita allowed almost an hour to elapse after its communications with 007 had suddenly been cut off before declaring an alert. While the Tokyo Rescue Co-ordination Centre was told at 19.15 GMT (4.15 am Tokyo time) that 007 was missing, several hours were to elapse before the RCC was given any further instruction. According to ICAO, it was between 21.00 and 23.00 (a mysteriously long and imprecise period – the ICAO Report details all other times to the last minute, even second) that the RCC decided to mount a search. It then ordered a large flotilla of rescue ships and planes to proceed to where 007 should have been if it had been on its right course. So twelve ships and five planes were then rushed off to a spot more than 300 miles away from where 007 had actually crashed. Then at 23.30 the Japanese Maritime Safety Agency (MSA) was told by the Japanese military of the Wakkanai radar track showing a plane disappearing from view off Sakhalin at 18.29, a whole five hours before: a piece of extraordinary and unexplained dilatoriness. The MSA clearly did not treat this news as seriously as it might. Two planes and two ships were dispatched to the area west of Sakhalin but the far larger fleet dispatched earlier was allowed to go on searching in the wrong place well into the next day. A further six hours and 40 minutes were allowed to elapse before the MSA began to concentrate any further attention on the Sakhalin crash site, and even then it took more than another eight further hours after that to dispatch more patrol boats to the area. Even the first two vessels sent did not arrive at the crash site until more than eight and a half hours after the shoot-down.[15] Had there been any survivors, such a delay could well have been fatal.

This was bad enough, but it was also bizarre when placed alongside the 'safe-on-Sakhalin' report, which came six and a half hours after the shoot-down. That is, the 'safe' report came at a time when search operations had already been ordered in two separate areas, and at least the former search (the one on the wrong site) was allowed to continue through the several hours when publicly, at least, all need for a search had been removed. Undoubtedly the 'safe' report contributed to the confusion and delays surrounding the search operations – a fact which can only increase the culpability of whoever authorised that misleading report.

It has to be emphasised that no rational reason can be given for all this confusion and delay, still less that US intelligence should have been the source of the confusion. For this part of the world is probably more densely covered by US military radars than any other. On Shemya Island, for example, the US maintains a great battery of radars: Cobra Dane, a gigantic phased-array radar used for tracking Soviet missiles, able to monitor 200 objects simultaneously and to pick up a baseball-sized object 2000 miles out in space;[16] Cobra Talon, a powerful Over-the-Horizon (OTH) Backscatter radar; and sundry other lesser devices. In the case of 007, there is no doubt that Cobra Talon would have been able to follow the plane almost throughout its whole flight, and certainly at the time of the shoot-down.

Apart from Cobra Talon, US intelligence could also rely on Cobra Judy,[17] a powerful radar installation aboard the USS *Observation Island*, then operating in the north Pacific; other US electronic listening posts at Kita-Kyushu Islands, Kamiseya (near Yokohama), at Hanza, Sobe and Futema (Okinawa); at Chitose and Wakkanai (Hokkaido) – which focus steadily on Sakhalin; and above all at Misawa (Honshu) where the US maintains the largest signal-intelligence station in the world outside the US. The Misawa facility covers not only Sakhalin, Kamchatka and the Seas of Japan and Okhotsk but sees far into Siberia. Finally, of course, the RC-135 which passed close to 007 would certainly have picked up the plane on its radar and it, like all the other listening posts, had its transmissions automatically relayed to the NSA headquarters at Fort Meade as well as to the vast (572 acres) NSA regional headquarters at Camp Fuchinobe, just west of Tokyo. In addition to all these the Japanese maintain their own military radar station at Wakkanai and twenty-seven other such stations around Japan. Even this far from exhausts the list of detection facilities available to the US: there may well have been other airborne intercept platforms aloft at the time and these would, when it came to pinpointing the crash site, have been powerfully complemented by a maritime reconnaissance network.[18]

It is worth pointing out that the monitoring of 007 (and, if necessary, warning it that it was off course) would have been fairly routine. In 1968 a DC-8 (flying with navigation instruments quite primitive in comparison to 007's) veered off course towards Soviet territory while on the Anchorage–Tokyo run. The deviation was immediately picked up both by the Americans at Shemya and the Japanese at Wakkanai.[19] Wakkanai radioed a warning directly to the DC-8, while Shemya immediately warned Anchorage ground control.[20]

Elwin Williamson, one of the Shemya radar operators that night,

recalls fascinated intercept operators following the entire incident through their keyhole to the Soviet radar network. Through their earphones they could hear as the Soviets began tracking the aircraft in international airspace, off the Kamchatka Peninsula. Excited intercept operators began calling out the co-ordinates as Soviet fighters took off to intercept the intruder. Other operators plotted the aircraft's harrowing path on a large wall map. 'We had a line on our board which they left up for about two weeks where you could see the [DC-8] plane come and stop,' said Williamson.[21]

In fact news reached the DC-8 too late to prevent it being intercepted by a MIG-17 which requested it to land on Iturbu (one of the Kurile Islands). The plane, belonging to Seaboard World Airways, was carrying 214 US soldiers to Cam Ranh Bay for service in the Vietnam War. Its pilot, Captain Joseph Tosolini, decided he must comply with the Soviet request. The plane put down, stayed overnight and was then allowed to fly on with its full complement of troops. The inquiry conducted by the Federal Aviation Administration showed that the DC-8 had not been carrying the navigation and weather radar equipment prescribed by the FAA. Seaboard was officially censured.[22]

The significance of this to 007 is not just that even with its 1968 equipment the DC-8 should not have been off course; nor that 007 carried both more and vastly superior equipment. It is simply that if both Wakkanai and Shemya could track and warn the plane with the detection abilities they had in 1968, it is unimaginable that, with the greatly reinforced capabilities of 1983, they could have failed to do so if they wished. This was certainly Williamson's own view: 'I would be willing to bet this Korean airplane was being tracked all the time,' he said.[23]

Similarly, it is ridiculous to suggest that the US had the ability to perform real-time tracking in 1968 but had somehow lost it fifteen years later. In fact data picked up by this immense radar net – potentially crucial in the event of war – is relayed automatically and instantaneously by satellite not only to NSA headquarters at Fort Meade, but also to the NORAD communications centre at Cheyenne, Colorado, and to the Foreign Technology Division of Wright-Patterson USAF base, Ohio.[24]

The fact that these US listening devices – all operating twenty-four hours a day – *did* pick up 007's flight is not disputed. Neither the *Washington Post* nor the *New York Times* had difficulty in finding US intelligence officials willing to admit this the day after the shoot-down.[25] This fact gave rise to several questions. Why had the US not acted to warn 007? How could the misleading report of the forced landing on Sakhalin ever have gained currency, particularly currency from the CIA itself? And why, when the US went public with the tapes of the Soviet pilots' conversations to ground, were only the data of the Japanese operating from Wakkanai released? And why was there apparently such a long delay in the relaying of information to Washington?

The response of the Reagan Administration was somewhat muffled. In general, official spokesmen tried to avoid the whole question of US monitoring of the flight, implying that important security considerations were at stake. Second, it was argued that there was no regular provision for military radar facilities to liaise with their civilian counterparts. Thirdly, it was asserted that the US did not have access to 'real-time' intelligence, merely to automatic recordings which were only examined later. And finally, it was claimed that the need to translate the Soviet pilots' conversations from Russian to Japanese to English caused inevitable delays.

Very little of this case can bear much examination. If there was military–civilian liaison in the 1968 case of the DC-8, it is hard to see why this should not have applied in 1983. Without doubt the capabilities of the US surveillance net is a high-security subject but the US, to Tokyo's considerable irritation,[26] had no compunction about revealing the equally high-security tapes from the Japanese listening post at Wakkanai. The necessity for translation through Japanese would hardly have arisen at the far more numerous and powerful US listening posts. But most of all, of course, the US surveillance net in the north Pacific is the American first line of defence against a surprise Soviet nuclear attack. If it sees strange planes or missiles in flight over Soviet territory it has imperatively to report this instantaneously to Washington: the very survival of the US might depend on that. It is absurd to believe that such data would wait around for hours on automatic recorders to be read: an ICBM takes only 20–30 minutes from launch to impact. Similarly, it is ludicrous to imagine that the US would, for the same reason, allow itself to be handicapped by lack of high-speed translation facilities.

A more revealing picture of the true situation was revealed right away after the disaster when the *Omaha World Herald* contacted a USAF officer in the Pentagon on the subject.

Nothing flies from, over or near Sakhalin that we don't monitor. The surveillance work routinely includes the eavesdropping by US and Japanese intelligence personnel on Soviet military radar transmissions, both ground-to-air and air-to-air conversations . . . The US listeners are graduates of military Russian-language training programs at Monterey, California, and Goodfellow Air Force Base at San Angelo, Texas . . . They listen to everything. They listen 24 hours a day, every day.

In particular, the officer said, the US relied on the radar at Misawa USAF base on the northern tip of Honshu Island which 'stares unblinkingly at Sakhalin'.[27]

With this sort of facilities routinely at work, 007's deviation from course would have been the subject of a CRITIC message for immediate White House attention, certainly no later than the point that the plane entered Soviet airspace for the first time. Citing 'intelligence sources', the *Washington Post* revealed how the procedure would have worked:

Monitoring-station operators write what they call a 'gist' for their superiors when they hear something alarming such as the conversation between the MIG pilots and their controllers. The gist usually triggers high-level attention and priority transcription by intelligence agencies of pertinent parts of the tape. The sources said the Soviet controllers followed their practice of radioing information about intruders from the border air bases up the command chain as far as Moscow, giving US and Japanese eavesdroppers several chances to record their messages.[28]

This astonishing admission reveals not merely that the US was following developments but that its attention extended to ground-level messages back to Moscow. The reference to 'several chances' almost certainly means that the US was intercepting such messages flowing back from Kamchatka, let alone the later messages back from Sakhalin to Moscow.

All of which leaves only three possibilities. Either there was a dramatic failure of normal US surveillance facilities so great as to have threatened American survival in case of nuclear war – and this would have to have been not a single failure but a whole simultaneous set of identical failures affecting all US listening posts throughout the north Pacific. The second possibility is that 007 was part of a preplanned surveillance mission, followed at every stage by US listening posts whose correct functioning is naturally being concealed. Or, thirdly, 007 was accidentally off course and was correctly tracked by US radar, but that the decision was taken to allow the flight to proceed for the sake of the intelligence about Soviet communications it would inevitably trigger. These possibilities must be continuously borne in mind in our examination of the reception of the news by the US Administration: if the US surveillance and communications network was working properly then the news of the tragedy must have been available to top policy makers several hours earlier than has been officially asserted. For the same reasons it should have been quite impossible for a false report that 007 had force-landed on Sakhalin to gain currency, much less for such a report to have been put out by the CIA itself.

# FIVE

# The Crisis Managers

The KAL tragedy impacted upon the US foreign policy establishment at a time of peculiar institutional weakness. Probably not since Warren Harding had the US had a president who knew less about foreign policy than Ronald Reagan. (The long series of financial scandals attaching to officers of the Administration was uncomfortably reminiscent of Harding too.) The State Department under George Shultz was further out in the cold and lacking in influence than it had been for more than a decade. Influence over foreign policy now depended not only on the normal bureaucratic infighting but on a series of Presidential buddy relationships which placed the heaviest responsibilities on men ill-fitted for the task. It was to these key decision-makers that the news of the KAL tragedy arrived first and it was the way in which they chose to handle the affair that helped ensure that it became one of the gravest crises in East–West relations for many years.

## The rise and rise of William P. Clark

Without doubt the key figure in this establishment – one is tempted to say maelstrom – was the President's National Security Adviser, William Clark. Nothing in Clark's career had prepared him for the awesome role he played in US foreign policy by 1983. A one-time student for the Catholic priesthood, he had tried his hand at many occupations without notable success before finally becoming a Californian lawyer. His extreme right-wing views had led him to play a key role in Reagan's election campaign for the California governorship in 1966. The two men became fast friends (their twin California ranches make them almost neighbours) and in 1967 Reagan had made Clark his chief of staff. Reagan's loyalty to Clark matched Clark's own towards him, as he showed by circumventing his own rules for judicial appointments to nominate Clark to the California Supreme Court over the outraged protests of the Bar Association. The two men remained close friends through the 1970s and it was always to Clark that Reagan turned for advice in times of trouble – a fact which alarmed more liberal spirits, for Clark often seemed comfortably to the right of Reagan.[1]

Clark only refused Reagan once: in 1980 Reagan's presidential campaign ran into difficulties and he turned to Clark – as ever – with the request that he take over as campaign manager. Clark said no – but his substitute nominee, the right-wing businessman and former intelligence operative, William J. Casey, was quickly accepted by Reagan. After the election Clark – who was perfectly happy to remain a Californian judge – was offered a variety of Cabinet posts (including the directorship of the CIA) by Reagan, who was determined to have his old buddy by his side.

In the end Clark was snapped up by Reagan's new Secretary of State, Alexander Haig, who wanted a Presidential intimate for his deputy. Haig recalled: 'The response to our inquiries in California about Clark had not been altogether positive. Questions had been raised about his ability to grasp complex issues . . . Also, he had not completed law school . . .'[2] Nonetheless, he offered Clark the job (though, doubtless, Clark would not have accepted without Reagan's say-so). Haig described Clark as having 'the simple manners of a rancher, which indeed he is; he wears a Stetson and Western boots . . . He has a very manly and open and easy-going manner. "I don't know a thing about foreign policy," he told me with amiable candour. I knew that already. It didn't matter . . . I needed a man who understood how the President did things. Clark knew . . .'[3] Such was the man who was shortly to become the chief overlord of US foreign policy. Not surprisingly, his confirmation hearings were a classic. Senators were startled to hear the new Deputy-Secretary of State confess to an almost total ignorance of foreign affairs. He could not name the heads of government of South Africa or Zimbabwe, knew nothing of developments in the British Labour party, and had no idea of European reaction to the placement of US nuclear missiles there.

Haig had little control over Clark. 'The President's aides,' he discovered, 'appeared to believe that foreign policy did not matter much.'[4] When foreign policy was discussed, Haig, though hardly a liberal, was appalled by the sheer wildness and irresponsibility of the Reagan inner circle: at his first Cabinet meeting he heard with incredulity a proposal that the US should publicly welsh on the Iranian hostages deal. Reagan seemed willing to go along until the horrified Haig intervened.[5] Similar wild initiatives followed in a steady stream.

Worse was to follow. At the end of 1981 Reagan's National Security Adviser, Richard Allen, became one of the first of the evergrowing list of Reagan appointees to attract charges of corruption and misconduct. Although an official Administration inquiry cleared Allen, there was a certain inconvenience in having someone running the National Security Council about whom bribery charges were erupting in the Japanese press and who was under investigation by the FBI. So Allen had to go. To replace him Reagan turned not to a foreign-policy expert but to an old buddy – Clark. It was an astonishing choice. That Clark could manage the job at all depended on his acquisition of a highly competent deputy, Robert ('Bud') McFarlane, a quiet, expert and loyal workaholic.

Ominously, given Clark's wholesale ignorance of foreign affairs, it was immediately announced that the role of National Security Adviser – now that it was filled by a Reagan buddy – would be 'upgraded'.[6] Haig quickly found that Clark 'seemed to be conducting a second foreign policy, using separate channels of communication'.[7] When he questioned Clark, Haig was effectively told that his day was over: 'Clark, drained of his old good fellowship, gave me a cryptic answer. "You've won a lot of battles in this Administration, Al," he said, "but you'd better understand that from now on it's going to be the *President's* foreign policy."'[8] There was nothing very cryptic about this and by July 1982 Clark had forced Haig out of office altogether. With Haig went the last pretence to any real expertise in foreign affairs. US foreign policy was now in the hands of a rancher who wore a Stetson and cowboy boots and cheerfully admitted he didn't know a thing about foreign affairs: it was almost the perfect representation of the John Wayne posture the Reaganauts so admired.

The new Secretary of State, George Shultz, came from the same Bechtel Corporation boardroom as Caspar Weinberger, the Defence Secretary. Shultz was chosen largely because of his dull, mild, consensus-seeking style – one strong man, it was felt after the Haig experience, was quite enough. The tacit assumption was that Clark would run things without contest from then on. As Shultz rather pathetically observed of Clark's infinitely closer relationship with Reagan, 'When the President and Bill are in the same room, it's not necessary for them to say many words.'[9]

Not that Clark was a power-seeker for its own sake. Having managed the somewhat unusual feat of elevation to the California Supreme Court without having even finished law school, he had not been keen to leave it – indeed no sooner had he accepted Haig's original offer of the Deputy-Secretaryship than he changed his mind and tried to stop his resignation as judge from being handed in. He was quite aware of his own unsuitability for his foreign policy role and anyway longed to be back on his ranch. By December 1982 he had become so depressed that he tried again to resign but Reagan wouldn't hear of it and the ever loyal Clark soldiered on.[10]

Clark's position thereafter was peculiar. On the one hand he frequently went home late from his office with bad headaches, only to be back early next morning for another fifteen-hour day. He was not happy and pined about his ranch being neglected in his absence. On the other hand he continued to amass power quite remorselessly. Clark saw his role as translating Reagan's policies into *action* and tended to OK proposals emanating from staff hawks or Casey's CIA in a fairly shoot-from-the-hip manner. Inevitably, he tended to see the State Department as full of professional softies and hesitaters who would only find arguments against doing things if they were told about them in advance. Better to leave them out.

The key to Clark's power was simple – his uniquely close relationship to Reagan on the one hand, and the coincidence of the President's gut instincts with his. This 'gut' kinship was the essense of their buddy relationship and it easily overrode normal bureaucratic constraints and, indeed, mere facts – the strong point of neither man. 'He is,' said one White House staffer of Clark, 'immune to information. If he was in the middle of the San Francisco earthquake, he wouldn't know if he was for or against earthquakes until he checked out the implications for Ronald Reagan.'[11] Clark could, moreover, always easily echo and awaken the President's ferociously anti-Soviet instincts – here the two men were as one. White House officials had many problems with the President on this score – he was always likely to come out suddenly with a fresh blast of anti-Soviet invective, often at diplomatically inopportune moments, forcing the White House staff into hurried denials that, in effect, what the President said had any significance. As one official put it, the President's anti-Soviet instinct was 'sort of like a clothes dryer. Everything is tumbling around, then lying quietly, and then someone puts a quarter in the machine and everything tumbles again.'[12] Clark was often the man to put the quarters in: observers noted 'the ease with which they [Clark and the President] can exchange views on how best to deal with the Communist menace in one-page mini-memos'.[13]

This somewhat Walt Disney combination was not to be taken lightly, though. Clark's awesome power was perhaps best revealed in the genesis of the 'Star Wars' programme. Clark's assistant, Robert McFarlane, had become an early advocate of the programme, but the scheme had little chance until Clark adopted it. Then he and McFarlane simply bounced the President into it at a lunch meeting supposedly held on quite another topic.[14] The President reacted like a happy sandboy. Had the scheme had to run the gauntlet of the normal bureaucratic channels, it would probably have had little chance. As it was, Clark and McFarlane not only secured the President's total commitment to it, but were able to do so while keeping the notion secret for a whole month from the Secretaries of State and Defense, Shultz and

Weinberger. By the time these men learned of it, it was a *fait accompli*. Of such manoeuvres is world history made.

Similarly, the short-lived (and ingloriously ended) US move into Lebanon owed more to Clark than to anyone else. In July 1983 the President took the whole area of arms-control policy away from State and Defence and put it under a Senior Arms Control Policy Group under Clark. When the question of possible Soviet violations of previous SALT treaties became a hot issue, a special verification panel was set up, again under Clark. In the developing undercover war against Nicaragua, Casey's proposals for covert action on an unprecedented scale were quickly OKed by Clark despite considerable reservations at State. On 1 August 1983 *Time* brought out a special issue on Central America with Clark on the cover – in charge. Shultz was mentioned only at the end as being 'too reticent to take control' and there were suggestions that the balance had tipped so far that the Secretary of State might as well resign.

The final straw came over the question of US naval exercises off Nicaragua in July 1983. Shultz was, as he thought, involved in all the key discussions on this, including the final decision to defer the matter for further discussion. Clark and Weinberger then went ahead with naval exercises of unprecedented size and duration – clearly threatening an invasion of Nicaragua – without telling Shultz. The news leaked out just as Shultz had to testify before Congress on Central American policy. He took a fearsome roasting over the exercises, which Congressmen had had to learn about from the press, not the Administration. Shultz managed to conceal the fact that the exercises were as much a surprise to him as they were to the House, but he could not prevent the House taking a major slap at the Administration by voting (228–195) to cut off CIA aid to the anti-Nicaraguan Contras. (Casey continued the aid, of course, using untied funds.) The House Speaker, Tip O'Neill, attributed the vote directly to the shock of the exercises. Shultz felt, and was, humiliated.[15]

Shultz had had enough and on 4 August managed at last to secure an audience with Reagan. The President was greatly taken aback as Shultz lost his temper completely: it had been assumed that Shultz was a mouse who never roared (indeed the occasion became famous as 'the day Shultz roared'). Terming the way that foreign policy was being made 'a disgrace', Shultz launched into a long laundry list of past grievances and strongly implied that he might resign. Vice-President Bush and Clark himself were hurriedly summoned to help soothe Shultz. In fact, of course, nothing much changed – Clark's power hardly diminished – but Reagan sought to keep Shultz mollified by inviting him for an occasional game of golf.[16]

But Shultz had been quite right: the foreign-policy process was in unparalleled disarray, and not just because (as was freely admitted) only 20 per cent of the time was spent making policy and the other 80 per cent on deciding how to present it to the media. The State Department itself had almost wholly lost control, and into that vacuum had sprung a whole host of powerful and individualist superhawks, many of them playing their own game with little regard for established procedures. The vast expansion of the military had given the Defence Secretary, Caspar Weinberger, even greater ability than usual to make foreign policy plays. Mrs Kirkpatrick at the UN was quite likely to make categorical hard-line statements off her own bat. The Assistant Defence Secretary, Richard Perle, had at the age of forty-one 'won almost unparalleled influence over US–Soviet relations'.[17] Like Clark and not a few others in the Reagan entourage, Perle was openly hostile to arms control. Perle was indeed so extreme – he was not merely anti-Communist but avowedly anti-Russian – that even among the right-wing Reagan entourage he was known as 'the Prince of Darkness'. *Business Week* – hardly noted for its liberal attitudes – commented that 'during the last fifteen years Perle has done as much as anyone to hamper arms-control progress and to sour economic relations between the two superpowers'.[18] Perle was famous for such *obiter dicta* as 'Soviet foreign policy is like a hotel burglar . . . when he finds an open door, in he goes',[19] but some of his own dealings had not escaped criticism, notably his urging of arms purchases from an Israeli company from which he had received a $50,000 payment before entering office.[20] In the context of the Reagan Administration this was, though, a fairly minor point: after all, one of Perle's Pentagon colleagues, Deputy Defence Secretary Paul Thayer, was to be sentenced to four years' jail for lying to government investigators about his stock-market activities.[21]

Perle was a major force when it came to arms control and East–West trade, but an even more formidable force across the board in US foreign policy was the 'new' CIA headed by William Casey. The CIA had been through a rough period in the wake of Watergate – its scale of operations cut back and subjected to embarrassing public scrutiny. The Reagan Administration had come to power with the avowed intention of reversing such policies. Casey had been selected to perform this task – one he performed with great speed and energy. Indeed, it had soon become clear that in appointing Casey Reagan had let loose a tiger.

## William Casey's CIA

William Casey was, in his way, as peculiar a man to find in his post as Clark was in his. Brought up on Buffalo Bill and Horatio Alger, in his brief and early career in the wartime oss under the legendary 'Wild Bill' Donovan, Casey had found the lure of secret work well-nigh irresistible. As Richard Helms (later to be CIA Director) who shared digs in wartime London with Casey, put it: 'He had what the Germans call *Fingerspitzengefuehl* – a feel for the clandestine.'[22] He also earned a reputation for being able to take tough, high-risk decisions even under the most extreme pressure. Even after he left the oss (later to become the CIA) Casey always kept up his secret-service interests and contacts – his National Strategy Information Center (set up in 1962 to lobby for higher arms spending) was widely believed to have CIA links.[23]

Casey's business career brought him multimillionaire status and a controversial reputation as someone who 'from the start ... favoured the bare-knuckled approach'[24] and was dogged by 'business problems'. During a plagiarism suit against him in the early 1960s – settled out of court – he told the opposing attorney: 'If you're not a gentleman, I'm going to kick your ass.'[25] Tough, obscene, and a self-made man, Casey was a right-wing hater of the Eastern WASP Establishment ('the white-shoe boys' as he called them)[26] and a can-do hurricane of energy. He was, above all, a high-risk taker. As one CIA agent put it, 'He just took fliers because that's how you get rich. You don't get rich by buying stock in General Electric.'[27]

Casey was active in right-wing politics from the 1940s on, playing a notable part in a number of presidential campaigns. Having set up the Citizens' Committee for Peace with Security to lobby for Nixon's foreign policy, he was ultimately rewarded in 1971 with the chairmanship of the Securities and Exchange Commission. Here too controversy followed him. As one SEC lawyer put it, 'I don't think Casey has any principles that can't be accommodated to get a good result.'[28] In a celebrated incident he outbid the Japanese government for a house on Embassy Row. When asked how the Nixon Administration was going to explain such rough treatment of the Japanese he merely replied, 'Tell them to remember Pearl Harbor'.[29] More serious was his involvement in the Vesco case, a Watergate sidelight: the financier Robert Vesco offered $200,000 to the Nixon campaign fund if the SEC would call off its investigation of him. Casey, after liaising with Nixon's campaign manager (and Attorney-General), John Mitchell, met with Vesco's representatives on three occasions, provoking later allegations that Vesco's approach had not been dismissed out of hand.[30] (The investigation of Vesco was indeed delayed, though the financier ultimately collapsed in a welter of fraud.) Similarly, Congress had not appreciated Casey's actions in the ITT case: as pressure mounted for an investigation of ITT, Casey, who had all the sensitive documents at the SEC and knew that Congress might soon subpoena them, had them all shipped off to the privileged sanctuary of Mitchell's Justice Department.[31] When Mitchell was forced to resign during the Watergate scandal Casey's close links with him also drew a certain amount of critical comment.

In 1980 Casey hedged his bets, contributing to both the Connally and Bush campaigns before becoming Reagan's campaign manager. An odd feature of the campaign was its links into the intelligence community. Carter's CIA Director, Admiral Stansfield Turner, had fired 800 agents from the CIA clandestine operations section: Turner had frowned on covert operations and had been appalled to find that some of the Nixon-era 'cowboys' were so incurably wedded to them that his initial restrictions were not always obeyed.[32] Some of these ex-agents had gravitated into the Bush campaign – not unnaturally Bush, as a former CIA director, was the Agency's favoured man.[33] When the Bush campaign amalgamated with Reagan's, this produced a pool of helpers eager to give proof of their new Reaganite loyalties: with Reagan committed to a major reinforcement of the CIA a Republican victory could only be good news for them. In July 1980 Casey announced that he was setting up 'an intelligence system' to make sure the Carter forces did not spring any surprises. This created alarm among some Reagan men (notably Ed Meese, the campaign chief of staff) and the phrase, at least, was dropped.[34] But for Casey, the lure of the clandestine was strong and he maintained a network which included not only ex-CIA and ex-FBI men but reached into the serving ranks of the CIA and FBI. (*Time* reported that Casey and his aide, Max Hugel, were the only members of the Reagan team willing to run the risk of maintaining such contacts, though Casey, whose hostility towards the press is undisguised, denied the reports.) Casey also maintained a network of ex-military officers under former admiral Robert Garrick to monitor and report back on unusual movements at US bases which might herald a sudden foreign policy move.[35] Later there were to be awkward questions about this phase of the campaign when it was discovered that some (secret) NSC documents had found their way to the Reagan campaign staff,[36] and, even more, when the Reagan forces managed to get hold of Carter's briefing notes for one of the TV debates. A furious row broke out over who was responsible for this. Casey denied he had anything to do with it but James Baker, Reagan's chief of White House staff, no less, testified that he had received the documents from Casey's office. It was a peculiar situation, with the Director of CIA and White House chief publicly calling one another liars. CIA men thought Baker had made a big mistake. As one agent put it, 'Casey is not the sort of man you want to be in a fight with. He could figure out more ways to cut off my balls than I could imagine.'[37]

Reagan's nomination of Casey as the new CIA Director did not go down well with Congress. In 1971 he had drawn Senate criticism for misleading the confirmation hearings over the question of the plagiarism suit against him. In 1981 all that the Senate Intelligence Committee chairman, Barry Goldwater, would grudgingly concede was that Casey was 'not unfit to serve'. It was only six months later, under pressure from the Committee, that Casey amended his financial statement, which the Committee had found 'deficient in several respects'. Casey had 'forgotten' to list a large number of lawsuits, directorships, debts, liabilities and payments. He had also 'forgotten' to list seventy former clients – one of which was the South Korean government.[38] To the fury of the Committee, Casey bluntly refused to comply with the official regulations requiring him to put his investments into a 'blind trust' while he was in office. Asked if the information to which he was now privy might not allow him to make stock-market killings, Casey allowed that this was so but told the Committee that such a notion was 'crap' and 'hogwash'. This led to cracks among the White House staff that CIA really stood for 'Casey Investing Again'.[39] The joke seemed less funny after Casey was finally pressured into agreeing to a blind trust in October 1983. It then emerged that Casey had been holding stock in a number of companies which had dealings with the CIA, including some which had contracts for secret operations ('national security' was invoked as a reason for disclosing no details of these, even then). It emerged, too, that a considerable amount of Agency time had indeed been spent on Casey's share transactions, with Agency memos examining Casey's holdings in oil stocks in light of the CIA's predictions of world oil supply, for example.[40] Even then Casey somehow managed to avoid placing in the blind trust a large block of shares in Capital Cities Communications Inc., the conglomerate which was to take over the American Broadcasting Corporation.[41]

Casey seemed to feel, in a word, that most of the normal rules and norms just did not apply to him. Thus at one point he launched plans to put the CIA back into domestic intelligence work in apparent rivalry with the FBI. The plan was scotched by bureaucratic resistance rather than through any consideration for the fact that it was illegal. But Casey's strength was that he had established a camaraderie with the President rivalled only by Meese and Clark, giving him an easy access to the Oval Office and a considerably enhanced role in the President's daily foreign-affairs briefings.[42] In effect this meant there was a protective White House umbrella over Casey which shielded him from the frequent outbursts of Congressional outrage against him. This could not, though, protect all those under him. Thus serious questions were raised in Congress over Casey's appointment of his campaign aide, Max Hugel, as head of CIA clandestine operations, and particularly about Hugel's previous business and stock-market dealings. These objections were furiously brushed aside by Casey but in the end Hugel had to resign. Goldwater icily asked Casey if he wouldn't like to resign too.[43] Hugel was replaced by John Stein (who in turn gave way to Clair George in June 1984).

This bad relationship continued to explode sporadically into bitter rows over Casey's alleged concealment of such matters as the CIA's secret mining of Nicaraguan harbours (an incident which caused Goldwater to write a celebrated letter to Casey in which he informed him: 'I am pissed off').[44] One Democrat bitterly asserted that 'Truth isn't part of his vocabulary',[45] but Casey's normal tactic was to push things through while leaving out key information so that afterwards he could usually claim, legalistically, not only that he had told no positive untruth but that others had actually endorsed his proposals. Another Committee member, Senator Durenberger, put it more exactly: 'Bill is just a salesman. He will tell you what he wants in order to sell a car. If you don't ask whether there's an engine or a steering wheel, he won't bring it up.'[46] What really concerned the Committee was not just Casey's cavalier approach to the law but the fact that he was a high-roller who saw all the normal restrictions as just so many obstacles to overcome. Every so often news of one or other of his schemes would leak out and he might have to climb down – but with the generally successful tightening of CIA security it seemed certain that he was involved in other high-risk operations of which they knew nothing.

What nobody doubted was that the CIA had never been so powerful as it quickly became under Casey. That Andropov, a former KGB chief, had succeeded to the Soviet leadership drew wide comment, but there was less recognition of the fact that, with one former CIA head as Vice-President and Casey the first CIA director to be given Cabinet status, Reagan's Cabinet now had not one but two intelligence men in the inner circle. Moreover, the Agency's budget grew at an annual compound rate of over 20 per cent, making it the fastest (indeed, under Reagan, almost the only) growing government department. Its staff was beefed up to 18,000, with many of those sacked by Stansfield Turner re-recruited. (Casey gave free rein to his hatred of the 'white-shoe boys' so most of the new recruits came from obscure western or Southern colleges.)[47] The Agency was rapidly returned to the 'cowboy' image it had enjoyed under Donovan.

The most startling increase was in clandestine and covert operations of every sort: in just three years a fivefold increase, according to David McMichael, an operative who left the Agency in protest.[48] By 1983 *Newsweek* estimated that there were twelve to fourteen 'major' covert operations under way in various parts of the world,[49] while *US News and World Report* put the number of 'minor' covert operations at around 50.[50] (The distinction is purely budgetary – a major operation is one costing $5 million or more.) The most spectacular was, of course, the building up of a 12,000-man army of anti-Sandinist Contras on Nicaragua's borders. In Africa alone, McMichael estimated, around twenty covert operations were under way by 1983.[51] Ruefully surveying what Casey had made of the CIA, his predecessor as director, Stansfield Turner, pointed out that Casey had two essential faults. First, he was the first CIA chief in history to take open and strongly partisan positions; and second, he was remodelling the CIA on the lines of the old wartime OSS. The OSS had operated in a situation where 'almost any covert action to help win the war was acceptable, and the more the better'. Casey was now applying the same philosophy in peacetime. 'What's been missing in the Reagan–Casey approach,' wrote Turner, 'is attention to the provision in the Hughes–Ryan Amendment that covert actions must be "important to national security".'[52]

This attitude to covert action was doubly dangerous because Casey was extremely successful in tightening security restrictions of every sort around the CIA, so that it became far harder than before for the media (or even Congress) to know what was going on. Indeed, just the day before 007's flight a fresh notice under the President's signature was circularised to federal employees in the foreign policy, defence and intelligence fields warning that disclosure of classified information could result in criminal prosecution.[53]

The seventy-year-old Casey dashed around his expanding empire in a state of some excitement – drawing criticism from within the Agency for his 'extremely risky' habit of flying on commercial airliners under assumed names.[54] Sometimes Casey would get so carried away by a new item of intelligence that he would dash to the White House, piece of paper in hand. In other ways he was a less good communicator: his rasping bullfrog mumbling caused even Reagan to joke that he would be the first CIA chief not to need a scrambler phone, while some Congressional Democrats found him so hard to follow (Nicaragua came out as 'Nicowawa') that they resolved not to approve plans to 'overthrow the government of any country Casey couldn't pronounce'.[55]

Casey was considerably larger than life, right down to living (like Gatsby) in a large mansion in West Egg. He also had the capability to carry out a completely separate and unofficial foreign policy if he wanted to. In fact he worked closely with Clark, as was only prudent. Casey had a close relationship with Reagan, but Clark's was closer and Casey was unlikely to forget that he had been recruited into the Reagan team only on Clark's say-so and had got the CIA job he so coveted only because Clark had turned it down. In any case the two men – both are Catholics – were friends and saw eye to eye. Their relationship gave US foreign policy what coherence it had, but the combination of Clark's ignorance and Casey's wild risk-taking seemed a dangerous mix to many.

Perhaps even more dangerous was the fact that many of the White House superhawks were fascinated by covert action. Straight away in 1981 Reagan had acceded to Casey's request for greater secrecy by setting up the National Security Planning Group with membership restricted to key White House and Cabinet officials (including Clark), but omitting the experts who normally gave advice. The result was alarming: 'There's nobody there', said one intelligence official, 'to tell these guys what the problems will be and what could go wrong', while another commented that 'people at the top of this Administration are fascinated with covert operations and find it easier to approve them than to discuss complicated diplomatic matters'.[56]

## On the eve of 007: the blind leading the blind

Undoubtedly, these 'people at the top' included William Clark, and from Shultz's point of view he remained the chief fly in the ointment, for he was the single most powerful figure and also the most ignorant. The situation became quite desperate in July 1983 when, to general astonishment, 'Bud' McFarlane, Clark's right-hand man, was named as the State Department's chief Middle East negotiator and flew off to the Middle East. Aside from the peculiarity of the fact that Shultz's man in the Middle East was now not his employee at all but Clark's, this left Clark without his one real expert and steadying influence. There was grave doubt that Clark could cope on his own at all. And he really was on his own, for the President himself showed his normal highly developed propensity to leave details to others and accept more or less whatever recommendations were put in front of him by his aides. Indeed, Clark had become openly frustrated in August 1983 when, loaded down with key decisions over the Middle East and arms control, he couldn't get Reagan to come along to any meetings of the National Security Council at all.[57] NSC business was backing up at a fearful rate and Clark would just have to take a lot of decisions on his own. The President had already declared that nothing would stop him and Nancy getting back to the ranch and it was a well established principle that the President's frequent holidays there had priority over almost anything short of a full-scale nuclear engagement.

The alarming picture of Clark in sole charge of foreign policy in August 1983 drove James Reston to the verdict:

Unlike Mr Kissinger or Mr Brzezinski, the Judge has no ambition and few ideas . . . Judge Clark is not the sort who would fiddle with the facts. He's too honest for that. It's just that he's more concerned with the political security of Ronald Reagan than with the security of the nation . . . the only top official here who knows less about foreign affairs than President Reagan is Mr Clark . . . the irony of this is not that Mr Clark strengthens the President, but dramatises his weaknesses. It's a case of the blind leading the blind . . .[58]

In mid-August the President and Mrs Reagan duly left for their California ranch, the President insisting that he could run the country just as well from there as from the White House. He was probably right in this: the two or three hours a day he spent on the phone at the ranch were not vastly different from the daily stint he put in in Washington. He would deal with the Lebanese crisis, nuclear arms control and so on in the intervals between horse rides, wood-stacking, fence-post mending and all the other little cowboy tasks the President so delighted in setting himself while home on the range. There was nothing for Clark to do except grit his teeth, arrange a whole set of NSC meetings back-to-back for September, and follow the President to California. He and Edwin Meese III – another of Reagan's close old cronies and now the most influential White House adviser – set up headquarters at the Biltmore Hotel, Santa Barbara, 20 miles from the Reagan ranch. Effectively, this made the Biltmore the temporary capital of the US and even of the Western world. Meese was to be the domestic policy supremo; indeed, despite his habit of awarding jobs to those who made him loans that he tended to forget about, he was soon to be elevated to the post of Attorney-General. Clark would be the foreign policy supremo. The arrangement was that they would conduct the affairs of government, staying close to the President but with the clear understanding that they were to bother him as sparingly as possible. The President, for his part, was already talking of taking another holiday in October . . .

## Getting the news: the impossible timetable

This, then, was the somewhat rickety state of the US foreign-policy process on the eve of the huge international crisis which the KAL tragedy was to produce. Given the centrality of Clark and Casey they would inevitably be the first two men to know the news, so the question of why there was apparently such a mysterious delay in the receipt of the news has to focus on them. This is not an easy task: Casey remained invisible throughout the crisis and Clark kept an extremely low profile, only emerging to make his first public statement on the affair two weeks later.

The shoot-down took place at 18.26 pm and 007 went off the radar screens at 18.38 – that is, 2.38 pm Washington time (Eastern Daylight Time – EDT). If the normal CRITIC system was working properly one would have expected the brute fact that 007 was down and the gist of the rapidly transcribed conversations of the Soviet pilots monitored by the US surveillance net to have reached Fort Meade and thence the White House no later than 3.00 pm. It would not have taken more than a minute or two for NSA or NSC officials to realise that this sort of information had to go straight to Clark in California. So Clark ought to have known the bare facts at, say, 3.10. (In fact, of course, such a schedule is far too leisurely: had US surveillance picked up Russian radio conversations suggesting a countdown to a surprise nuclear attack, it would have been essential for translation and communication to take no more than five minutes at the most. This would suggest that the news should have been available at 2.45 at the latest, perhaps even 2.30. But, for the sake of argument, let us allow 3.10.)

According to White House spokesman Larry Speakes, it was not until 7.30 pm California time (10.30 pm EDT – eight whole hours after the shoot-down) that William Clark phoned the President to tell him that 007 was 'missing', and at that point it was still unclear what had happened to the plane, so the President was just told 'the extent of our information on it and all viewpoints on it'.[59] At 10.30 pm (1.30 am EDT) Clark phoned Reagan again to update him, but the picture was still unclear. As Speakes described the call, 'It was a little clearer, and we had some speculation, and I would judge fairly hard information at 10.30 based on intelligence reports. But then again we were still assessing, as we did throughout the night.'[60] This was eleven hours after the shoot-down and some ten and a half hours after Clark should have had full information if the CRITIC system had worked properly.

Richard Burt, Assistant Secretary of State for European Affairs, gave journalists a blow-by-blow account of how news of the 007 tragedy was received through the night at the State Department. According to Burt it was only at 10.30 pm EDT – a full eight hours after the shoot-down – that State set up a special operations group to monitor the affair, comprising members from the Pentagon, the White House and the intelligence agencies. Only at midnight was the Department sure enough of its ground to contact the Soviet chargé d'affaires in Washington, Oleg M. Sokolov, to ask for an explanation of the plane's fate. Simultaneously the US Embassy in Moscow was reached and took up the matter there. Both enquiries met no response. At 2.15 am Shultz phoned Clark to say he was going to have to make a statement about the affair and wanting to clear with Clark the text of what he would say on TV. There is no (public) record of Clark having bothered to get in touch with Shultz before that.

At 3.00 am EDT White House officials were told that 007 had been shot down. But according to Speakes the picture available to those in Washington was still far from clear: 'we still did not have, that it had disappeared from radar. So we still did not have a detailed assessment of why it was there. We did not know whether it had been forced down or whether it had actually been fired on.'[61]

According to Speakes the process of 'assessment' of what had happened continued in Washington 'throughout the night'. Even Clark, he claimed, had not been fully aware of the facts when he spoke to Reagan at 1.30 am EDT – all he knew was that there was 'reason to believe' that 007 'was in the water'.[62] Clark does not seem to have had much sleep that night for at 5 am California time he was on the phone to Shultz, though according to Speakes, things were still not completely clear. Finally, Clark phoned the President at 7.10 am (10.10 EDT) to tell him that 007 had definitely been shot down by the Russians. Speakes (who had also followed the President to California and was stationed at the Santa Barbara Sheraton) was immediately pressed by an incredulous press corps. It had taken almost seventeen hours since the shoot-down for the definitive news of it to reach the President. How could it possibly have taken so long? At what time was the news of the shoot-down known to be definitive? Speakes became noticeably irritable about such probing: 'The point is that we did not know, did not have final, firm confirmation and a willingness to go public with it until shortly before the President was informed of it. As soon as they were certain on it [sic], they informed the President on it. Now, that was 7.10 am for you tick-tock fanatics.'[63]

The press corps could be excused their incredulity (though they seemed, almost instantly, to forget it), for the timetable provided by the White House is very hard to believe. A delay as long as this would imply a massive and simultaneous breakdown in a whole series of US surveillance and/or communications facilities which would have placed national security in extremely grave peril. Such a breakdown would seem to be inexplicable and indeed no explanation for it has been offered. Beyond that, however, there is a whole string of further oddities to this timetable.

Frederic N. Smith, assistant to Larry McDonald, had become concerned about the Congressman's fate and at 8.30 pm EDT had phoned the State Department's operations office to ask if something had happened to 007. He was told that the US Embassy in Seoul had already reported that the plane was 'in the water'.[64] Then, at about 9 pm, the South Korean Ambassador in Washington, Lew Biong Hion, contacted the State Department to express concern that 007 might have strayed off course over Soviet territory.[65] This is the first mention of 007 being off course and it is a remarkable feature of the White House version of events that the South Koreans (who depend entirely on the US for sophisticated surveillance information) should have come out with this notion before the US itself did.

Thus at this stage – around 9 pm EDT – the US Embassy in Seoul and the South Korean Embassy in Washington had the bare bones of the story: 007 had strayed off course over Soviet territory and had then ended up 'in the water'. All this one and a half hours before Clark made his first phone call to the President when, we are told, he was still unclear about the situation; and three hours before the State Department even set up its special monitoring group on the matter. This is simply incredible. Even if there had been a long and inexplicable delay in acquiring hard information before, these two reports would undoubtedly have triggered rapid transcription of the taped conversations of the Soviet pilots – which furnished conclusive proof of the shoot-down.

It is not difficult to believe that the State Department might have been very slow to learn the facts. As the example of the US Navy exercises off Nicaragua only two months before had shown, State could be kept ignorant, even for days, about what large-scale US forces were doing in America's back garden: not only Clark but the Pentagon and the CIA and NSA would have known all about those exercises and they had all kept their information from State. But thanks to these Embassy reports – if nothing else – State had a fair idea of the facts by 9 pm. Then, according to Richard Burt, the Assistant Secretary of State, at 10.00 or 10.30 (he couldn't remember which), the Department had definite confirmation that 007 had strayed off course. But then, said Burt, they received reports that 007 had force-landed on Sakhalin and this threw them off for a while. It was shortly after this ('between 10 and 11') that Larry McDonald's wife, Kathryn, was phoned by 'someone in the State Department'[66] and given the safe-on-Sakhalin story. Larry McDonald's brother, Harold, and the Congressman's press secretary, Tommy Toles, were similarly contacted.[67] Thus State was just as fooled by the CIA report as KAL and the South Korean Foreign Ministry had been. It was absurd: as soon as it got the safe-on-Sakhalin story the Japanese Broadcasting Corporation simply telephoned Sakhalin airport and were told that 007 was definitely not there.[68]

From Burt's account and the phone call to Kathryn McDonald it seems clear that the CIA report of the Sakhalin forced landing reached State at around 10.30 pm EDT – eight hours after the shoot-down. This is very peculiar indeed, for the same report had reached the Seoul Foreign Ministry only six and a half hours after shoot-down. Thus to reconcile this timetable we have to believe that the CIA – or someone within the CIA – came up with the false report, handed it to Seoul but kept State in the dark, and then still believed in the report sufficiently to hand it on to State one and a half hours later. There is, in a word, something dreadfully fishy about the whole CIA report. One cannot but observe that it arrived in Seoul just as the passengers' relatives were becoming hysterical because they knew the plane must be out of fuel wherever it was. The report headed off an inevitable explosion here and sent the relatives home happy for a few hours. Similarly in Washington, it was just as State received definite confirmation that 007 had strayed off course – and were thus on the verge of the truth – that the false CIA report arrived to throw them off the track for another hour. Whatever the purpose of whoever originated the report, its function was exactly the same in Seoul and at State: it headed off the truth for a further period and prolonged the uncertainty.

But there are other impossibilities here too. At 9 pm EDT State had firm reports that 007 had strayed off course over Soviet territory and then crashed. Even if one accepts – something it is very difficult to do – that US intelligence had not made a thorough check of all its data in the previous six and a half hours since the shoot-down, there is no doubt that such a grave report would have led to a rapid check of all the radar readings, tape transcripts and electronic intercepts available to the US. This data would have made quite plain what had happened and it seems certain that Clark must have had all this data to hand when he made his first phone call to Reagan at 10.30 pm EDT (he probably wouldn't have disturbed him otherwise). This means that the story that Clark was still unsure of his facts at that point must be untrue. But, more important, such a check would have placed the same data in the hands of the Pentagon, NSA and CIA. This should have made it quite impossible for the CIA to come out with the false report of the Sakhalin forced landing at any stage, let alone at two separate points across an interval of an hour and a half.

On the other hand it seems clear that neither Clark, the NSC, the CIA or the Pentagon handed on the tape transcripts to State: otherwise State could not have been fooled by the false report of the forced landing. Nonetheless, State was concerned enough to set up its special monitoring group, pulling in experts from the Pentagon and the intelligence community: after the Nicaraguan exercises affair they must have been well aware of the possibility that they were being kept in the dark. But if they were concerned enough to do this, it is odd indeed that State should have phoned Kathryn McDonald to give her cruelly false reassurance.

The special operations group would doubtless have called for further intelligence data and, according to Burt, 'within the hour (i.e. by 11.30 pm) there were other indications that much more tragic circumstances had taken place'.[69] But all this turned out to mean was that State was told only that the CIA could not confirm that 007 had landed on Sakhalin: State still did not have the tapes.

Larry McDonald's assistant, Frederic Smith, had meanwhile realised that Defence might know more than State and had contacted the Pentagon. He was invited to a special briefing session at 1.00 am in the National Military Command Center, in a bunker under the Pentagon. He was not only told that 007 had definitely been shot down by the Russians, but had some of the tape intercepts read to him.[70] Smith, it should be noted, was merely a humble Congressional assistant: he would have been a long way down on any need-to-know list. Indeed, revealing the tape information to Smith implied not only that the Pentagon had had the tapes for some time – long enough for many others to see them – but that a decision had already been taken that the Administration would go public with them. It is important to note that this occurred a half-hour before Clark's second phone call to Reagan. It is possible – though hardly conceivable – that the relatively humble Smith would be given access to this information before the President, but it seems certain that Reagan had in fact been told of them in Clark's earlier call, which in turn meant that Clark had had them for some time before that. The White House version of Clark's second call – that he was still not fully sure of the situation – is thus obviously untrue. *A fortiori*, the claim that the final truth of the matter was only known shortly before Clark's next call to the President at 10.10 am EDT the next morning is also a lie.

Thus by 1.00 am the whole matter had actually been digested in substance and the question of its media presentation – in the Reagan Administration always a far longer debate – also worked out. This is confirmed by Shultz's 2.15 am call to Clark to clear his speech with him. Nobody pretended that Shultz was more than a front man (one notes who cleared speeches with whom), but even he must by then have known the facts for some time. It would normally take his aides a few hours at least to draft a major speech due to achieve immense international coverage and impact. One does not commission such a speech or arrange for its TV coverage without being sure of the facts.

Given all this it was hardly surprising that the press corps reacted with such incredulity the next day when informed of the White House version of events.

Indeed, when the *Washington Post* checked with its usual 'intelligence sources' it found that one of them 'suggested that the information arrived in Washington sooner than has been publicly acknowledged'.[71] But, over-whelmed by the sheer horror of the shoot-down, the press quickly regained its credulity over what seemed, in comparison, a minor technical matter.

Later, though, suspicions began to grow.[72] According to Sampson and Bittorf,[73] NSA headquarters at Fort Meade had, within 30 minutes of the shoot-down, received news of an incident over southern Sakhalin and also knew that a South Korean airliner had been involved: this information they received from the Misawa signal-intelligence station. By 5.00 pm EDT the NSA confirmed the full facts of the shoot-down to Clark, who thereupon called a teleconference with Meese, Burt, Shultz, Eagleburger and Casey to consider how the incident should be handled. Burt, they report, was particu-larly concerned not to give a fillip to the European peace movement (which always tended to emphasise the dangers of accidental war). Thus it was essential that the incident be presented as a deliberate and conscious Soviet action above all else. Clark and several of the others were, apparently, more worried about a possible repetition of the U-2 affair of 1960; that is, that the Russians might have evidence which could then be used to embarrass the US in front of the world. This bespoke a need to achieve maximum coordination with the Japanese and South Koreans, to procure the tapes which would best support the presentation made by the US. To make time for this coordination effort to be put together, the false CIA report of the Sakhalin forced landing was put out as a holding operation. All this, Sampson and Bittorf report, was worked out by the teleconference before the President was told anything. A somewhat similar report appeared in the monthly, *New York*, citing an (unnamed) intelligence source to the effect that this teleconference took place 'just hours' after the shoot-down and was concerned with 'exploiting' the incident so that it 'could be used to quell European opposition to Pershing missiles'.[74] Certainly those familiar with the US military information system from the inside – such as former admiral Eugene Carroll[75] – felt certain that everyone at the top would have been bound to receive full information of the incident very quickly indeed.

In fact Sampson and Bittorf report that the official Administration version of lengthy delays while the news was processed and checked was deeply resented by NSA professionals. It was a matter of great pride to them that they could get their information fast: as Admiral Bobby Inman, the former NSA director, put it, 'We want to know what's happening before it happens.' According to their NSA sources, the NSA had monitored live all the air-to-ground and ground-to-air conversations of the Soviet pilots over Kamchatka, through the services of the USS *Observation Island*. From there on, the NSA monitored everything live. The reason why 007 had not been warned, the NSA source said, was that while those monitoring its flight were aware that the plane wasn't one of their own RC-135s, they hadn't been sure exactly what it was, other than that it was civilian. To be sure, they could have called Anchorage and told them to check on planes under their control – but such links to civilian ground controllers were not part of NSA routine.[76]

## Japan: The front line

Japan was the front line both in terms of intelligence and news throughout most of the 007 affair. If one puts together the information gleaned by M. Katayama,[77] Sampson and Bittorf,[78] and other reporters there, it is clear that the situation in Washington was closely paralleled in Tokyo, with news of the tragedy arriving quickly and then being delayed for hours – no doubt at Washington's request.

News of the tragedy caught the Japanese evening papers on the hop: just after the closing time for their evening editions the official line on 007 changed abruptly from 'all safe' to 'no hope'. Only one paper – the right-wing and pro-Government *Sankei* got in not just the bare news but also the fact of a possible Soviet shoot-down. *Sankei*, it turned out, had got its information from Nibetsu or 'the rabbit's ears', as it is popularly known.

One of the side-effects of the 007 affair was the fresh light it shed on Nibetsu[79] – officially the 'Annex Chamber of the Second Section, Investigation Division, of the Ground Self-Defence Forces'. Headquartered at Ichigaya Camp, Tokyo, Nibetsu employs over 1100 people, runs nine intercept stations and deploys the whole range of modern technology in a highly efficient intelligence-gathering operation. Thanks largely to Nibetsu, Japan has in recent years been ahead of the US in learning of a number of major developments. Thus Japan had the first word of the Sino–Vietnamese border war of February 1979, learned of the successful test of a Chinese submarine-launched missile in October 1982, and has been able to pass on valuable information to the US about Soviet troop movements on the Chinese border. Nibetsu is so tightly tied into the US NSA structure that it is virtually a division of the NSA. In Japan its chief peculiarity is that it does not report to the Self-Defence Agency but directly to the Prime Minister's Cabinet Research Office.[80] It is the Prime Minister and Cabinet Secretary who decide what, if anything, of this information is to be passed on to the SDA. This system allows for a particularly fast and secure liaison between the White House and the Japanese head of government in sensitive intelligence matters.

Nibetsu was, naturally, quick to learn of what had happened to 007. Both the SDA and Nibetsu regard Sakhalin as almost home ground – as *Yomiuri* put it, the SDA 'gets almost all there is to know about Soviet Far East armed forces covering the maritime provinces of Siberia, Sakhalin and the northern islands'.[81] On this occasion it got its information from its intercept stations at Wakkanai, Nemuro and Abashiri (Hokkaido).

Narita had informed the Air Self-Defence Force (ASDF) that 007 was missing around 5.00 am Tokyo time (20.00 GMT – one and a half hours after the shoot-down) – but in fact the Wakkanai radar had already reported to the SDA by then (which means that Nibetsu had already been in touch with the Cabinet Research Office and got clearance to do this). Kazuho Tanikawa, the head of the SDA, immediately demanded full information on the matter and by 8.00 am Tokyo time (23.00 GMT) he knew the full story. Tanikawa went straight to a business breakfast with the Cabinet Secretary, Masaharu Gotoda. Gotoda then phoned the Prime Minister, Yasuhiro Nakasone, who in turn called a meeting of his inner Cabinet for 9.30. Even before the meeting, though, Nakasone had already been contacted by Washington by backchannel (i.e. a secure, nonofficial communications route). Washington impressed on Nakasone its wish for the tightest possible coordination and collaboration: in particular it wanted no independent actions or announcements made by Nakasone. 'Above all,' the backchannel communication ran (according to Sampson and Bittorf), 'and until further notice, in any pronouncements on the missing airliner anything about a shoot-down by the Soviets or North Koreans [sic] is to be mentioned as only one possibility among others.' Nakasone agreed to this – partly because he is wont to go along with what Washington wants, but also because he had no particular desire for Japan to lead the condemnation of the Russians. If the Americans wanted to be the ones to break the news with a great public splash (and thus to be the ones to set the terms of debate), Nakasone had no objection. But it did leave Nakasone and Gotoda with a considerable job of news management.[82]

In this the Japanese Government was largely but not wholly successful. The big problem was that the SDA knew the story and could not be prevented from leaking some of it. Thus Shunji Taoka, the military correspondent of *Asahi Shimbun*, had got onto his sources at the SDA and learned the true story shortly after 9.30. He found he couldn't use it, though – no newspaper or television station wanted to go public before there had been an official announcement. (This sounds rather as if they may have been responding to an official request.) Meanwhile, there was complete confusion at Wakkanai: the first rescue boats had gone to the wrong place. Then at 8.30 the SDA told the Maritime Safety Agency (MSA) of the right crash location, but in the absence of any official announcement about the plane, uncertainty naturally persisted.

Meanwhile – as the SDA later openly revealed to journalists – Mr Natsume, the head of the SDA civil service, visited Gotoda just after 10.00 to discuss the shoot-down, and at 10.25 Tanikawa, the SDA head, went to see Nakasone about it, presumably so that Nakasone could explain to them the need for silence. At 2.30 pm Mr Kamakura, head of the Cabinet Research Department, told journalists at the Prime Minister's residence that a shoot-down was one possibility among others. At that stage 007 had been down for eleven hours and the top Government figures had known about it for over six hours. What this meant was that the Government had allowed the safe-on-Sakhalin story to stand for many hours, though knowing it to be false. Later, the Government was effectively to admit this but to plead that they hadn't wanted to go public until further checks had been carried out.

In fact, of course, if the safe-on-Sakhalin story was to have any currency at all, it must have been necessary for Washington to tell Tokyo that the story was false – otherwise there would have been some danger of the Japanese giving the lie to it. It is even possible that the false story was invented largely with an eye to the Japanese situation: with Europe asleep and the US going to sleep, the only place where the story could break 'prematurely' was Japan (South Korea was less of a problem, having no real equivalent to Nibetsu or the NSA). But 'holding' the news blackout in Japan would be very difficult – the truth had already begun to seep out and, in the absence of any contrary lead, journalists were bound to converge on it. There had to be *some* explanation of what had happened to 007, after all. Better, then, to give them that explanation – a false hare to chase for a few hours at least. If this was the tactic, it did work: when Shultz went on US nationwide TV with his charges of a Soviet 'cover-up', he had the stage all to himself.

It seems certain, then, that the official version of how the news was received in Washington, so elaborately presented by Burt, Speakes and others, was a deliberate cover. (Speakes, no doubt, was never given the facts. This happened not infrequently: the day before the US invasion of Grenada, Speakes, acting on authoritative assurances from above, informed the media that any notion that the US might invade the island was 'preposterous'.[83]) Not only did Clark and other top decision-makers know the key facts within half an hour but by 1 am (when Frederic Smith was read the tape transcripts) it had effectively been decided to go public. The notion that the facts were not known for a full nine hours after that simply won't wash. Speakes was nearer the mark when he implied the need for delay until the Administration had 'the willingness to go public'.

One implication of the Sampson/Bittorf/M. Katayama/*New York* version of events is that all the important decisions in Washington were taken without reference to the President, and that the delay in informing him was much longer than has been admitted. This is not difficult to accept. Indeed, such a delay would have best accorded with the President's own preferences. As the 1981 incident of the shooting down of the Libyan MIGs revealed, Reagan's aides would not lightly disturb the President, *a fortiori* when he was on holiday. They knew better than to ring him with a complicated mass of raw data and alternative hypotheses. The President, to put it kindly, was not at his best when thus treated. His strong preference – one his aides were only too happy to observe – was that they should do all the analysis and make most of the primary decisions, only then serving him up with ready-cooked solutions which, almost invariably, he was quick and happy to endorse. One must assume that Clark's two phone calls to the President, at 7.30 and 10.30 pm, did this much and that this was why there was no need for any further communication to him from Clark for almost another nine hours. Indeed, by the time Reagan was phoned next morning – according to Speakes, to get the full news of the affair for the first time – Shultz's press conference was already scheduled and it was all systems go for a massive media explosion on the affair, which Reagan would have been too late to affect either way. (One notes in passing that Reagan had no contact at all with Shultz until after Shultz's press conference: a fair measure of how far Presidential delegation to Clark – and the distancing of Shultz – had gone.)

Two elements in the Sampson/Bittorf account are, though, quite explosive. To suggest that Clark feared that the Soviets might have embarrassing evidence to reveal, as in the U-2 affair, is close to suggesting that 007's flight had had some surveillance purpose: the U-2 had, after all, been a spy flight and it is difficult to imagine what the embarrassing evidence could be other than US collusion in the 007 flight. It is worth noting that, according to the *Washington Post*, 'top US officials anticipated that the Soviets would claim the airliner was on a spy mission'.[84] Accordingly, said the *Post*, Clark did not dismiss such a possibility out of hand but phoned the CIA 'to check whether there were any grounds for such a charge'. He spoke to Casey's deputy director, John N. McMahon, who 'assured Clark that there were none'.[85] It is difficult to know what to make of this report: Clark would undoubtedly have wanted to speak to Casey and, according to Sampson/Bittorf, did so. This should have obviated any need to speak to McMahon.

Almost equally explosive is the suggestion that the false CIA report was put out as a deliberate stratagem to gain time. This report not only had the effect of throwing the South Korean Government and KAL off the track, with a delay in the launching of air–sea rescue operations which could, in other circumstances, have proved fatal, but had extremely cruel consequences for Kathryn McDonald and all the other relatives and friends of the victims. If the reports of an early teleconference are correct, Clark and the other top Administration officials concerned cannot avoid responsibility for the misleading CIA report: even if they did not originate the report, they had the means to deny it and instead let it stand for five fateful hours.

It seems virtually certain, then, that the Reagan Administration did receive news of the 007 tragedy far earlier than it admitted, and that it deliberately sought to give currency to a misleading timetable of its own reactions. This exercise in news management was, though, a remarkable success: the press did not even ask the obvious questions posed by the cover story itself. To argue that there had been such an extraordinary delay in the US learning of a violent Soviet action by their armed forces against a plane flying from a US airport with US citizens aboard – in this hypersensitive area above all – was tantamount to suggesting that the whole US surveillance network had been subject to the worst national security failure since Pearl Harbor. At the very least, Clark, as the National Security supremo, might have expected some hard probing over such a notion, let alone the reports of a far earlier meeting. (In fact Clark remained inaccessible to the press after the incident and did not speak publicly about it until 14 September.) As it was, the Administration successfully diverted attention away from all such questions by focusing the media's attention as hard as possible on the sheer, brutal fact of the Soviet shoot-down – which was, in all conscience, heinous enough.

When Larry Speakes faced reporters on Thursday morning (1 September) they naturally wanted to know how the President had taken the news. He was very upset, said Speakes. He then went on to issue his normal bulletin of the President's activities for the day ahead: 'The President, as usual, is planning a horse-back ride this morning and will generally work around the ranch in the afternoon.'[86] In fact the President's staff had already suggested that an early return to Washington might be politically wise: a Congressman had been killed and Capitol Hill might take it amiss if the President appeared to ignore the fact. The President refused – he was determined to have his holiday.

This produced a degree of incredulity among the press and within hours the White House staff had convinced Reagan that an early return to Washington was essential. Finally, Reagan said he would go back on Saturday. This produced further lively reaction in Washington and by

Thursday afternoon Speakes told the press that the President would go back on Friday. He was taking the crisis very seriously. Next morning TV cameras captured the President and Mrs Reagan out for their normal carefree horse ride, leading Speakes to inveigh, not for the first time, at the grossly unfair way in which the media depicted the President.

As is well known by the Washington press, Larry Speakes keeps a card by his desk with his favourite quotation (from himself) on it: 'You don't tell us how to stage the news and we don't tell you how to cover it.'[87] Given the scale and audacious scope of the news management exercise the Administration had now launched, Speakes could have afforded to feel proud. But these 'insensitive' pictures of the President and Mrs Reagan suggested that things were still not working in quite the mutually satisfactory way desired. This was to be very much the story of the unprecedented media blitz now launched by the Administration over 007: overall it was a stunning success, but some awkward details were to be left hanging at the end . . .

# SIX

# The Media War

The Reagan Administration's stress on presentation rather than substance in policy-making has inevitably generated much criticism, but the KAL tragedy was one case where presentation really was of vital importance. The incident took place at a time of maximal Cold War tension, with both the superpowers engaged in an ominous new deployment of nuclear missiles in Europe and Asia and with key arms-control talks at a stage of great delicacy. Given this situation there was clearly a danger that the incident would tip the superpowers over the edge into a yet further increase in tension and further acceleration in the arms race. If this was to be avoided it was essential that the Administration took a firm but unprovocative line over the shoot-down.

The 'obvious' line to take in that sense was for the Administration to restrict itself to a simple statement that 007 had been shot down by the Russians, that the US deplored the loss of life but could not imagine that the USSR would have knowingly and deliberately carried out such an atrocity, and was accordingly seeking further clarification from the Soviet leaders. The object would have been to get the Soviet Union to admit the event, give its own explanation of how it had occurred, and make a clear apology with full compensation for the victims. This would have been exceedingly embarrassing for the Russians and would have given the US a great moral advantage in the international arena, but it might have avoided some of the grosser dangers of further Cold War escalation. The Russians would have hated such a loss of face but would have known that the US was reacting responsibly and that if there was no Soviet apology or admission of guilt, the US could simply put the Russians in the dock by releasing the tapes.

The key question was whether the Russians had shot down 007 knowing it was a civilian airliner. If that was so, there would be no alternative to denouncing them, bell, book and candle, right away. But the US had no certain knowledge that this was the case – indeed, further CIA analysis was to show that it had not been the case. Until that evidence was in there was much to be lost in an American rush to judgement. The Russians would then have taken their costs up front and would have nothing much further to lose in the court of world opinion. They would be furiously resentful, would probably refuse to apologise and the Cold War would intensify.

There is no evidence that this fairly obvious approach in responsible diplomacy was ever considered by Reagan's rabidly anti-Soviet advisers. Most of them regarded the USSR as a simple embodiment of evil – indeed it was only three weeks before the 007 tragedy that the President himself had solemnly declared the Russians to be 'the focus of evil in the modern world'. Men like Clark, Casey and Perle often seemed to speak of the Russians as if they were not people at all, just malignly misprogrammed robots. These men were not merely extremely right-wing – the fact that political exploitation of the tragedy would hurt the cause of arms control would not have bothered them for they did not much believe in arms control anyway – but they were also wild and incautious. In such a circle it is doubtful if the 'responsible' diplomatic option was even considered. Any debate over presentation was always likely to have assumed that the US would attempt to cause the Soviet Union the maximum possible embarrassment, and to have concerned itself instead with how far the US was willing to reveal its precious intelligence data to that end.

This emphasis was strongly apparent even in Shultz's first press conference on the affair. Shultz, his voice breaking with emotion, gave a lengthy account of the incident, citing evidence from the tapes in US possession (though never actually revealing the tapes). According to Shultz, there was little doubt that the Russians had shot down the plane while knowing it was an airliner and without any attempt to warn it. The Russians had tracked the plane for two and a half hours and had sent up as many as eight fighters after it. The fighter that fired the fatal missile was, said Shultz, 'close enough for visual inspection' (though in fact it never got nearer than 2 km) and there was no evidence of any attempt to warn 007. Indeed, 'there was no, apparently no ability to communicate between the two aircraft.'[1] This was, of course, tantamount to an accusation of deliberate mass murder.

The first reaction of Soviet diplomats was simply to deny the whole story. Vladimir Pavlov, the Soviet Ambassador to Japan, did this quite flatly on 2 September and added that he 'did not know why . . . Shultz had made such an accusation and on what he based such a charge'.[2] All this meant, though, was that Soviet diplomats had no clear line on the story from Moscow and were, accordingly, stonewalling. Far more culpable was the first TASS statement – slipped in as the last item on the Moscow TV news on 2 September. Expressing the 'regret' of the Soviet leadership at the loss of life, TASS laid the blame squarely on the US: the plane had been flying a surveillance mission, had shown no navigation lights, did not respond to queries and had ignored the tracer shells fired past it. All this was contentious but at least arguable. But TASS continued: 'Soon after this the intruder plane left the limits of Soviet airspace and continued its flight towards the Sea of Japan. For about ten minutes it was within the observation zone of radio-location means, after which it could be observed no more.'[3] Not only was there no admission that Soviet fighters had shot down 007 but the statement contained a clear attempt to avoid responsibility altogether.

There is, moreover, no doubt that this effectively mendacious statement had been authorised by the Politburo itself. The Soviet leader, Yuri Andropov, had been rushed back to Moscow from the spa in the Caucasus where he had been convalescing and had chaired a gruelling Politburo meeting which sat in almost continuous session on the affair on 1–2 September:[4] the TASS statement came only after that. Moreover, Party cell meetings were hurriedly called all over the USSR for 2–3 September in order to push out the TASS version to the grassroots.[5]

What can explain this reluctance to tell the truth? No doubt the tone of early American statements and the general context of Cold War tension produced an immediate defensive reflex, but the Russians must have been sufficiently conscious of US intelligence capabilities to know that proof of the shoot-down would soon be available. It is also true that the Russians do not give the same publicity to air crashes as the West: many internal Soviet crashes are reported late or not at all and even when the TU-144 ('Concordski') crashed at the Paris air show in 1973, *Pravda* gave it only a forty-word mention. But 007 was different and the frantic activity of the Party and the Politburo signalled clearly that the Russians knew they had a major crisis on their hands.

It is possible that the Russians were at first confused as to what had happened. As we have seen, there had been a query whether both Major Kasmin's missiles had hit 007; there had been evident Soviet radar difficulties; the fighters had failed to find the plane after the shoot-down – and it had stayed on the radar for 12 minutes. Perhaps it had somehow managed to slip beneath the radar net and then get away after all? An hour elapsed before it was light enough for the Russians to conduct a sea search and all their planes found then was a kerosene patch on the water. True, US intelligence monitored Soviet ground-station conversations four hours after the shoot-down and overheard discussions between Soviet pilots and controllers about a report that a passenger plane was down and a search effort was under way[6] – but the Russians would have been very slow to admit responsibility while even a shred of doubt remained. Nonetheless, it is impossible to believe that the Politburo did not know the central fact of the shoot-down when it met.

It seems likely, then, that the Russians knew the truth perfectly well but that the Politburo decided, all the same, to try to avoid admitting it. There were probably two reasons for this. The Soviet military apparently took the lead at the Politburo meeting in asserting that 007 had been part of a surveillance mission, and their assertion gained sufficient acceptance to appear in the TASS statement. Nonetheless, the Politburo ordered an immediate inquiry. The statement may thus have represented both a holding operation (until the inquiry had reported) and a compromise between Politburo factions. If there was evidence for the surveillance-mission claim, the USSR would feel itself the injured party and an admission of guilt would seem psychologically inappropriate. An apology would imply that the USSR would not knowingly shoot down any further civilian plane even if it was being used for surveillance purposes and it is doubtful whether the Politburo would have wished to encourage the notion that such planes could be used to spy with impunity.

Probably even more on the Politburo's mind was the crisis it faced with Soviet public opinion. The Moscow correspondent of the *New York Times*[7] found that when he first put the news to Soviet citizens their reaction was invariably one of horror and sheer incredulity. Whatever criticisms might be made of other institutions in Soviet society, the Soviet armed forces were widely and deeply believed to be essentially honourable. Such an accusation against them must be a provocation: they would not have shot down a civilian airliner under any circumstances whatsoever. The Soviet leadership, knowing full well the depth of such attitudes, were doubtless concerned to protect the domestic good name of the armed forces at almost all costs. If so, the posture they adopted was short-sighted as well as culpable, for the truth was bound to come out. Ultimately nothing could excuse the shooting down of a civilian airliner and there was no substitute for a frank and immediate apology.

## The propaganda barrage

The Soviet failure to admit the truth immediately played right into the hands of the enormous American propaganda campaign which began within hours of the news being received. The US decision to treat the affair as a major propaganda coup brought a new and remarkable character to centre stage, Charles Z. Wick, Director of the US Information Agency (USIA).

Given that the President himself was an actor it was perhaps not surprising that he should have turned to Hollywood for his chief executive for US information and cultural affairs abroad. Wick, a former music arranger and show-business agent, was another long-time buddy of Reagan's and had created considerable controversy by bringing a 'box-office' approach to the

USIA, transforming it from a rather stodgy bureaucracy to a Hollywood-style production in which Wick is unquestionably the star.[8] Wick's own style was decidedly flashy and luxurious: the day after his confirmation hearings he set off on a three-week tour of European capitals and in his first two years he spent 177 days travelling abroad, always travelling first-class or by Concorde with a team of bodyguards, staying in luxury hotels, tipping heavily and using big limousines, his trips lavishly chronicled in *USIA World*.[9] Since this was almost wholly paid for out of government money (Reagan had doubled the USIA budget), Congressmen who were having to vote cuts in social programmes became somewhat restive. Trouble erupted when it was discovered that Wick had spent $32,000 of government money installing elaborate home-security systems at his private residence and he was made to pay $22,000 back.[10] Further trouble followed over Wick's attempt to cut USIA educational and cultural programmes by 50 per cent; over the USIA jobs distributed by Wick to eight children, relatives and other friends of various top Administration officials, including Weinberger, Shultz and Clark;[11] over the existence of a USIA 'blacklist' of American personalities thought too liberal to represent America abroad;[12] and over Wick's habit of secretly taping the telephone conversations of his USIA employees and (among others) Senator Mark Hatfield, the White House chief of staff, James Baker III, the former ambassador, Walter Annenberg, and the actor, Kirk Douglas.[13] (Wick at first denied these charges but, faced with the transcripts, admitted he had been lying. The taping of Baker had been illegal but, luckily for Wick, Baker did not press charges.[14])

Most of all, concern was felt over Wick's headlong politicisation of the USIA – an empire which includes more than 1000 press and cultural affairs officers in 209 embassies and consulates, over 4000 employees in Washington, and the Voice of America. Wick not only began to hire actors to be sent abroad to give a Reaganite hard sell for the virtues of capitalism, to make considerable USIA donations to conservative think-tanks, and to provide expenses-paid foreign trips for many leading Administration hard-liners (trips frequently combined with family vacations), but he also made more than sixty political appointments to top jobs – invariably to highly partisan right-wingers.[15] (This was clearly done with White House encouragement – indeed Reagan himself nominated the outspoken right-winger, Paul Harvey, to the Corporation for Public Broadcasting – the body which makes grants to public TV and radio: Harvey proudly proclaimed, 'I've never been objective or pretended to be.'[16]) The same spirit now invaded the USIA and VOA, making them more and more an international propaganda arm of Reaganism. The gaudy figure of Wick presided over all this with a quite new approach to the provision of international information: 'It's like box office. This is a star performance. The better the box office, the greater impact you can make for your post.'[17] Wick was always in search of the movie spectacular – he masterminded coverage of the Polish events of 1981–82 with the controversial TV spectacular, *Let Poland be Poland* (starring Ronald Reagan). The dramatic tragedy of KAL 007 could, in this sense, have been made for Charles Wick.

By 5 September the VOA had added no fewer than 56 transmitter hours a day to its schedule in an attempt to get the Administration's version of events over to Soviet-bloc citizens and by 7 September the figure was an extra 90 hours a day, with a overall doubling of transmitters in use.[18] So intense was the effort that equipment which should have been receiving maintenance was snatched back into use: to avoid Soviet jamming, the VOA used multiple frequencies with surprise jumps from one frequency to another. The rest of the USIA machine around the world was flung into top gear with endless press conferences, handouts, briefings and so on.

Members of the Administration were not slow to give Wick the copy he needed. Within a few hours of his first press conference Shultz, at Reagan's instigation,[19] held a second one in order to refute the TASS report. Charging the USSR with a 'cover-up', Shultz angrily dismissed the allegation of a surveillance mission: 'The world is waiting for the Soviet Union to tell the truth.' Shultz asserted again that the SU-15 had been quite close enough to see that 007 was an airliner and denied that there was any evidence that the SU-15 had tried to warn 007 by firing tracers. Indeed, he claimed, NATO information was that SU-15s carried no guns, only missiles, and thus couldn't fire tracers.[20] (This was odd: most standard reference works such as *Janes's* describe the SU-15 as carrying guns, Administration spokesmen admitted in the next few days.[21]) The general tone of Shultz's remarks was such that while his text referred to the Russians as 'inhumane', in his speech Shultz changed this to 'inhuman'.[22]

The President himself used the incident to suggest that there was now little point in talking to the Soviet Union at all: 'What can we think of a regime that so broadly trumpets its visions of peace and global disarmament and yet so callously and quickly commits a terrorist act? . . . what can be the scope of legitimate mutual discourse with a state whose values permit such atrocities?' Other official US spokesmen took up the same tone – at the UN Charles Lichenstein, deputy to Mrs Kirkpatrick, termed the Russian action a 'wanton, calculated, deliberate murder'.

By this stage statements of public condemnation had grown to a torrent – even the astronauts aboard the space shuttle, *Challenger*, were interviewed to add their condemnation from space. There were angry demonstrations outside the UN, and many American politicians seemed almost to compete with one another in the fury of their rhetoric. The governors of many American states outlawed the sale of Russian vodka – though barkeepers frequently beat them to it, some even going in for public orgies of bottle smashing. At the University of Texas, Austin, arcade video games were hurriedly reprogrammed to suit the public mood: in Robotron, for example, one played a game to save the human race from 'the Communist mutant from outer space, Andropov'.[23]

The Russians – while still not admitting to the shoot-down – continued to assert that 007 had been flying without lights and had looked like a reconnaissance plane. On 4 September TASS quoted Colonel-General Semyon F. Romanov, chief of staff at Soviet Air Defence headquarters, as saying that 007 had resembled an RC-135.[24] This was the first mention of an RC-135 in the whole affair: the continuing series of US intelligence 'leaks' from the tape transcripts had made no mention of such a plane. Romanov went on to say that it was hardly surprising that the USSR should have thought it was an RC-135 – in 1983 there had already been nine violations of Soviet airspace in the Kurile Island region by USAF planes, and further such violations in the Bering Strait region.[25]

This Soviet mention of the RC-135 seems to have given the Administration a jolt: if the news that an RC-135 had crossed 007's path was going to come out, it would be far better that the US admitted it first. Accordingly the President's briefing session with Congressional leaders was, unusually, moved up to a Sunday (4 September) and doubled in length.[26] The meeting had other unusual aspects too. Although the meeting was exclusively about 007 and although the President was flanked by almost his entire Cabinet and the head of the Joint Chiefs of Staff, the single and remarkable absentee was William Clark,[27] the man who had been in charge of dealing with the crisis. The President immediately created a mood of sober consensus by opening the meeting with a prayer for the victims of the tragedy, played excerpts from the tapes – and then allowed the fact to slip out that an RC-135 had been in the vicinity of 007 at one point in its flight. There seems little doubt that this was a calculated leak – one of the Congressmen present would surely be bound to tell the press. This duly and immediately occurred.

The press, which was by this stage becoming fed up with having the tapes endlessly quoted at them but not released to them, was shaken by this belated admission. How long had the President known about the RC-135? The White House refused to say. Had the Russians genuinely mistaken 007 for an RC-135? Had they ever actually referred to 007 as an RC-135, for example?

The House Majority Leader, Jim Wright, had no doubt about that: 'Yes, that's true. At at least one point they referred to it by that designation.'[28] This produced a flurry of White House denials: Representative Wright was quite mistaken about this, said Larry Speakes; the Russians had made no mention of an RC-135. Under repeated questioning Speakes weakened this to 'if there was any reference' to an RC-135, 'it took place well in advance'. Finally, he admitted that the Russians 'did identify an aircraft as a US reconnaissance flight', but only one and a half to two hours before the shoot-down.[29] Later, an Administration official, speaking to the *New York Times* on condition that he not be identified, said, 'The Soviets tracked the Korean plane and first misidentified it as an RC-135 . . . then they changed their identification of it to "unidentified".'[30]

While this served to muddy the waters somewhat, the inconsistencies in the US version of events were wholly overshadowed both by the sheer horror of the event and the far greater inconsistencies of the Soviet version. By this stage Moscow's line was: it is a slanderous attack on the USSR to say we shot down 007. We don't admit that at all – indeed, we saw it proceed on towards the Sea of Japan. But it was a terrible provocation that the plane was over our territory and we would have been quite justified in shooting it down because it was on a preplanned spy mission. And in any case, we confused it with an RC-135.

On 5 September President Reagan went on television to fire a further great barrage in the propaganda war. Recapitulating the US version, which he illustrated with excerpts from the tape of the Soviet pilots ('We only have the voices from the pilots. The Soviet ground-to-air transmissions were not recorded'), the President dismissed all notion that the Russians had not known exactly what they were doing. Visibility had been quite reasonable – 'it was a clear night with a half moon' – and the RC-135 had been 'back at his base in Alaska' well before the shoot-down occurred. 'It was,' said the President, 'an act of barbarism born of a society which wantonly disregards human rights and the value of human life and seeks to expand and dominate other nations.' Moreover, the Russians had not only failed to warn 007 but had actually lacked the ability to do so: 'Among the rest of us there is one protective measure: an international radio wavelength on which pilots can communicate with planes of other nations if they are in trouble or lost. Soviet military planes are not so equipped because that would make it easier for pilots who might want to defect.'[31]

What, then, should America do? The President had little doubt: 'We shouldn't be surprised by such inhuman brutality. Memories come back of Czechoslovakia, Hungary, Poland, the gassing of villages in Afghanistan.'

The best thing the US could do was to push through the MX programme now before Congress, 'vital to restore America's parity with the Soviets'. America was up against a peculiarly ruthless foe, for 'the Soviets reveal that, yes, shooting down a plane, even one with hundreds of innocent men, women, children and babies, is a part of their normal procedure if that plane is in what they claim as their airspace.'[32]

Reagan's performance was chiefly for domestic US consumption – hence the strong push for Congress to pass the MX programme. In purely theatrical terms it paled by comparison with the show mounted for international opinion by Mrs Jeane Kirkpatrick the following day. In a Charles Wick spectacular – witnessed on TV screens around the world– Mrs Kirkpatrick, addressing the UN Security Council, played the tapes of the Soviet fighters to the world (the tapes were henceforth on general release). Before the embarrassed Soviet delegate and a world audience Mrs Kirkpatrick played a (simulated) video tape on five TV screens to drive home her points: 007 had had its lights on; no tracers had been fired; no warnings had been given; the Soviet fighters did not even carry the right equipment to give such warnings; and 'violence and lies are regular instruments of Soviet policy'.[33] It was a bravura performance of the sort for which Mrs Kirkpatrick was justly famous – and its international impact was enormous. Without doubt this was the high point of the entire US propaganda campaign: for the world audience the enduring image of the whole 007 tragedy was probably that of the thin-lipped and furious Mrs Kirkpatrick using her audio–video presentation to accuse the Soviet Union before the world.

Not long afterwards Charles Wick was off on his travels again and gave an interesting, if somewhat indiscreet, account of this USIA coup to the Israel–America Chamber of Commerce in Tel Aviv. This account – hitherto unpublished – is worth quoting at length:

I will leave you with just one delineation of what USIA has done very recently about which we are very proud and Mauri Lee suggested I might share this with you. President Reagan returned from – shortening his vacation on Friday night, September 2nd, following the shoot-down of the Korean airliner 007 on Thursday, September 1st. I was invited to the National Security Council at six o'clock at the White House about forty minutes after his plane touched down, and we were trying to determine what would be the most effective way of communicating the information that a starved world, many nations were pouring in questions what exactly happened. And we felt that the best authoritative documentable way would be to play the tapes that had been recorded by Japan . . .

Now, we didn't have the tapes of the ground station to the pilots because of the curvature of the earth – the Japanese listening post being so far away could not record that. But from the pilots, up about thirty-three or thirty-five thousand feet, they got a clear transcription. So we listened to the scratchy recordings in Russian, marred by the static of the radar, and we decided that that would be rather frustrating and it would be a little hard, really, to convey the impact of what really happened. So, we determined in USIA that what we would do is, we would take the audio tapes and we would make a video tape. That Jeane Kirkpatrick who was going to address the Security Council – our Ambassador to the United Nations – on Tuesday, September 6th. What we decided to do was, we would have the audio for your ear and in the video we would have the GMT time here, that was correlated with what each of the three pilots were saying at that given point and time, we would have an English translation here, and a Russian translation there. Our people at our broadcast studio stayed up all night Saturday, Sunday. Monday, we met at the State Department with Jeane Kirkpatrick – it was our Labor Day holiday – and the other State Department people and we were just really impacted with the history that we were watching with that video tape and listening to those Soviet pilots, and seeing on the translation near the end of the tape the very grim line, 'Target destroyed.' 'Target destroyed', 269 lives and the whole world watching the unmasking of the real Soviets. And contrary to their peaceful intentions manifested by them. However, the thing went so fast, the video tape in synchronization with the voices, that we all had a feeling of frustration, that you could not quite digest all of it. So what we decided to do on Monday 5th, knowing that we had to go to the Security Council on the 6th, was to freeze-frame it. In other words, instead of going on with the tape, we didn't want to alter the audio tape because we didn't want of being accused in any way of impairing the quality or in some way distorting it. After each pilot's transmission ended, and the next pilot began, we just held on that and held the voice. So there is common natural finish and you were prepared to go on. And that's the way we did it.

We met on the next morning, Tuesday morning, at eight o'clock in Ambassador Kirkpatrick's office at the State Department. She was to catch the nine-o'clock shuttle to go to the Security Council at the United Nations in New York. At nine o'clock and she was supposed to speak at eleven o'clock. We watched this tape and it was terribly exciting because you got the full impact. I think you've seen portions of that on television and the various magazines around the world carried it. And then I showed Jeane Kirkpatrick a plan of where we were going to place the video monitors in the Security Council so you could see the tape and hear it. And she said, 'But Charles, it's never been done before in the Security Council.' I said, 'Well, so what!' She said, 'Well, the Russians will protest.' I said, 'Well, let them protest, we'll show it somewhere else and let them be on the record as not wanting the truth to come out.' She said, 'Well, that's fine.'

She went to the Security Council, barely made the plane. There was a hold-up of half an hour, the Soviets protested and they wanted to discuss the removal of those video monitors off the record. And Ambassador Kirkpatrick said no, it must be on the record. They withdrew their protest. And I think you saw those pictures. We placed one of the monitors behind the Ambassador, Troyanovski – the Soviet Ambassador to the UN – so you saw these pictures of him looking back at the unmasking of the Soviets through the transcription of their pilots' tapes, and the rest is world history and in USIA we were very proud that we were given the privilege of using the communications in a rare classic symbol of how penetrating and impacting the truth can be.[34]

Apart from conveying the authentic Wick style, this passage tells one much of the Reagan Administration's emphasis on presentation. It is not just a matter of feeling concern about having a good press. All Administrations want that. What marks the Reagan Administration is a belief that events themselves can be shaped decisively by the way they are presented – that truth itself is a malleable quantity – a subject, like any other, for 'good management'. (The President himself has always lived in such a world and still does. After the US invasion of Grenada he became very testy with reporters, objecting to 'your frequent use of the word "invasion".'[35])

Certainly, presentation was the dominating topic at the National Security Council's crisis meeting on 007 on 2 September. And, quite largely, it was what Mrs Kirkpatrick's performance at the UN was about. The Security Council was, in effect, used as a television set to get the message across in an 'impacting' way. The production itself – involving an American voice-over with Cyrillic and English text flashing up on the screen with timings altered on what was anyway a quite imaginary video – was pure Hollywood, right down to the carefully judged camera angles of the Soviet Ambassador juxtaposed with the monitor screen. (Finding a Cyrillic typewriter among the props to give the final bogus cinéma-vérité touch was inspired Wickery.) The irony clearly escaped Wick – as well as much of his audience, no doubt – that what he was watching was not 'world history' but his own carefully mocked-up production. The only authentic part of the show was the fuzzy voice tape, and that had had its timing altered and was indecipherable even to Russian speakers. More seriously, it emerged a little later that parts of it had been incorrectly translated. Most notably, the phrase 'I am firing cannon [tracer] bursts' had been simply left out; a phrase first translated as 'I have enough time' now became 'They don't [seem to] see me'; and 'Now I will try a rocket' became 'Now I will try rockets'. Naturally, these late corrections – which all tended to weaken Mrs Kirkpatrick's version slightly – achieved nothing like the same publicity and impact as the original bravura performance.

This blast elicited an immediate Soviet response: on the Moscow TV news that evening TASS issued a lengthy statement[36] on behalf of the Soviet Government, following the report of the special investigation set afoot on 1 September. Admitting that 007 had indeed been shot down by a Soviet fighter, the Soviet Government 'expresses regret over the death of innocent people and shares the sorrow of their bereaved relatives and friends', said TASS. The statement took furious issue with Reagan's statement that it was 'normal' for the Soviet Union to shoot down a civilian plane within its airspace: dozens of international flight routes led across the USSR and thousands of foreign planes had used them for years without incident. But 007 had been different. It had rendezvoused with an RC-135 just off Kamchatka, and had ignored the signals of the Soviet fighters that had intercepted it there and again over Sakhalin. It was, the statement continued, 'flying without navigation lights at the height of night in conditions of bad visibility' and had taken a path leading directly over highly sensitive installations. The Soviet control services had several times picked up short coded radio signals transmitted from 007 of a type normally used for transmitting intelligence information. Not only had it ignored all signals but it had also taken evasive action when approached. In these circumstances the Soviet authorities had concluded that they were dealing with a surveillance mission of some sort and, on the orders of his ground controller, the lead Soviet fighter had shot it down. This statement was in many ways a more sensitive one than that first issued but the only important fact in the eyes of international opinion was that it had taken the USSR six full days to admit the truth of the shoot-down.

There was no doubt that the Reagan Administration viewed the 007 tragedy primarily as a heaven-sent opportunity to exploit a major propaganda advantage over the USSR, thus providing a political following wind which would assist the passage of key defence programmes through Congress and the deployment of US missiles in Europe. As one White House adviser put it on 2 September, 'It's going to make some things easier for us, and that's a bad trade-off for the Russians.'[37] In the days that followed, innumerable Administration officials appeared on a host of radio and TV news and chat shows to ram home the advantage. Retired admiral Eugene Carroll appeared on CBS news with Assistant Secretary of State Richard Burt and the former US Ambassador to the USSR, Malcolm Tune, and was appalled: 'Not much happened on the air. But prior to going on the air I was amazed at the attitude of Burt and Tune. They were convinced we had the Russians down, and now we could kick them. They seemed bent on slamming the communication door.'[38] The ever sensitive barometer of Wall Street quickly reflected the new mood as the 007 affair touched off a major boom in defence stocks, notably Avco Corporation (with a big stake in the MX), Lockheed, Loral Corporation, and other firms with a major stake in electronic warfare systems such as Litton Industries and E-Systems Inc.[39] As Wolfgang H. Demisch, First Boston Corporation's aerospace analyst, put it, 'The Korean jetliner incident provided a spark for a more positive reappraisal of the defence industry.'[40] But as Philip Brannon, Merrill Lynch's vice-president for defence electronics research, added, 'More important is that politically it has firmed up Reagan's position in calling for a stronger defence.'[41]

Wall Street had got it right. Caspar Weinberger, the Defence Secretary, was not a man to miss an opportunity such as this and, with the support of William Clark, now began urging on the President an accelerated Star Wars programme, with $18–$27 billion to be spent over the next five years.[42] Even

White House officials winced, though, when Weinberger followed this up by slapping down a new $322.5-billion defence budget – a whole 22 per cent up on the amount Congress had approved for the previous year – itself easily a peacetime record.[43]

President Reagan himself, with his big TV appearance behind him, quickly evinced a desire to get back on holiday to his ranch. But he now faced a difficult political situation, for while it suited the Administration to bang the drum loudly over 007 in order to put pressure on Congress and world opinion, the impassioned climate of anti-Sovietism engendered by such drum-banging quickly threatened to take events out of the Administration's control.

Even by the time Congress reassembled on 12 September, it was clear that 007 would dominate proceedings. As Representative Mike Synar, an Oklahoma Democrat, put it, in his district, as in others, 'that's all people are talking about'.[44] Representative Joseph Addabo (New York – Democrat), the subcommittee chairman in charge of defence appropriations and a leading opponent of the MX, had to concede almost immediately that his cause was in tatters: 'These things give people a big visible vote to say "Well, I got back at the Russians".'[45] Representative Les Aspin (Wisconsin – Democrat) of the House Armed Services Committee agreed: 'What do the MX, nerve gas or aid to Nicaraguan rebels have to do with the Soviets shooting down a Korean commercial jet? In a rational world there is no obvious connection. But in the political world these things do have a connection. Our attitude toward the Soviet Union and defence issues is driven by events.'[46] The expectation that the House Speaker, Tip O'Neill, would lead the opposition to the MX died quickly, while in the Senate the proponents of a nuclear freeze decided not to push things to a vote.[47]

O'Neill more or less conceded defeat in advance: 'the MX would have been in deep trouble' before 007, he averred, but would now probably go through. Indeed, O'Neill and a number of other House liberals tried to outdo the conservatives in calling for tough sanctions against the USSR. Reagan was even compared unfavourably with President Carter by O'Neill: Carter had taken real sanctions against the Russians over Afghanistan while all Reagan had offered to date was words.[48] To the Administration's embarrassment, pressure quickly mounted for a grain embargo and diplomatic sanctions. As we have seen, a new five-year grain deal with the Russians had been signed only a week before the shoot-down. The very hint of an embargo had sent grain and soya prices plunging immediately[49] and the Administration was too concerned to keep the farm vote in 1984 to want to see that continue. Moreover, the imposition of major trade or diplomatic sanctions would be taken to mean that the US had summarily lost all interest in the arms-control talks then under way. This would so alarm European opinion that emplacement of the new US missiles in Europe might be endangered.

Immediately, such dangers were headed off. Instead Congress voted 416–0 to denounce the 'brutal massacre' of 007, the result of a 'cold-blooded barbarous attack' and 'one of the most infamous and reprehensible acts in history'.[50] The same motion was passed 95–0 in the Senate where the ultraconservatives under Jesse Helms forced a whole series of votes on proposals for a variety of tough sanctions. But the essential point was that the defence budget sailed through. Not only did the MX pass but the House voted by the astonishing margin of 266–152 to authorise production of the Bigeye nerve gas, thus ending President Nixon's 1969 pledge to halt all chemical-weapons production and President Ford's agreement that the US would at last comply with the 1925 Geneva Protocol banning first use of poison gas. That the House could now agree to overturn restraints which had been so recently agreeable even to conservative Republican presidents was some measure of the fevered climate. But as the *New York Times* commented, all discussion of these weapons as such was 'overcome by arguments that centred on sending a message to the Russians'.[51]

## Reaction on the Right

The Reagan Administration was particularly sensitive to the feelings of the American far Right, many of whose leaders were enjoying a hitherto unparalleled access into all corners of the Administration, and which was likely to be of considerable electoral importance to Reagan in 1984. The far Right in turn had its own particular reasons for its enraged reaction to the 007 tragedy, reasons which went beyond even its normal bitter anti-Sovietism. Ever since the days of the China Lobby in the 1940s, the Right had cultivated close relations with the fiercely anti-Communist South Korean regime. This axis led to a rich and luxuriant undergrowth of other ties – not just economic and diplomatic, but the extremely close relationship between the CIA and the Korean CIA (KCIA), and the peculiar phenomenon of the Moonies: South Korean-based, rigidly anti-Communist and with a considerable presence in Washington, notably through the Moonies' ownership of the *Washington Times*.[52] This nexus of interests provided a hothouse environment for extreme right-wing views and a dense network of personal contacts on the far Right. It also meant that an incident involving a major confrontation between the Soviet military and South Korea not only pulled in all manner of military superhawks, but activated many other nerve ends on the far Right.

Finally, of course, the Right had lost one of its leaders aboard 007, Larry McDonald, who immediately became both a martyr and a symbol: the Moral Majority leader, the Reverend Jerry Falwell, was merely the first to take up the refrain that the Russians had shot down 007 in order to assassinate McDonald. McDonald was an unlikely martyr figure. Sitting for an ultraconservative, rich, rural district in Cobb County, Georgia – home to Lockheed, sundry other high-tech defence concerns and a flourishing chapter of the Klu Klux Klan[53] – McDonald had been unquestionably the most right-wing man in Congress. A somewhat unorthodox doctor – he had recommended patients with terminal cancer to eat laetrile and had encouraged them to contribute to his vast (200 plus) collection of guns[54] – he had been buoyed in his political career by his close friendship with the oil billionaire (and fellow John Bircher), Nelson Bunker Hunt. Hunt and the Birchers had spent huge sums to provide McDonald with an invincible electoral machine, a favour McDonald had repaid in 1979 by getting Congress to refuse permission for the sale of silver from the government's strategic stockpile. (Such a move would have cost Hunt dear, for he was then engaged in an attempt to corner the world silver market.)[55]

This had, however, been an isolated success in McDonald's career. His attempt to nominate Rudolph Hess for the Nobel Peace Prize – with the object of showing that even a Nazi war criminal was a useful asset in the struggle against Communism – had not attracted widespread support.[56] Much of McDonald's time and plentiful resources had been devoted to his Western Goals Foundation – an 'anti-terrorist intelligence organisation' (with two generals and an admiral on its board), which sought continually to lay its computerised lists of alleged terrorists and Communist agents before the American public – without noticeable effect.

A great deal of media attention was now focused, however, on the simple fact that a Congressman had been killed. McDonald's attractive young widow, Kathryn, immediately announced that she took the view that the shoot-down had essentially been a successful assassination attempt on her husband – and that she would be running for his vacant Congressional seat. 'I think I could step in better than anyone else,' said Mrs McDonald, herself a keen Bircher. Mourning, she said, was 'a luxury I can't afford'.[57] President Reagan sought to keep his lines open to the forces Mrs McDonald represented by speaking of the way in which 'her composure and eloquence on the day of her husband's death moved us all', but Mrs McDonald was having none of it, attacking even this speech of Reagan's for not being tough enough with the Russians.[58] The Right took the straightforward view that sixty-one Americans had died on 007 and that the US had to take some concrete action to revenge them. The problem for Reagan was that with trade and diplomatic sanctions ruled out and the need to keep the arms-control talks going, even symbolic gestures were hard to find. Aeroflot flights to the US had been suspended over Afghanistan in 1980 and the US was keen that the Russians should come to the 1984 Olympics in Los Angeles. All that was left were speeches and securing the toughest possible condemnation of the Russians at the UN and elsewhere. In the eyes of the Right, this was nothing like enough. As Richard Viguerie, the influential publisher of the *Conservative Digest*, put it, Reagan had 'just walked away from the town bully without pulling his gun',[59] while the *New York Times* columnist, William Safire, accused Reagan of being led astray by a State Department still full of 'détenteniks'.[60] Gibes such as these and that Reagan was 'making Jimmy Carter look like Charles Atlas'[61] were intended to hurt, but what the Right sensed was the opportunity for a historic hardening of US policy towards the USSR right across the board. As Senator Jesse Helms put it to fellow conservatives in Seoul, 'This is the best chance we ever had to paint these bastards into a corner.'[62]

The Administration could not but be conscious of the potent electoral power of the conservative Political Action Committees, particularly the National Conservative PAC (NICPAC). On 7 September William Clark received NICPAC's director, John Dolan, together with Larry McDonald's son, Tryggvi, who demanded a complete cessation of US trade and diplomatic links with the USSR. Tryggvi McDonald then spoke at a rally organised by various right-wing groups and the Moonies at which an effigy of Andropov was burned outside the White House. This rally was timed to coincide with the mass funeral for 007 victims, attended by 100,000 people in Seoul, which quickly turned into a near-hysterical display of anti-Soviet feeling whose anguished images were relayed around the world.

In Washington somewhat similar scenes were to be witnessed at the funeral for Larry McDonald attended by 3000 conservatives (bumper stickers reading 'Remember Flight 7. Honk if you hate massacres' were handed out).[63] Speaker after speaker, greeted with standing ovations, called for the toughest possible action against the Russians. The US should only talk about arms control to the USSR, said the Reverend Jerry Falwell, when it had 'the pure, raw, brute strength' to force arms reductions on them. 'There are,' he added, 'some things worse than war, and one of them is slavery.'[64] Congressman Philip M. Crane struck a similar note. The Russians were, he said, 'psychopathic subhumans. They are obscene. They violate the laws of God and nature.'[65] The funeral/rally was perhaps most notable for the constellation of personalities assembled in the Right's cause. Alongside the Reverend Falwell stood the former chairman of the US Joint Chiefs of Staff, Thomas H.

Moorer, and Major-General John K. Singlaub, the former chief of staff of US forces in Korea (fired by President Carter for having publicly resisted the notion of a retreat of US forces from Korea), and the South Korean Ambassador, Lew Byong Hion, for long the chief of South Korean Anti-Infiltration Operations (i.e. the campaign to root out 'internal subversion') and then the chairman of the South Korean Joint Chiefs of Staff. Unembarrassed by his diplomatic status, Ambassador Hion made it clear that South Korea, 'America's most faithful ally', would like to see a much tougher line taken by President Reagan.[66] The Right's general tone was such as to alarm even so seasoned a conservative as Barry Goldwater: 'I think some of the conservatives are just crazy as hell. What do they want to do – go to war? If you get right down to it, it was a plane from another country.'[67]

President Reagan – who had been invited to the McDonald funeral but declined to go – used another Washington memorial service held for the 007 victims to answer the Right. Flanked by Meese, Clark and other Administration luminaries, Reagan told the congregation of the National Cathedral: 'Vengeance isn't the name of the game in this. Short of going to war, what would they have us do?'[68] Bishop John T. Walker, officiating at the ceremony, used his sermon to castigate the USSR as 'an outlaw in the family of nations' and called for prayers for 'our enemies' – but praised Reagan for his 'controlled anger'.[69]

Nevertheless, Reagan felt the need to stay in tune with his constituency on the Right and returned frequently to the theme of the 007 tragedy in the weeks that followed. On 10 September he reminded an audience that he had been taken to task two years before for his allegation that the Russians regularly lied and cheated, but the 007 affair had shown again that they 'reserve unto themselves the right to commit any crime'. And, he suggested, since 'the Soviets are terrified of the truth', the best thing for Congress to do was to vote further funds for Charles Wick's VOA and the establishment of a new Radio Marti network to be operated by anti-Castro Cuban exiles.[70] Four days later the President followed up by alleging that the Russians had 'abrogated many times' the informal agreement between Kennedy and Khrushchev after the 1962 missile crisis, and that Castro had set out to 'infiltrate subversives into our country'.[71] (This produced more embarrassment for Larry Speakes who had to admit that there was no evidence of 'subversive infiltration' to hand and that the 1962 agreement that no nuclear-capable weapons would be introduced into Cuba had not in fact been broken at all.[72]) On 18 September the President returned to the theme that the 007 tragedy was a powerful argument for the MX. Referring to the Russians as 'brutal', 'savage', and 'cruel', Reagan criticised earlier US leaders who had talked of 'our inordinate fear of Communism' and announced: 'This nation is through with hand-wringing and apologising.'[73] On 24 September the President repeated some of these themes in a VOA broadcast aimed at the USSR, adding: 'Your airline, Aeroflot, has violated sensitive US airspace scores of times'[74] – though again no hard evidence for this charge was provided.

## The airline boycott

Reagan, in his search for a symbolic gesture with which to placate the Right, would no doubt have liked to lead a boycott of Aeroflot. Given that Aeroflot had already been banned from running scheduled flights to the US for three years already, however, this weapon was not available. Clearly, the next best thing would be if Canada could lead the way, which indeed she did, in a move timed to coincide with Mrs Kirkpatrick's UN speech. The Canadians announced that all Aeroflot flights to Montreal would be banned for sixty days and that further sanctions would be considered if the USSR did not own up. This was no mean threat (and may explain why the USSR owned up so promptly thereafter): the Russians rely on Canada's Gander International Airport (Newfoundland) for their regular refuelling stop *en route* to Cuba and would have been gravely embarrassed if that facility had been withdrawn. (In fact it never was.)[75]

The Canadian ban quickly drew support from the International Federation of Airline Pilots' Associations (IFALPA). But IFALPA's fury at the fate of 007 was mixed with a certain queasiness: as the IFALPA deputy president put it, 'The pilots have put themselves on the tip of the spear and now it's up to their governments to make this work.'[76] In fact a number of governments were distinctly unhappy about such a proposal – notably the Japanese, Austrians, Finns, French, Greeks and West Germans. Immediately the Japanese government attempted to evade the ban by suggesting that it would merely stop government employees from travelling on Aeroflot.[77] The problem was partly that such countries did not wish to endanger their own relations with Moscow, partly that they felt the US was overreacting. Moreover, while IFALPA represented sixty airlines, only seventeen of them ran flights to the USSR and these seventeen would be bound to suffer retaliation of which the other forty-three (including US carriers) ran no risk.

Behind the scenes, though, US pressure was intense. President Reagan was eager to show that, as he put it, 'The Soviet Union stands alone against the world' and that the 007 episode had produced 'a fundamental and long-overdue reappraisal'.[78] Commenting on this speech, the *New York Times* noted that 'the US has been spearheading a campaign to get as many countries as possible to take action against Moscow . . . Today Mr Reagan suggested that this campaign should go beyond the airliner incident and have a longer-lasting effect.'[79] There was an attempt to get NATO to take a collective line on the matter – and the British and Scandinavians not only agreed to a ban on Aeroflot but also forbade Russian flights to Cuba from overflying their territory. (Instead the Russians had to fly over the North Pole or across the Mediterranean, refuelling in Greece.) But the best that could be achieved was a NATO decision for a two-week ban from 12 September, and the French, Danes, Turks, Greeks and Spaniards immediately announced that they would not comply even with this. (When Air France pilots decided to observe the ban, the French government merely used non-union pilots to maintain services.) With considerable reluctance, the Japanese finally complied. Finland announced it would not comply with the ban. When Finnair pilots took independent action to stop the airline's Moscow service, the Finnair President, Gunnar Korhonen, reacted angrily by saying that primary blame for the tragedy had to lie with KAL and that any boycott should include South Korea. Korhonen also added extra flights to Finnair's Helsinki–Leningrad run, thus compensating for the loss of the Moscow service.[80] Other countries refusing to comply with the ban included India and Austria.

The result was a mess. The Russians never ceased to be able to fly their own planes out and the chief effect was merely to strand a large number of angry Westerners in the USSR, thus providing something of a bonanza for those Western airlines which did continue their flights. Moreover, when the two-week deadline ran out IFALPA found itself quite unable to maintain its sixty-day ban and had to call its action off from 3 October. By then, moreover, IFALPA had begun to change its views somewhat, pointing out that the Russians had not merely deplored the tragedy but had come up with a number of constructive proposals to ensure that no such tragedy could recur in the future.[81] Not unnaturally, the Russians treated the collapse of the boycott as a triumph and TASS regaled its readers with a long list of Western airlines once again landing at Sheremetyevo airport (Moscow) – a rather odd performance for TASS had previously given the boycott minimal coverage. All that it did now was alert the Soviet public to just how extensive the boycott had been.[82]

## Overshoot at the UN

The Reagan Administration had pinned considerable hopes on the prospect that its propaganda barrage – and most particularly Mrs Kirkpatrick's *coup de théâtre* – would result in a sweeping condemnation of the USSR at the UN, with America leading a thoroughly mobilised world opinion to isolate the Russians in a way not seen since the 1950s. This tended to assume that other UN members viewed the USSR through the same tinted glass as the Administration and led the US seriously to overplay its hand. Around the world there was a general horror at the shoot-down, but also a real uncertainty about what 007 had been doing so far off course in the first place, and an underlying concern not to allow the incident to lead to a wider Cold War escalation.

This caution was very obvious in Japan. The Prime Minister, Nakasone, though notably hawkish by custom, avoided any immediate denunciation of the USSR, and the Foreign Minister, Shintaro Abe, commented only that much depended on how the Russians handled the affair. On 4 September Abe termed the incident a 'temporary' problem and said that no sanctions were called for.[83] Only with great reluctance and under great US pressure was Japan shifted from this line. The Chinese expressed 'shock and regret' at the incident, but refrained from the anti-Soviet diatribe which might have been expected. The main Saudi Arabian paper, *Al Medina*, actually criticised the US for its 'relentless' attack on the USSR, contrasting this unfavourably with the American attitude towards Israel when 'the Jews' had shot down a Libyan airliner in 1973.[84] Many Western leaders were simply silent, no doubt waiting for their own intelligence reports on the matter. Remarkably, Mrs Thatcher, Reagan's most dependable ally, waited seventeen days before mentioning the matter at all. This stirred suspicions in some quarters that Western leaders believed there was more to the incident than immediately met the eye. As one Labour backbencher remarked of Mrs Thatcher's silence: 'Why did it take her seventeen days to comment . . . ? What has prevented such a voluble, talkative woman from commenting during this period? . . . It seems completely out of character unless there is some other reason.'[85]

In fact Mrs Thatcher rallied to Reagan's line but an attempt to get the EEC to condemn the USSR for the shoot-down failed. As luck would have it, the EEC Foreign Ministers met in Athens, which meant that the Greek Foreign Minister, Mr Ioannis Haralambopoulos, was in the chair. To the fury of the other nine EEC members, he used this position to evade any discussion of 007 and adamantly refused to put Greece's signature to a motion of condemnation, arguing that Greece was keen to see what sort of explanation could be given of why the airliner had been off course: the most Greece could support was a motion regretting the tragedy and calling for an inquiry. In the end a fairly anodyne motion was adopted as the price of unanimity.[86] The US Embassy in Athens protested bitterly at the Greek Government's attitude, though this was as nothing compared to the American fury felt later on when the Greek Premier, Mr Papandreou, stated that it seemed clear that 007 had been on a surveillance mission.

The problem with Greece was indicative of quite widespread international misgivings over the Reagan line on the affair, while the Reagan Administration reacted with furious incomprehension that any other view was even possible. Without doubt the Reagan Administration included far more officials and spokesmen with a more parochially American view than had been common in the past. Its spokesmen, feeling the huge surge of American domestic opinion on the issue, tended simply to assume an international unanimity behind the US view – and were disconcerted, as well as infuriated, to find that this was not so.

This led to a near disaster for the US at the UN. While there was universal revulsion against the shoot-down, many states began to resist quite strongly the US attempt to steamroller through a motion which denounced the Soviet Union explicitly. India expressed the typical Third World view when it called for caution, given the many uncertainties still surrounding the affair, while Guyana publicly complained that the US had broken with previous Security Council practice by failing to negotiate the terms of its resolution with other members. Mrs Kirkpatrick and her deputy, Charles Lichenstein, continued to press their motion for an explicit condemnation of the USSR until 9 September, when they suddenly realised that they were on the brink of a momentous defeat, with only seven of the fifteen Security Council members willing to support the US motion. Even the anti-Soviet Chinese had backed away in the end. The US hurriedly snatched back its motion and postponed the vote without explanation.[87] A weaker motion was then presented which did not condemn the Soviet Union explicitly but merely noted that the Security Council was 'gravely disturbed' that 007 had been 'shot down by Soviet military aircraft' and 'deplored the destruction' of the plane. Even this motion only squeaked through at the last moment when Malta was finally persuaded to change its vote, though still protesting that there was 'too much uncertainty' about the whole affair.[88] This did, however, achieve the US objective of forcing the USSR to use its veto against the motion. The US had become a little embarrassed by the fact that since 1980 it had exercised its Security Council veto five times as often as the USSR[89] and this would do something to right that imbalance. But a far larger objective had been lost. The way the Reagan Administration had handled the affair had brought American popular feeling to fever pitch and created a political need to hit back at the USSR hard and publicly. With the failure at the UN this popular need was still dangerously unsatisfied.

It was this which explained the bombshell of 16 September when the State

Department announced that it had told the Soviet Foreign Minister, Mr Gromyko, that he would not be allowed to land at Kennedy International Airport (New York) on his visit to attend the new opening session of the UN: if he wanted to come he would have to use a military airport instead. The Russians furiously cancelled the Gromyko visit altogether, alleging (though this was denied by the US) that the US had failed to guarantee Gromyko's safe arrival or the servicing of his Aeroflot plane. It was a major break with tradition: Gromyko was a UN founder and for twenty-seven years had provided a review of Soviet foreign policy to the opening session – it was the oldest ritual the UN had.

The decision not to allow the Gromyko landing had in fact been taken by the Port Authority of New York and New Jersey as a result of a decision by Governors Mario Cuomo of New York and Thomas Kean of New Jersey. The State Department had been horrified when it first heard of the decision but had quickly retreated when the White House made it known that it agreed with the Governors' decision.[90] As the UN Secretary-General's office speedily made clear, this meant that the US was breaking the terms of the 1947 treaty siting the UN in New York, which explicitly stated that no US Federal, State or local authority should enforce any impediments to travel to or from UN headquarters by the representatives of any member nation. The US had, moreover, also agreed in the treaty that this provision should apply *whatever* the state of relations between the governments involved.[91] Governor Cuomo, when asked if he had no reservations over this deliberate disregard for international treaty obligations, replied, 'You can tell you're right when the guy running the elevator or driving the cab stops you and says "Right on, Governor".'[92] Larry Speakes reacted in similar vein when told by White House reporters that an anonymous State Department official had admitted to them that New York and New Jersey were acting in violation of international law. 'We'll find out who he is and see how long he lasts,' said Speakes. Intrigued, the reporters asked who precisely was making this threat? Speakes was, it turned out, only 'speaking for myself'.[93]

Inevitably, the Russians brought a furious complaint before the UN's Host Country Committee, accusing the US of breaking the 1947 treaty. There could hardly be any doubt of the verdict. The US representative, Charles Lichenstein, apparently maddened by a situation in which the US, not the USSR, would end up getting condemned by name, furiously announced that he would be quite happy to see the UN get out of New York and America anyway. It was a remarkable statement – which Lichenstein never withdrew. Not the least remarkable aspect of the affair was that Lichenstein must have known that, as the representative of the UN's host country (and chief contributor of funds), his words were bound to carry great weight – and yet he had made the speech off his own bat, with no official authorisation at all. For the man who had been the ghostwriter to Richard Nixon for his book, *Six Crises*,[94] it was a surprising demonstration of how to lose one's temper in a crisis and make it that much worse.

This pronouncement had the effect of making Lichenstein – a long-time friend of Mrs Kirkpatrick, a former CIA official and hard-liner – a hero with the American Right. Larry Speakes was less thrilled, for he was immediately surrounded by White House reporters demanding to know if Lichenstein's speech represented official US policy. This Speakes firmly denied: Lichenstein had been speaking 'off the cuff' and his statement was not 'White House-approved'. 'His remarks should be understood as a response to a deliberate provocation, not as any new departure in US policy.'[95]

This seemed clear enough for a day or two, until President Reagan cheerfully announced that he endorsed Lichenstein and that the UN was welcome to leave New York. This speech caused utter consternation around the world, especially since the US Senate voted the next day to cut the US contribution to the UN by 21 per cent immediately and then by 10 per cent in each of the three following years – a $500-million cut in four years. This would clearly lead to the collapse of the UN and, very possibly, to its removal from America. Both the Republican Majority Leader, Senator Howard Baker, and the Republican Chairman of the Foreign Relations Committee, Senator Charles Percy, professed themselves appalled at the Senate vote, but with the President apparently backing such a move they were powerless to stop it (it was passed 66–23).

This produced a special White House briefing the next day to 'clarify' the US position. The President now stressed his 'strong support' for the UN and said that he was entirely against the Senate resolution and wanted it reversed.[96] A few days later the President announced to foreign diplomats at a reception that the US was 'proud to be the home' of the UN.[97] Finally, in his address to the UN General Assembly on 26 September, the President spoke of his 'unwavering support' for the UN: 'The UN has a proud history . . . Our goals are those that guide this very body.'[98] Although some might cavil at his use of the adjective 'unwavering', this made it clear enough that the storm was over. Even Ed Koch, the populist mayor of New York, admitted as much. The UN should stay in New York, he said, 'because every country needs a cesspool'.[99] Actually – as everyone knew – the presence of the UN in the city makes New York something like the world capital, with a financial, cultural and diplomatic spin-off which was never likely to be lightly surrendered. It was clear that the Senate would have to reverse its vote: if it didn't the US would lose its own UN seat in two years – and that too was unthinkable.

None of this made a very favourable impression on most UN delegates. Just how exasperated many of the Third World states were feeling was vividly illustrated by the inaugural speech of the new President of the Assembly, Mr Jorge Illueca, the Vice-President of Panama. Illueca compared the 007 affair with the Sarajevo assassination in 1914 and laid blame quite equally on the two superpowers for the Cold War tensions which threatened to overwhelm the UN.[100] Inevitably, such sentiments, coming from a state on whose support the US could normally rely, did little to soothe American feelings.

Reagan's own speech to the General Assembly took several strong swipes at the USSR – alleging the use of biological weapons in Afghanistan and Soviet violations of SALT, as well as a further reference to the 007 affair: it was 'new unwelcome evidence of brutal disregard for life and truth' and 'a timely reminder of just how different the Soviets' concept of truth and international cooperation is from that of the rest of the world'.[101] The State Department later revealed the thinking behind the speech: 'as a result of the airliner incident and the latest arms-control proposals, the President has achieved a significant propaganda coup over the Russians, and we are trying to hold on to it.'[102] On the other hand, the speech had been softened quite deliberately from its ferocious first-draft state – 'the rhetoric was becoming too heavy – we were beating the drum too loudly and it was time for Ronald Reagan the peacemaker to consolidate his image.'[103]

Undoubtedly, this decision in part reflected a White House awareness that maintaining the propaganda effort at fever pitch was generating uncontrollable right-wing pressures which served only to embarrass the President. Moreover, it was tolerably clear that the US was far ahead in its propaganda war with the Russians; it was a good time to cash in one's chips.

## The Soviet reply

The Russians had, belatedly, mounted a major propaganda effort of their own in which the chief event had been the extraordinary press conference held in Moscow on 9 September by the Chief of Staff of the Soviet Armed Forces, Marshal Nikolai Ogarkov, to publicise the results of the official Soviet commission of inquiry into the 007 affair.[104] This too had been a bravura performance, perhaps the first time ever that a top Soviet military leader had exposed himself to hours of spontaneous questions by hundreds of Western press correspondents. Flanked by maps, confident, assured and unruffled, Ogarkov spelled out the Soviet case that 007 had been on a surveillance mission. Thousands of foreign planes flew over or near the

USSR, he said, and sometimes they made mistakes in their flight course. The Soviet Union was quite used to this and knew the difference between a mistake and a reconnaissance mission. Throughout the flight the Soviet fighter bases had 'operated in full contact with the Government authorities' – though Ogarkov did not deny the possible confusion of 007 with an RC-135 for all that. But the shoot-down itself had been quite deliberate. 'What was left to us?' he asked. Asked whether any pretext had been good enough to justify the loss of 269 lives (Soviet journalists were shocked by the sheer bluntness of such questions), Ogarkov appealed to the defensive reflex which, since 1941, has been the deepest and most elemental part of Soviet popular feeling: 'Protection of the sacred, inviolable borders of our country, and our political system, was worth to us – as you know very well – many, many millions of lives.' Clearly, if the Soviet leadership could get the Russian populace to perform the feat of regarding 007 within the same mental framework as Hitler's Panzer columns, the home propaganda front, at least, would be secure. The fact that such an appeal could be made at all showed, though, just how far the Russians had been thrown on the defensive: in Soviet political discourse this was to reach for the ultimate weapon. Ogarkov likened the case to that of the American U-2 spy plane shot down over the USSR in 1960, whose existence President Eisenhower had at first denied. On that occasion the US President had 'recovered his manliness and courage' and admitted culpability. The question was whether President Reagan would show the same qualities: 'Let's hope that this will come soon.'

Ogarkov, in full dress uniform, with nine rows of medals and the large gold stars of a marshal of the USSR on his shoulders, made an impressive figure as he fielded questions with good humour for two hours. Soviet reporters gaped at the spectacle, particularly the map of the Soviet Far Eastern defence system and the open talk of SAM launchers, nuclear bases and other ultrasecret material never normally publicly mentioned in the USSR. The civilian officials with Ogarkov (the First Deputy Foreign Minister, Georgi Korniyenko, and the head of the Central Committee's International Information Department, Leonid Zamyatin) were clearly far less at ease under the unwonted pressure of public questioning: indeed, Ogarkov's sudden demotion a year later caused some to wonder if this new and difficult standard in public-relations work had been altogether popular with those less able to meet it. The whole performance (relayed live by cable TV to the US) was clearly seen as a major propaganda riposte. After the meeting, Soviet Foreign Ministry press officials mingled with Western journalists, anxiously asking them for their impressions of the affair – hardly something they would have done except under instruction.

The Ogarkov press conference had considerable impact, not least, doubt-less, on Soviet home opinion – though only a censored version of the conference was permitted to be seen on Soviet TV. But overall there was no doubt who had won the propaganda war. The US had been far quicker, slicker and more forthright, its presentation far more expert and better amplified. The Russians had begun by denying everything, had then made vague allegations of a surveillance mission, basing themselves heavily on data which had already appeared in the Western media; had given the appearance of having the truth only gradually dragged out of them, admitting the fact of the shoot-down after a whole six days had passed; and had not presented their best case until nine days afterwards. Moreover the Russians released none of the further information which must have been in their possession: they denied the veracity of the tapes produced by the US but did not, for example, provide their own version of them. Without doubt the routinely defensive and secretive style of Soviet behaviour goes far to explain these gaffes, but when contrasted with the much more open style of the Americans this proved, as usual, an insurmountable propaganda handicap.

Several Russian officials in the West frankly admitted the deficiencies in the Soviet case. Professor Viktor Afanasiev, editor-in-chief of *Pravda* and a Central Committee member, admitted on BBC TV on 18 September that the initial Soviet reports had been misleading: 'I think in this respect our military people are guilty. Probably they let some inaccuracies slip by . . . I would not say I was very pleased with our first reports.' He was particularly critical of the early report that 007 had 'continued its flight' towards the Sea of Japan.'[105]

Viktor Linnik, a member of the USSR Institute for the Study of the USA and Canada (and a consultant to the Central Committee) went even further in another BBC interview, terming the whole shoot-down a mistake:

They [the Soviet fighters] never thought it was a civilian plane. If they did, the signal would have been totally different. I'm absolutely certain of that. But the fact was, you know, the US reconnaissance planes were overflying the area all the time . . . They were about to monitor the would-be tests, the tests of Soviet intercontinental missiles, and the very tension that the pilots in that area are telling you about is so high that I was not surprised that they would react in this – what's the expression – yes, trigger-happy manner.[106]

Afanasiev disowned his speech on returning home,[107] but the influential *Izvestia* columnist, Alexsandr Bovin, when interviewed in Moscow, told Western reporters that he was '150 per cent sure' that the Soviet pilots would not have shot 007 down if they had known it was an airliner. Bovin also implied that an apology – or at least a less strident defence of its action – might have been forthcoming from the USSR had the US not gone public with its version of the incident and condemned the USSR so strongly in the same speech. The Russians, he said, had still been finding out exactly what happened when 'a tidal wave of propaganda came down on us'.[108] Bovin clearly regarded this as having 'forced' the USSR into replying in kind – though such an assumption is questionable.

Both Linnik and Bovin were clearly contradicting Ogarkov – and some of the later Soviet 'corrections' to their case[109] suggest strongly that there was a greater diversity and uncertainty to Soviet views of the tragedy than Soviet official pronouncements made clear. (None of the comments by Afanasiev, Linnik and Bovin appeared in the Soviet press – they were wholly for external consumption, and have to be treated with reserve as a possible PR exercise to present a more 'human face' abroad.) What was not in doubt was that the USSR had made a poor, belated and, indeed, an at least initially untruthful presentation of its case, and this had cost it dear before the court of world opinion.

## Assessing the media war

The US undoubtedly won the propaganda war over 007, but its advantage tended to diminish the longer the war went on. Indeed, the US version of events was not wholly believed even by the American electorate: on 14 September a poll jointly commissioned by the *New York Times* and CBS found that only 21 per cent of Americans believed that their government had told them all it knew about the 007 incident, while 61 per cent believed that the Government was 'holding back information that people ought to know'.[110] Some of the probable reasons for this were set forth by the conservative Georgia Democrat, Senator Sam Nunn, widely regarded as the most militarily knowledgeable man in Congress:

We would have been much better had we ascertained the facts and put out the worst side of our case first, rather than having it creep out incrementally. There's a real obligation of leadership in a crisis, in spite of the huge pressures, to try and get as complete a picture as possible before going to the world with charges, particularly in a nuclear age . . . Mistakes in the past, false charges, have never been that serious. Now they are . . . the Administration has got to realise that . . . it's enormously important to hold your tongue unless you really know all the facts.[111]

There was no doubt that the Reagan Administration's handling of the crisis had created a new low in Soviet–American relations: the Russians even recalled Soviet students studying in the US, saying they feared for their physical safety – thus halting a programme which had hitherto survived every twist and turn of the Cold War. For a while American commentators drew comfort from the fact that Soviet comment on the affair seemed largely to have been left in the hands of the military and the news agencies and that the Soviet political leadership was keeping its distance, as if trying to throw the blame on the military. Such false comfort was sharply dispelled on 28 September when President Andropov issued a blistering statement on the affair. This was, indeed, a notable departure from precedent – the top Soviet leadership in recent years has tended to be relatively cautious in its statements about the US, and Andropov in particular had taken a notably calm and unpolemical tone. It was a quite different Andropov now who spoke of Mr Reagan's 'obscenities' and his 'malicious' attitude:

The sophisticated provocation masterminded by the US special services with the use of a South Korean plane is an example of extreme adventurism in politics . . . The guilt of its organisers, no matter how hard they may dodge and what false versions they may put forward, has been proved.

The Soviet leadership expressed regret over the loss of human life resulting from that unprecedented criminal subversion. It is on the conscience of those who would like to assume the right not to reckon with the sovereignty of states and the inviolability of borders, who masterminded and carried out the provocation, who literally on the following day hastily pushed through Congress colossal military spending and are now rubbing their hands with pleasure. Thus the 'humanism' of statesmen who are seeking to lay the blame for the deaths of people who were aboard the plane on others is turning into new heaps of weapons of mass destruction from MX missiles to nerve-gas containers.[112]

Andropov was saying, in effect, that there was little point left in trying to deal with the US. Most Westerners were too convinced of Soviet guilt in the affair to realise the full extent of Russian fury. Given that the Soviet leadership was clearly convinced that the US had used 007 as part of a surveillance probe, had then sought to turn the blame for the tragedy on the USSR, and had further used it to pave the way towards a major escalation in the arms race, the bitterness and anger felt by the Soviet leaders must have been deep indeed. In the months before the shoot-down it looked as if the Soviet leadership had been nerving itself to attempt a new effort at détente with the US – a preliminary, perhaps, to a crucial concession in the arms-control talks. Now all this was gone. Andropov's blast was accompanied by repeated Soviet comparisons of Hitler with Reagan and talk of a 'fascist frenzy' sweeping the American people.[113] The Soviet TV commentator, Gendrikh Borovik, for example, claimed that the US had used innocent passengers as a cover for surveillance purposes. 'When the Hitlerites made an attack, they forced women and children in front of them,' he said. 'I do not think this comparison is too strong. I think it is just right.'[114] In a country which lost 20 million dead to Hitler, this is the ultimate condemnation.

Andropov returned with a further furious blast in January 1984 over the question of US accusations of Soviet violations of SALT. Pointing out that the

Administration had not bothered to raise any of its charges in the special US–USSR commission where they could be reviewed by experts, but had simply published them as a sort of media event, Andropov spoke of Reagan's willingness to rely instead on 'the service of ill-willed and incompetent "specialists" from his own entourage to back up these ridiculous allegations'.[115] Other Soviet commentators went even further. Thus Alexander Yakovlev, Director of the Soviet Institute of the World Economy and International Relations, launched a bitter personal attack on Reagan in *Izvestia* on 12 September 1983. Reagan, he said, 'has a lot more horses in his stable than books in his library. He believes in flying saucers, consults the predictions of astrologers and does not question the effects of evil spirits.'[116]

The Reagan Administration gave no public impression of being bothered by the parlous state of US–Soviet relations, but no doubt it was the realisation of just how dangerously provoked the Russians were feeling that led to the Administration's desire to wind down its propaganda campaign. But the Administration was now bottled in by that very campaign. It could not admit the frightening extent of the Soviets' 'self-righteous' anger without creating the impression that such anger might have some possible justification. So, publicly at least, Soviet reactions were played down as just so much predictable mouthing.

This was an extremely dangerous ploy, for the Russians were not merely upset but jumpy. (As the search for the wreckage of 007 got under way, the Soviet Far Eastern defences were at peak alert, with fighter pilots and SAM batteries so nervous that one Russian fighter came within an ace of shooting down another: the pursuing pilot was prepared to fire his missiles when his 'prey' was identified as a Soviet craft.[117]) Only on 16 October did the *Washington Post*'s Murrey Marder call attention to the fact that 'US relations with the Soviet Union are in a far more precarious and volatile state than any high official of the Reagan Administration is admitting publicly, even though Soviet officials in Moscow are making no attempt to conceal it.'[118]

## The irreplaceable Larry McDonald

The sudden winding down of the US propaganda campaign boded ill for Kathryn McDonald's attempt to succeed to her late husband's Congressional seat. Although supported by the financial might of the Birchers (including Nelson Bunker Hunt), her campaign quickly ran into trouble. Many of Larry McDonald's former supporters were so ultrareactionary that they found the notion of electing a woman – any woman – repugnant. But she was dogged, too, by a whispering campaign which suggested that she and Larry had been on the edge of divorce. Her campaign billed her as Larry's second wife, but court records showed that she was his third: the Congressman's second wife had sued him for divorce alleging that he had beaten her with a garden tool while she was pregnant and that he had called a five-year moratorium on their sex life on the grounds 'that we were in the Third World War and that people did not make love during war'.[119]

Mrs McDonald fought an energetic right-wing campaign – demanding the revival of the Un-American Activities Committee and the cutting off of all federal aid to education – and did well enough to make the run-off contest with another conservative Democrat, George Washington Darden III. But although she avoided almost all contacts with reporters she was unable to shake off persistent questioning as to how she could fling herself into the electoral fray without any period of mourning for her late husband. Mrs McDonald complained about being called 'the Ice Lady', but she had undoubtedly affronted strong local mores about the way that recently widowed ladies were expected to behave. One Vietnam veteran told a reporter that 'fish ain't even started eating him yet, and she was running for office'.[120] In the end Mrs McDonald was easily beaten by Darden. She retired from the scene with the comment, 'It's very difficult to put your whole heart in something when half of it is broken.'[121]

The media war over 007 was over. Without doubt, the US had won it. In the West, at least, the Soviet case had gone largely by default, and the many awkward questions surrounding the affair had been largely glossed over in the general wave of anti-Soviet feeling. It is that case and those questions which we must now review.

# SEVEN

# The Soviet Case

The Soviet case over KAL 007 was so badly presented that few in the West paid very much heed to its details. The important thing seemed only that the Russians had shot the plane down; that they had lied about it for days; that they had then come up with a story about a surveillance mission which sounded very much like a belated excuse, and a very partial excuse since the killing of hundreds of innocent civilians was unjustified whatever 007's reason for being off course. If it was really true that the Russians had misidentified the plane as an RC-135, this was still extremely culpable: it was their duty to make a correct identification before loosing off missiles at any plane. Since this moral case was fairly well unanswerable, it was easy enough to assume that the Soviet theses were a pack of lies from beginning to end. If so, the details hardly mattered.

The Soviet case, like its American counterparts, came out in instalments. On 4 September 1983 the chief of the main headquarters staff of the Soviet air defence forces, Colonel-General Semyon F. Romanov, gave an initial account to TASS. Romanov alleged that 007 had been flying with both its navigation and collision-prevention lights extinguished. The outlines of a 747, he said, 'much resemble those of the American reconnaissance plane, RC-135'. Referring always to a Soviet pilot in the singular, he claimed that the Soviet pilot

undertook for a long period repeated attempts to lead the intruder plane to the closest Soviet airfield. The Soviet pilot failed, despite all his attempts, to establish radio communication with the intruder since its crew did not respond to radio signals he sent . . . Then the pilot resorted to a change in aircraft attitude: wing-rock. At that, our interceptor flew with his lights on, flashing them in order to attract the attention of the intruder's crew. The intruder plane continued . . . The plane seemed to be stalking under cover of night above our territory . . .[1]

The intrusion had, claimed Romanov, to be viewed in the context of repeated US violations of Soviet Far Eastern airspace. Already in 1983 there had been nine such incidents in the Kurile Island region by US combat planes. In addition other US planes had made incursions in the Bering Straits in the region of Ratmanov Island. It was clear, he asserted, that all these intrusions had been quite deliberate.[2]

On 6 September *Pravda* published further details. From 13.45 to 18.49 GMT (i.e. for four and three-quarter hours before the shoot-down and more than 20 minutes after it) Soviet radar had, it claimed, tracked seven RC-135s off the Soviet Far Eastern coast, plus three US naval vessels just outside Soviet territorial waters at the same time.[3] Thus, according to Moscow, a veritable fleet of US planes and boats took up position along the line of 007's flight at about the time that 007 was passing Bethel, and waited for it to approach. *Pravda* added that the USSR had actually shown considerable restraint, for SAMs could have been used at an early stage. 007 had, it said, overflown a naval base on Kamchatka, causing a fighter group there to scramble to intercept it. 007 had also veered over southern Sakhalin to take it over an air base and it was only after this that tracer shells had been fired past it. Moreover, 007 had radioed its Japanese ground control that it had 'success-fully' overflown Soviet territory. Meanwhile Soviet TV suggested that the job of the RC-135, which the US had admitted to, had been to 'correct' 007's flight and that the RC-135 had flown parallel to 007's flight path.[4] TASS suggested that the US had sent 007 on its mission with the expectation of creating a crisis which would wreck the arms talks and thus enhance the US bid for nuclear superiority.[5] A slight further twist was given by the Soviet journalist, Alexan-der Ignatov, speaking on French TV. There had, he said, been not one but eight RC-135s and three or four 'American boats specialised in intelligence service' off the Soviet coast. 007 had been acting as 'bait'. Asked for proof of these allegations, Ignatov just referred to 'our intelligence services'.[6]

On the evening of 6 September TASS issued a longer statement, saying that the USSR had now completed its special investigation and could give a fuller account. When 007 entered Soviet airspace over Kamchatka, with the RC-135 flying close by and at the same altitude, one Soviet fighter had been dispatched to 'control' the RC-135 and another to intercept 007. This latter signalled to 007 that it was intruding but its (unspecified) signals were ignored. 007 had then proceeded to overfly 'a most important base of the strategic nuclear force' on Kamchatka. When 007 proceeded over Sakhalin it encountered more Soviet fighters, which used the international emergency radio frequency of 121.5 MHz to contact the plane: all Soviet air defence planes were, TASS said, equipped to transmit on this frequency. They met with no response but 'the Soviet radio control services picked up short coded radio signals transmitted from time to time, such signals that are usually used in transmitting intelligence information'. TASS repeated earlier Soviet claims that there had been no way of knowing that the intruder had been a civilian craft, owing to its lack of lights, the night, poor visibility and the fact that the plane's configuration resembled that of an RC-135.[7]

## Ogarkov or never apologise

Marshal Ogarkov filled this picture out considerably at his press conference of 9 September,[8] basing himself, he said, on the official report of the State Aviation Inspectorate of the USSR, whose members had visited all the key Soviet bases and radar stations, interviewing pilots, ground controllers, electronics specialists and so forth. Ogarkov said that 007 had been first picked up by Soviet radar when it was 500 miles northeast of Petropavlovsk naval base (Kamchatka). Although Ogarkov's wall map showed seven other US reconnaissance planes at various points along the Soviet coast, he laid particular stress on the RC-135 whose course had crossed 007's to the east of Kamchatka. This RC-135, he said, had first appeared on Soviet radar at 15.51 GMT. It was flying 'a strange patrol', consisting of wide loops which converged with 007's course so that ultimately the two planes flew together, parallel, for ten minutes. Then the RC-135 turned back to its base while 007 made a definite turn westwards towards Petropavlovsk. 'Naturally,' said Ogarkov, 'the conclusion was made at Soviet anti-aircraft defence command posts: an intelligence plane is approaching the USSR's airspace.' Ogarkov laid considerable stress on the role of the RC-135, suggesting both that it had been monitoring and controlling 007's flight and that its purpose had been to confuse Soviet radars below. (According to Ogarkov, 007 and the RC-135 flew so close that their two radar blips actually merged into one. Thus when one of the two blips separated the Russians assumed that the plane now approaching them was an RC-135.) Both planes, Ogarkov said, were flying at the same height – 8000 metres.

As the two planes diverged, said Ogarkov, one (the RC-135) headed back to base but the other (007) veered westwards off its previous course and headed towards Petropavlovsk. At 16.30 the plane entered Kamchatka airspace 'heading straight towards a major base of the USSR's strategic nuclear forces' and skirting an emplacement of SAM-5 missile batteries. Four Soviet fighters were scrambled at 16.37. Both these fighters and also Soviet ground control stations attempted to establish contact with 007 'including with the help of the general call signal at the fixed international distress frequency of 121.5 Megahertz', and attempted to compel the intruder to land at the nearest Soviet airfield. 'But,' said Ogarkov, 'these attempts failed.' But at the same time 'radio-monitoring stations detected periodically transmitted brief coded signals, which are usually used for transmitting intelligence data.' At 17.08 the intruder exited from Kamchatka airspace and the Soviet fighters simultaneously returned to base.

The intruder, continued Ogarkov, then crossed the Sea of Okhotsk and entered Sakhalin airspace, with six Soviet fighters scrambling to meet it at 17.42. All these planes too, he said, were 'fitted out with communications facilities incorporating the international emergency frequency, 121.5 MHZ. They repeatedly tried to contact the intruder on that frequency, but the intruder did not respond.' It was over Sakhalin, Ogarkov claimed, that 007's actions 'became outrageous. As announced earlier, it had not responded to the warning shots of the Soviet interceptor planes. Moreover, it began to change simultaneously the direction, altitude and speed of flight, obviously trying to evade the air-defence planes.' Moreover, at 18.02 'the intruder plane, sharply changing course, circumvented the positions of our air-defence missile units and passed over important military facilities in the southern part of Sakhalin Island.' This led to a final attempt to warn the plane – the firing of 120 tracer shells at 18.20 – but this too was ignored and at 18.24 the shoot-down order was given. Many Western correspondents at Ogarkov's press conference had been speculating that the actual shoot-down must have been a low-level decision and that the Russians would not accept high-level responsibility for such a horrendous action. Ogarkov flatly ruled out all such notions: the order to fire had been given by the commander of the Blys military region but throughout the intrusion 'Soviet Air Defence Forces operated in full contact with the Government authorities'.

Ogarkov was, indeed, quite unapologetic. The USSR had, he said, 'used every warning measure possible'. It could easily have shot the plane down with SAM-5s over Kamchatka without ever bothering with fighter interception. The plane had spent lengthy periods in Soviet airspace and had done so 'in the dead of night and under conditions of cloud cover, along the upper edge of which the intruder was flying' – it had been shot down at 18.24 with dawn not due till 19.11 and sunrise at 19.49. (President Reagan had spoken of a 'clear night with a half-moon'.) The plane had 'stubbornly ignored all the warnings' and had 'acted exactly like' the KAL plane which had intruded over Soviet Karelia in 1978 – 'it was the same hand'. After all that, 'What was left to us?'

Ogarkov was so impressive a figure that he might have got away with a good press but for two utterly appalling statements. When he was questioned about why the USSR had taken so long to admit to the shoot-down he replied that 'the information that the flight was terminated was made in the first TASS dispatch. You should have read it attentively. Perhaps we understand better our own language than you understand Russian.'[9] This was a lie compounding a lie. Secondly, when asked why the USSR had given so little domestic publicity to the fact that 269 people had died aboard the plane, Ogarkov replied, 'We did not conclude that it was a commercial flight. Why should we report that it had so-and-so many on board? As to how many there were, it will be found out later.'[10] There is little need for moral comment on such statements. Politically, one can only wonder when the USSR will learn that this form of attack is the worst form of defence.

Several other points emerged in the question-and-answer session which followed Ogarkov's presentation. Western correspondents pointed out that the tapes of the Soviet fighters' conversations published by the US showed that twice there had been reference to flashing lights on the intruder plane. Did this not contradict the Soviet assertion that 007 had been flying without navigation lights? To this there were two answers: that actually this was a reference by one of the Soviet pilots to the fact that another of the Soviet planes (not 007) was flashing its lights in an attempt to warn 007; and that, in any case, 'the alleged "recordings" had been falsified from beginning to end'. The USSR had its own tapes of its fighters' conversations and the State Commission had examined them, but it was not Soviet policy to publish these tapes. Why had the US not published the tapes of the conversations of its other planes in the vicinity, including the RC-135?

Ogarkov also alleged that 007's intrusion was merely the latest in a series of violations of Soviet airspace in the same general region. 'In 1983 alone US planes repeatedly violated the boundary of the Soviet Union's airspace in that region, including in the area of the lesser Kurile chain, with US naval planes from the aircraft carriers *Midway* and *Enterprise* going up to 30 km deep, and with US civilian planes in the area of Chukotka.' All the USSR's official protests about such flights had, he said, been ignored. Ogarkov repeatedly returned to the fact that 007's flight must have been visible throughout to US surveillance facilities, but that no attempt had been made to contact the Soviet authorities about it, even though there was a direct radio link between Japanese air-control services and their Soviet counterparts at Khabarovsk. There had been no doubt at any level of the Soviet command structure that they were dealing with a spy plane: 'In the General Staff we were all informed . . . there is probably no general staff in the world which, in such a situation, would not receive full reports of such an incident.' The Marshal was, though, less clear on the question of whether one or two missiles had been fired at 007, sometimes talking as if only one missile had been fired, sometimes as if more than one had. In general, though, the Russians talked about one missile only.

Several points deserve to be highlighted in Ogarkov's presentation. His assertion – ignored though not contradicted by the US – that 007's flight followed a series of intrusions into Soviet airspace by US military *and civilian* planes cuts both ways. That is, if the assertion is to be credited, any notion of a surveillance mission by 007 has to suggest an objective for which these other intrusions had been insufficient. Similarly, although Ogarkov laid repeated stress on the role of the RC-135 as 007's 'controller', his map showed a virtual flotilla of other US reconnaissance planes in the general vicinity. The US again merely ignored rather than contradicted this assertion, but neither Ogarkov nor the US gave any explanation for their presence. US sources also made no comment on Ogarkov's assertion that 007 was at 8000 metres' (26,250 feet) altitude when picked up by Soviet radar and during its 'rendezvous' with the RC-135 – although this was in stark contradiction with 007's own claim to have been flying at 31,000 feet until 16.06 when it ascended to 33,000 feet. Either Ogarkov, for reasons difficult to discern, was guilty of giving a false altitude report, or 007 was, via KAL 015, relaying false altitude reports as well as false position reports.

It is worth noting, too, that Ogarkov left much unexplained about the interception of 007 over Kamchatka. According to his own account Soviet fighters did not scramble there until 16.37 – a full seven minutes after 007 had entered Kamchatka airspace even though, according to his account, Soviet radar had had 007 in view when it was still 500 kilometres away. Since normal procedure would have entailed the interception of 007 at the edge of the Airspace Defence Identification Zone (60 miles out), Ogarkov's account implied a serious failure either in Soviet radar identification or in interception procedures. An air-defence system which does not even scramble fighters until an intruder is some 60 miles inland is clearly malfunctioning badly. Ogarkov also gave a fairly minimal account of the actual interception, recording merely that the Soviet fighters attempted to establish radio contact and persuade 007 to land on a Kamchatka airfield: he avoided any actual assertion, for example, that the Soviet fighters had made a visual sighting of 007 and merely concluded that their interception 'attempts failed'. The next day, as we have seen, as if to correct this impression, in the Soviet press surfaced (unnamed) Kamchatka pilots who gave graphic descriptions of actual, visual interceptions.[11]

## Puffing the PVO

It seems not impossible that the Soviet authorities, realising that Ogarkov's account implied an extremely serious failure of the Soviet air-defence system, hurried the next day to 'correct' such a notion.

This certainly seems to have been the main concern of the Soviet TV programme devoted to the 007 incident on 11 September. Colonel-General Nikolai I. Moskvitelev, a three-star general in the PVO (Voiska Protivovozdushnoi Oborony – the Soviet Air Defence Force), was now wheeled to the front. His claims should be seen, no doubt, as an attempt to dress up a lamentable performance by the PVO. Appearing on the regular Sunday night programme, *I Serve the Soviet Union* (which deals with military affairs and aims particularly at Soviet youth), he went to considerable lengths to reassure his audience of the PVO's efficacy.[12] The Soviet fighters had indeed intercepted 007 over Kamchatka, he said, but when they failed to evoke any response they had simply withdrawn, having determined that 'the intruder aircraft had no need of assistance and . . . that everything on board was in working condition'. This was a remarkable assertion – not only that the fighters had ascertained that everything aboard 007 'was in working condition' despite failing to get any response at all from it, but also that an intruder plane could be allowed to fly serenely on its way provided only that it 'had no need of assistance'. (*Izvestia* of 12 September followed this up with a description of how one Soviet pilot had flown parallel with 007 over Kamchatka – 'a large dark silhouette' – under very poor weather conditions, with a gusting wind and 'thick, multi-layered clouds'.[13] *Izvestia*'s weather report was accurate but, as we shall see, the rest was fiction.) Moskvitelev also argued that 'The RC-135 reconnaissance plane and the passenger plane Boeing 747 are of one type – they have an identical form and geometric dimensions' and 'analogous radar signatures'. 'They have,' he continued, 'an identical flight speed. They can be distinguished in the air only during the day, visually and from a close distance. For a pilot to do this at night is totally impossible.' Now, while it is true that both the RC-135 and the Boeing 747 are four-engined jets with similar cruising speeds which might well be difficult to tell apart in the dark at any distance, it is simply not true that they have 'an identical form and geometric dimensions': the 747 has a distinctive 'hump' and is 231 feet long, 195 feet in wing span and 63 feet in height, while the 135 is 152 feet long, with a 145 feet wing span and is 42 feet in height.[14] It seems likely, in other words, that Moskvitelev was stretching a point in order to reassure his Soviet audience as to the efficacy of Soviet air defence. His account of the Kamchatka interception should, too, be regarded as strictly for internal consumption.

It is, indeed, a peculiarity of the Soviet system that more and bigger lies are told for internal consumption than spokesmen often feel it safe to venture before external audiences. Thus, for example, some of the data revealed at Ogarkov's press conference was thought too sensitive for Soviet audiences to have access to it: the actual number of casualties aboard 007 (269) was only mentioned twice in all the Soviet press coverage;[15] and Soviet audiences only learned of the full extent of the airline boycott when it was on the point of collapse. It is, in effect, assumed that many Soviet citizens get their 'real' news from foreign broadcasts – and one ludicrous result of the Soviet propaganda style is that the gaps left by the Soviet media virtually encourage them to do so.

In fact the implications of the fiasco over Kamchatka could not be long concealed. On 11 October Associated Press reported that a Soviet official source – speaking on condition that he not be identified – had admitted that two out of three radar installations on Kamchatka had not worked properly; that the local air-defence command had been thrown into confusion by the intrusion; that the commanders had not known the intruder was a civilian airliner; and that the intrusion was not confirmed until 007 had reached Sakhalin. The actual decision to shoot down 007, the source added, had been made by top military officials in Moscow and the Soviet civilian leadership had never been consulted. This all rang true – and was generally admitted before long by Soviet commentators.[16] This meant admitting, in effect, that a large number of very public lies had been told about the 'Kamchatka interception' – including, presumably, a fictional 'interview' with the Kamchatka fighter pilots. Certainly, US intelligence had rapidly come to the conclusion that no interception at all was made over Kamchatka. Given that the Russians knew that the US had been monitoring their activity over Kamchatka, it is difficult to see how they could ever have believed they could deceive the US about that. That is, the whole 'Kamchatka interception' story was probably always primarily for internal consumption.

The question was, where did that leave the PVO? The PVO is a wholly separate service arm alongside the Army, Navy, Air Force and Strategic Missile Force. It controls 2250 fighter aircraft, 10,000 SAM missiles and a vast radar defence network, and it has to compete with the other service arms for scarce resources.[17] These budget battles lead the PVO to stress how Soviet borders are under constant threat of aerial penetration and that the PVO alone can prevent that. Perhaps the fictional interview with the Kamchatka pilots (or were real PVO pilots made to mouth the untruths?) was an act of self-protection by a hideously embarrassed PVO? But it was clearly no good: 007 had got clean away over Kamchatka, had spent nearly two and a half hours in Soviet airspace and over the Sea of Okhotsk without being positively identified; and when Major Kasmin finally saved the PVO's bacon, he did it only after 007 was on the point of leaving Soviet airspace for the second time. Had Kasmin not been good enough not to be fooled by 007's apparent last-minute evasive tactics, the PVO's disgrace would have been complete.

Almost the worst thing was that it had happened before, with the 1978 KAL incursion over Murmansk. The fact that that plane, KAL 902, had been able to stray 1000 kilometres into Soviet airspace, overfly the Red Navy's biggest base, and even manage to keep flying for one and a half hours after it had been shot and damaged by Soviet fighters, had drawn attention to the poor state of the PVO. A purge had followed in which, according to Western intelligence, several senior PVO officers were sacked or possibly even shot, but the PVO had also been reorganised to allow greater autonomy to its regional commanders. It had remained a rigidly compartmentalised force, with control of radars, fighters and missiles separated into wholly separate sections, and even these sections are rigidly subdivided so that, for example, the monitoring of USAF radio transmissions is kept quite separate from the PVO group in charge of radar detection. Moreover, all air defence is ground-controlled – reliance on airborne command platforms is minimal and Soviet fighter pilots are kept on such a tight leash from the ground that the USAF tends to regard them as little more than human guided missiles. This emphasis on ground control means that the PVO is utterly reliant on its radars, a field in which Soviet technology lags the US by a considerable distance.

Just as in 1978, the 1983 intrusion led to a considerable shake-up within the PVO. By early October the Far Eastern Command of the PVO was in the firing line.[18] The Soviet High Command in Moscow was reported to be furious with Kamchatka's poor performance in particular. (Note that Ogarkov had carefully made no mention of any 'Kamchatka interception', and nor did Kirsanov (see below). They probably knew what was to come – indeed, were probably the ones to take action themselves.) Later the Kamchatka PVO commander was reported to have been transferred – and later to have died.[19] This may even have been an execution. There was no mention of such action within the Sakhalin command which had, after all, stopped the intruder in the end.

On 13 September *Krasnaya Zvezda*, the official Soviet military newspaper, gave further details of how the confusion over Kamchatka occurred[20] – a far more realistic-sounding account. When the RC-135 and 007 had parted company just short of the Kamchatka coast, the RC-135 had dived beneath radar cover and sped away southwards along the edge of the Kamchatka coastline. This, the paper said, had distracted Soviet radar at just the moment that 007 had begun to move over Kamchatka. Certainly, this would have had a confusing effect if, as the Russians alleged, the two planes had previously been close enough to one another to produce a single blip on radar screens. As one blip dived below the radar screen close to the Soviet coastline while the other blip carried on straight towards Kamchatka, Soviet ground controllers would have needed to scramble fighters towards the disappearing blip (the RC-135) in case it was planning to infringe Soviet airspace below radar level. They would probably have assumed that the blip carrying on steadily towards Soviet airspace (007) within radar vision was the plane 'selling a dummy' to cover for the RC-135. It would have seemed too obvious a ploy for a plane to steer steadily in a straight line, at easy radar level, towards forbidden airspace. If so, the Russians would have had a nasty shock when they realised they had been sold a 'double dummy' – which might help to explain why Soviet fighters were scrambled late, behind 007, as it crossed Kamchatka.

## KAL and Captain Chun again

On 16 September *Krasnaya Zvezda* followed up with further unsubstantiated allegations.[21] the US, it said, had taken an interest in KAL in the late 1960s, when the company had been 'on the verge of bankruptcy', and that around 1970 'a top-secret agreement was concluded between the Central Intelligence Agency of the USA and the airline KAL for the use of passenger planes to gather intelligence from Soviet territory. In connection with this agreement several planes, and initially Boeing planes of American make, were specially equipped with spying photo and radio devices.' In return for this, the newspaper alleged, KAL had received fourteen Boeing 747s, seven Boeing 707s, and five McDonnell Douglas DC-10s at special low prices. This had enabled KAL to cut its fare prices and thus return to profitability. Under the agreement, the paper continued, a considerable number of South Korean pilots underwent training at US flying schools and at Boeing and McDonnell Douglas, at which companies 'one will permanently find 10 to 15 pilots and 25 to 30 specialists of the Korean Air Lines technical services'. A number of directors of both companies, it added, were former KAF officers, and these officers were 'fully controlled' by the South Korean Transport Ministry, which in turn was always headed by retired South Korean generals. The Minister himself, Lee Hi Sung, was 'notorious for his pro-American views and having personal links with the US secret services'.

As for Captain Chun, said *Krasnaya Zvezda*, he was not only a colonel in the KAF reserve, but had 'boasted to his close friends that he was carrying out special tasks of American intelligence and to some of them he showed spy equipment on his plane which was used for surveying Soviet military objects during flights *en route* from New York to Seoul.' Chun's impressive record, the paper added, made

the attempts look so clumsy to present him as a debutant who lost his way in airspace and started his flight with defective navigation and communication equipment. However, it is significant that in spite of his apparently successful career, Chun Byung-in intended soon to leave the company, as he told people close to him, because of the big risk for life connected with fulfilling intelligence tasks for the CIA.

It is impossible to evaluate any of these assertions by *Krasnaya Zvezda*, for the newspaper provided no evidence whatsoever for any of them and nor did it cite sources. No doubt some particulars are true – it would be unsurprising if South Korean pilots received training in the US or if the South Korean Transport Minister held pro-American views, for example. Other parts seem highly improbable. Thus, to take but one example, the notion of Chun taking such wild risks as to show off surveillance equipment or to boast openly of espionage missions seems very out of character with all that is known both of his somewhat taciturn nature or, indeed, his sheer professionalism. Had Chun performed such missions one would have expected him to be a model of silent discretion. The *New York Times* (17 September 1983) was, though, sufficiently intrigued by these allegations to question a former CIA officer about them. This source could say nothing of the early 1970s, but did say that the CIA had had no data-gathering operations in progress through KAL in the late 1970s or as late as summer 1982. It was, though, the source said, impossible to say whether or not some such arrangement might have existed with the KCIA.

## Kirsanov and the 'Ferret'

On 20 September *Pravda* published a new and striking analysis by a Soviet Air Force Marshal, Piotr Kirsanov.[22] Although Kirsanov's article received less publicity than Ogarkov's press conference, it was actually more important, for it contained an essentially new interpretation of the 007 'mission', backed up by more specific detail, and it also signalled a clear alteration in the Soviet stance towards the affair.

The aim of the 007 'mission', said Kirsanov, was to gain for the US 'as full information as possible about the Soviet anti-aircraft defence system in the Far East' – that is, the plane had been a passive probe. Gone was any mention of surveillance equipment carried by 007 itself, for on a passive probe mission the intruder plane itself may be wholly 'clean' of surveillance devices, its object being to trigger radar, radio communication and other electronic systems whose intelligence fruits can then be monitored and recorded by other facilities. 007 had had, according to Kirsanov, 'a whole set of strategic and political objectives' – though he did not elaborate on the latter. The plane had, he said, carried eleven intelligence specialists in addition to its normal crew of eighteen (in the shape of the extra, dead-heading crew taken on at Anchorage and the unexplained five surplus crew members with which 007 had started).

The 007 'mission', alleged Kirsanov, had been very precisely timed and

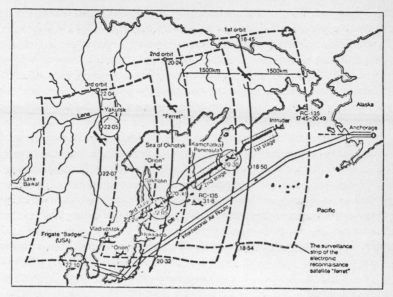

6  The Soviet depiction of US ELINT platforms and the overpassing satellite at the time of KAL 007's flight. *Source*: The map above is reproduced from P. Q. Mann, 'Reassessing the Sakhalin Incident', *Defence Attaché* (London) no. 3, 1984, p. 48. Mann, in turn, has merely reproduced the map accompanying Kirsanov's *Pravda* article, but has helpfully translated the Russian notations into English.

coordinated. The 40-minute delay at Anchorage before taking off had been crucial to achieving an exact coordination with the overflights of a US ELINT satellite, a 'Ferret-D'. Kirsanov's article was accompanied by a map (reproduced above) showing how this coincidence worked. The satellite's first pass, over the eastern edge of Siberia and parallel to Kamchatka, occurred before 007 entered Soviet airspace. According to Kirsanov.

the satellite had the opportunity right before the South Korean plane's intrusion into Soviet airspace to hear the Soviet radio electronic systems in the Chukchi peninsula and Kamchatka that worked in their routine on-combat duty mode, and clarify their where-abouts and the level of activity, thus assuring the first stage of the flight of the intruder plane.

The satellite's second pass, bisecting the Sea of Okhotsk between Kamchatka and Sakhalin, coincided exactly with 007's penetration of Soviet airspace over Kamchatka, enabling it to monitor 'a doubling of the intensive-ness of the work of our radio and radio technical equipment' occasioned by the intrusion. The third pass by the satellite, to the east of Sakhalin and close to Vladivostok, also coincided with 007's intrusion into Sakhalin airspace, said Kirsanov, and thus allowed the monitoring of the whole Soviet C3 (command, communications and control) system during the final interception and shoot-down. The satellite's electronic monitoring had, claimed Kirsanov, been backed up by a whole battery of other US surveillance platforms – apart from the RC-135 that had rendezvoused with 007 off Kamchatka, a second such plane had been flying a mission course off the southern tip of Kamchatka, and there were two Lockheed P-3C Orion planes, one cruising over the Sea of Okhotsk near the northern tip of Sakhalin, and the other over the Sea of Japan. In addition, the USS *Badger* had been cruising off Vladivostok – thus positioning an electronic reconnaissance craft in close proximity to the Soviet communications nerve centre for the Far East. Kirsanov also claimed that a Boeing E-3 Sentry (AWACS) plane had been in the vicinity, but his map did not show its alleged whereabouts. Finally, the entire operation – including the whole flight of 007 from start to finish – had been monitored, said Kirsanov, by US ground tracking stations in Japan, Hawaii and the Aleutians. These had 'recorded the work of all additionally switched-on electronic devices of our anti-aircraft defence system in Sakhalin, the Kurile Islands and maritime territory'.

The Kirsanov article clearly represented a mature Soviet assessment of 007's flight and was remarkable in its detailed attempt to substantiate the notion of a surveillance mission. Not only was Ogarkov's version of the flight implicitly altered towards that of a passive probe mission, but the number of US planes alleged to have been in the area was reduced from Ogarkov's seven to five. Similarly, Ogarkov had not even mentioned the Ferret-D satellite at all, nor had he given such chapter and verse about both US and Soviet electronic capabilities and facilities.

Kirsanov's article also represented a notable hardening of the Soviet attitude as to the political responsibility for the flight of 007. When Gary Powers' U-2 spy plane had been shot down over the USSR in 1960, Khrushchev had gone to elaborate lengths to suggest that Eisenhower himself had probably known nothing of the mission and that it had merely been an aberrant act by the CIA – the point being to allow Eisenhower an escape route and thus prevent the incident from damaging the plans for the forthcoming Paris summit talks: Khrushchev had been correspondingly furious when Eisenhower had insisted on taking direct personal responsibility for the flight (even though this had involved admitting that he had publicly lied earlier on when he had denied the whole spy-flight story). Given that the 007 shoot-down occurred just as the Geneva arms-control talks were nearing their climax, Soviet spokesmen might have been expected to adopt a similar attitude now – but Kirsanov did the opposite. 'It is impossible to imagine,' he wrote, 'that such an operation was worked out by special services without the corresponding authorisation. It was doubtless being prepared for a long time with the approval of, or on direct assignment from the US Administration.' Indeed, the whole operation had been so carefully prepared, Kirsanov suggested, that President Reagan himself had been privy to its planning. Since the incident, he claimed, 'the most stringent censorship' had been imposed on links between the CIA and KCIA.

Such language not merely implied that the Russians had already given up real hope for the Geneva talks but also reflected a more fundamental pessimism. There was no doubting – as visitors to Moscow repeatedly confirmed – that the Russians *did* believe their own version of the 007 incident. If that view was taken, then it followed that the USSR was dealing with a US Administration which had cynically and carefully prepared a most intricate mission (the coincidence of the 'Ferret' and all the other surveillance platforms alleged to be in the area clearly bespoke a coordination and clearance of the project at a very high level); which had done all this even while ultrasensitive arms-control talks were in progress; and which was now seeking to throw all the blame onto the USSR. If one believed this then there was very little point in attempting to negotiate with such an Administration, and every incentive to drop the normal Soviet tendency to speak in generalities (attributing moves one did not like to 'American imperialism', 'militarist forces', etc.) and instead point the finger at those one thought to be the guilty men. And, as we have seen, it was very much this spirit which lay behind Andropov's blistering speech of 28 September in which he effectively suggested there was nothing more to be done with a US Administration capable of (in the Soviet view) such bad faith.

## Assessing Kirsanov

Perhaps the best way to confront Kirsanov's main charges is to evaluate them in the light of the objections made by James Oberg.[23] Oberg, who is employed by a major Pentagon contractor and is an expert on UFOs and related topics, has emerged as one of the most energetic defenders of the Reagan Administration's line on the 007 affair. In particular, Oberg has published the fullest and most severe critique of Kirsanov, so to measure Kirsanov against Oberg's objections is to put this part of the Soviet case to its most acid test.

First, there is the question of US ELINT planes operating off the Siberian coastline at the time of 007's flight. Oberg does not commit himself to any particular view of how many such planes there were, or where exactly they were, but he does point out, quite rightly, that the Russians provided three different maps showing such aircraft – Ogarkov's, Kirsanov's, and one for submission to ICAO. There is at least some variation in each of these maps as to the number or position of the US planes. To Oberg this proves that the Russians 'were just making it up as they went along'. This seems extremely unlikely – for then, doubtless, they would have made up a single story and stuck to it. It seems more probable that these changes result from a continuing Soviet attempt to reassess their data, and rather likely that they reflect a real confusion (due to jamming?) in the Soviet radar system. It is worth pointing out that as this reassessment proceeded, the Russians revised their estimate of US planes downwards – while sheer propaganda concerns might have led them to do the opposite.

Oberg also makes strenuous objection to Kirsanov's version of the over-passing satellite, and produces a revision in his estimate of the satellite's actual path. (Oberg's projection of the satellite path is not confirmed by other astronomers. But there is a rough measure of agreement – and all differ somewhat from Kirsanov.[24]) Just two months before the 007 tragedy, the Reagan Administration suddenly stopped providing the customary data on all satellite paths (a fact which Oberg does not mention). Nonetheless, all astronomers who have examined the matter concur that the satellite could only be the 1982-41C ELINT satellite launched on 11 May 1982 in conjunction with a KH-9 Big Bird satellite. Probably the most authoritative version of 1982-41C's track is that provided by Dr Bhupendra Jasani (see map 7). We do not, however, know what type of satellite 1982-41C was, other than that it was designated for electronic reconnaissance.[25] The Russians termed it a 'Ferret-D', but this can only be their own idiosyncratic term – it is not a designation used by the US. The term 'Ferret satellite' is a broad generic term, encompassing all SIGINT (signals intelligence) satellites.[26] Accordingly, one has to refer to it, rather clumsily, as 1982-41C.

As will be seen from Dr Jasani's projection of the satellite's track, Oberg is quite right to pour scorn on Kirsanov's version of 1982-41C's orbit (though Jasani's tracks differ, too, from those shown by Oberg). Kirsanov shows the orbits bending in the wrong direction and, indeed, actually changing direction – a physical impossibility. Similarly, Kirsanov shows the satellite's tracks too close together – suggesting that he thought 1982-41C was orbiting considerably faster than it was. Finally, Kirsanov's depiction of the tracks starts slightly too far to the west. This may not be an innocent error. But all told, these errors are so elementary that it is utterly astonishing that the

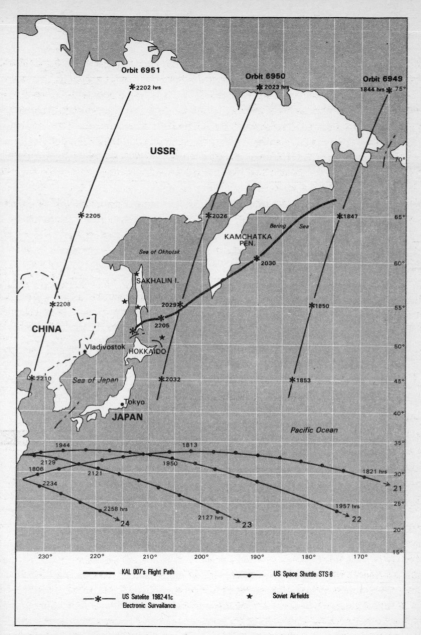

7 Ground tracks of the US electronic reconnaissance satellite 1982–41C launched on 11 May 1982, during orbits 6949, 6950 and 6951; and the tracks of the US space shuttle STS-8, launched on 30 August 1983. The tracks were made on 31 August 1983. The figures indicate the Moscow Standard Time for various positions of the spacecraft. *Source*: Bhupendra Jasani and G. E. Perry, 'The Military Use of Outer Space', in SIPRI, *World Armaments and Disarmament. SIPRI Yearbook 1985, p. 138.*

Russians could make them, especially since no clear propaganda point was served by several of the errors.

There is, moreover, another huge error. As Oberg points out, Kirsanov's estimate of the satellite's viewing range is 'off by a factor of two'. This is perfectly correct – but Oberg fails to note that actually this error helps Kirsanov's case. Astonishingly, Kirsanov seemed to think that the half-width of the satellite's track was 1500 kilometres, whereas it was actually 1500 nautical miles (2793 km).[27] Thus the viewing range was almost twice what Kirsanov thought it was.

It is difficult to believe that anything other than quite appalling incompetence can explain such an error: the Russians had every reason not to make such a mistake.

None of this invalidates Kirsanov's main point that there was a rough synchronisation of the satellite's overpasses and 007's flight across Kamchatka and Sakhalin. However, Oberg is also unwilling to accept at all easily the notion that these overpasses would have yielded much electronic information, suggesting that its path was not optimal for radar beams emanating from Kamchatka and Sakhalin. He grudgingly accepts that the satellite would have picked up any 360-degree search radars, but suggests that other radar beams might have been too narrowly focused for 1982-41C to pick them up.

It is this – the crucial part – of Oberg's objection which appears to be completely wrong. First, of course, the satellite might have been interested in radar and other electronic installations far beyond Kamchatka and Sakhalin. With its effective range nearly twice what Kirsanov suggested, an enormous span of such impulse-emitting installations would have been within its purview. It is true that radar beams can be fairly narrowly focused, but powerful radars emit a considerable backward-leaking, back-scatter effect. Radio astronomers simply scoff at the notion that a sensitive ELINT satellite would not have found such back-scatter effects more than adequate to its purposes. These are millions of times the strength of pulse necessary to detection, so even a relatively weak back-scatter effect is still quite strong enough for satellite reception, particularly a satellite reflecting US technology as at May 1982.

According to Ernest Volkman, the defence analyst and editor of *Defense Science*, the 007 intrusion had the effect of turning on 'just about every single Soviet electro-magnetic transmission over a period of about four hours and an area of approximately 7000 square miles'.[28] There is no doubt that 1982-41C's repeated passes over the eastern USSR (at 98.8 minute intervals)[29] would have yielded an enormous intelligence harvest under such conditions. It really would have mattered not at all whether its actual track was as Kirsanov, Oberg or others have depicted: given the satellite's enormous range, sophistication and power, it was simply bound to pick up enough data to keep US analysts busy for a very long time. Moreover, we *know* that the satellite did pick up data. The *Asahi Evening News* (Tokyo) conducted interviews with Japanese government sources who agreed that Japanese intelligence on 007's flight 'was checked against information obtained by the US from satellites and American facilities within Japan and confirmed as accurate'.[30] It is possible that more than one satellite was involved – a relay satellite for example – but only 1982-41C was in the right places at the right times for us to have a clear certainty about it.

While this crucial part of Oberg's argument cannot be sustained, it remains true that Kirsanov's satellite data was, mysteriously, most incompetently presented. It is also true, of course, that the mere overpassage of the satellite cannot bear the whole explanatory weight placed on it by the Russians. Doubtless, once the Russians noticed the coincidence of the satellite track and the plane's flight, it would have dawned on them what a huge intelligence harvest the US had garnered – and that the satellite would have seen far, far more than the ELINT platforms operating off the Siberian coast. That is, in intelligence-gathering terms the 1982-41C was clearly the crucial piece of ELINT hardware deployed that night. But to jump from the mere size of the secrets thus lost to the certain conviction that 007 was definitely on a passive probe mission was still purely circumstantial.

## The spy Shuttle?

A point which the Russians did not originally make themselves was the possible coincidence of the orbiting space shuttle with 007's overflight of Soviet airspace. This argument was first put forward by P. Q. Mann (a pseudonym) in an article in *Defence Attaché*[31] which implied, in the words of the airline's lawyer, that KAL 'consciously and intentionally took part in an adventure likely to result in disaster'. When KAL sued, the magazine apologized for making this allegation, and paid substantial damages and costs. The Russians naturally seized upon Mann's hypothesis about the shuttle *Challenger* (Mission STS-8) and the question of the shuttle's involvement quickly became part of the groundswell which has followed the 007 case. As will be seen from the tracks drawn by Dr Jasani (see map 7), the shuttle did make four passes over the northern Pacific area on the night in question, though all rather to the south of 007's flight path.

Mann suggested that *Challenger*, lifting off just 36 hours before the shoot-down in the first-ever night launch of a shuttle, flew its 23rd, 24th and

25th orbits at times which coincided reasonably with key events in 007's flight, and that these passes might have been close enough to allow *Challenger* to eavesdrop electronically on some of the Soviet communications activity occasioned by 007's intrusion. In particular, its passes coincided with the 007-RC-135 'rendezvous'; with the moment when 007 had just left Kamchatka airspace and begun to proceed towards Sakhalin; and again when 007, had it survived, would have just emerged from Sakhalin airspace. Mann pointed out that the shuttle, which, from the beginning, has had militarily designated functions, was launched 17 minutes late – and that the coincidence would have been even better had the launch been on time. He also pointed out that the launch time had been set about one month in advance, thus indicating a time-horizon for the planning of the entire surveillance mission – if, indeed, that is what it was.

Against this Oberg urged several objections.[32] A night shuttle launch had, he pointed out (quite correctly), long been an objective of the shuttle programme: there was nothing necessarily sinister about that. Secondly, Oberg insisted that given the type of radio gear carried by *Challenger*, the shuttle was always beyond maximum radio range of 007 and that no relay satellite of sufficient power was within range either. Finally, there was the exceptionally crowded programme of duties being carried out by *Challenger*'s commander, Captain Richard H. Truly, and his crew. During the first 'pass' the astronauts were preparing to speak direct to President Reagan, on the second they were having supper, and on the third they were asleep.

An initial point to be made here is that a degree of suspicion about shuttle launch times is not out of order. It has now been revealed, for example, that the second shuttle mission (STS-2), piloted, as it happens, by Captain Richard H. Truly and Colonel Joe H. Engle, 'used in effect a phony launch time to cover the real launch target ... At the time NASA management said the extra hold time was inserted to settle some launch-team questions that arose on vehicle status. In reality it was inserted to ensure the orbiter *Columbia* was at the right place in space at the right time to allow a KH-11 to view it properly.'[33] (The KH-11 'Keyhole' satellite is the most advanced of all US reconnaissance satellites.[34]) It is quite striking that, as early as the second shuttle mission, Captain Truly and his launch team had experience of a deception over timing. This makes it rather difficult to argue that it was impossible that the timing of the eighth shuttle mission was necessarily immune from similar secondary motives. (Oberg omits this point.)

Oberg also failed to note a last-moment change in *Challenger*'s mission objectives. The STS-8 had always been intended to launch Insat-1B – a communications satellite to serve India. But the other satellite it was supposed to launch was withdrawn as unready at the last moment and so, we are told, *Challenger* substituted a 7460-pound dummy for it.[35] This was noteworthy: the whole shuttle programme is extremely expensive and has been under continuous pressure to justify itself in terms of military utility. Carrying a 3.5-ton dummy satellite into space can hardly have seemed a good way to do that. Why, after all, could the mission not have been delayed until the second satellite was ready? Officially the night launch was necessitated by the need to place Insat-1B into the right orbit at the right time – but the manager of Shuttle Operations Integration, Jay Honeycutt, said that actually there was no need for this to be done on the early morning of 31 August to achieve that: there would have been an opportunity to do it on the third morning of the flight anyway.[36] So the launch could have been delayed without prejudice to its primary mission, but it was decided instead to go ahead just before 007 took off, even though this meant carrying a 3.5-ton dummy into space.

*Challenger* STS-8 also marked up some other 'firsts'.[37] It experimented by dropping 50 miles in height to test new orbits; it gave 'the clearest space television transmission ever beamed to earth'; the timing of the flight gave the crew 'the first night-time glimpse of parts of the Northern Hemisphere'; and it took 'photographs of parts of the Earth never seen before by men from space'. Captain Truly and his crew repeatedly commented on the remarkable accuracy of *Challenger*'s photographs – they could see every street within whole cities as if they were taking their snaps from next door, and so on. Moreover, on 2 September the astronauts 'communicated through the satellite secretly, using an encryption technique that is being used for the first time'. This method of coding would 'allow secret communication on military shuttle missions'.

None of this answers Oberg's objections. If the *Challenger* did not have a greater radio capability than he suggests, he must be right. Moreover, it would have taken an almost impossibly cynical team of astronauts to have first played an active part in monitoring 007's mission and, only shortly thereafter, to pop up on the ether to lend their voices to the swelling chorus of condemnation of the Russians.[38] And Oberg is right that they did have other things to do at the time of their nearest approaches to 007. Moreover, given the plenitude of other land, sea, air and satellite ELINT platforms operating that night to monitor Soviet communications activity, the shuttle would hardly have been an essential extra platform. Mann suggests that there would have been a strong temptation to utilise the shuttle's capabilities in order to help convince the military of the real usefulness of the programme to them. Perhaps so; only perhaps.

Nonetheless, it is impossible to rule out the possibility that *Challenger* carried radio gear and detector devices in excess of what Oberg alleges; and it would hardly be difficult to install a device which operated passively and automatically, without the astronauts having to play any active part in its operation – perhaps without their even knowing what it was. One would, in a word, like to know more about the 3.5-ton dummy satellite which *Challenger* so expensively carried into space just before the 007 flight. Given that this dummy was substituted at the very last moment, the astronauts could hardly have known much about it. One would, too, like to know more about what data was sent back from *Challenger* in the new, specially encrypted code. If only for these reasons, it is difficult to come to a final conclusion as to whether *Challenger* played any part in the ELINT-gathering operation that night. Even such speculation as this will, however, be harder to entertain in the future: in November 1984 it was announced that all future shuttle launches would take place in complete secrecy for national security reasons.[39] This emphasised yet again the clear military and surveillance functions of the shuttle programme.

Soviet commentators eagerly picked up on Mann's article as soon as it appeared, enthusiastically repeating as fact what he had put forward as mere hypothesis, although mention of the shuttle had been entirely absent from the 'authoritative' Soviet accounts by Ogarkov, Romanov and Kirsanov to date. This was, indeed, very much the pattern of the Soviet response throughout: the Russians tended to pick up on articles in the Western press about 007 and happily repeat them – without permission and without qualifications.[40] Similarly, it was only after the role of KAL 015 in the whole affair had aroused considerable controversy among Western followers of the 007 case that the Soviet commentator, Vladimir Nakaryakov, claimed in a Novosti press release that KAL 015 had been used as a decoy for 007 and sent false radio messages. Indeed, 007's delayed departure from Anchorage was now explained as much in terms of the need to shorten the gap between it and 015 as to harmonise with the overpassage of 1982-41C.[41]

## The politics of the Soviet case

The Soviet case on 007 suffered from many deficiencies and oddities. In part this doubtless resulted from the sheer initial confusion of the Soviet air defence system as it dealt with 007. This was then compounded by the cumbersome reactions of a Soviet political and media bureaucracy, unused to having to confront the multiple, rapid-fire diversity of the Western media. The immediate propaganda onslaught from the Reagan Administration caught the Russians utterly flat-footed, and immediately activated the deep defensive reflexes of Soviet official opinion: put up the shutters and deny everything. The Russians were also torn between the need to reassure Soviet domestic opinion that the USSR was both blameless and had an air-defence system which was something less than a shambles, and the conflicting need to confront Western criticism with a more honest and understanding response. Without doubt – as was true, too, in the US – the priorities dictated by the state of domestic opinion easily won the day.

The presentation of the Soviet case may well have also been affected by the tensions the affair generated within the Soviet establishment. The political leadership can hardly have been other than extremely displeased when the Soviet military deposited this explosive and tragic incident in their laps, just as that leadership was nearing the climactic stages of its campaign for an arms-control agreement and to woo West European opinion against the emplacement of cruise and Pershing II. Suddenly, all their hopes, previous efforts and plans were as nothing; indeed, were ashes in their mouth. Their disappointment and bitterness must have been correspondingly great. No doubt there was some embittered reflection upon the fact that the military had taken the fatal decision to shoot down 007 without ever bothering to seek the advice of the political leadership. (One can feel some sympathy for the Soviet High Command in this: who, in the middle of a crisis where minutes counted, would care to disturb a gravely ill and septuagenarian Andropov on holiday, in the early hours of the morning? Or the septuagenarian Minister of Defence, Ustinov? But such arguments could hardly be openly used. On the American side, as we have seen, there was a similar disinclination to awaken a septuagenarian President.)

The PVO's unimpressive performance would also doubtless have served to fuel political criticism and inter-service sniping. If, after all, 007 had been a bomber (a slow-moving one at that) it could clearly have wiped out the vast Soviet missile and submarine base at Petropavlovsk (Kamchatka) and got clean away. And Petropavlovsk houses a good one-third of the USSR's seaborne nuclear deterrent force: the implications were catastrophic. The PVO, and indeed the military as a whole, would no doubt have realised that their heads were potentially on the block, and it would not have been an unnatural human response to bluster one's way out. This may help explain the long list of military men who went up front to 'explain' the affair – and it is not impossible that some of their 'explanations' were intended primarily to fob off an angry Politburo as much as domestic or foreign opinion. Kirsanov's depiction of the overpassing satellite's tracks might not pass muster among foreign analysts, but it may have been enough to bamboozle the Politburo.

Which Soviet military analyst, after all, would wish to take responsibility for suggesting that Kirsanov, a Marshal of the Soviet Union, had presented a picture which included blunders so elementary that they could hardly be undeliberate?

Finally, of course, the always supersecretive Russians were presented with a tough dilemma about military security. Just as the US (and the Japanese) knew a great deal more than they were willing to reveal, so, very probably, did the Russians. Their own ELINT apparatus – perhaps their spy networks in the US and elsewhere as well – must surely have provided them with considerably more information about US ELINT activities off their coast, the affair's ramifications in Seoul, Tokyo and Washington, and so on than they revealed. As it was, the USSR was willing to go further than was at all normal in revealing security-sensitive matters in order to counter the American propaganda onslaught. But – probably at a fairly early stage – a decision must have been taken that it was foolish to throw good money after bad. Quite quickly, the chief questions would have become: how much had US ELINT learned from its monitoring of Soviet responses; how could this damage be rectified; and how could the PVO be strengthened to make both identification and interception of intruders quicker and more certain? As for the public-relations side, well, it was clear that the USSR had taken a bruising defeat on that front. However much this rankled – and it clearly did and does – better not to compromise security further in a vain attempt to play Canute against the tide. Instead one could just follow up possible leads in the Western media on the affair, without volunteering any more data oneself. Whatever the rationalisation, this is certainly a fair description of how the Russians behaved in practice.

None of this, of course, in any way excuses the presentation of the Soviet case. Quite clearly and culpably the Russians had lied badly and at length about the initial shoot-down. They also lied again over the 'Kamchatka interception', including the production of a bogus TV interview with Kamchatka pilots. They exaggerated the similarities between a 747 and an RC-135 to the point where, absurdly, they were made to sound like identical planes. They produced a map which falsified the tracks of the overpassing US satellite in a manner which was either deliberate or unbelievably incompetent. They never had a good case to present – there was no excuse for shooting down an airliner full of civilians, whatever it was doing. But they could and should have apologised. It is no moral answer to these charges to show – as our next chapter does – that the US presentation of its case, though far more skilful, was similarly riddled with inconsistency and dishonesty.

# EIGHT

# Contradictions and Further Questions

The initial US propaganda blast and the answering Soviet counterblast left innumerable contradictions and unanswered questions hanging in the air. In addition, however, a further penumbra of uncertainty rapidly accumulated over some of the secondary details of the tragedy. The general effect, as these later (and often less noticed) facts dribbled out, was to weaken the US case quite considerably. In the first place, there were a series of awkward questions about the crucial tapes.

## 007 to ground control: The Anchorage and Narita tapes

The press were, naturally, extremely loud in their demand for the 007–ground control tapes so that they could judge for themselves what had gone wrong. This should have been quite routine but, extraordinarily, they were not forthcoming. The Russians quickly added their voice to the clamour, suggesting that the tapes might include incriminating material indicating a surveillance mission. These demands reached a new pitch when Mrs Kirkpatrick released the tape of the Soviet fighters' conversation with their ground control on 6 September: if such potentially top-secret data could be released, why on earth the hold-up over the routine civilian tapes of 007 talking to its ground controllers? Mrs Kirkpatrick agreed, under this pressure, that these tapes would indeed be released. The next day, however, the State Department threw some doubt on this statement, saying that the tapes of 007 talking to Narita were under the control of the Japanese Ministry of Transportation and that it was up to Tokyo whether or not they were released.[1] (This did not explain why the Anchorage section of the tapes – under the control of the US government – had also not been released.) The clamour continued but it was only on 13 September that both the Narita and Anchorage tapes were released.

Naturally, this lengthy and inexplicable delay led to Soviet suggestions that the tapes had, in the meanwhile, been 'cleaned' of all dubious material. In fact the only part of the tapes which excited critical comment was the portion at which 007 was due to report its first waypoint beyond Alaska, at NABIE. At this point, as we have seen, Anchorage tried to call 007 no less than four times. Although it could get no clear answer from 007, it did pick up an unknown plane, using an unknown call sign, and speaking in Korean. This more or less had to be 007: Anchorage was having no difficulty talking to KAL 015, after all, and 007 was the only other Korean plane known to be operating in the area. But if so, the mystery only deepens, for the unknown plane did not behave at all as a plane which has to report a waypoint should, merely telling Anchorage to call again and, when it did, to 'wait for a while'. It has to be emphasised that an airliner must, imperatively, report waypoints: there is no 'wait for a while' allowed. And, if it was 007, what was it doing using an unknown call sign? The fact that 007 was a whole 12 minutes late reporting this waypoint – and never spoke to Anchorage ground control even then – also excited sharp comment, as well it might.

A second curiosity was that 007 was using the wrong code on its transponder (i.e. the device which picks up radar emissions from others and transmits back to them). The code 007 would normally have used was SSR code 2000, although if it were intercepted it had to switch immediately to SSR emergency code 7700. Not only did 007 never switch to the emergency code, but it was actually using a 'squawking' code, SSR code 1300. The ICAO Air Navigation Commission expressed bafflement at this. Such a code may be used if a radar facility whose coverage a plane is leaving (i.e., in this case, Anchorage) specifically assigns it to that plane – but Anchorage did no such thing.[2]

The published radio tapes did not reveal any sign of the bursts of coded electronic data the Russians claimed to have picked up, nor was there any sign of the call which the Russians alleged 007 had made to Tokyo confirming that it had successfully crossed Soviet territory. Interestingly, though, in the period before the Narita tape was finally disclosed, the Kyodo Press Agency in Tokyo (which frequently has good sources within the Japanese military and intelligence community) reported that more than an hour after Soviet fighters had first attempted to intercept 007 over Kamchatka, 007 had sent a 'telegram' confirming that 'the plane's navigational equipment is operating normally'.[3] There was, though, no confirmation of this and certainly nothing like it on the published tape.

Three days later, however, Matsumi Suzuki, the Director of the Japan Sound Research Centre, issued a further translation of the last, semi-intelligible bit of the tape. Fifty seconds after the plane was hit, the copilot's voice reported 'rapid decompression ... one-zero-one ... Delta'. The suggestion was made that 'one-zero-one' referred to loss of pressure and 'Delta' to a change in altitude (though such an interpretation was not obvious).[4] In the ICAO transcript this was altered on a 'best interpretation' basis to 'rapid decompression . . . descending to one zero thousand': there was no mention of 'Delta'.

The ICAO alteration was fairly arbitrary, and several acoustics experts gave their opinion that the last phrase was actually 'one-zero-one-zero Delta'.[5] What is agreed by all is that this last phrase was shouted at the top of the pilot's voice. There is, in fact, no civilian air term which can explain the 'Delta', while 'IOIO' is strongly redolent of the military surveillance world. The US KH-II Keyhole satellite is coded IOIO to indicate its surveillance function.[6] Similarly, Gary Powers, the U-2 pilot shot down over the USSR in 1960, served in a special CIA surveillance group – Detachment 10-10. Indeed, what gave Powers away was that in his wallet, confiscated by the Russians, alongside his ID card identifying him as a USAF civilian employee, was a card listing his Detachment as 10-10.[7] To some, 007's apparent use of the 'IOIO' call thus had immediate sinister implications – but it would be wrong, of course, to make too much of this: the tape is difficult to listen to; it is in dispute; and there are alternative meanings. That said, Matsumi Suzuki undoubtedly had far better voice-enhancement facilities than did ICAO, and his translation of the tape is thus more authoritative.

## The Soviet fighters' tapes

Some awkward questions also surround the tapes produced with such éclat by Mrs Kirkpatrick at the UN on 6 September. It is clear, as we have seen, that US officials had copies of these tapes within hours of the shoot-down and that Shultz used them in preparing his 1 September press conference. There is little doubt that in the following five days they would have been the subject of the most intense analysis by the US defence and intelligence community. It is, then, extremely difficult to explain how the transcript provided by Mrs Kirkpatrick should have required correction in several respects a whole five days later still, especially since one of those corrections (about the firing of warning tracer bursts by the SU-15) was quite crucial to the interpretation placed on the entire incident. The official reason given for this mistake was difficulty in deciphering the tapes, but at least one expert who later heard the tapes voiced criticism of this and claimed that actually there was no great difficulty in understanding them.[8]

Meanwhile the Japanese had released their own transcript of the tapes – which, given that it was their tapes being translated from Russian into Japanese and then into English, should have been the authoritative version. However, not only did the Japanese transcript make the same initial errors as the US-provided one, but there were considerable differences between the two. It was not just that the Japanese tapes made no mention of the Soviet radar stations, Karnaval, Deputat and Trikotazh, and even gave a slightly different time (18.26 and 21 seconds) for the shoot-down (the US version gave 18.26 and 22 seconds). M. Katayama made an exact analysis of the two transcripts and found that there were small but sometimes important differences throughout, so that only the last two sentences of the entire transcript were actually identical in Japanese and English versions.[9] When he went back to the original Russian he found that such key phrases as 'the target's lights are flashing' were actually not there at all: instead the pilot had just said, 'It's flashing'. There was simply no way of knowing – *pace* Mrs Kirkpatrick – whether the Soviet pilot had been referring to 007's lights, his own or those of another of the Soviet fighters. It is known that before the tapes were handed over to Charles Wick's USIA (and thence to Mrs Kirkpatrick) their actual translation was effected by the CIA and it seems not impossible, to put it mildly, that there was an element of positive disinformation involved in the transcript so theatrically produced at the UN.

There were, however, much larger questions about the tapes and their provenance. The transcript actually produced covered only the last 30 minutes of 007's flight, plus the conversations of the Soviet pilots in the 20 minutes after that, and the tapes were said to come from the Japanese monitoring unit at Wakkanai. This left hanging the question whether the US (which also maintains facilities at Wakkanai) did not have tapes of its own and whether these might cover a far longer period. Almost immediately after the shoot-down, rumours began to circulate of a far greater body of intelligence data which was being held back, and by 3 September the Japanese Broadcasting Corporation was authoritatively reporting that 'conversations between Soviet pilots and ground control stations had been taped throughout the two and a half hours that Soviet planes reportedly tracked the passenger airliner'.[10] The operation had, the JBC reported, been closely monitored by both Japanese and US intelligence. This brought forth immediate assertions from US intelligence officials that there were no separate US tapes and that the Japanese alone had tapes of the Soviet fighters' conversation.[11] This line was thereafter repeatedly maintained by Administration spokesmen, who insisted that the Japanese alone had tapes of the crucial conversations and that any transcript would therefore have to be made from them.

This line was never very plausible: the notion that US intelligence would be content to have monitoring capabilities inferior to the Japanese was ludicrous. The US possesses by far the best surveillance electronics capability in the world – by the 1970s the US Embassy in Moscow had equipment so good that it could monitor the private conversations of senior Kremlin officials as they talked over their car phones.[12] But in any case the US is not in the habit of placing itself in a position dependent on third parties in such matters.

Sampson and Bittorf reveal a very different[13] – and far more convincing – account of what happened. When Nakasone was first contacted by back-channel from Washington in the early hours after the crash, the chief US demand, apart from Japanese silence on the whole affair, was that they hand over their tapes of the Soviet fighters' conversations. The demand from the State Department was, they say, both peremptory and furiously insistent – despite the fact that the US had better, fuller and clearer tapes of its own at the Misawa NSA facility. In the end Nakasone agreed to this request on two conditions: first, that the Japanese tapes should not be made public without Japan's permission; second, that if they were made public, so should the US data too. This was agreed. This casts an interesting sidelight: clearly US policy-makers had already decided on their entire propaganda strategy – and decided to make the tapes central to that effort – in the first few hours after the shoot-down. This, no doubt, must have been one of the key items for discussion at the Clark–Meese–Burt–Eagleburger–Casey–Shultz teleconference shortly after the shoot-down.

Nakasone encountered strong resistance from the SDA (and, no doubt, Nibetsu) to the idea of publishing the Japanese tapes – to do so would severely compromise Japanese intelligence activities. But Nakasone and his Cabinet Secretary, Gotoda, overruled the SDA on their own, without ever taking the matter to the Cabinet.[14] It must have been hugely embarrassing to Nakasone and Gotoda when their tapes were finally revealed without the US revealing any of their own: a straight double-cross. Sampson talked to a somewhat embittered SDA official about this: 'The CIA were very mean,' he said. 'They only considered their own national interest, and they were very touchy about their spy plane. We should have been warned by the name of the White House spokesman. The trouble with Larry Speakes is – he speaks.'[15]

It seems likely that Nakasone and Gotoda were finally bulldozed at very short notice into acquiescing in the release of their tapes at the UN. For it was just a few hours before Mrs Kirkpatrick rose to speak at the UN that Gotoda convened a press conference in great haste to give advance details of the tape transcripts.[16] Clearly, it was felt that Japan had at least to give the impression of being a full partner in the initiative to reveal the tapes, rather than suffer the humiliation of having its intelligence revealed by another state. Even so, the Japanese acknowledged that not even everything they knew had been revealed – only what was 'necessary and sufficient'.[17] In fact the Japanese had been treated extremely shabbily: while Nakasone and Gotoda may have had only hours' notice about the coming revelation of their tapes, we know from

Wick's account[18] that he, Mrs Kirkpatrick and others had been happily preparing the *coup de théâtre* with the tapes at the UN for days previously.

It is, then, clear that the US had tapes of the conversation of Soviet fighter pilots throughout the 007 intrusion, including the period of the failed interception over Kamchatka.[19] It is hardly surprising that the US was unwilling to compromise its own intelligence monitoring capabilities, but the questions thus raised were sharper than that: what were the intercept platforms being operated by the US? We know that one RC-135 was on mission for part of 007's flight – and, as we shall see, this implied that there really had to be a second RC-135 as well. We also know that the USS *Observation Island*, operating radar Cobra Judy, was on station, and we know that a great battery of land-based radars – at Wakkanai, Misawa, Chitose and elsewhere – would routinely have followed 007's flight, as would Cobra Talon on Shemya. And, under pressure, the US did admit that an (ELINT) Orion P-3C was also airborne in the general vicinity at the time.[20] (According to the Russians there were other US planes aloft too, of course.) And we know, from an official US source, that the US attempt to follow up all the Soviet electronic traffic engendered by 007's intrusion 'plumbs the depths of US intelligence capabilities, and may never be made public'.[21] Finally, we know that, at least an hour before the shoot-down, US intelligence agencies – no doubt following the procedures outlined by General Keegan[22] – had already picked up signs of heightened Soviet air-defence activity in the area, and had monitored the launching of the Soviet fighters.[23] What all this surely has to mean is that, at the very least, the US was monitoring 007's flight (in real time) and benefiting from the intelligence it produced – without using its ability to warn the aircraft of the mortal danger it was in.

A further remarkable element in the affair was the US willingness to double-cross Nakasone and risk the wrath of this all-important ally. For, in the wake of the tape revelations at the UN, the Soviet military commands to the north of Japan immediately changed all the codes and frequencies of their airborne radio transmissions, with the result that the Japanese intelligence monitors suffered a 40 per cent drop in the information they could pick up.[24] This produced great fury within the Japanese defence and intelligence communities, the more so since they had warned both Nakasone and Gotoda of just such a consequence beforehand. Nakasone was thus humiliated before his own defence chiefs, especially when the US failed to deliver on its side of the bargain. 'Our peepholes have been closed,' one intelligence officer was quoted as saying, while some experts thought that Japanese intelligence-gathering might have been set back by as much as five years.[25] While the 007 affair turned out as an intelligence bonanza for the US, it was an intelligence disaster for Japan.

All of this bespeaks not only a settled US determination to create the maximum embarrassment for the USSR (through publication of the tapes), but also an apparent inability to come clean with Nakasone on why the US had to be so reticent with its own information. One cannot but suspect that the revelation of the US tapes might indeed have revealed the presence of various US intercept platforms in the area, something which would have gone some way to confirming suspicions of a coordinated intelligence operation of the type the Russians alleged. No wonder that Sampson found that the Japanese 'have their own deep suspicions'[26] or that they found the US 'very touchy' about the RC-135 – for this may have been one of the intercept platforms involved.

## The Soviet ground-to-air tapes

In the immediate aftermath of the shoot-down a great deal of attention was fastened on the question of whether the Soviet fighter pilot had acted on his own initiative or whether he had received orders from higher authority to bring down 007. The US was emphatic (rightly) that the latter was the case. This naturally led to questions of whether tapes existed not only of the Soviet fighters talking to their ground control, but of their ground controller's transmissions back to them.

The existence of such ground-to-air tapes was immediately confirmed by the Kyodo Press Agency, which actually provided a version of both sides of the conversation as the ground controller gave the crucial order to fire on the airliner,[27] while US intelligence sources told the *Washington Post* that even Soviet ground-to-ground conversations had been monitored as the bases on the Soviet borders radioed back up the command chain to Moscow.[28] The influential *Asahi* papers in Tokyo also quoted Japanese military sources as saying that both sides of the air–ground conversation had been recorded, while the Japanese Broadcasting Corporation repeatedly suggested the same thing, quoting both Japanese government and intelligence sources.[29] Indeed, it was suggested that should the USSR continue to attempt to evade responsibility for the shoot-down, the damning section of the ground tape (giving the order to fire) would be released to nail the lie. Finally, at his 6 September press conference, Mr Gotoda officially confirmed, in answer to persistent press questioning, that Japan also had tapes of the Soviet ground communications to the fighters – but would not release them.[30] It is doubtful if Mr Gotoda realised what a huge cat he was letting out of the bag: he had, we have seen, summoned the press conference at very short notice and may well have been inadequately prepared. Luckily for him, the world's press made nothing of the awesome implications of this admission.

Gotoda's statement must have created consternation in Washington, for only the day before President Reagan had announced, 'We only have the voices of the pilots; the Soviet ground-to-air transmissions were not recorded.'[31] US intelligence officials, following Gotoda's statement, were quick to confirm the Reagan version, pointing out that while it was not difficult for Japanese ground listening stations to pick up the transmissions from Soviet fighters broadcasting from a height of six miles, it was impossible for them to monitor transmissions from ground level. 'Normal radio conversations from ground stations, they said, are blocked by the earth's curvature and are beyond range of distant radio stations such as those in Japan.'[32] For this was indeed the crux. To monitor ground transmissions one would have to have been operating either a ground-level intercept platform (e.g. an electronic reconnaissance ship) close to the source of the ground transmitter or an airborne intercept platform not too far off. In other words, to admit to the existence of ground-to-air tapes was to admit to the presence in the vicinity of 007 of other intelligence-gathering ships or planes – which was, after all, just what the Russians were alleging (the Orion P-3s, RC-135s and the satellite). Moreover, such intelligence platforms typically make 'real-time' translations of what they are picking up, so this implies that the US knew that 007 was off course but failed to act to avert the tragedy. Thus the US could not admit to the existence of the ground tapes without lending credibility to a key part of the Soviet version of events and, by extension, the notion of a surveillance mission.

The trouble was that the ground tapes clearly did exist and a lot of people knew that they did. Some of these were, moreover, political figures who did not realise the intelligence implications of admitting to their existence. Thus on 6 September a 'senior Administration official' told the *New York Times* that tapes existed of a sufficient amount of 'ground chatter' for the US to know that the shoot-down had been ordered from the ground.[33] The next day Larry Speakes, the White House spokesman, was questioned about this and confirmed that the US did have tapes of the Soviet ground controllers talking to their fighters, but that some of these were unintelligible.[34] This admission presumably caused a strong reaction from the CIA, for a few hours later Speakes denied his earlier statement and said the US did not have the ground tapes after all: the Japanese had some such tapes but it was up to them whether they were released or not.[35] Other Administration officials rushed to minimise the damage and averred that the 'ground chatter' 'did not necessarily include transmissions of any kind from ground–air traffic control stations. Instead, one official said, the radio intercepts were of ground-station and ocean-based communications, perhaps any fishermen in the area.'[36] No journalist was awake enough to point out that this invalidated the earlier statement that the 'ground chatter' had proved that the shoot-down order had been given from the ground: only the monitoring of the Soviet military ground controllers could have proved that.

Meanwhile the ground tapes story refused to lie down. At the UN on 8 September the USSR charged that since the Japanese had been monitoring Soviet transmissions so closely they had clearly had the capability to warn 007 it was in danger. The Japanese, unaccustomed to finding themselves in such a hot seat in the Cold War, reacted very sharply.[37] Thereafter the Japanese government, despite Gotoda's earlier admission about the tapes, clammed up entirely and refused to confirm or deny their existence, although on 9 September the Japanese press unanimously announced that Japan did have the ground tapes. This led the government to adopt the official attitude that it did not have any such tapes at all. This did not prevent wide and continuing reports in the Japanese press that the government did indeed have such tapes. Privately, Japanese intelligence officials admitted that they had the tapes but that it would be too compromising to security to release them.[38]

As one looks back at the affair of the ground tapes one cannot but be struck by the extraordinarily incurious attitude of the American press. The President had stated quite bluntly that the US did not have the ground tapes. But it was tolerably clear that the Japanese did; and if the Japanese did, so did the US. The possession of such tapes almost certainly bespoke the presence of airborne ELINT platforms in the vicinity of the disaster, which implied real-time monitoring, which in turn implied an ability to warn 007 had the US wished. The trail was clearly marked, but no major paper followed it.

## The RC-135

Hand in hand with US dissimulation about the ground-to-air tapes went a marked effort to spread disinformation about the RC-135 whose path had crossed that of 007 just before it had ventured into Soviet airspace over Kamchatka. In the first place, as we have seen, the US said nothing at all about this plane until it seemed likely that the Russians were going to beat them to it.[39] The question then arose, how did the RC-135 just so happen to be in that place at that time? The US answer was that the meeting or near-meeting with 007 was just a coincidence of timing, and that the plane had been there to monitor a new Soviet missile, the PL-5, being launched towards the Kamchatka testing ground. Had there been such a test? Well, no, there hadn't. There was going to be one and then it got cancelled. At the last minute. Too late for the RC-135 to stop its mission. So it just happened to be there all the same, when 007 came wandering along, off course. Two coincidences on the same night. The damnedest thing.

At first, however, this suggestion of an abortive Soviet missile test came from purely off-the-record leaks. The press was naturally curious. The *New York Times*[40] contacted 'intelligence officials' about the capabilities of the RC-135. These sources confirmed that the plane's sophisticated ELINT capabilities meant that it could 'provide access to certain Soviet military activity that cannot be obtained by satellites or high-flying reconnaissance planes like the U-2 or the SR-71'. In particular, an RC-135 at its normal ceiling of 35,000 feet could monitor 'air-defence systems on the ground' with great clarity at a range of 150 miles; indeed, when conditions were right it could monitor radio, radar and microwave communications at ranges up to 1000 miles. Because of this emphasis on the monitoring of Soviet ground-and-air-defence communications systems, the typical RC-135 carried not merely a USAF flight crew but also a number of NSA specialists, particularly techni-cians and translators. (Sampson and Bittorf confirmed from their sources that translators were part of a typical RC-135's total complement of around 25.[41])

What, though, of the specific RC-135 which had been cruising off Kam-chatka on the night of 31 August? The intelligence officials said they could give no details other than that the plane had been based in Alaska and had been 'round-tripping' to Shemya on a mission which took it 'over the northern Pacific'. There was no mention of a missile test – but all the emphasis was on the RC-135's suitability for quite different tasks. And it sounded rather as if the plane had taken off from mainland Alaska and flown down to Shemya.

Next day the *Washington Post*[42] contacted its own sources within the USAF. These sources confirmed that a tight secrecy lid had been clamped on the whole question of the RC-135's flight, but that it was known that it 'was recording Soviet voice and electronic communications'. This fitted with the RC-135's general capabilities, which were to track the Soviet 'electronic order of battle, which includes how radar stations react to intruders, and forward air defences, such as how many fighters have moved to what bases and when'. But what about the leaked reports that it was there to monitor the telemetry (i.e. coded electronic impulses emitted by a missile in flight) of a PL-5 test? The *Post*'s sources thought this pretty unlikely: 'The RC-135 . . . was most likely involved only tangentially in gathering missile data. More specialised intelligence-gathering, including that by planes flying out of Shemya Air Force Base . . . focuses on missile activity.' This would make sense, after all, Shemya being only some 320 miles from Kamchatka – a plane could cruise for hours off the Soviet coast from that base. Well then, where had the RC-135 come from? From the 6th wing of the US Strategic Air Command based at Eielson Air Force Base, 26 miles southeast of Fairbanks, Alaska.

In one sense, this was not very surprising news. All RC-135s from SAC are part of the 55th Strategic Reconnaissance Wing on Offut Air Force Base (Nebraska), but there are also three permanent RC-135 detachments elsewhere: at Mildenhall (England), at Kadena (Okinawa, Japan) – and at Eielson.[43] Those stationed at Eielson form the 24th Reconnaissance Squadron (part of the SAC 6th Wing).

Typically, such planes carry SLAR – Sideways-Looking Airborne Radar, placed like whiskers along both sides of the front fuselage. The Eielson RC-135s fly over the Bering Sea, along Kamchatka, the Kuriles and Sakhalin, finally landing at Shemya, spying on Soviet electronic communications and radars as they go. After refuelling at Shemya they round-trip back to Eielson. It is a long trip. The direct route from Shemya to Eielson alone is 1564 miles – but the RC-135 will typically fly at least that far again as it diverges from that direct path to hug the Soviet coastline and go far beyond Shemya to Sakhalin. (The RC-135 has a mission radius of 3450 miles, so it can cope with these long patrols.) Such lengthy missions are ideal for the RC-135's principal task – monitoring Soviet radar and communications along a vast stretch of the Soviet coastline.

The significance of this was not widely grasped. Marshal Ogarkov insisted that the RC-135 had taken off from Shemya, rendezvoused with 007 as part of a figure-of-eight flight pattern, and finally flown off towards mainland Alaska – that is, round-tripping back towards Eielson. The US, on the other hand, insisted that the plane had both taken off from and then returned to Shemya. What the *Post*'s and *Times*'s sources were saying was not incompatible with the missile-monitoring story, and some RC-135s have been modified to play telemetry intelligence (TELINT) roles. But on the whole their information leaned far more towards the Ogarkov rather than the US version. That is, most RC-135s were not well suited to monitor missile tests – but were ideally suited to deal with just the situation which the 007 incursion created, and the plane probably was round-tripping back to Eielson, just as the Russians claimed. Such round-tripping was also not very compatible with a missile-monitoring role – far better to use a Shemya-based plane with greater mission endurance. To hang in the air at slow speeds near a missile test ground the slower-moving P-3C Orion, with its phenomenal sixteen-hour mission endurance, would probably have been ideal.

The fact that the RC-135 carries translators was also of great significance, for that would mean that the planes were equipped for the real-time translation of Soviet communications, news of which could be flashed back to NSA headquarters at Fort Meade. With such capabilities the RC-135 would have been bound to know what exactly was going on during the 007 incursion – at the time that it was happening. At the least, this implied a capability to warn 007 it was off course – one that was not used. Just how such a capability might work had, after all, been perfectly illustrated in September 1980 when an RC-135, monitoring Libyan radar and communications, eavesdropped on a ground controller ordering up MIG-23s to shoot down the RC-135. The RC-135, thanks to its (Arabic) translators, knew immediately what was up and fled to safety.[44] Given the nature of its work, the presence of such translators on board is indispensable.

As if alarmed by these stories in the *Post* and *Times* – although the press did not grasp their full potential significance – the Reagan Administration immediately began to spread a very different account of the RC-135's capabilities and its presence near Kamchatka. (This was, in fact, the first time any administration had ever volunteered details about the operational mission of any electronic surveillance plane.) Officials now averred (though still not for attribution) that the RC-135 had indeed been on a mission to monitor a missile test; that it was based at Shemya, not at Eielson; and that it had not been round-tripping.

The same officials denied that the 135 had overheard either Soviet ground transmissions or 007's transmissions to its ground controllers. RC-135s, they said, 'rarely' listened to wavelengths used by commercial airliners and anyway its listening devices would have been tuned to missile communications, not anything else. In any case, they added, a RC-135's crew rarely had a knowledge of Russian and merely taped what they heard for later decipherment.[45] The picture now given of the RC-135 was of a passive intercept platform, able to perform only one task at a time, and unaware even that 007 had been in its close vicinity. In the days that followed, Administration spokesmen energetically took up the theme that the RC-135 had been on station purely to monitor a missile test. Interestingly, this explanation had not been officially offered in the original Presidential briefing on the RC-135 but only began to appear as a suggestion in later briefings.

Then on 8 September the ultraconservative columnist, William Safire, who has good sources on the wilder right-wing fringes of the Pentagon and the Administration, gave a fuller account: the RC-135 had been there to monitor a PL-5 missile test, but 007's incursion had caused the USSR to call the test off, and this was why the 135 had then flown off to Shemya.[46] Three days later this was officially confirmed as the Administration's line on the matter.[47]

There is little doubt that most of what the Administration and its spokesmen had to say about the RC-135 was straightforward disinformation. Even after the Administration came out with its extraordinary picture of the RC-135 as a single-purpose and almost blind aircraft, the *New York Times* was able to find military sources willing to admit that the RC-135 would quite certainly have known 007 was in its vicinity and off course, for as a matter of basic aerial safety it would have 'painted' it with its radar net.[48]

Secondly, there are oddities about the PL-5 missile test which the Administration said they had expected on August 31. On 3 September the Russians did launch their new SS-X-24 into the Kamchatka test ground from its launch pad at Plesetsk. This was, presumably, the PL-5 (PL-5 simply means the fifth firing in a series from Plesetsk). But the suggestion that this missile test had been expected four days earlier – made only after 3 September – was at first informally leaked as if testing the waters, and then only when it seemed possible the Russians were about to surface the fact of the RC-135's presence on their own. The four day delay seems rather long too. There never has been independent confirmation that a test was expected on 31 August. Suspicion lingers that the whole missile-monitoring explanation for the RC-135's presence was a blind – particularly since the USAF itself had originally denied any such explanation of the 135's mission, and given a mission description and trajectory for the RC-135 which was wholly incompatible with such a notion.

The RC-135, it should be pointed out, is a considerable electronic wonder. The Boeing 707 (of which it is the military variant) carries up to 189 passengers and 45 tons of cargo. In the RC-135 all this capacity has been converted to vast banks of electronic gadgetry of every kind. It has gone through many variants – James Bamford, the intelligence writer, talks of the RC-135(U), for example, as 'so crammed with sophisticated eavesdropping equipment that special sensors and antennas cover almost its entire airframe'.[50] It was always very unlikely that the Administration's cover story on the RC-135 would stand muster, but it was hardly to be expected that it would be exposed by two veteran RC-135 pilots who had flown missions over the same East Asian theatre. This was now exactly what happened.

The two pilots, Tom Bernard and Edward Eskelson (who had been based at Okinawa, Japan), published a furious article in the *Denver Post*[51] accusing the Reagan Administration of 'a major effort ... to bewilder the public concerning the capabilities of the US Air Force RC-135 and, more important-ly, the National Security Agency'. The view of the RC-135 as merely a passive intercept platform for monitoring missile tests was, they said, ludicrous. On the contrary, the plane had a number of capabilities which 'we view as being offensive in nature' – every plane carrying equipment to jam enemy radar and radio, for example. The notion that an RC-135 did not make real-time analyses of data was, they wrote, equally fantastic. An on-board communica-tions system 'permits instantaneous reporting of tactical intelligence to the highest levels of government, including the president, from any location in the world'. Indeed, any really urgent RC-135 message 'is required to be in the president's hands no more than 10 minutes after the time of transmission' from any point in the world. Moreover, Bernard and Eskelson emphasised, the RC-135 had multiple and extremely extensive capabilities – it could receive and transmit 'over an extremely broad range of frequencies, including those used by other aircraft, both civilian and military, ships, ground stations and air controllers'. During the Vietnam War, they added, RC-135s had been able to warn US bombers whenever they were picked up by North Vietnamese radars, thus enabling them to take advance evasive action against SAM missiles and interceptors sent up against them. (In the case of 007 this would have meant not only that the RC-135 would have been aware of 007's presence close by, but would have been able to warn it over civilian frequencies, and even to tell it about Soviet radar, ground communications and interceptor activity directed against it, or to jam those radars and radio communications if it wished to.) And the RC-135 would certainly have been aware of such Soviet activity even if the plane's primary mission had lain elsewhere, for the RC-135 had an internal warning system which monitored all the tactical air activity and air-defence radars of a potential antagonist. This enabled the RC-135 crew to make instantaneous detection of any 'hostile activity' directed against itself or any friendly plane in the vicinity.

Finally, Bernard and Eskelson dismissed as simply 'unbelievable' Reagan's claim that the RC-135, having been in 007's close vicinity as it headed into Soviet airspace, would simply have flown off leaving 007 to its fate. The 135, they pointed out, flies figure eights on its missions and 'it is always relieved on its orbit by yet another RC-135 just prior to the conclusion of its mission'. (This tended, of course, to lend credence to the Soviet claims of other US intelligence planes being present in the general vicinity – including another RC-135.) Bernard and Eskelson concluded:

We believe that the entire sweep of events – from the time the Soviets first began tracking KAL flight 007, to 'confusing' it with the American reconnaissance aircraft, to the time of the shoot-down – was meticulously monitored and analysed simultaneously by US intelligence . . . There are serious questions in our minds as to not only what specific role did the capabilities of the RC-135 play in the eventual shooting down of the KAL airliner, but also why these capabilities were never utilised in an attempt to head off the tragedy.

No attempt to deny – or even confront – any of this was made by any Administration official; indeed, it would have been difficult to do so, for Bernard and Eskelson had had many years' experience of what they were talking about. And while the press gave wide mention to the Bernard and Eskelson article, there was a peculiar failure to face Administration spokesmen with the fact that these revelations had comprehensively undermined their own version of the RC-135's presence and capabilities. Instead, the Administration just kept repeating this version as if nothing had happened, made blanket and summary denials of the presence of any other US intercept platforms (planes, ships or satellites) in the area at the time of the tragedy, and clamped down a complete blackout on any further information relating to the RC-135.

Not until several weeks later did the *New York Times* return to the problem of why US surveillance capabilities had not been sufficient to allow 007 to be warned that it was off course. The official answer to this was that US military radar had only had the capacity to track 007 for the first 250 miles of its flight. Leslie H. Gelb, the *New York Times*[52] reporter on the story, found, however, that 'the former intelligence officials' he spoke to could not accept this version, pointing out that the US had over-the-horizon (OTH) and other radar capabilities which enabled it to track a plane anywhere in the world; that Japanese radars which feed into the US intelligence system would also have been tracking 007; and that the RC-135 was, even on the US version of events, easily close enough to 007 to warn it that it was off course. Moreover, while intelligence officials were now willing to admit that they had been aware of 'an unusual level' of USSR radar surveillance and the dispatch of interceptors an hour before the shoot-down (this must have been over Kamchatka), they specifically said this could have nothing to do with the RC-135 which had, reportedly, landed at Shemya by that time. If so, this could only mean that the US had been aware of such activity via other intercept platforms in the vicinity or by radar with OTH capability. Gelb found, however, that he could gain no official comment at all about the RC-135 and what it had seen or said to 007. He concluded by asking his intelligence sources, 'What is some of the information being withheld by the US?' The answer he received was stunning: 'Worldwide American radio and radar abilities; any communications between the RC-135 and KAL Flight 007, and between Flight 007 and the somewhat earlier [sic] KAL flight from Anchorage to Seoul, and communications between Soviet ground controllers and fighter planes.' Gelb's sources added that 'Based on what is known of Soviet radar ability, they were tracking the Korean plane almost from take-off' – a line which Administration officials strongly endorsed. In fact, of course, so had US military radars at King Salmon, Cape Newenham and Shemya – the King Salmon radar observed 007 14 miles off course by the time it left the Alaskan coast, though the official US line remained either that these radars had no idea that 007 was an airliner or that it was in any case none of their business to warn civilian craft that they were off course.

The blanket US denial that it had any other ELINT platforms operating further down 007's route could not be sustained. After a while, it was grudgingly conceded that in addition to the RC-135 the US had also had an Orion P-3C ELINT plane somewhere in the vicinity.[53] Later it was admitted that the ELINT ship, USS *Observation Island*, operating its Cobra Judy radar, had also been on station, and that at least one US observation satellite had been overhead.[54] Given Bernard and Eskelson's statement, it would probably be prudent to add at least one other RC-135 to this list, replacing the first one as it went off station. There was no denial that 007 would have been well within range of several of the giant US radars in Japan. Replying to questions as to how this vast battery of ELINT devices could possibly have failed to know what was going on, a State Department official – speaking a whole year later, on the first anniversary of the shoot-down – claimed, 'Our equipment is designed to track unidentified aircraft moving in our direction, not aircraft moving in their direction.'[55]

This statement is, of course, wholly incredible. A radar system which operates in one direction only is technically difficult to believe in and would be fairly useless if it existed. Presumably this would have to mean that when RC-135s fly in 'tickling' operations off the Soviet coast, they are invisible to US radar in the crucial period when they are flying towards the USSR, and only become visible as they veer away. The notion that the US could or would operate such a radar system is simply insulting.

## The Japanese radar tapes

As we have seen, the Japanese conceded that they had not revealed all they knew – only what was 'necessary and sufficient'. What in practice that meant was that they released a tape to the public of the Soviet fighters' conversations which ran from 17.56:58 GMT to 18.46:09 – and that they announced some of their findings based on the Wakkanai radar tape. They did not release the radar tape itself: instead ICAO and everybody else had to rely simply on what the Japanese reported about that tape. According to this disclosure the

Wakkanai radar picked up 007 at 18.12 and followed it until 18.29 when, according to the Japanese (though not the US) the plane disappeared from the screen. Great stress was laid on this radar tape at many points in the inquiry, but questions about it remain.

The first point is that, as the Japanese finally conceded,[56] 007 had not just been tracked by the Wakkanai radar but by two other Japanese ASDF radars at Abashiri and Nemuro, on the north coast of Hokkaido. The radar tape was actually a synthesised version, they said, of all three radar tapes, with the synthesis carried out at the SDF's Misawa Air Defence Control Command. At 18.12 the straight-line distances of these radars from 007 were 160, 220 and 270 nautical miles. Now these are really very small distances for such radars. The Japanese refuse to say anything about the range capabilities or even the heights of the three radars above sea level, in case that helped one to know their range. But it is known that the Japanese are second only to the US in the sophistication and power of their electronic detection technology – hardly a surprising fact when one considers the remarkable Japanese industrial and commercial progress in all the obvious related high-tech fields. Yet, according to the official Japanese version, even a high-security radar like the one at Wakkanai, tracking a plane 30,000 feet up, could only see it 160 nautical miles away. This is quite impossible to believe. It seems quite clear that the Japanese must have tracked 007 (and its pursuers) long before 18.12 – perhaps all the time that they were using their radio-intercept devices to record the Soviet pilots' conversations, perhaps even longer. Indeed, how could one have one form of radio-based device (to hear the Soviet pilots) with so much longer a range than another, similarly radio-based device (radar)? Without doubt, it is these earlier parts of the radar tape(s) which the Japanese regarded it as not 'necessary and sufficient' to report on.

It will be remembered that ICAO reported that they had been told by the Japanese that their radar had shown 007 making a shallower turn over Sakhalin than the Russians reported. If we were actually able to examine the Japanese radar tape, we would be able to see if that was indeed true. But if we had a radar tape which stretched back well before 18.12 we would also be able to verify if many other parts of 007's behaviour, as reported by the Russians, were true or not. We would be able to see whether 007 began its turn before Sakhalin, whether it was flying in a straight line before then, what its height was, and whether it was making any altitude or speed changes. As things stand, it is impossible to say whether the Russians are telling the truth about all these things. But, virtually certainly, the answers lie on the Japanese radar tapes – and these are not being released. All that we can say is that US and Japanese attempts to refute the Soviet version of 007's behaviour would be a great deal more impressive if they were not unwilling to release the data in their possession which could confirm or deny it. (Equally, of course, if the Russians want us to believe their version, they ought to publish their radar tapes, not just give us 'reports' on them.)

## 007's line of flight

A further oddity lies in the early US descriptions of 007's flight path. In the weeks following the shoot-down American newspapers repeatedly published maps (see map 8) showing 007 proceeding normally along route Romeo 20 until late in the flight, and then taking a path which barely skirted Kamchatka and Sakhalin. These maps were based on the repeated assertion of Administration officials that 007 had stayed on its right course until late in its flight. President Reagan himself gave this version official blessing by insisting on 007's 'straight-line course'.[57] Even when, on 5 September, the Administration published a map which admitted that 007 had made a turn over Sakhalin, the US continued to insist that 007 had remained on a correct track for

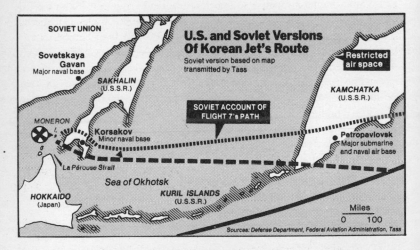

8  Classic disinformation tactics: the US version of the route taken by KAL 007, provided to the *New York Times* (6 September 1983) and the rest of the world's media by the US Defense Department and the Federal Aviation Administration. The map suggests that 007 was on its correct course until just before Kamchatka; that it only just skirted Kamchatka and Sakhalin; and that the configuration of its final turn over Sakhalin was quite different from that actually taken. Yet this map was provided many days after US radars had revealed the truth – which would, in this case, have largely confirmed the Soviet version of 007's route.

something like the first 1500 miles of its flight. Moreover, the turn over Sakhalin was shown as having been an arc in a southerly direction. All this, of course, contrasted sharply with the Soviet version of 007's flight path which showed 007 well off track long before it reached Kamchatka, had the plane crossing Kamchatka and Sakhalin far to the north of the US-provided flight path, and showed the final turn over Sakhalin as a northerly arc.

It is difficult to see how this official US version of the flight path could have been other than deliberate disinformation, for as the ICAO investigation was to confirm, it was the Soviet version which was correct in main essentials (ICAO agreed that 007 had made a northerly arc over Sakhalin, but suggested it might not have been quite as sharp as the Russians showed it).[58] Of crucial importance was the early radar track of 007 already well to the north of Bethel on passing this, the first of its waypoints – showing that 007 had indeed begun to deviate from its due course almost immediately after takeoff. The point is, of course, that even if the US Administration was really as slow as it said it was to process its radar readings, it must have known the full details of 007's flight path (including the crucial Bethel and Wakkanai readings and the position in which the RC-135 would have 'painted' 007 way off course before Kamchatka) by 2 September at the very latest. One can only conclude that the President and the other Administration officials either knew that they were disseminating a false picture of 007's flight path, or were being briefed by those who knew the truth but were concealing it even from the Administration's leader and top officials.


## Soviet attempts to contact 007

A key element in the US charge against the USSR was that the Soviet fighters had made no serious attempt to warn 007 before the shoot-down. In making this charge US spokesmen – notably President Reagan and Mrs Kirkpatrick – made a number of allegations, all of which on further examination turned out to be untrue:

i.  Among the rest of us there is one protective measure, an international radio wavelength on which pilots can communicate with planes of other nations if they are in trouble or lost. Soviet planes are not so equipped because that would make it easier for pilots who want to defect. (President Reagan, 5 September.)[59]

The wavelength referred to by the President was the standard 121.5 MHZ distress frequency – which the Russians claimed to have used both from its ground stations and fighters. In fact, Major-General George Keegan, the former head of USAF Intelligence, immediately stated that both types of

Soviet fighters used in the interception – MIG-23s and SU-15s – did carry 121.5 MHZ transmitters.[60] Soviet officials added that the SU-15 carried equipment which, when switched on (as it was, they claimed, in this case), automatically emits internationally recognisable signals on the 121.5 MHZ band.[61]

ii. Contrary to Soviet statements, the pilot makes no mention of firing any warning shots. (Mrs Kirkpatrick at the UN, 6 September.)[62]

As we have seen, warning shots were fired, but this emerged only after the version of the tape transcript provided by Mrs Kirkpatrick had been corrected.

iii. Contrary to Soviet statements, there is no indication whatsoever that the interceptor pilot made any attempt either to communicate with the airliner, or to signal it to land. (Mrs Kirkpatrick.)

Again, this rested on the faulty translation of the tape transcript provided by Mrs Kirkpatrick. The corrected version later showed that not only did the Soviet pilot fire warning shots but also said, on another occasion, 'The target does not respond to an enquiry.'

iv. The only activity bearing on the identity of the aircraft was a statement by the pilot of the attacking interceptor that 'the target isn't responding to IFF' (Identification Friend or Foe, a purely military identification system). But, of course, the Korean airliner could not have responded to IFF, because commercial aircraft are not equipped to do so. (Mrs Kirkpatrick.)

This statement was untrue on several different counts. First, the tape transcript was wrong: the actual tape makes no mention of IFF at any point. Astonishingly, the sentence 'The target does not respond to an enquiry' was mistranslated as a reference to IFF. By the same token, an enquiry as to identity *was* made. And finally, KAL 007 was equipped with IFF anyway. This emerged from a talk to the Tokyo Foreign Correspondents' Club given by General Goro Takeda, the recently retired head of the Japanese Air Self-Defence Force (and former chairman of the Japanese Joint Chiefs of Staff) on 8 September 1983.[63] Certainly, it would not have been more than ordinary prudence to equip planes flying Romeo 20 – so close to such sensitive airspace – with IFF.

It is impossible not to suspect that these various untruths were part of a deliberate disinformation strategy by the Reagan Administration. It is quite possible that neither President Reagan nor Mrs Kirkpatrick knew that they were telling untruths. But in that case those who briefed them or handed them tape transcripts so systematically 'mistranslated' to favour the US case at every turn, must have known what they were doing – and must have been taking the political risk of offending the US President and UN Representative when these untruths were revealed. After all, as the BBC news programme, *Panorama*, put it, Mrs Kirkpatrick was using 'material which would be in breach of civil law in Britain if she were selling soap powder on television ads'.[64] Similarly, if General Keegan, though in retirement, knew that such ancient fighter types as the MIG-23 and SU-15 were equipped with 121.5 MHZ radio, those in the Pentagon or CIA who briefed the President and Mrs Kirkpatrick to say the opposite must have known these were lies. But the fact was, of course, that Administration spokesmen have not been overscrupulous about using any information, however dubious, to attack the USSR, and there is no doubt that the impact made by the original Reagan–Kirkpatrick allegations was far greater than the subsequent revisions to their case, which generally received minimal publicity. In an Administration hyperconscious of presentational impact, that alone would probably have justified the use of such faulty material.

Finally, it is worth noting that the first report from US intelligence sources was that the Russians *had* succeeded in making contact with 007, at least to a point where 007 had been aware of its interception. Under the headline, 'Korean Jet Signalled Russians, US Says', the *New York Times* reporter, Philip Taubman, based his report[65] on conversations with 'senior American intelligence officials' after NSA analysts had 'spent two days and nights' examining not just the tapes of the Soviet fighters, but other fragments of Soviet communications at their disposal. According to these officials there was no evidence of radio contact between the Russians and 007, but 'Soviet communications include conversations that indicate that the Korean plane either rocked its wings, flashed its navigational lights or took some other form of action to show that it knew it was in trouble . . . it is apparent that the Korean crew realised that they were being intercepted'. As Taubman commented, this report 'raised more questions than it answered' for 'The officials could not explain why the Korean crew did not notify Japanese authorities they were being tracked by Soviet planes.' Indeed, it was difficult to see how any explanation other than a deliberate deception of their ground controllers by 007's pilots could explain the position. The implications were clearly explosive.

Oddly, this report was never again mentioned, explained or even explicitly retracted. Certainly the tapes, in their published version, provided no evidence for such an interpretation – but then there were many faults in that published version and Taubman's sources clearly had access to material beyond just the tapes. It is difficult to believe that Taubman's sources were simply in error – two days and nights of intensive analysis should have made that impossible. At the least, it seems clear that in the early days after the tragedy by no means all of the US intelligence community were toeing what quickly became the Administration line on the matter: indeed, the day after Taubman's report the *New York Times* carried another story citing 'US intelligence analysts' saying that they could not rule out the possibility that 007 had overflown Soviet territory 'intentionally'.[66] Immediately thereafter, however, both President Reagan and Mrs Kirkpatrick came thundering out with the Administration's line and leaks such as these from the intelligence community abruptly stopped.

## Did the Russians know they were shooting down an airliner?

In the immediate aftermath of the tragedy, the Reagan Administration insisted strongly that the Russians must have known that they were shooting down an airliner – indeed, several Administration spokesmen, including the President, suggested that the airliner might even have been in international airspace when it was shot down, thus compounding the crime.

The possibility that 007 might have been confused with a military RC-135 did not emerge until the presence of an RC-135 near 007 off Kamchatka was revealed to the Congressional briefing on 4 September. The House Majority Leader, Representative Jim Wright, immediately asked whether confusion with the 135 had not been possible but was emphatically told by both the Defence Secretary, Caspar Weinberger, and the Chairman of the Joint Chiefs of Staff, General John W. Vessey, that such a confusion had been impossible because the Soviet pilot had approached to within two kilometres of 007.[67] Wright did, nonetheless, report that on the tapes he had heard the Russians had referred to 007 as an RC-135 at one stage. This interpretation was hurriedly denied by Larry Speakes, the White House spokesman: Congressman Wright had, he said, been mistaken in what he thought he heard.[68] The White House seemed, indeed, very concerned to squash any notion that the Russians could have been confused about 007's identity. After the Congressional briefing, Senator Howard Baker, the Republican Majority Leader, was given 'additional information' which, his aides said, showed there could have been no possible confusion between 007 and the 135: the Russians had assigned different numbers to them and had tracked their separate courses.[69]

None of this was really conclusive and almost immediately a senior Administration official effectively admitted that Congressman Wright had been correct and Larry Speakes wrong: 'The Soviets tracked the Korean plane and first misidentified it as an RC-135. It went over their territory . . . Then they changed their identification of it to "unidentified".[70] This admission was then confirmed by an official White House statement.[71] The possibility thus clearly existed that not only had the Russians originally misidentified the plane – and never managed to identify it positively – but that they might have thought it was another RC-135.

This ambiguous position did not sit at all well with the Administration's clear wish to maximise the Russians' culpability and the next day President Reagan attempted to sweep all such doubts aside. 'There was no way,' he averred, 'a pilot could mistake this for anything other than an airliner . . . it was a clear night with a half-moon . . . It flew in a straight line at 30–35,000 feet. Only civilian airliners fly in such a fashion.'[72] This latter point was taken up by other Administration officials, who argued that 007 had flown with lights on at a steady 32,000 feet while RC-135s tended to make altitude changes, to fly at higher altitudes and to show no lights.[73] Finally, of course, it was argued that confusion between a 747 airliner and an RC-135 was almost impossible because a 747 was so much bigger and also had a telltale hump.

This case crumbled on closer examination; the White House must have known that substantial parts of its accusations were based on untruths. Thus Major Kasmin's SU-15 did not approach 'within 2 km' of 007: Kasmin never reported getting closer than two kilometres. Secondly, versions of the RC-135 do exist with much the same hump configuration as a 747.[74] The issue of what lights, if any, 007 was showing was never conclusively resolved one way or another; in any case both the Orion P-3C surveillance plane (used both by the Japanese and the USAF) and the large aerial tankers used by the USAF all carry the same strobe lighting as did 007.[75]

More remarkable still were the statements made by President Reagan that it was a clear night, that 007 flew a straight line and maintained a steady altitude. Every single one of these statements was untrue and the President, if he did not know the truth, certainly had the means by which he could have known it. As we have seen, 007 did not fly a straight line – and US radar readings showing its turns were available long before the President made his claim. Secondly, 007 did not by any means fly at a steady height but, as we have seen, made a number of altitude alterations and actually deceived Narita ground control to do so.[76] This too must have been well known to US intelligence before the President made his claim. And finally, it was not 'a clear night with a half-moon'; indeed, TASS's description of its being 'the height of night in conditions of bad visibility' was a great deal nearer the truth. The ICAO report made no bones about this. 'There was extensive coverage of low, medium and high level clouds over southern Kamchatka' while over southern Sakhalin there was 'a condition of mostly overcast low cloud with scattered medium and high clouds . . . The moon was in the last quarter with approximately 45 per cent of the disc illuminated.' Both Sakhalin and Kamchatka were in darkness, with sunrise over Sakhalin due more than one and three-quarter hours after the shoot-down took place. The adverse winds were sending the clouds scudding towards 007 and its pursuers at between 40 and 65 knots.[77] It is difficult to believe that this meteorological information was unavailable to President Reagan.

Reviewing these conditions, General Goro Takeda, the former head of the Japanese Air Self-Defence Force (and chairman of the Japanese Joint Chiefs of Staff), gave an altogether different picture from that provided by President Reagan:

. . . it was difficult for the Soviets to tell the kind of aircraft or where it had come from. I checked on how light it was at that altitude on the day of the tragedy. The moon was in the 23rd day of its phase, and sunrise was at 4.52 am [local time]. The incident occurred at about 3.25 am, more than an hour and a half before sunrise. Allowing 20 minutes for an earlier sunrise at that latitude and altitude, it would still have been dark. Self-Defence Force pilots concur that at that hour there is only a faint glow on the horizon. [The Soviet pilot] could tell that it was a large aircraft and may have seen its four engines. But in the darkness, he could not have discerned the craft's silhouette, much less its insignia. I believe the Russians were telling the truth when they said they did not know what kind of plane they were tracking . . . The only sure method of identification is to get within 300 feet of a suspect craft and note the number of windows. All the Soviets probably knew was that the plane was not one of theirs and that it was large, but not whether it was civilian or military.[78]

Moreover, although General Takeda assumed throughout that 007 was showing all the requisite lights, he dismissed the idea that the Soviet pilot would have seen its hump – to do this, he said, the fighter would have had to come with 1000 feet of the airliner and would have to have been either above or in front of it.[79] It soon emerged that the fighter had consistently remained below and behind 007 – and, of course, had never come closer than 6500 feet.[80]

Given all of this, it was fairly remarkable that the notion that the Russians had known they were shooting down an airliner should ever have gained such wide currency. But in fact it was only on 7 October – five weeks after the shoot-down – that the *New York Times* revealed that US intelligence analysts did now concede that the Russians had not realised they were shooting down an airliner. What had happened, intelligence experts told the paper, was that a Soviet radar operator had told the Kamchatka command that he had picked up an RC-135 as 007 first entered Soviet airspace. No Soviet interceptor had got closer than 20 miles away from 007 over Kamchatka, but later radar operators had reported the plane as 'unidentified' and as 'an intruder'. Finally, Soviet SAM batteries had been ordered (in vain) to shoot at 007 in order to stop 'the RC-135'. 'As a result of a review of the evidence intelligence experts said they believed that the decision to shoot down the 747 was all but made once Soviet radar operators misidentified the jetliner as an RC-135 when it first entered Soviet airspace two hours before it was shot down.' The fact that Soviet fighters had always remained below the aircraft had been a contributory factor, but what had perhaps been most important was that 'the initial identification of the jetliner as a military reconnaissance aircraft became fixed in the minds of Soviet air defence officials and was strengthened after Soviet interceptors were unable to locate the plane for two hours'.[81]

The *New York Times* report was a bombshell: it made nonsense of the President's statement that 'There was no way a pilot could mistake this for anything other than a civilian airliner', and Mrs Kirkpatrick's equally emphatic claim that the tape transcripts had proved that 'the Soviets decided to shoot down a civilian airliner'. Moreover, the information on which this new intelligence assessment was based had become known to US intelligence 'in the days after the downing' of 007 and the fact that the Soviet fighters had stayed below 007 had been known during 'the week of September 12'. The whole assessment had been passed to the White House 'about two weeks after the attack'.[82] And yet in the three weeks which had elapsed between then and the *New York Times* revelation neither the President nor Mrs Kirkpatrick had made any attempt to qualify their original accusations – and had, indeed, continued to speak as if they still fully believed them.

The White House never did come clean over this. Questioned by reporters, the State Department spokesman, Alan Romberg, when pressed as to whether the Administration had not alleged that the Russians had known they were shooting down an airliner, replied, 'How could we possibly know for sure? We've never said we did.'[83] Mr Romberg's statement is so remarkable that it ranks alongside Larry Speakes' famous attempt to dismiss questions: 'What's history is history, be it be fact or fiction.'[84] Worse was to come. On 13 October William Pfaff, a columnist for the *International Herald Tribune*, wrote an article criticising the Administration for its failure to face up to the implications of the CIA disclosure of Soviet misidentification of 007. The only comment this drew from the Administration was one from USIA which said that Pfaff's column 'must delight Soviet propagandists'.[85]

Thereafter, although Administration spokesmen were willing to admit in off-the-record sessions that the Russians had misidentified 007 as an

RC-135, there was no further official comment. It was only on the first anniversary of the shoot-down that an official State Department briefing confirmed that the US now acknowledged that 007 had been shot down in error, in the belief that it was on a surveillance mission.[86]

## 'The Russians do this sort of thing all the time'

Finally, some mention should be made of the repeated Administration accusation that the Russians had no ground for complaint even if 007 *had* been spying, because the Russians themselves did this sort of thing all the time. Again, President Reagan himself was the most explicit. Broadcasting over VOA to the USSR he alleged: 'Your airline, Aeroflot, has violated sensitive US airspace scores of times.'[87]

Now in one sense this was fair enough. Aeroflot is organised as almost an integral part of the Soviet military establishment and it seems tolerably clear that both the superpowers (and some of the lesser ones too) have, over the years, taken frequent opportunities for aerial espionage – the CIA has even admitted to the use of civilian airliners for espionage over East Germany,[88] and the prodigious record of Air America – once the world's largest airline – in covert operations of every sort has also been documented.[89] Russian capabilities in this direction have always lagged far behind those of the US, but there is no reason to doubt that they have made full use of what they have had.

On another level, though, President Reagan's accusations – and the host of similar accusations made by Administration spokesmen – were wide of the mark, for the record of Soviet aerial espionage over the US is decidedly thin. Typically, the Reagan Administration made much of the fact that two separate Aeroflot flights on 8 November 1981 had overflown the Trident submarine base at New London, Connecticut, and the Pease (SAC) Air Force Base in New Hampshire – but failed to mention that Aeroflot had actually obtained advance US permission for both flights. The Russians had filed flight plans asking to make deviations from their normal routes which would take them over these sensitive facilities and the Federal Aviation Administration – then busy breaking the air controllers' strike with thousands of inexperienced non-union workers – had OKed them. The State Department had belatedly discovered the flights, furiously accused the Russians of 'intentional deviations', and suspended Aeroflot's Moscow–Washington service for a week in reprisal. A reprisal against the FAA might, perhaps, have been easier to understand.[90]

This somewhat comic-opera incident apart, there had been no recent opportunity at all for Soviet aerial espionage over the US, since President

Reagan had suspended all Aeroflot flights to the US in January 1982 in response to the Jaruzelski coup in Poland. The only recent Soviet intrusions into US airspace (not even over the US itself) were the seventy or so occasions each year when Tupelov Bear reconnaissance planes tested the Aerospace Defence Identification Zone (ADIZ) which extends 60–200 miles beyond the US coastline. These were generally regarded as 'fence-testing' exercises and the Soviet planes always veered away once US fighters were sent up. Finally, about twenty times a year Aeroflot planes on the Moscow–Havana route trespassed into the ADIZ outside Florida but their pilots normally resumed their correct course once radioed to do so. All these incursions were merely into the ADIZ, and there are no reports of any Soviet plane getting near the US coastline itself, let alone near to 'sensitive' facilities.

Despite this, the Reagan Administration strove to give the impression that Soviet civilian planes almost routinely made the same sort of intrusions over the US that KAL 007 had made over the USSR. At the 6 October hearing of the Senate Foreign Relations Committee's subcommittee on East Asian and Pacific Affairs, the subcommittee's chairman, Senator Frank H. Muskowski (Alaska), questioned Lieutenant-General Bruce K. Brown, Chief of the Alaskan Air Defense Command, about Soviet aerial incursions. Senator Muskowski related that he had been told by the State Department and Pentagon that 'the Soviets intrude continually into US airspace' and that 'in Alaska alone there have been nearly 90 interceptions of Soviet aircraft since January 1974'. Lieutenant-General Brown replied that this was quite wrong: there had certainly been many interceptions of Soviet planes, but these had occurred in international airspace. The only Soviet intrusions he knew of at all had been in Alaskan airspace (which extends as far as Shemya) – 'since 1964 we think they have done that seven times'.[91]

It is, perhaps, rather remarkable that both the State Department and the Pentagon should have been priming Senator Muskowski with untruths, but it is surely more remarkable that President Reagan himself should have alleged 'scores' of 'sensitive' violations. Not for the first time in the affair of KAL 007 one finds that the US President was not a wholly reliable witness.

# NINE

# Finding the Black Box?

The speculation concerning 007's flight and the many questions it left unanswered gave a very special urgency to the hunt to recover the plane's 'black box'. Actually the term 'black box' is misleading: there were two of them and they were painted orange, for purposes of better visibility. The cockpit voice recorder would contain all cockpit sounds and conversation (including radio communications) for the last 30 minutes of the flight, while the flight-data recorder would contain the last three hours of all signals from the plane, with data on airspeed, altitude, roll, pitch, flap position and so forth. Both boxes were installed above the left-hand rear door of the passenger cabin, just where the tail section rounds into the top of the fuselage. Both boxes were effectively indestructible: the flight-data recorder was thermally insulated and the cockpit recorder was protected by an armoured shield. Somewhere, at the bottom of the Sea of Japan, these boxes lay and, with them, the answers to all the key questions about the flight. (Following convention and for simplicity's sake, I have, in the account which follows, referred to the boxes as a single entity – 'the black box'.)

## A midair explosion?

As we have seen, the official US version (provided by George Shultz, the Secretary of State) of the 007 shoot-down was that the Wakkanai radar showed 007 disappearing below the radar net of 1000 feet at 18.38 GMT – 12 minutes after it had been hit by a Soviet missile.[1] One assumes this must have been the US radar at Wakkanai that Shultz was talking about, for the Japanese reported a quite different picture from their radar at Wakkanai. I have followed this State Department version in trying to set out the last moments of 007 – but it is of some importance to say that this version of events was quite hotly contested by the Japanese, who reported that their own radar showed 007 disappearing from the screen at 18.29 – just three minutes after it had been hit. The Japanese version suggested a dreadful midair explosion, followed by a vertical plunge at top speed into the depths. It would, of course, be perfectly simple to resolve this conflict if either or both the Japanese and US were willing to release their radar tapes – but neither was willing to do that.

One is bound to say that the balance of circumstantial evidence is overwhelmingly in favour of the Japanese version of events (in which case the lengthy agony of 007's passengers and crew depicted in Chapter One is, mercifully, inaccurate).

This was certainly the view taken by General Goro Takeda, the former head of the Japanese Air Self-Defence Force. Calling the 3.29 timing 'solid', he pointed out that 007 had had its IFF radio beam switched on. 'You can catch this beam on radar clearly. Therefore there is no possibility that the ASDF lost their plot,' he averred. Moreover, he pointed out that the Japanese radar had pinpointed the crash as being just north of Moneron Island, off the west coast of Sakhalin. It was here that not only the Japanese and American but also the Soviet search efforts were concentrated – suggesting that Soviet radar had shown the same crashpoint. Had 007 carried on flying for another nine minutes, as the US insisted, then, said Takeda, it would have crashed at least 45 miles further away.[2] Against this, of course, the US version had 007 descending in a series of spirals, so that it was possible that the final crash point was the same on both explanations: nonetheless, one has to agree with Takeda that the odds against such a coincidence would be very high.

But as the search brought up its grisly remnants, further evidence in favour of the Japanese version mounted. No single whole human body was retrieved – merely shattered torsos, thighs and other limbs, and some of these had glass and metal fragments embedded in them – bespeaking an explosion of enormous force. Experts at Boeing who examined fragments of the wreckage were aghast at the power of the explosion required to create such damage: the 747 is one of the world's strongest planes – 'a tough, tough airplane' – which has in the past survived bombs, lightning bolts, midair collisions, and engines and parts of wings breaking off.[3] Moreover, the wreckage that was found was spread over a wide area. It is also worth noting that when Air India 747 went down off the west of Ireland in June 1985, the victim of a powerful midair (bomb) explosion, the plane took just three minutes to crash into the sea – the same interval the Japanese observed for 007.[4]

The discrepancy between the US and Japanese accounts of the shoot-down is only one of a number of differences in the versions of events offered by the two countries. Thus the Japanese Self-Defence Agency (SDA) continued for some time to insist that the aircraft which had shot down 007 was a MIG-23, not an SU-15.[5] Early on, the White House also insisted it had been a MIG-23 – even while the Pentagon was saying it had been an SU-15.[6] The US soon settled (correctly) on an SU-15, but the SDA maintained its version. (This suggests that the US had different and superior intelligence to the Japanese.)

Then again, as we have seen, the US and Japanese versions of the Soviet fighters' tapes were not exactly the same. And while it took the CIA a long time to conclude that the Russians had shot down 007 without realising it was an airliner, Mr Nakasone warned the Japanese Cabinet that this might be the case on 9 September.[7] There were many other small discrepancies of this sort, though one gains the powerful impression of the Japanese version being forced gradually into line with the 'official' US version.

This was, indeed, what happened in the case of the shoot-down, with Mr Gotoda finally taking it upon himself to confirm that the Wakkanai radar did indeed show 007 disappearing at 18.38, not 18.29.[8] The SDA refused to comment either way on this, but no SDA official was ever willing to come forward and deny the version they had earlier – and quite emphatically – provided. One has the impression that Mr Gotoda was removing a potentially embarrassing discrepancy for essentially political reasons, and that the Japanese military never really agreed with him.

If the US was, for some reason, not telling the truth about this aspect of the shoot-down – and one must wonder – then one has the further mystery of why it should have wanted to, particularly since the 18.38 time throws up the extra mystery of why the Korean pilots did not use that extra 12 minutes to send out a Mayday distress call – or even, if the plane was still under their control, not attempt to limp home on one or two engines (a 747 will fly on only one engine).

This contradiction between the 18.29 and 18.38 versions of 007's final plunge was never really resolved. But one thing all parties quickly agreed: the search for the vital black box must concentrate on a small area north of Moneron Island.

## The search begins

Search and rescue operations were, as we have seen, held up for over five hours after the crash, thanks to the false report of 007's safe landing on Sakhalin and to the dispatch of the Japanese Maritime Safety Agency (MSA) ships and planes to the wrong place. When MSA craft eventually got to the right spot, they reported that two Russian ships and five planes were already searching in the same area, just outside Soviet territorial waters.[9] Within a few hours the MSA patrol boat, *Chitose*, had found an oil slick 100 yards wide 33 miles northwest of Moneron.[10] Within a day the search had been joined by ninety Japanese fishing boats, further MSA craft and increasing numbers of Soviet craft. Tension between this growing armada of vessels inevitably ran high, especially since the Russians were evidently quite determined to prevent any non-Soviet vessel from trespassing into Soviet waters. Given that

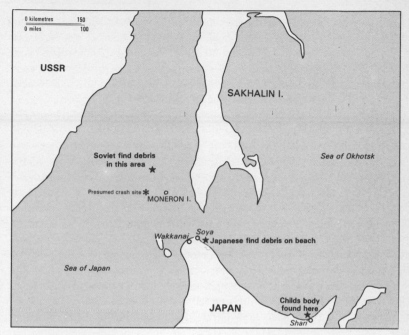

0 kilometres 150
0 miles 100

USSR

SAKHALIN I.

Sea of Okhotsk

Soviet find debris
in this area ★

Presumed crash site ✳ ○
MONERON I.

Wakkanai ○ Soya
○ ★ Japanese find debris on beach

Sea of Japan

JAPAN

Childs body
found here ★
Shari ○

9 The Search Operation after the shoot-down.

the central search site was just on the edge of the Soviet 12-mile territorial limit and that that limit lacked the visible definition of a land border, clashes and near collisions multiplied.

An extremely odd feature of the search operation was the tight security blackout clamped on the whole question of US involvement in it. Given the massive and permanent US naval presence in the area and the supreme political importance Washington had attached to the KAL affair, it was only to be expected that US vessels would play a leading role, and indeed the first report of the search mentioned 'several US Navy vessels' participating in it.[11] When, however, American journalists asked the US Embassy in Tokyo for details, officials refused to say anything at all about the nature of the US effort and referred all enquiries to Washington – which said nothing.[12] Similarly, early Japanese reports spoke of the deployment of several American 'advanced search and rescue aircraft'[13] in the search, but no further details could be gained. Thereafter the daily reports of the search relayed by the press (who relied principally on what the MSA told them – no journalists were allowed into the search area itself) omitted all mention of US ships or planes. It was only on the ninth day of the search that the *New York Times* mentioned that several US Navy vessels and also Orion P-3CS and HC-130 Hercules were taking part in the search.[14] No further details were given and for the next week the sparse press comment again mentioned only Japanese vessels involved in the search. It was only on 14 September that a Pentagon spokesman, Commander Fred Leeder, claimed that the US had actually had the first three ships on the scene of the crash – the frigate, USS *Badger*, the destroyer, USS *Eliot*, and a coastguard cutter, the USS *Munro*.[15] (It will be remembered that the USS *Badger* was the electronic-surveillance frigate which the Russians had shown as being stationed off Vladivostok at the time of the flight and which had, they alleged, played a key part in the electronic coordination of KAL 007's entire 'mission'.) Meanwhile, said Commander Leeder, they had been joined by the ocean-going tug, *Narragansett*, and would shortly be joined by another, *Conserver*. Commander Leeder spoke of the US as mounting a major and urgent recovery effort;[16] which, no doubt, it was – the oddity was that it had taken two weeks to make serious mention of it. There could not, after all, have been any real need for security precautions – with Soviet ships and planes ceaselessly in action around the American ships, it was absurd to think that the Russians had not been fully cognisant of the presence and identity of the US Navy craft from the first moment of their arrival. Moreover, the recovery operation was supposed to be a humanitarian effort in connection with a civilian tragedy, not an operation of any military significance.

Meanwhile, the State Department had not been slow to consolidate what was in fact the leading US role in the salvage operation, drawing up documents whereby South Korea designated the US and Japan as search and salvage agents. The aim was to make it illegal for the Russians to search and salvage 007. Provided the wreckage lay – as it was universally believed to do – in international waters, the US would now be legally entitled to use force against the Russians, if necessary, to prevent their retrieval of any part of the plane. Meanwhile the Russians maintained a large presence in the area, with between eighteen and fifty vessels in close proximity to the US–Japanese flotilla. Prevented from searching in international waters, the Russians set up their own salvage operation just inside their own territorial limit – an exercise the Americans viewed with derision – and shadowed the American ships ceaselessly.

As time went by, the Japanese role diminished considerably. Partly this was just because the US, of all the nations involved, had the only really sophisticated deep-sea retrieval capabilities: if anything was going to be found, it was certain that the Americans, not the Japanese, would do it. But the truth was that the tense skirmishing between the superpowers around Moneron was both alarming and a nuisance to the Japanese, and particularly to the city of Wakkanai, the inevitable hub of the search effort. Wakkanai depends utterly on the fishing industry – the city has no less than 151 fish-processing factories – and as a matter of life and death its fishermen need to fish unimpeded in Soviet territorial waters near Sakhalin. Soviet goodwill is thus vital to Wakkanai – and the big fishing interests have built a Japanese–Soviet Friendship Hall in the city centre. Wakkanai fishermen trespass into Soviet waters all the time but the Russians have normally treated such trespass in a flexible and casual way: Soviet fish inspectors routinely board Wakkanai boats and exact spot fines. These are happily paid by the fishermen – who then go on trespassing and 'poaching'. This, at least, was how it had all worked before. Now, however, the tension was beginning to tell: suddenly there were a lot more Soviet fish inspectors, they were levying far steeper fines, and the Wakkanai boats were getting pushed out of their traditional poaching grounds. In Wakkanai, the search operation for 007 had quickly become extremely unpopular.[17]

At the end of a fortnight's search a number of remnants of wreckage and several human limbs had been washed up on the northern shores of Hokkaido, and the Russians reported a number of similar finds, which they agreed to turn over to the Japanese authorities. Within the main search area itself, however, no finds at all were reported. Meanwhile, a number of American politicians had begun to warn the public not to trust any 'evidence' the Russians might find.

## 'The Russians will fake it'

The news that the Russians were picking up wreckage seems to have alarmed Washington conservatives. The conservative columnist, William Safire, basing himself on Pentagon and CIA sources, was the first to vent a new theory of Soviet duplicity, in a *New York Times* column of 8 September: 'The KGB's disinformation unit will now create and plant "proof" that the airliner was on a spying mission. We can expect Western electronic spying gear – perhaps an artfully recreated recording in a Boeing black box – to be dunked in salt water and then "recovered" from the real wreckage.'[18] The next day the refrain was picked up by the Defence Secretary, Caspar Weinberger:

You have to bear in mind the most worrisome thing the Soviets are doing right now is refusing any of the nations . . . the rights to enter the area where the plane was shot down. I think the reason they're doing that is because they are going to try to manufacture some sort of evidence and come up with some black box dripping with seaweed and claim that the Korean pilot was a spy or some nonsense like that.[19]

The most remarkable speech, however, was given by William Clark, the President's National Security Adviser and the man who, we have seen, was the central figure in the Administration's handling of the crisis when it broke. Clark was not a man given to public speaking and tended to avoid the press quite systematically – he had, indeed, been almost invisible since the early days after the shoot-down. Thus it was doubly striking that he should have chosen to make a speech to the Air Force Association in Washington on 14 September.

The absolute and incontrovertible fact is that KAL 007 was not on an intelligence-gathering mission of any kind. On the other hand, the Soviets and their surrogates do use passenger aircraft for espionage purposes and have overflown the US on spying missions . . . We believe they will take further initiatives to cover up. We must anticipate the Soviets will fabricate so-called 'newly discovered evidence' to prove the spy plane thesis.

But, added Clark, somewhat incongruously, perhaps some good might come out of the 007 tragedy, for its end result might be to bring the two superpowers closer together. It might, he said, even produce a new summit.[20]

These speeches had a peculiar ring. Although some members of the Administration, including the President, had sought to suggest that 007 might have been in international airspace when it was shot, Weinberger was now suggesting that it had been so deep into Soviet airspace that it had even come down inside Soviet territorial waters. Moreover, long before he spoke both the Japanese and the US Navy had pinpointed a crash site outside Soviet territorial waters. No sense could be made of this. More remarkably, of course, senior figures in the Administration were actively preparing public opinion for the retrieval of a black box which would suggest that 007 had been on an intelligence mission – and attempting to get them to discount any such evidence in advance. What this amounted to was the suggestion that the black box, if found, should not be believed unless it supported what the Administration had been saying. If one entertained the possibility that 007 *had* been on an intelligence mission, then it would follow that the Administration was hardly likely to come up with a black box which proved its own guilt – but would be deeply worried lest the other side find the box first. All one can say is that Weinberger, Clark *et al.* were behaving like the accused in a court case who, pre-emptively, attempt to deny the veracity of any evidence the prosecution might bring even before that evidence is produced.

To emphasise its point, on 16 September the State Department released a set of documents which, it said, were actually clever forgeries and part of a KGB disinformation campaign. (The documents purported to show that the US had connived with Israel over the invasion of Lebanon; that there was a close working relationship between the US and South African governments and that Mrs Kirkpatrick had received a gift from the South Africans; that the US and Italy had cooked up evidence attempting to link the Bulgarians to the plot to kill the Pope; and that the CIA had been intriguing to overthrow the Ghanaian government. It was a curious list, for there was reason to believe that at least some of these things were true.[21]) The State Department spokesman warned the press that they must expect the Russians to produce faked tapes or a bogus black box 'proving' that 007 had been on a spy mission. 'We're watching. It certainly would not be surprising for the Soviets to try something like this.'[22]

In fact the notion that the USSR might beat the US in finding the (real) black box was far-fetched: the US is by far the world leader in the technology of underwater retrieval. Indeed, its capabilities were such as to make it highly probable that it would find the vital box, and all but certain that it would find it before anyone else.

## US retrieval capabilities

It was with the launching of the first atomic-powered submarine, the USS *Nautilus*, in 1955 that the US fully grasped the potentially crucial significance of underwater detection and retrieval. The first step was the top-secret Project Caesar programme which had, by the early 1960s, eventuated in the 'Sea Spider', a gigantic underwater detection system.[23] The best known element of this is the SOSUS (Sound Surveillance System) – a worldwide grid of underwater hydrophones, arranged in line and vertical array. These sonic devices are so sensitive that they are capable of detecting not only the presence of objects on or under the water, but their direction, size and design. Augmenting these sonic devices are others which detect heat or specific parts of the electromagnetic spectrum. The whole network of such devices is connected back to a central computer, producing an instant and detailed picture of marine activity of every kind. Naturally, this system is clustered particularly thickly around the Soviet coastline, enabling the US to detect Soviet submarines almost immediately they have left port. It is known that such devices ring the Sea of Okhotsk[24] – where, undoubtedly, the US naval presence includes considerable submarine activity – and feed their information back to US Pacific headquarters on the island of Oahu. It seems entirely possible that 007's plunge into the Sea of Japan was picked up by this system – the crash of the huge plane, even in several pieces, would have created opportunities for the detection of sound, heat and electromagnetic phenomena. There is no doubt that the airliner would have crashed into the sea well within SOSUS range. Writing in 1983 one intelligence expert noted that 'SOSUS is certainly known to have reasonable sensitivity and was reported some years ago to be able to detect some of the noisier Soviet submarines at ranges of "several hundred kilometres"' – though the same expert hints that SOSUS ranges may well have been extended since then.[25] Once SOSUS had given an (instantaneous) position reading on the airliner crash site, the next step would have been to dispatch one of the many US ASW (Anti-Submarine Warfare) aircraft in the vicinity to drop sonobuoys at the site, relaying their information back up to the circling plane or helicopter.[26] This in turn could be complemented by the information collected at considerable ranges and depths by the use of OTH (Over-The-Horizon) back-scatter radar – which produces so great a volume of raw data that it is fed into a giant Illiac-4 computer for real-time analysis.[27] In case of rough weather, the US has also devised special Variable Depth Sonar (VDS).[28] Even this by no means exhausts the list of detection devices available to the US, but there is really no need to go on. Suffice it to say that all of these systems are devised to detect merely passive lumps of metal under the water (i.e. silent, hiding submarines), and the steady pulse of the pinger from the black box should have made detection extremely simple. Had the whole system been working anything like normally one would have expected 007's crash site to have been known instantly to within a very small radius; for OTH radar to have provided a cross-fix; and for ASW aircraft to have pinpointed both the wreck and the black box within an hour of the crash.

Thereafter the task of retrieval could be turned over to US naval craft. Here again, the US has developed quite awesome capabilities for deep-sea location and retrieval. A striking example of this technology is the USS *Mizar*, now in service for over twenty years.[29] The *Mizar* is equipped with every sort of high-tech detection device including the fascinating technique of acoustical holography. This system effectively translated sonar waves into light waves, and with the aid of laser technology can then translate this into three-dimensional pictures. So powerful is this technology that the *Mizar* can scan even the deepest ocean floor and, despite the utter blackness there, throw up clear three-dimensional TV pictures of all the objects on the bottom, sunken wrecks and all. The *Mizar* was used to locate the two lost US nuclear submarines, the USS *Thresher* (sunk in 1963, at a depth of 6000 feet) and the USS *Scorpion* (lost in 1968 at 12,000–14,000 feet), and also found the

'November' class Soviet nuclear submarine lost off Portugal in April 1970, as well as performing extensive mapping operations of the ocean bottom.[30] But the *Mizar*'s most famous coup came with the loss of a Soviet 'Golf' class submarine in 1968 in the North Pacific, and the mounting of the ultrasecret 'Project Jennifer' to recover the craft for the US. Even today the full details of Project Jennifer are not wholly revealed, but it is known that the *Mizar* located the submarine wreck at a depth of around 16,000 feet and that at least half of it was recovered by stealth[31] by the remarkable *Hughes Glomar Explorer*, which possessed not merely the same detection technology as the *Mizar*, but the ability to haul the 3000-ton submarine – code books, nuclear missiles and all – from a depth of more than three miles. All this, moreover, was performed with such secrecy that it was possible to do this under the noses of the watching Russians without their knowledge.

By the early 1970s the technology pioneered by the *Mizar* and Howard Hughes's *Glomar Explorer* had enabled the US to pull off a continuous series of retrieval coups. In one operation an American hydrogen bomb, which had fallen into the sea after a midair collision, was successfully located at 2500 feet and recovered.[32] In 1970 a Soviet aircraft which had crashed into the Sea of Japan was secretly located and the nuclear weapon it was carrying recovered by the US. In 1971 the electronic surveillance equipment from an American spy trawler was recovered and in 1972 a joint US–UK operation successfully found and recovered a Soviet plane from the bottom of the North Sea, relieving it of its electronic gear.[33] Without doubt only a tight security blanket prevents us from knowing of a number of similar operations in the period since then. Not the least notable feature of such operations has been the ability to effect retrieval in complete secrecy, despite Soviet surveillance. (This is necessary not merely for the obvious military reasons, but because the recovery or salvage of another nation's craft is strictly illegal. Project Jennifer was certainly a technological triumph – but it was also a clear infringement of international law.)

The significance of all this to the KAL 007 tragedy was that it seemed quite certain that the US had the capability to find the plane (even in pieces) and with it the black box. The Soviet capability was, by contrast, a stone-age affair. Most of the Soviet ships near the crash site were trawlers which literally fished for the wreckage by making line-abreast sweeps with their nets. The Russians also deployed a midget yellow submarine,[34] but this more truly belonged in a Beatles song than in a serious competition with the Americans. Quite quickly the Russians were reduced to bad-tempered spoiling tactics, harassing the American ships in their search, cutting sharply across them and sometimes producing near-collisions. Apart from a desire to discourage this

large US presence near their coast, it is difficult not to put such tactics down to
sheer frustration.

## The search heats up

It was hardly surprising, given US capabilities, that Commander Leeder, the
Pentagon spokesman, should have struck a highly optimistic note about the
search for the black box when he spoke to the press on 14 September. The
water in the search area, he pointed out, was only a few hundred feet deep[35]
and both the *Narragansett* and the *Conserver* carried sophisticated special
detection equipment. Moreover, both were equipped with robot submersible
drones which operated at depths up to 6000 feet. These drones carried lights,
television cameras and had the ability to lift objects of up to 350 pounds'
weight to the surface, or tie lines over heavier objects which could then be
hauled in by other craft.[36] There was no need for manned research submers-
ibles – the equipment already on site should easily be enough. Moreover, the
radio transmitter in the flight recorder – the 'pinger' – had water-operated
batteries and would send out signals for a steady thirty days after the crash.
The pinger could be picked up by detection equipment at ranges of 2000 to
4000 yards.[37] In addition to the two specialist tugs, of course, the search
would be able to rely on the (very considerable) detection capabilities of the
Navy vessels and the Orion P-3Cs, whose advanced submarine-hunting
technology would be highly germane to the task in hand.

Journalists were still not allowed anywhere near the actual search operation, but relied instead on what Pentagon officials in Washington were willing
to tell them and the occasional leaks percolating to the Japanese news
agencies from Japanese military sources. On 20 September the *Washington
Post* quoted 'informed sources' in Washington to the effect that the pinger
had indeed been picked up – and it was assumed that the Russians had heard
it too. 'There is one helluva race going on out there,' one official was quoted
as saying. 'American sources,' the *Post* continued, 'said there appeared to be
several large pieces of wreckage, and that they seemed to be strewn over a
wide area.'[38] Meanwhile, the *Post* noted, there appeared to be something of a
conflict between the Japanese and the US versions of the search site: while
earliest reports had suggested that the water there was only a few hundred
feet deep, the Japanese now put it as 600–900 feet, while the US put it at
900–1200 feet.[39]

The *Post* story prompted an official Pentagon briefing later that day.
Benjamin Welles, the Pentagon spokesman, said that US vessels had begun
picking up the pinger's signal 'beginning last weekend' (17–18 September);

that the box seemed to be international waters; and that on 19 September both the *Conserver* and the *Narragansett* had got 'a strong fix on the pinger for about an hour. Then the signal was lost. Later it was picked up steadily again for 20 minutes, then lost.' Welles, though now revising the estimate of the water's depth up to 2500 feet, claimed that 'We're quite certain that what we've got is what we're looking for.'[40] Welles talked of the search going on over a 3000-square-mile area, but Japanese sources spoke of an area of just nine square miles.[41] The US Navy did its best to play down these strong indications that they were on the point of finding the black box. A Navy spokesman, while admitting that the search ships had picked up what seemed to be the right radio signals several times a day for the last week, suggested that one could still not be certain that they were really from the recorders. Both recorders send signals on 37.5 kilohertz, while all the spokesman would say of the signals received was that they were within the 30–40-kilohertz range (a strange piece of coyness, this – it would be impossible not to know the frequency exactly). In fact Administration officials happily confirmed that the signals received had been precisely at 37.5 kilohertz, indicating positive identification.[42] Throughout the search this was to be the pattern, with Washington spokesmen admitting to information which those closer to the search seemed far less willing to reveal.

But the oddities in the situation went well beyond that. According to Welles (and the Navy spokesman, Lieutenant Commander Mark Ncuhart), the pinger had been picked up for several days – but the Administration had said nothing about it and the impression was clear that they would have carried on saying nothing but for the jolt of the *Post* story. Whence such secrecy? Secondly, it was really very remarkable to have lost contact with the pinger after it had been picked up by both specialist ships. They should have been able to pinpoint it exactly and produce TV images of it in well under an hour. And finally, it was absurd to be searching over a huge area like 3000 square miles if one had already located the black box to within a maximum of a few thousand yards at the very worst.

Welles's press conference was immediately followed by a statement by Rear Admiral Masayoshi Kato of the Japanese MSA that the US seemed to have located 'crucial portions' of 007's wreckage.[43] The result was an irresistible press rush to the search area – the first time reporters had been allowed near. There they found seven US ships – the *Narragansett*, the *Conserver*, the *Munro*, the *Badger*, a guided missile destroyer, the USS *Callaghan*, a supply ship, the USS *Wichita*, and a guided missile cruiser, the USS *Sterett*. Headquartered on the *Sterett* was the man in charge of the operation, Rear-Admiral William A. Cockell. Cockell was, however, curiously reticent. All he would say was that the search had been narrowed to an area of 350 square miles and that there was 'some reasonable prospect' of finding the black box. He refused absolutely to answer any questions at all about the pinger – where it was, how often it had been picked up, or whether it was still being heard. Cockell said, indeed, that the US search had only begun on 15 September. Reporters queried this somewhat incredulously but all Cockell would say was that 'preparation time was needed'. He refused all other comment. It seemed clear that a tight security blanket had been thrown over the whole ship, for when the *New York Times* reporter, Clyde Haberman, decided to seek out the opinions of others on board, he got nowhere. Approaching 'a senior Navy officer', Haberman asked him if the pinging continued and was still being detected. The only answer he could get was 'It could be.'[44] With such minimal enlightenment, the press departed, not to return.

Almost a week passed with no further news of any sort. Then on 26 September several Japanese news agencies reported that the US ships had definitively pinpointed the location of the black box in international waters just to the west of Moneron at a depth of 2500 feet.[45] For the last several days, the agencies reported, both the US and Russians had been concentrating their search on the same area of 15 square miles.[46] Reporters pressed the US Embassy in Tokyo for details but the press attaché, Carol Ludwig, denied that the US had found the box at all.[47] This was immediately contradicted by Japanese Foreign Ministry officials, who confirmed that the box had been pinpointed and that it could now be recovered at any time. The only reason for delay, they said, was that it had been agreed that officials of the International Civil Aviation Organisation (ICAO) and of the Japanese Transport Ministry and the MSA should be present on board when the box was actually hauled up.[48] There followed a direct Japanese government announcement that Japan had received an official request to assist in the retrieval of the black box[49] (i.e. not just the search for it, but its actual retrieval). The Cabinet Secretary, Mr Gotoda – reputedly the second most powerful man in Japan – confirmed all this but added that 'it is not known whether the US has already recovered the black box'. This was an extremely curious thing to say, for it suggested that Mr Gotoda believed that the US might have broken its agreement with Japan and ICAO and gone ahead with the retrieval of the black box on its own. Moreover, there was a clear hint that the Japanese government was not confident that it was being kept fully informed about the retrieval operation. This prompted a hurried announcement from the State Department in Washington that the US had neither found the black box nor was yet prepared to retrieve it.[50] Nonetheless, Japanese and ICAO officials were rushed out to the search site ready to participate in a retrieval operation. They were to spend three wholly fruitless days there.

For the day after Mr Gotoda's statement, the tone of excited optimism was suddenly turned right down. Mr Gotoda himself appeared to make an announcement effectively denying what he had said the day before. There had, he now said, been no official US request to Japan concerning the retrieval of the black box – and he now felt he could not say whether retrieval of the box was possible or not.[51] Mr Gotoda must have come under considerable pressure, one feels: he cannot have enjoyed having to eat his words so publicly and hurriedly.

Meanwhile, it was now clear that the official line had changed: every new announcement played down the possibilities of retrieval, mentioned the great difficulties in the way, and generally prepared opinion for a disappointment. Pentagon officials now averred that the signals earlier picked up from the pinger had been followed by the detection of only 'a few intermittent sounds'.[52] This had not enabled the US ships to pinpoint the black box. The search was complicated by the water's depth, which they now put at up to 5000 feet.[53] The whole operation had been set back by windy weather too, although, the officials conceded, the pinger had been picked up at repeated intervals through the last week. This all sounded very pessimistic and reporters pointed out that the pinger's batteries would fade out on about 30 September anyway – in only two days' time. That was not so serious, the officials said: the 15-square-mile area had been marked off with ocean-bed sonar buoys and it would be perfectly possible to carry on using sonar equipment to locate the plane and the black box even when the pinger was exhausted. '"There's no magic drop-dead date", a Pentagon official said.'[54] This was certainly a valid point: after all, in previous retrieval operations the US had succeeded in locating sunken submarines at far greater depths with no pinger to help them.

On 29 September the Japanese and ICAO officials returned to Japan from the search area. One of the MSA officials, Kazumi Mino, said that the American attitude was 'We don't know', but overall there was a feeling of considerable pessimism.[55] The officers in charge of the search had stressed their worry that the pinger might now be exhausted – and made no mention of the possibilities of further sonar detection. Mr Gotoda told a press conference that the search for the black box 'may take time', but promised that independent third-party officials would be present when and if the box was found.[56] This reassurance was made necessary by the growing tide of rumour in Japan that the US had actually found the black box and was keeping it to itself.

It is possible that feelings such as these lay behind the announcement by the MSA on 30 September that it was calling off its participation in the search for the black box forthwith.[57] Given what Mr Gotoda had said the day before about a continuing search and the earlier hopeful statements of there being 'no drop-dead date', the MSA announcement was a rather surprising volte-face. Certainly, the announcement was not welcome to the US, which immediately requested that the Japanese continue their participation in the search.[58] After a few days the Japanese gave way and two Japanese salvage boats were dispatched to rejoin the search,[59] which remained concentrated in a small area 30 miles north of Moneron.

Thereafter news of the search operation was extremely sparse. On 15 October the *Washington Post* reported that the 14-square-mile (sic) search area had now been almost wholly searched, but that Navy officials in the Pentagon were still confident that 'US sonar could find almost any piece of wreckage'. 'The search will continue until we find what we are looking for,' said the Pentagon spokesman, 'or the on-scene commander determines that further effort would be fruitless. With the current logistics lines we can keep units up there indefinitely.'[60] Two days later another Pentagon spokesman said that the search area had been rewidened to an area of 65 square miles. Later this became 150 square miles. Finally, on 26 October, the Pentagon announced that the whole of the enlarged area had now also been exhaustively searched and the situation looked just about hopeless. The officials now spoke of the operation being hampered by an underwater mountain range, bad weather and Soviet harassment.[61] Meanwhile, the remaining Russian ships had clustered in a tight knot at one particular spot (in international waters) and had hauled several pieces of debris, including one piece of metal, to the surface.[62] US officials now began to talk of the likelihood of the search having to be abandoned due to bad weather, and gloomily speculated that perhaps the plane was in smithereens.[63] On 6 November the US called off its search, having searched an area of 150 square miles, citing bad weather, and their example was followed on 9 November by the Japanese and on 10 November by the Russians. The Russians handed over several hundred items of wreckage to the Japanese, saying they had been found in the water or washed up on Moneron or Sakhalin. The items were mainly small pieces of aircraft wreckage – five oxygen cylinders, an engine cover, a piece of the tailplane – and personal effects (bags, shoes, spectacle cases and clothes). The grieving relatives of the plane's victims who travelled to Hokkaido to identify these items were left to grieve bitterly that so much effort had brought to light only these few pitiful objects.

## Was the Black Box found?

Ever since the abandonment of the search there have been recurrent rumours that the US did indeed find the black box and kept it to itself – and that much of the search was, in effect, a charade. As will be evident, there was certainly much about the search that is both mysterious and suspicious. One has, indeed, continually to remind oneself that this was supposed to be a search operation for an ordinary civilian airliner – yet it was never treated like that. If it had been, surely either or both the US and the Japanese would have been willing, in the normal, routine way, to release their radar tapes in order to clear up immediately the question of where the plane crashed? The US story, after all, is that it did not have real-time radar recordings and that they took time to process. While the 'no real-time' argument is clearly nonsense, from this point of view it doesn't matter: they admit they do have the tapes. Why not release them?

But, of course, the oddities go far beyond that. The tight security maintained throughout the search had no place in a search operation for an ordinary civilian airliner. The attempt to throw a security blanket over the presence and identity of the US ships involved in the search for weeks on end was also hard to explain. Why did leading members of the Reagan Administration repeatedly seek to warn the public not to pay any heed to the discovery of a black box which appeared to 'prove' a surveillance mission? Why did they give an account of the pinger's sonar range which was so dramatically at odds with that of Boeing's spokesman on the subject?[64] And, above all, given the fabulous resources of US undersea retrieval technology, should it not have been a relatively simple matter to find the remains of several hundred tons of aircraft? Given the US version of the crash – the gradual descent over 12 minutes – the plane had to be in one piece or several large pieces, after all. Each of 007's wings spanned over 80 feet and its fuselage was over 231 feet long. Yet at the end of over two months' search of a 150-square-mile area, the Pentagon claimed that the only metal object found was an old ship's cooking pot.[65]

This is clearly quite incredible. The early radar fix of the crash site – agreed by both the Japanese and US – indicated an area with a water depth of only 600 feet. Pinpointing of this site should have been instantaneously refined by the data available from SOSUS and the underwater heat and electromagnetic detectors, and within an hour or two the P-3Cs should have been able to confirm such findings with a considerable degree of accuracy. Thereafter one would have expected the absolute pinpointing of the two recorders to have been a relatively simple and quick task for the extremely sophisticated craft available to the US Navy. The notion that all this technical wizardry was unable even to locate a single piece of wreckage is a very tall order indeed.

Indeed, Pentagon sources had told the *Washington Post* as early as 19 September that 'several large pieces of wreckage' had been found. So where were they? And if the Russians, with their greatly inferior retrieval capabilities could find several hundred items of wreckage, how could the US claim to have found no single item at all? Sonar which can pick up metal objects as small as a cooking pot should have no difficulty with 80-foot wings.

Then again, the reports of the pinger being repeatedly picked up and then lost are simply absurd. Even on the US account, the pinger was heard for several periods of up to an hour. This would have given more than enough time to get a triangulated fix which would have pinpointed the black box's location quite definitively. Even if – though it is quite incredible – a fix had not been obtained, then the search ship would have known that the box could not be more than 4000 yards away (if we accept the Administration's version of the pinger's range), and it would have a straight directional bearing on it, at least. With that the search could have been narrowed to a small and quite definitive area of five square miles: once the pinger had been picked up, even for a minute, it would be ridiculous ever to expand the area of search again. Then again, the refusal of the US Navy officers in charge of the search to answer any questions at all about the pinger is little less than fantastic. No wonder the Japanese were so certain the box had been found – and the evidence of conflict between the Japanese MSA and the US is pretty clear cut. The Japanese acted as if they wanted to end their participation in the search because they had decided that the black box had already been found and they wanted no more to do with an empty charade.

One notes, too, the steady escalation of the water depths, from 500 to 800 to 1200 to 2500 and finally 5000 feet. This is utterly absurd: the US sonars would have given a clear-cut picture of the ocean bottom and the sea depths right away – the picture couldn't change after that. No doubt the Pentagon spokesmen asked to dish out this nonsense knew little enough of what was actually going on off Moneron Island and did what they were told. But even they must have wondered. The ICAO inquiry reported quite flatly: 'The search area consisted of an underwater ridge with an average depth of 200 metres (656 feet), and an area west of the ridge, where the depth varies between 500 and 800 metres (1640 and 2624 feet).'[66]

Finally, of course, the notion that such depths presented any problems to a retrieval technology which, even nine years before, had, with no aid from 'pingers' of any sort, been able to find objects at 16,000 feet – is simply laughable.

A benchmark is provided by the Air India tragedy of June 1985, when a 747 plummeted into the Atlantic in just three minutes from 31,000 feet. Two RAF Nimrods – which are certainly not superior to the American P-3C Orions – were immediately able to locate the wreckage to within 1.5 miles, even though it was 7000 feet down on the sea bottom. Within eleven days the black box's pinger had been picked up (and was not lost) and a Scarab II submersible drone had provided TV pictures of the wreckage with even rivets visible. Despite the plunge from six miles up the plane was still in large pieces and many dead passengers were still strapped in their seats. One hundred and thirty-one bodies were recovered. A few days after the wreckage had been found both the cockpit voice and digital flight recorders had been recovered, some two miles away from the main wreckage, despite a far greater water depth than that which applied to 007. The search seems to have used just two planes and three ships. But while most reports mentioned only a British, a French and a Canadian vessel, one report did also mention another ship – 'the American vessel which took part in the unsuccessful search for the flight recorder of the Korean 747 shot down by the Russians off Sakhalin Island'.[67]

It is thus almost impossible to believe the official version of the search for the black box. It seems possible that the box was recovered by the US – perhaps at a very early stage, just conceivably in the first few hours of confusion and delay while the search was being mounted in the wrong place and the 'safe on Sakhalin' story was put out. It is even possible that all the stories of the pinger being picked up were a false trail, deliberately laid, and that the 'search' was bogus throughout.

There is also a final point to ponder. The search was called off in November 1983, with bad weather cited as the principal reason. But the search was not resumed in spring or summer 1984 or 1985. Yet if the US had truly not recovered the black box, this would have meant leaving it for the Russians to find at their leisure. It is quite inconceivable that the US could have tolerated such a position. Little wonder that the rumour has spread that the black box was found.

## Implications

The implications of the box(es) being found but concealed do not require a great deal of spelling out. But there is one issue here which has enormous implications for the whole inquiry into the KAL 007 affair.

Everything suggests, quite overwhelmingly, that the Japanese SDA was right to insist on an 18.29 crash time. Goro Takeda's arguments alone are convincing enough, but our examination of the search operation produces further evidence all pointing in the same direction. First, there is the fact that when the earliest MSA craft arrived on the scene, they found Soviet vessels already on the same spot. This can only mean that the Soviet radars showed 007 plunging into the same place. That is, the Japanese radar track and the Soviet one must check with one another: it is the State Department version of the crash with its 18.38 timing which is aberrant.

Secondly, the fact that the wreckage was in small pieces and that no single whole human body was found clearly suggests an immense midair explosion. This tallies far better with the Japanese version than the US one. Finally, it should be noted that even if, for whatever reason, the US and Japanese found pieces of wreckage at the crash site which they did not disclose, the Russians too reported finding relatively little at the crash site. Most of the actual wreckage and personal effects recovered were washed up on the neighbouring shores of Sakhalin and Wakkanai. This suggests that these might have been pieces flung outwards by an immense explosion which, nearer its epicentre, left almost nothing intact. (An explosion that great really might have destroyed the black boxes too, of course.)

We must, accordingly, view with great suspicion the early – and always unsubstantiated – US claim of an 18.38 crash time. But, as we saw, to produce that time created several large problems for the US version: why, then, no attempt by 007 to limp home on one engine or more? Why no large pieces of wreckage, even a wholly intact plane? Why, above all, no Mayday message from Captain Chun? So, if the US version is false, what possible motive could the US have had for producing a false version which only multiplied the difficult questions that the Administration had to face over the 007 tragedy?

There is only one possible answer: if one accepts the 18.29 crash time, then one cannot accept the published version of 007's conversations with ground control, which showed the pilots still on the air nearly a minute after missile impact. As it is, that last minute of conversation is fraught with difficulties. It shows, for example, 007 apparently calling up twice after the missile impact – once 38 seconds afterwards and once 48 seconds afterwards – and both times starting off with the routine call sign: 'Tokyo Korean Air zero zero seven' and then 'Korean Air zero zero seven'. Yet standard emergency procedure is to abandon all such routine and just shout 'Mayday' three times. Even if we imagine that Captain Chun was off course by design, it is very hard to imagine that he would have not responded to this utter emergency in the necessary way. But if we accept the 18.29 crash time, then we must also accept an instant and complete loss of control by 007's pilots. To fall over 30,000 feet in under three minutes means losing altitude at over 10,000 feet a minute – and a 747's maximum safe descent rate is 4000 feet a minute. So if the 18.29 crash time is correct – and everything points to that conclusion – then neither Captain Chun, nor First Officer Son, nor anybody else on 007, made those last calls.

But the calls were made. So who made them? One can only speculate. But one suggestion which has been made is that more or less throughout the flight some other, unknown plane was actually 'impersonating' 007, sending in reports to keep the ground controllers busy and happy, while 007's crew devoted themselves to their maximum-risk trip through Soviet airspace. Such messages would also have had the effect of helping to bamboozle Soviet ground controllers. There would have been no need, of course, for such messages to have had any relation at all to what 007 was actually doing. If 007 wanted to weave up and down or make turns, the impostor plane could simply send out messages relating to quite different manoeuvres. But the impostor plane would not know immediately that 007 had been hit by a missile. Even if the impostor was in contact with 007 on some special frequency, all he would have heard would have been static, confusion and silence. So he might have continued the imposture for another 40 or 50 seconds or more, before being alerted to the situation. Then the last phrase about 'rapid decompression' might have been an unscheduled snatch of conversation between the impostor and someone else – a moment of panic and confusion which the ground controllers were allowed to catch. One can only speculate, and quite wildly at that. But if we accept that 007 did not make those last calls, we have to do just that.

If the notion of an impostor plane pretending to be 007 is accepted, it does suggest answers to several otherwise inexplicable questions. It would explain why the US had a motive to come up with an 18.38 crash time – to do otherwise would have been a *de facto* admission that the 007-to-ground tape was an impossibility. And it would help one understand the extraordinary delay and apparent US resistance to the release of these tapes in the first place: twice as long was taken to publish them (or some version of them?) as was taken to reveal the supersecret tapes of the Soviet fighters in conversation with their ground control, even though these were supposed to be routine civil aviation tapes. It would also explain the clearly contradictory situation between Major Kasmin, who broke off his action right away because the 'target' was 'destroyed', and his ground controller, who, presumably listening to the continuing, calm call signs from 007, could not believe this was so. And finally, of course, it would explain why the Soviet fighters were unable then to find 007, even though diving after it at great speed.

Again, it is instructive to return to the comparable case of the 1985 Air India 747. When analysts examined tapes of the doomed airliner's conversations with ground control all they could find at the moment of the explosion was 'something like a shout or a screech . . . it lasted just a fraction of a second'.[68] This is what one might have expected of the 007 tape too: calm call signs 40 and 50 seconds after a midair explosion are simply incredible.

But the Air India case still leaves a mystery. Even a midair explosion sufficient to send that plane plunging to its death from 30,000 feet in just three minutes was still not sufficient to reduce the wreck to the sort of smithereens which, if we are to credit official accounts, 007 was reduced to. So, if those accounts are correct, one has to visualise a midair explosion of quite extraordinary magnitude aboard 007.

Let us go back to the only possible eyewitnesses of that explosion – the Japanese crew of *Chidori Maru No. 58* some six miles below.[69] Earlier, we have suggested that the bangs and flashes they saw might have been Major Kasmin's tracer shells, and that the time they gave for these sights, 'about three o'clock in the morning' (i.e. 18.00 GMT), was too early for this to have been the shoot-down. But that may be wrong. One is talking about fishermen who are not in the habit of looking constantly at their wristwatches in the pitch dark of night. But what they described was an explosion far too big to allow for leisurely call signs. First, they said, they heard a loud bang. Then, two or three seconds later, they saw 'a glowing orange-coloured, expanding fireball'. This fireball's illumination lasted, they said, for five or six seconds. This was then followed by a second bang and then a second fireball a few moments later, not as bright as the first one.[70] It is such reports – subject to all the normal reservations about later, collective memories playing tricks even on well-meaning witnesses – that have led to speculation that 007 might even have been destroyed in the end by a bomb placed in its hold.[71] (Presumably, we have to envisage a remote-controlled device used to abort a surveillance mission and destroy evidence – a sort of mechanical equivalent to the cyanide pill provided to human spies, but in this case one triggered by a 'controller' monitoring 007.) But to enter such realms of speculation is really just to allow our imagination free rein without anything like the evidence we need. And, after all, we do not need such a hypothesis: perhaps the effect of the missile's impact was simply far greater than we first imagined. Even if we jettison such speculations, however, it is somewhat harder to avoid the suspicion that perhaps an impostor plane was involved; that the 007-to-ground tape is thus not a true record; that the whole US version of 007's 'last 12 minutes' is distinctly dubious; and that it looks as if 007 was destroyed by a quite extraordinary explosion. The sole happy result of such speculations is to prompt the thought that those aboard 007 may have died almost instantaneously and, in the case of those asleep beforehand, almost unconsciously.

# TEN

# The Mysterious Exit of William Clark

As we have seen, the man at the centre of the handling of the 007 crisis – indeed, at the centre of the entire US foreign policy process – was William Clark, the President's close friend and National Security Adviser. Clark's position seemed enviable to many – he was the most powerful man in US foreign policy since Henry Kissinger. Yet, just six weeks after the 007 crisis broke, Clark stunned Washington by a sudden departure into relative obscurity. The Russians were not slow to point a finger at Clark and to allege that his abrupt and astonishing exit was a direct consequence of the 007 tragedy. If only for this reason, it is worth examining how this extraordinary change occurred.

On 21 September the US Secretary of the Interior, James G. Watt, addressing the US Chamber of Commerce, countered criticisms of the Reagan Administration's attitude towards minorities by genially pointing out that the new coal advisory commission he had appointed included 'a black, a woman, two Jews and a cripple'.[1] Although this remark was greeted by a gasp of laughter, there followed an immediate and enormous uproar.

Outside a hardline right-wing constituency, Watt had never been exactly popular – he owed his position essentially to the patronage of the right-wing brewery magnate, Joseph Coors, who was an intimate of Reagan's.[2] Among the environmentalist groups that lobbied the Interior Department, he was anathema – indeed, Watt had likened such groups to the forces that had supported Nazism (just as he had likened pro-abortion campaigners to 'the forces that created the Holocaust'). Similarly, his way of referring to Democrats and Republicans ('liberals and Americans') or to Indian reservations ('examples of the failure of socialism in America') or his attempt to ban the Beach Boys from the capital's Fourth of July celebrations (as being prone to attract drug-takers and drunks) had not gained Watt a particularly strong reputation for diplomacy.[3] Similarly, his reported threat to the Israeli ambassador that US aid to Israel might be cut off if American Jews did not stop opposing his off-shore drilling programme[4] had helped Watt to enrage a wider audience than an Interior Secretary usually gets.

At first the White House attempted to play down Watt's 'cripple' remark (for which Watt apologised). Reagan's stress on buddy relationships – Watt was a friend of the President's, who found his wisecracks genuinely funny – had made Watt a protected species. It seemed at first that this would save Watt yet again – after a week's uproar Ed Meese told reporters that Watt was not expected to resign and that the President 'considers this a closed issue now'.[5] However, a number of Republican Senators then made it clear that they were willing to vote for the censure motion being mounted against Watt and on 9 October Watt resigned.

The search for his successor began immediately. The Interior Secretary's job is not one of Washington's plums (Presidents have often used it as a sinecure from which one of their henchmen runs their re-election campaigns) and not surprisingly the White House made it clear that no other member of the Cabinet would be shifted to fill Watt's job.[6] 'Let's face it,' said one Republican, 'the job isn't necessarily the most attractive in the world, with less than a year and a half to go and an announcement from everyone that Watt's mission has been accomplished.'[7] It quickly became known that a number of those approached (e.g. ex-Senator James Buckley, now running Radio Free Europe and Radio Liberty) had turned the job down.[8] Then, on 13 October, the President announced that William Clark would take Watt's position, giving up his national security role. Explaining the move, Reagan said, 'He is a God-fearing Westerner, a fourth-generation rancher and a person I trust.'[9] This was to beg the question: the foreign policy supremo had been abruptly removed – with no successor in sight – despite a major foreign crisis then under way in the Lebanon, an invasion of Grenada imminent, the arms-control talks nearing their climax, the emplacement of cruise and Pershing II in Europe only days away, and relations between the superpowers at an all-time low. And the decision had been made so suddenly that neither the NATO allies, nor Cabinet members, nor White House staff, nor Congressional leaders had been informed – not even Secretary of State Shultz himself. It was a bombshell.

Clark had, though, given the impression of a man whose job was becoming too much for him. Apparently eager to reverse his August defeat over the sale of oil equipment to Russia, Clark had managed to get the question of future such sales referred to an inter-agency committee on which the Defence Department, the NSC and CIA were represented. In the climate engendered by the airliner tragedy it was not difficult to get the committee to recommend a sweeping ban on the sale of seventeen different categories of oil and gas equipment. 'It's a 180-degree turn from the decision to decontrol pipe-layers,' admitted one trade official.[10] William A. Root, the State Department's director for East–West trade, furiously tendered his resignation, claiming that since the airliner tragedy the US had 'been redoubling our efforts to convey to our Allies that their views do not count, that we know best and that they had better shape up'. The 'arrogance of the US Government', he warned, would lead to a 'major, justified explosion of Allied resentment'.[11] Shultz and Baldridge were similarly horrified, knowing that the Administration was now set on course for a hideous clash with Europe and Japan.

Shultz and Baldridge temporised, hoping to reverse the decision. Clark then went over the top, sending a letter to the two men on 19 September in which he effectively ordered them to go ahead and carry out the committee's decision, explicitly citing the KAL 007 tragedy as an extra reason for the ban.[12] Clark had no authority to do this – he was effectively trying to act as if he were the President and prevent the matter even surfacing in Cabinet. The letter – likened to 'a hand grenade in the chicken coop'[13] – produced a furious confrontation between Clark, Shultz and Baldridge. To the dismay of his backers, Clark summarily and completely backed down. The committee report was overturned. The sales would go ahead. Root was reinstated. This was not characteristic behaviour for Clark. It was quite unrealistic to imagine that the President would allow himself to be steered back into a headlong conflict with his allies less than a year after the last bruising (and losing) bout, especially with large US firms pressing for the contracts (Hughes Tool had just landed one of them).[14] To try, after that, to pre-empt the Cabinet and to act as if he was usurping the President's role was quite crazily unwise. (And Clark was a notable absentee from the Cabinet meeting of mid-September.)[15] Finally, having got this far, Clark – normally nothing if not a tough fighter in such situations – simply collapsed in front of Baldridge's and Shultz's wrath, leaving those who had backed him on the inter-agency committee twisting in the wind (there was even talk that Shultz wanted some of them sacked).[16] These were, surely, the actions of a man under considerable stress.

None of this, however, had prepared official Washington for the astonishing notion that Clark might move to the Interior Department. 'Environmentalists responded with rage,' reported the *Washington Post*,

conservatives with scepticism, Republican members of Congress with restraint and almost all of them with disbelief as word of [Clark's] appointment as Secretary of the Interior spread yesterday. The immediate reaction from environmental groups was that the appointment was a joke . . . 'It's a preposterous appointment, an insult to the environment,' said William Turnage, executive director of the Wilderness Society . . . Officials throughout Interior expressed bafflement at Clark's choice . . . 'I guess the appointment will play well with the right wing, but it doesn't indicate much reverence for anything we do over here,' said a high-level career official who has been in the department through several administrations. 'What a bird. God help us all over again.'[17]

The *New York Times* commented:

the prevailing opinion in Washington appeared to be that the President had made this decision for reasons having little to do with foreign policy and much to do with Mr Clark ... Nonetheless, the way the switch was managed by Mr Reagan has raised some foreign policy questions that neither White House nor State Department officials were able to answer today. They had all been caught by surprise ... The questions being most urgently asked were: Why did the President move so precipitously to name Mr Clark as Interior Secretary without at the same time settling on his replacement? And why had the President not consulted with Secretary of State George P. Shultz, to see if Mr Clark's sudden departure would cause any harm?[18]

Even four days after the announcement the newspaper was reporting that Washington was still 'stunned' by the news.[19] The former senior editor of the *New York Times*, John B. Oakes, wrote a blistering column in which he argued that Mr Watt had 'presided over the most destructive giveaways of America's publicly owned natural resources to private interests since Teapot Dome' but that the President had nonetheless accomplished the apparently impossible in finding a successor to Mr Watt even less qualified for the job.[20]

Gradually it became possible to piece together a more complete picture of what had happened. It emerged that on 1 October Clark had made a sudden and secret trip to Rome to meet Caspar Weinberger, the Defence Secretary, and Robert McFarlane, Clark's deputy, who was still based in the Italian capital in his somewhat anomalous position as the State Department envoy to the Middle East who was not in the State Department's employ. 'The reasons for Clark's sudden trip,' the *Washington Post* commented when, two weeks later, news of it leaked out, 'have remained something of a Washington mystery', especially since the trip had been 'undertaken without advance discussion between Clark and Shultz'.[21] The Secretary of State was reportedly extremely upset for he had no idea of what Clark was up to.[22] It seems possible, however, that Clark already had it in mind to leave his National Security post and wanted to consult with McFarlane, his trusted subordinate, about the change. It is certainly known that one of the items of discussion was McFarlane's future role[23] – and Clark was to push strongly for McFarlane to succeed him.

Returning to Washington, Clark had phoned Reagan on 8 October and told the President that he was determined to give up his job.[24] (At first the White House attempted to portray the decision as having been taken by the President, but finally conceded that the initiative had been Clark's.[25]) 'The President wanted to accommodate Bill', as one White House official put it.[26] Clark, who took the position that he had already decided to leave his National Security job,[27] was then offered an appointment to the Supreme Court by

Reagan, but said he didn't want to go back to the judiciary at any level.[28] Clark suggested to Reagan that he might, instead, go to Interior – that is, a day before Watt resigned, making one wonder whether Reagan's determination to keep Clark in his Cabinet may not have given the final push to Watt's resignation: until then, after all, the President's position had been that Watt was staying on. At this stage, however, the idea remained a secret between the two men. The President apparently had some difficulty in believing that Clark could really be serious about wanting to move to Interior. Clark then 'had long conversations with Edwin Meese III, the White House counsellor', a White House official later revealed, and Mr Meese 'provided a facilitating role' in persuading the President that Clark was indeed deadly serious about moving to Interior.[29] These talks were held, though, under conditions of the most absolute secrecy – so much so that neither of the other two top men in the White House troika, James A. Baker or Michael K. Deaver, knew that they had occurred.[30]

This rather extraordinary cloak-and-dagger act was maintained up to the last moment, with neither Meese nor Clark nor Reagan giving any clue, even to their closest advisers, of what was in the wind, and with White House officials allowed to go on opining wisely about the still long list of possible candidates for the Interior post. On 12 October Mrs Kirkpatrick returned to Washington from a Central American trip. She had got on well with Clark, whom she felt to be on the same wavelength as herself, and he had frequently told her that he thought she would do his National Security job better than he did it himself.[31] On 13 October Clark and Mrs Kirkpatrick went together to see the President to discuss Central America but neither Clark nor Reagan allowed any hint to drop[32] of the seismic change which was to take place within hours in the management of US foreign policy – an extraordinary and surely not accidental omission. Clark also saw the President on his own that morning to clinch the matter of the Interior job[33] – and then had lunch with the President, Shultz and McFarlane. Even more remarkably, Shultz was not told of the impending change[34] – though one suspects McFarlane must already have known, leaving Shultz, the man formally charged with the management of foreign policy, as the only one at the table not to have known of Clark's move. Straight after lunch Reagan broke the news to Baker and Deaver[35] and then immediately made it public. It was, to say the least, extremely unusual for Reagan to take a decision of this magnitude without discussions with the senior White House staff: there can be no doubt that the strict secrecy with which the whole matter was handled was highly deliberate.

Shultz, on hearing the news, 'was as surprised as everyone else'.[36] It was not till two hours later that the White House's Congressional liaison officer,

Kenneth M. Duberstein, got the news to Congressional leaders.[37] Senator Howard Baker, the Republican majority leader, greeted the news 'with disbelief'.[38] The Speaker of the House, Tip O'Neill, actually learned of the change from the TV news: 'I was shocked, to be perfectly truthful,' he said. 'It's a strange appointment.'[39] Clark himself quickly went to ground. He had been due to be the main speaker at the launch of the USS *Henry M. Jackson*, America's latest Trident submarine, but immediately cancelled the appearance and sent his wife, Joan, instead.[40] The whole episode was distinctly peculiar – not least because Clark had always told his friends that he would stay in the National Security job just as long as the President wanted him to.[41] He had not only changed his mind but had then made the most startling change seen in Washington for many administrations past, moving from the most powerful job to one of the most humble – at his own behest. He had, moreover, moved to a job about which he knew so little – far less than Watt, who had been an anti-environmentalist lawyer for years – that it is impossible to believe that he took it out of any real feeling of enthusiasm for what it involved. And the whole thing had been managed in an astonishingly secret fashion – Clark never explained publicly why he had done it. As the conservative political activist, Richard Viguerie, not unreasonably commented, 'I'm afraid there could be a lot more to this than meets the eye.'[42] The only person who seemed straightforwardly delighted was Watt, who described Clark as 'a prince of a fellow'.[43]

## A surprising succession

Clark's sudden exit was the signal for a frantic competition for the succession to his job, whose eventual outcome was almost as surprising as the way in which the vacancy occurred.

Clark had made it clear to Reagan that he felt Robert 'Bud' McFarlane – 'Clark's faithful executor', as the *Washington Post* called him[44] – should succeed to the National Security job, and Reagan seems to have given a commitment to do this, for White House officials coupled the announcement of Clark's departure with suggestions that McFarlane was expected to take over. In fact such an appointment was anything but predictable. No one had previously supposed that McFarlane was the man to fill a post previously held by giants such as Bundy, Kissinger and Brzezinski. Retiring as a Marine Lieutenant-Colonel only seven years before, he had cheerfully acknowledged that he had not had the intellectual qualities for promotion within the military.[45] He had been a junior assistant to Kissinger – something which the Right believed had tarred him for ever with the fatal brush of détente. He had then continued as an assistant to Ford's National Security Adviser, Brent Scowcroft, but was seen by most as an anonymous apparatchik. In 1981 a White House official had described him as 'the perfect No. 2 man or maybe No. 2½',[46] while Paul Weyrich, the New Right activist, claimed that McFarlane 'was created by God to disappear into crowds'.[47] His chief virtues were simply that he was self-effacing, deferential, hard-working and completely loyal to Clark. True, he knew a great deal more about foreign policy than Clark, but this was hardly a large achievement.

Almost nobody among the top foreign-policy advisers wanted McFarlane to succeed. Shultz had become increasingly critical of McFarlane's role in the Lebanese crisis: McFarlane had pushed strongly for the US military intervention in Lebanon in 1983 and given a positive estimate of the capabilities of the (Christian) Lebanese Army.[48] US troops had gone in and the Lebanese Army had folded up like a pack of cards. The situation had begun to unravel towards the utter dénouement of US withdrawal, following the death of over 240 US Marines in the Beirut truck-bombing. Shultz advised Reagan to recall McFarlane's old National Security boss, Brent Scowcroft, instead.[49]

The President's right-wing constituency were almost hysterically opposed to McFarlane, whom they viewed as a dangerous moderate. Not only did McFarlane maintain his links with Kissinger, but it was known that he had been instrumental in convincing the President that the US would have to be seen to negotiate seriously for an arms-control agreement if there was to be any hope of getting the MX and other military programmes through Congress.[50] The Right had felt that Clark was their man, but conservatives in and out of Congress lobbied strongly against McFarlane. Howard Phillips, the chairman of the Conservative Caucus, even suggested that a McFarlane appointment might lead his group not to campaign for Reagan in 1984: 'A McFarlane appointment would freeze conservatives out of all foreign policy-making and would result in terminal despondency for conservatives,'[51] he said. The favoured candidate of the Right was Jeane Kirkpatrick.

Casey and Weinberger also lobbied the President strongly against McFarlane and for Kirkpatrick. Apart from feeling a greater personal and political camaraderie with Kirkpatrick, they also argued that McFarlane was insufficiently forceful and that he would not well represent their views to the President. The result, they feared, would be that foreign policy issues would simply drop off the White House agenda. More specifically, they worried that McFarlane would be unable to stand up to the White House chief of staff, James A. Baker III.[52] Like other conservatives, Weinberger and Casey did not trust Baker: he had been a Bush supporter, not a true believer, and was thus regarded as harbouring worryingly dovish tendencies. In addition, of course,

Casey and Baker had publicly called each other liars over the question of the purloined debating notes for Jimmy Carter:[53] anything which strengthened Baker's hand was bad news for Casey.

Baker and his deputy, Michael Deaver, had ideas of their own. Deaver, a one-time friend of Clark, had quarrelled with him, but his White House position was secure because he was Nancy Reagan's favourite. Baker now conceived the idea that he would like to succeed Clark himself and agreed with Deaver that, in return for his support, he would support Deaver to become the new White House chief of staff. Having worked out this private deal – in much the same way that Baker and the Treasury Secretary, Donald Regan, were later to agree to swap jobs and then persuade Reagan to bless the deal – the two men approached the President and got him to agree to their mutual new appointments.[54]

Meanwhile Mrs Kirkpatrick, to her immense frustration, had had to take to her bed with a bout of flu and bronchitis contracted on her Central American trip. It was in this state – with a high fever and hardly able to speak – that she heard of the bombshell of Clark's resignation from the National Security job. Mrs Kirkpatrick had never hidden her feeling that her UN job was too small for her talents. She had managed to elicit regular invitations to sit on the NSC – whose importance far eclipses that of the Cabinet.[55] When Richard Allen had been forced out as National Security Adviser, she had seen herself as a leading candidate for the post and had been upset to be passed over for Clark.[56] Nonetheless, she had worked well with Clark, whose gut right-wing instincts she shared. When McFarlane had gone off to the Middle East Mrs Kirkpatrick had been quick to suggest to Clark that he now needed a new deputy – and that she would be the one for the job.[57] Clark, though her close associate – and though he certainly had needed someone to replace the invaluable McFarlane – had passed the offer up.

Mrs Kirkpatrick was undoubtedly upset that Clark had made his sudden move while keeping her so deliberately in the dark – and it was noticeable that Clark kept his distance from her throughout the intense palace politicking which followed. Mrs Kirkpatrick was keen to have Clark's job for herself, but, failing that, she wanted Clark to reverse his decision and stay, for she had found him an invaluable conduit of her views to the President – indeed, she relied on Clark for access to the President. She had no reason to believe that McFarlane would play the same role. Accordingly, she was quickly up from her sickbed and into action, lobbying for Clark to stay on, while her own candidacy was pushed hard by Casey and Weinberger – and resisted, with equal force, by Shultz. Mrs Kirkpatrick was as much opposed to Baker taking the National Security job as she was to McFarlane, but with Baker and

Deaver playing their own game and Clark staying out of contact with her, she was shut out of the White House manoeuvering.

Meanwhile, the word from the White House was that McFarlane was the favourite for the job. With Baker, Deaver, Weinberger, Casey, Shultz, Kirkpatrick and the true believers of the Right all fiercely opposed to him, it might have been thought that the uncharismatic McFarlane had little hope. But he had one asset which outweighed all of these: Clark was determined that McFarlane be appointed and willing to use his unrivalled influence with Reagan to the full to ensure this happened. Thus when Clark learned of the Baker bid for power, he immediately rounded up Ed Meese and the two men prevailed upon Reagan to back down.[58] If he had promised the job to Baker already, that was too bad: he'd just have to un-promise it. Reagan did. But the President was hardly used to acting in the face of such concerted opposition from his supporters and delayed taking any positive step. By 15 October a White House official suggested that 'the process of picking Clark's successor had become one of "trying to round people up" and "build a consensus" for McFarlane'.[59] What this meant in particular was Reagan personally assuring Casey and Weinberger that McFarlane would be all right.[60] Shultz did not need much convincing: he would have preferred Scowcroft but the truth was that, from his point of view, McFarlane would be a great deal better than Clark.

This left the formidable Mrs Kirkpatrick to be reconciled. She was livid about the growing consensus for McFarlane and it was quite clear that the Presidential interview with her would be neither easy nor particularly pleasant. The President knew he would have to see her – she was quite capable of resigning in a huff if he made the appointment before seeing her – but it was clearly not a job he looked forward to: for several days he kept putting off such a confrontation.[61] Finally, Clark called Kirkpatrick on the morning of 17 October to suggest she come and see the President. When she called Clark back to arrange the time of the meeting, it seemed as if Reagan had had cold feet again: she was now told that the Presidential schedule was too tight for him to see her that morning after all. Mrs Kirkpatrick persisted and finally an appointment was made for that afternoon. Later she was to complain that she had been whisked in and out of the White House in a way designed to get the whole thing over with the minimum public attention, but she claimed she had spent a whole hour with the President. A White House spokesman said she had spent just 15 minutes with Reagan. The President tried as hard as he could to mollify her, praising her performance at the UN and successively offering her posts as head of the Agency for International Development (AID), as a White House counsellor, and finally as deputy to

McFarlane.[62] Mrs Kirkpatrick repulsed all these offers – no doubt taking the last as a virtual insult. But the President was adamant that McFarlane was to be appointed – and now made the news official.

There was a predictable uproar from the Right and Mrs Kirkpatrick was unable to hide her own feelings. While indignantly denying that she had been pushing her own candidacy, she announced bitterly: 'I believe it is terribly undesirable for Bill Clark to leave and impossible for anyone else to do the job he was doing. It is an unmitigated disaster for him to leave. That decision shouldn't have been made. And once made, it should have been rescinded.'[63] This amounted to a public declaration of hostility to the new National Security Adviser and it was hardly surprising that word was soon abroad that Mrs Kirkpatrick was determined to resign her UN job. In fact she stayed at the UN for over a year more. When she finally resigned she was again to be offered all manner of number-two jobs but resolutely declined them all. It had been number one or nothing.

These strange convulsions did not pass unnoticed in Moscow. Although Soviet commentary is generally slow to personalise, *Pravda* made an exception in the case of William Clark. Clark, it said, was 'a militant adventurist who brought nothing but disgrace to the White House'. Now he was being used as a 'scapegoat'. For his 'unbridled aggressiveness led to a number of ruthless actions' – including, specifically, the flight of KAL 007. 'In the judgement of knowledgeable observers, Clark, together with the leaders of the Pentagon and special services, gave the green light to the South Korean airliner's espionage flight,'[64] said *Pravda*. *Pravda* did not, of course, say which 'knowledgeable observers' it was quoting, and the accusation was treated with a bare, derisive mention in the American press. This was odd, given how unusual it was for the Russians to attempt to interpret personnel changes within the US Administration, and also how unusual it was for them to attempt to fasten responsibility for particular (alleged) actions on individual actors rather than 'the forces of American imperialism' etc. Beyond that, of course, there was the question of the substantive accusation itself. What one can say with some certainty is that *if* KAL 007 was indeed sent on a US-sponsored surveillance mission, it *would* have been difficult for this to occur without Clark having had to give the go-ahead. And Clark's extraordinary speech on 14 September in which he had attempted to suggest that some good might come out of the 007 tragedy after all, *had* sounded rather like a man searching for a *post facto* justification after a disaster. And if Clark *had* decided to quit under such (hypothetical) circumstances, then no doubt he *would* have wanted someone utterly loyal to him to fill his place and sweep up any untidy pieces: a McFarlane, in fact – someone who was not only personally loyal to Clark, but who knew that he could not possibly have attained the top foreign policy job without Clark's determined patronage.

But no American newspaper was willing to air speculations such as these. To publish an article which even entertained the notion of a surveillance mission seriously was to risk the Administration's furious wrath and accusations of being a Soviet stooge and a virtual accomplice to the murder of KAL 007's passengers. There is no doubt that much of the American press was simply intimidated by the scale of Reagan's general political success and the fierceness of his anti-Soviet campaign in particular. In that atmosphere to publish articles which appeared to take the Soviet accusations at all seriously would have seemed variously provocative, unwise and downright unpatriotic. Larry Flynt, the maverick editor of *Hustler*, tested these waters in mid-October when he sought to place a full-page ad in a number of American newspapers suggesting that there were far too many fishy things about the KAL 007 story for the allegation of a surveillance mission to be dismissed out of hand. Although Flynt was able to offer extremely large cheques paid fully in advance, he found many newspapers unwilling to print the ad. The *Los Angeles Times* finally agreed to print it only if textual changes were made. The *Washington Post* refused to accept it until the son of the proprietor, Katherine Graham, had given his personal go-ahead. The *New York Times* simply refused to accept it altogether, saying it was 'unfit to print'.[65] Similarly, when the potentially explosive data about 007's deception of Tokyo ground control and evasive tactics in the last moments of flight was released to the Japanese Diet in May 1985, the *New York Times* simply failed to print the news. Readers of David Halberstam's *The Powers That Be* will not find it difficult to imagine the pressures which led to decisions such as these.

What does seem possible is that the 007 tragedy did have something to do with Clark's departure, at least to this extent: there is no reason to doubt that the Soviet leadership sincerely believed the plane had been on a surveillance mission, or that they genuinely believed that Clark was responsible for it. Given the enormous political damage the USSR suffered as a result of the 007 affair, the Russians must have felt a great bitterness towards Clark – perhaps even intimated that they could do no further business with the US while he remained in control of US foreign policy. If so, with the crucial arms-control talks nearing their climax, Clark's position could have become virtually untenable.

It is interesting to reconstruct the events leading up to Clark's surprise resignation in the light of such a hypothesis. Prior to the 007 tragedy Clark had been heading the special committee on arms control and the tricky question of possible Soviet SALT violations – especially the Krasnoyarsk radar – had landed in his lap. Although preoccupied with such concerns, he had also been a member of the select committee which oversaw CIA covert operations. Hence, if it had been decided to launch a passive probe mission to test the Soviet radar network, Clark would have been in *both* the key positions to know of such a move – which could hardly have gone ahead without his say-so. Clark was also both a close associate of the head of the CIA, William Casey, and a man who had the President's confidence to a degree where he could have felt able to authorise even high-risk operations without telling the President until after they had been carried out.

Clark was, we have seen, at the very centre of the small inner group which dealt with the immediate repercussions of the 007 tragedy – and it was he who broke the news of it to the President. Indeed, other policy-makers such as Shultz were so cut out that all the President's early information on the affair came from Clark.

Thereafter Clark was strangely invisible. He did not attend Cabinet meetings and he did not, extraordinarily, attend the special Presidential briefing of leading Congressmen and Senators on the 007 affair – which even far junior Cabinet members attended. At least after his resignation, reports of the stress he suffered in this period were legion. True, he had continued to press ahead with proposals to restrict trade with the USSR – but then, as we have seen, had uncharacteristically collapsed under pressure, having previously gone over the top and acted almost as if he were President. These too were surely signs of a man under exceptional strain.

Then came Clark's remarkable speech of 14 September. While he reached new heights of bitterness in his condemnation of the Russians for shooting down 007, he also – somewhat peculiarly, and despite the all-time low in Soviet–American relations – suggested that some good might come of the 007 tragedy. Perhaps it would bring a new coming together of the superpowers, perhaps even a new summit. Given that Reagan had scrupulously avoided anything resembling a summit – no doubt on Clark's advice – this was a curious reversal.

It is not difficult to see how Soviet observers might have viewed this strange behaviour pattern. If they believed that there had been an '007 mission' and Clark had been the man behind it, it would have been easy to view Clark's behaviour as that of a man suffering the pangs of remorse and self-doubt. The promise of a possible summit would then appear as a holding-out of a last-ditch olive branch. Similarly, the unexpected softening of the US line in late September would have been interpreted as the gradual workings of an

American guilty conscience over 007. And certainly there was a growing realisation on the US side that something needed to be done to rescue their relations with the USSR from their 'volatile and precarious' state. Thus Reagan's UN address of 26 September was, a State Department spokesman admitted, deliberately softened from an earlier version, with some of the stronger anti-Soviet statements taken out. 'The rhetoric was becoming too heavy,' he said. 'We were beating the drum too loudly.'[66]

Clearly, from the Soviet point of view, this was still far from good enough – hence the remarkable personal intervention of Andropov on 28 September in which he said, in almost as many words, that it was impossible to deal with those currently running US foreign policy.[67] It must have been in the day or two following this broadside that Clark decided he might have to resign – hence his surprise flying visit to see McFarlane in Rome on 1 October. However, Clark did not make any move to see the President about a possible resignation in the days after his return. On 7 October came the revelation that the CIA was now conceding that the Russians had, after all, never realised that they had been shooting down a civilian plane. It was the day after this that Clark told the President that he was leaving the National Security Adviser job. If the Russians believed that Clark had been the man behind the 007 flight, it is not too difficult to imagine how Moscow would have interpreted this sequence of events. One cannot but wonder, too, what the intention was behind that crucial CIA leak – for the effect was, of course, to take a considerable amount of the sting out of the entire campaign against the Russians for having 'deliberately' shot down a civilian plane.

Finally, at a press conference just two weeks later, President Reagan announced: 'I do believe in the right of a country, when it believes that its interests are best served, to practise covert activity.' (Administration officials hurriedly amended this to mean that it was all right only for the US to conduct such activities, not others.)[68] Again, the Russians must, given what they believed, have seen this statement as essentially a justification for the flight of KAL 007.

Clark's tenure at Interior did not fulfil the worst fears of the environmental-ists – indeed, he adopted a very low profile and seemed to have little stomach for continuing the bruising battles with them that Watt had so delighted in. His time at Interior was, indeed, so uneventful as to stir further wonderment as to why he had moved there at all – he evinced no positive enthusiasm for the job and left it and the Administration altogether a year later. It was as if Clark had decided that he had urgently needed to quit as National Security Adviser and had simply gone to Interior to sit out time and create a 'decent interval' before his ultimate withdrawal. For, quite clearly, his sudden decision to leave the pinnacle of power in October 1983 had been the real end. For the first time in twenty years Reagan was without his most faithful buddy, Bill Clark – something Clark had said would never happen. The press talked vaguely about Clark's wish to be back at his ranch, but it is doubtful if such an explanation would have been accepted as adequate had Brzezinski or Kissinger abruptly resigned at the peak of their power.

No explanation ever did emerge as to why Clark acted as he did in October 1983; why he made his move with such extreme secrecy; and why he was willing to affront his natural constituency and take on almost every leading Administration figure to ensure McFarlane's succession. The mystery remains.

# ELEVEN

# Indecision at ICAO

The Reagan Administration had achieved less than it had desired at the UN. It had wanted a swingeing condemnation of the USSR by the international body and, as we have seen, the final resolution adopted there not only avoided this but only just got the nine votes needed for adoption at all.[1] There was some satisfaction in forcing the USSR to use its veto, but the impact of the famous 'Nyet' has been considerably dulled in recent years by the fact that the US has used its veto far more frequently than the Russians (since 1980, fifteen US vetoes to three Soviet ones).[2] With the Administration still under strong pressure from its Right wing to show more concrete results, American attention turned to the possibilities presented by the International Civil Aviation Organisation (ICAO). The day after the shoot-down Canada (the host country to ICAO, which is based in Montreal) and South Korea had asked for an emergency ICAO Council meeting to consider the position. It was immediately obvious that in some respects ICAO represented a better forum than the UN. Although ICAO has 151 members (East Germany is the only major state unrepresented), most of its work is done by its 33-member Council. Since ICAO's constitution specifies that the Council ought to include particularly states 'of chief importance in air transport' and those which 'make the largest contribution to the provision of facilities for international civil air navigation',[3] this ensures in effect that the Council is dominated by the Western states which run most of the world's major airlines. Moreover, ICAO has an authoritative reputation for technical expertise in the aviation world – so a condemnation of the USSR by it would carry considerable weight. And, most importantly, there is no provision for any veto power within the Council, so the USSR would not be able to block an ICAO resolution as it had the UN one.

For ICAO the affair of KAL 007 was both a crisis and an embarrassment. ICAO was founded in 1944 (a year before the UN) and was able for many years to remain a comfortably consensual body, without significant political divisions. Not until 1969 did the USSR or any other Communist states join ICAO, and although a large number of Third World countries joined in the 1960s, they were more important in the Assembly than in the Council. With the Council sitting permanently and the Assembly rarely, this meant that in practice the ethos of apolitical consensus has remained the organisation's dominant cultural inheritance. ICAO fears political entanglement of any kind and has always been extremely nervous of having anything to do with the wide range of aviation matters with military implications. Above all, ICAO wishes to devote itself to technical, procedural and standardisation issues and the intrusion of international politics is seen as a threat to those primary purposes. The politicisation of other specialist UN agencies such as UNESCO, the ILO, FAO and UNIDO is viewed with horror by ICAO, for it has meant that these bodies have been frequently wracked by heated political standoffs and even the withdrawal of major states like the US. If ICAO allows itself to be politicised, this is the awful fate which awaits it. For all these reasons ICAO was less than thrilled to have the KAL 007 affair dropped in its lap. While the tragedy was certainly of the gravest significance for ICAO, it was also the hottest of political hot potatoes. ICAO, which tries hard to rock no political boats at all, was now to be asked to deliver a veritable judgement of Paris in the Cold War.[4]

The Reagan Administration's attitude to the ICAO meeting was made quite clear when it was announced that, exceptionally, J. Lynn Helms, the head of the Federal Aviation Administration (FAA) would lead the US delegation at ICAO. Helms was no neutral administrator, but a hard-line Reaganite whose chief achievement had been the smashing of the air controllers' union. Helms had, indeed, been at the first NSC meeting held to discuss 007 and could be relied upon to take a strong Administration line. Helms, together with the other US delegates, actually had a meeting at the White House with Reagan the day before ICAO met.[5] Helms 'predicted' that ICAO would vote to carry out its own inquiry into the tragedy, and that the USSR 'would not dare' to ignore such an inquiry.[6] The point was that ICAO does not normally carry out investigations into aircraft crashes.

ICAO's revulsion from politics extends to a disinclination to get involved in matters which might lead it to find fault with (frequently government-owned) national airlines for possible negligence or incompetence: some governments would resent such 'interference' and of course the commercial damage to an airline would be all the greater for the fact that such a verdict bore the authoritative stamp of ICAO. At the UN, however, both the US and several other Western states had called for an ICAO investigation. In the end the compromise motion submitted by the Netherlands and reluctantly supported by the US had merely called for ICAO to 'consider' the incident – and, of course, even this motion had been vetoed. What Helms was making clear was that the US was now going to try to get from ICAO what it had been unable to get at the UN.

Just how tough the US was prepared to be in exerting leverage for its cause was shown by the sharp reversal of US policy towards Poland. With the lifting of martial law and the release of many political prisoners, the Poles had carried out their part of a bargain whereby the US would, in return, allow Polish ships to fish in US waters and also expedite negotations on the rescheduling of the Polish debt. But in mid-September – against the anguished protests of some State Department officials – the US called off these concessions, citing Polish support for the USSR at the UN over 007 as the reason.[7] This meant Poland could get no new Western loans. The numerous Third World states with debt problems no doubt took worried note of how much might hang on their attitude to the 007 case.

But the most significant point about the demand for an ICAO inquiry was that someone, somewhere clearly had to conduct a proper accident investigation and publish the results. But neither the US nor South Korea appeared at all keen to do this. In the end both these governments produced official White Papers on the affair of a highly political sort – and, of course, the Russians carried out an investigation all on their own. But the US Administration seemed singularly determined to avoid the normal type of accident investigation. Normally, because 007 was an American-built plane, with American passengers aboard, leaving from an American airport, there would routinely have been an investigation into the disaster by the US National Transportation Safety Board (NTSB). The NTSB did indeed open just such an investigation but was summarily (and illegally) ordered by the State Department to halt it and to turn over all its documentation on the disaster.[8] This was the last ever heard of these documents, or of the legally necessary inquiry in the US. Clearly, the Administration's hope was that an ICAO inquiry would head off the demand for an inquiry by anyone else. And ICAO had the supreme advantage of being an intergovernmental organisation which can only consider information or evidence that its member governments decide to bring before it. What this meant was that ICAO would have no independent power of inquiry and could not pose to the US any of the very large number of embarrassing questions which the affair had raised about US behaviour.

There was no other forum in which the Reagan Administration could hope to control the flow of evidence so readily: clearly the South Koreans and Japanese would do what they were told by the US in this respect. And who, in the atmosphere which was bound to prevail, would listen to the Russians?

## ICAO meets

ICAO had certainly never been designed to carry out such investigations but its Convention was not definitive about the matter. Article 26 laid down the normal procedure: in case of accident involving death or serious injury, the state in whose territory the accident had taken place (in this case the USSR) was bound to conduct an inquiry into the affair, complying with ICAO procedures 'so far as its laws permit'. The state of registration (in this case South Korea) should be allowed to appoint observers to attend such an inquiry.[9] Annexe 13 to the Convention broadens this out to allow the state under whose air-navigation control the plane was (in this case Japan) and the state of the plane's manufacture (in this case the US) to attend the inquiry as well.

The Russians stood hard on these provisions, with which they promised their 'strict compliance'[10] – though it was notable that their delegate issued invitations to the South Koreans and Japanese to attend the official Russian inquiry under way, but not to the US. Given their compliance with ICAO rules, they argued, there was no ground at all for an ICAO inquiry, which would, indeed, be an infringement of ICAO rules. In fact neither the US, the Japanese nor the South Koreans made any move to attend the Soviet inquiry (though one can imagine the Americans enjoying a tour of the radar installations and fighter bases of Sakhalin and Kamchatka). Given that the USSR had already prejudged its inquiry entirely by accusing KAL 007 of carrying out a surveillance mission, this reluctance by the other three states to lend legitimacy to that inquiry was not very surprising.

J. Lynn Helms, when he spoke, made it equally clear that the US had in effect prejudged any inquiry too, for he argued both for an inquiry and condemnation of the USSR by ICAO in advance of that inquiry. Against the Soviet contentions, the US and its allies had three arguments: first that ICAO should observe 'the spirit' of its Convention; second that when the Libyan airliner had been shot down in 1973 the USSR had argued that ICAO could not stand aloof from such an event and should conduct an inquiry of its own (the ICAO Assembly had voted unanimously for such an inquiry (the only other ICAO inquiry ever held) but the Israelis had made it effectively redundant by admitting their fault and apologising); and third, Article 55(e) of the Convention empowered ICAO to investigate 'any situation which may appear to present avoidable obstacles to the development of international air navigation'.[11] While the Russians argued that this clause had never been intended to countermand Article 26, the fact was that 55(e) was the sort of saving clause lawyers love and would have permitted ICAO to stage inquiries into flying saucers or fairies if it wanted to.

The ICAO Council debate was the fairly predictable international slanging match which the UN is well used to – though ICAO is not. The French, seeking an independent position as ever, introduced an amendment trying to turn the issue into one of how to prevent the use of force against civilian airliners in the future. But it was immediately apparent that there was a large pro-Western majority and that the USSR was isolated, save for Czechoslovakia. The really serious problems came over the question of whether the USSR was to be condemned. The US, together with South Korea, exerted maximum pressure to this end but, as at the UN, they encountered stiff resistance from a number of Third World states. The really difficult case was India: almost alone the Indians pointed out that while the shoot-down was to be deeply deplored, there were many questions remaining unanswered about how on earth KAL 007 came to be so far off course, and how the pilots could possibly have been ignorant of the fact. India thus favoured an inquiry but concluded that 'until all the facts are in, judgement must necessarily be suspended'.[12] These sentiments were deeply unwelcome to the US and several other Western states in the highly emotional atmosphere which still clouded the whole affair only a fortnight after the shoot-down. Both superpowers attempted to broaden the issue out into the more general one of surveillance of their territories. The Russians handed in a long list of airspace violations they had allegedly suffered in the recent past. Not to be outdone, Lynn Helms made a dramatic counter: 'I have here in my hand a detailed list of over a page of Aeroflot violations in US airspace, showing the date and the aircraft.' The press showed a lively interest in this and asked Helms exactly how many violations there had been. He wasn't sure – 'twelve or fourteen'. Well, could journalists see the list? Absolutely not, said Helms's staff, though giving no reason. The list was not heard of again.[13]

In the end it was apparent that while there was a clear majority for an inquiry, even the strongest US pressure could not secure an outright condemnation of the USSR in advance of the inquiry's findings. The final, compromise resolution 'deeply deplored' the destruction of a civilian airliner and spoke of the use of force against an airliner being 'incompatible with the norms governing international behaviour and elementary considerations of humanity', but the only direct criticism of the USSR came in a clause which expressed 'concern' that the USSR 'has not so far acknowledged the paramount importance of the safety and lives of passengers and crew when dealing with civil aircraft intercepted in or near its territorial airspace'.[14] Faced with this cunningly drawn composite resolution, India asked for a clause-by-clause vote but was defeated. In the end the resolution passed by 26–2, with India, China and Algeria abstaining and Tanzania and Iraq absenting themselves from the vote. Helms professed himself delighted with the vote but the South Korean representative, Park Kun, commented bitterly that 'the resolution is far, far behind our expectations'.[15]

## The ICAO investigation

The ICAO investigation team went to work at once. Headquartered at ICAO's Bangkok office, the team had to visit South Korea, Japan, the US and the Sea of Japan. They wanted, of course, to visit the USSR too, but the Russians said they could not accept the team, reiterating their stance on Article 26 and Annexe 13 and claiming that the ICAO inquiry was illegal under ICAO's own rules. Nonetheless, the team worked with such speed that not much more than a month later they were able to present a lengthy interim report. At this stage the USSR appeared to relent somewhat and invited both the ICAO Secretary General, Yves Lambert, and the head of the ICAO inquiry team to Moscow. There they had meetings with the Minister of Civil Aviation and with the Soviet Commission of Inquiry into the 007 affair. They were taken to a Soviet fighter base where they were given a demonstration of a SU-15, replete with a 121.5 MHz radio transmitter. The Soviet inquiry also handed over some of its initial data to the Secretary General.[16] While this sort of assistance was a gesture, it fell a long way short of the full cooperation the ICAO really needed.

But the ICAO inquiry was handicapped above all by the political need for a speedy report and the fact that it wasn't equipped to carry out such investigations. As Duane Freer, head of ICAO's Air Navigation Commission, pointed out, 'We're not in the business of doing that. We had a short time-frame to determine the technical aspects of the accident. A full-fledged state investigation goes into greater detail.' Freer made the comparison with the US National Transportation Safety Board's inquiry into the crash of a DC-10 at O'Hare Airport (Chicago) in 1979. More than a hundred people had worked for seven months on that NTSB inquiry, while in the 007 case ICAO had five full-time and four part-time investigators with only sixty days to complete their job.[17] Thus while the 007 disaster was the most controversial of all the great aviation tragedies of recent time, it has also been the least thoroughly professionally investigated.

## The ICAO report

The inquiry's final report was presented to the ICAO Council at its session of 12–13 December. The report was a curate's egg: a mass of professionally assembled technical data with a commentary and analysis which left almost every important question unanswered – a classic piece of UN-ese, in fact. There can be little doubt that the inquiry team was heavily constrained, not only by the fact that they could only examine evidence put before them by the four governments concerned (privately, ICAO officials were indignant at the fact that all four were clearly holding back a great deal of information); but by the consciousness that theirs was destined to be the most-read ICAO report in history; and by that thumping Council majority which could have been considerably embarrassed by a more searching report.

The truth is that if one wants an awkward investigation carried out, the last body in the world one should go to is a UN affiliate, whose main concern is to give the least offence to all concerned. A recent classic of this genus was the UN inquiry into the invasion of Guinea in 1970. The Guineans furiously accused Portugal, and a large body of circumstantial evidence certainly pointed in that direction. The UN inquiry, with nothing less than the armed invasion of a member state at issue, concluded that it was impossible to blame anyone in particular. Four years later the Portuguese revolution took place and Portugal's initiative in launching the invasion was admitted, thus confirming what large numbers of soldiers, bureaucrats, politicians and even moderately informed journalists had known all along.

In the case of the ICAO report, the whole question of whether KAL 007 might have been on a surveillance mission was disposed of in just eight lines of the 113-page report. The USSR had claimed that 007's departure from Anchorage had been delayed by 40 minutes in order to allow it to coincide with the overpassage of a reconnaissance satellite later on. ICAO found that there was a satisfactorily innocent explanation of the delayed departure time: allowing for *en route* wind conditions, it would still have allowed KAL 007 to reach Kimpo International Airport, Seoul, at the standard 6 am arrival time.[18] Astonishingly, on this slender basis alone, ICAO concluded that it was therefore possible to ignore the surveillance hypothesis entirely – which is what the rest of the report proceeded to do. That is to say, ICAO's refutation of the hypothesis consisted simply of noting the wind conditions along Romeo 20, a glance at the standard KAL flight schedules, and an argument based on KAL 007's behaviour at Anchorage – before the flight had even begun.

It was, of course, quite ridiculous to treat the arrival time at Kimpo as conclusive. KAL planes quite normally arrive before 6 am. That is simply the time that the Kimpo customs section starts duty but the control tower is, of course, manned around the clock. Pilots are typically keen just to get in and finish the flight. Taxiing in, getting all the passengers and their hand luggage off the plane, into the terminal and through the arrival lounge will always take

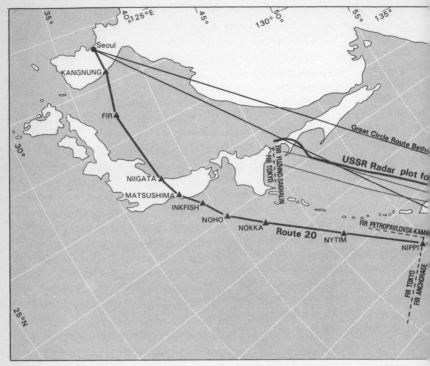

10  ICAO's simulations of possible accidental routes taken by KAL 007.

a good few extra minutes anyway. If the customs officers have to be dragged on to duty (or the passengers have to wait a little), this will not normally worry the pilots and crew who, having done their job, can get their sleep. There was, of course, nothing necessarily suspect about KAL 007's delayed departure time from Anchorage – but to treat this issue as the utterly crucial one was absurd.

What was needed was a careful, step-by-step attempt to examine – and then confirm or refute – the surveillance hypothesis. Instead, ICAO's determination to keep away from areas of military and political sensitivity meant that it preferred simply to ignore the question. It was a classic UN-style cop-out.

Thereafter, with the help of Boeing, Litton (the makers of the INS), the FAA and KAL, ICAO carried out exhaustive simulations of all the possible ways in which 007 might have accidentally gone off course. There turned out to be six of these (for the tracks produced by these simulations see Map 10 – the

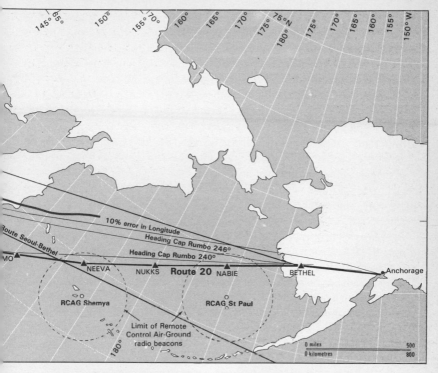

fifth and sixth simulations produced exactly the same track, so the map shows just five possible tracks).

The first possibility was that 007 had somehow selected a Great Circle – effectively, as the crow flies – track to Seoul from its position twelve miles north of Bethel. This produced a track far to the north of where 007 had been in fact. This alternative clearly wouldn't work and was discarded.

A second possibility was that 007 had somehow selected a Great Circle route somewhere along R20 which would have taken it direct to Seoul on a path which *did* coincide with its last known track over Sakhalin. This track was then extrapolated backwards and suggested that 007 would have had to make such an error just after passing NEEVA. This too had to be discarded – it couldn't account for 007's track over Kamchatka and it had to assume that 007 had stayed correctly on R20 all the way to NEEVA – while it was known it had been badly off course even at Bethel.

Next to be examined was the possibility that 007 had somehow got locked onto a 240° magnetic heading at its position north of Bethel. The resulting track failed quite hopelessly to coincide with what was known of 007's flight-path and this possibility too had to be summarily abandoned.

Another hypothesis which was carefully simulated only to be abandoned was that an erroneous ramp (take-off) position, 10° too far to the east, had somehow been programmed into all three INS at Anchorage. But in that case it would have been virtually impossible to pass position reports and estimates of waypoint times without reading them off the INS – which clearly displayed the fact of increasing cross-track error. So had this happened the crew would have to have seen they were off course. Had they carried on all the same, their deviation could only have been deliberate.

This left just two possibilities – that the same 10° error of longitude had been programmed into just one INS, or that 007 had somehow been locked onto a 246° magnetic heading. The problem was – as ICAO's own map showed – that neither of these two scenarios could explain the course 007 had actually taken.[19]

Despite this glaring hole in the argument, ICAO concluded that these were both possible explanations for the course 007 had taken. This clear illogicality was then covered over with the statement, 'Each of those postulations assumed a considerable degree of lack of alertness and attentiveness on the part of the entire flight crew but not to a degree that was unknown in international civil aviation.'[20] While, of course, gross negligence is by no means unheard of in the aviation world, this was a fairly startling statement, and not only in the light of the known proficiency and utter professionalism of 007's pilot. As the International Federation of Air Line Pilots' Associations (IFALPA) indignantly pointed out, ICAO had adduced no shred of evidence for such an assumption. IFALPA announced that it preferred 'to keep an open mind on the reason as to why the aircraft deviated from its track'.[21]

In sum, then, the ICAO judgement was that the surveillance mission hypothesis should be summarily dealt with on the basis of the plane's departure time alone, and then ignored; that only accidental explanations would be seriously considered; that when none of these really worked, ICAO would nonetheless settle on two of them as possible explanations; and that it would support this by making a further assumption for which it had no evidence at all.

Not surprisingly, the report pleased almost nobody. The USSR dismissed it out of hand and said the ICAO inquiry should never have taken place anyway. KAL was not best pleased by the assumption that its pilots might endanger their passengers by gross negligence. The US was not pleased by paragraphs in the report which suggested that its military radar facilities might have done more to avert the tragedy.[22] IFALPA was indignant. The press was contemptuous that the inquiry had laboured to bring forth a mouse. On the other hand the report was, in political terms, a skilful job. Nobody was wholly vindicated or condemned, or not more than they had been before the inquiry started. Everyone could feel disgruntled, but no one outraged. The report's conclusions were so tentative that no one had to accept any of them if they didn't want to – and the tension which remained could slowly be dissipated in a healing fog of confusion.

It makes more sense, in fact, not to view the ICAO report as an authoritative attempt to deliver the last word on the 007 tragedy – manifestly it was not that – but as an exercise in political damage limitation. Had the report attempted to insist that the plane could only have been off course by accident, there might have been grounds for a political condemnation of the USSR, or even its expulsion from ICAO. On the other hand, had the report concluded that 007's deviation from course could only have been deliberate, and taken the surveillance hypothesis really seriously, ICAO might have faced walkouts by South Korea and the US – the latter being the organisation's chief paymaster. To return a completely open verdict, giving equal treatment to the accidental and surveillance hypotheses, would still have enraged the US and would, from the point of view of the Council majority, have had the unfortunate effect of vindicating the troublesome Third World doubters. Instead, the report avoided all these problematic outcomes and thus fulfilled the categorical imperative of all bureaucracies, the maintenance of organisational unity. With a sigh of relief, ICAO was now able to return to the smoother, quieter waters it so much preferred.

When the ICAO Council met again on 12–15 December the US FAA head, J. Lynn Helms, attempted again to secure a condemnation of the USSR, arguing that the ICAO report had 'rebuffed'[23] the allegation of a surveillance mission by 007. The Council, having resisted strong American pressures over three months to move in this direction, now responded by deciding to defer detailed consideration of the report until the ICAO Air Navigation Commission (the ANC – a specialist technical body) had reviewed it. This was to be the end of Helms's efforts – shortly afterwards he was to join the long list of Reagan appointees forced to resign over allegations related to his business dealings while in office.[24]

## The ANC report

The ANC report[25] – delivered in February 1984 – was something of a bombshell and suggested that there were serious misgivings within ICAO about the first (the Secretary General's) report. Although the ANC's language was carefully chosen, several passages in its report amounted to little less than a rebuke to the framers of the first report. Such open criticism was extremely unusual in the benignly diplomatic atmosphere of ICAO.

The ANC made a large number of detailed points. For example, in the transcript of the Soviet fighters' conversations provided by Japan and the US, one of the key sentences had been 'the strobe light is flashing'. This had been taken as definitive proof by Mrs Kirkpatrick and other American spokesmen that 007's lights had been on and had been seen. Actually, as the ANC pointed out, 007 was 'not equipped with white strobe anti-collision lights', only with red, flashing (non-strobe) lights.[26] This threw a major element in the US case into confusion and raised further questions about the translation of the transcripts. On a more general level, the ANC could not go along with any of the accident scenarios postulated by the first report 'because any one of them contained some points which could not be explained satisfactorily'.[27] This was, pretty clearly, dynamite, for if doubt was thrown on the accident scenarios, what was left? This the ANC simply left open: it was 'unable to establish the exact cause for the significant deviation from track. The magnitude of the diversion cannot be explained . . .'[28] All the ANC would say on the other side was that it had been 'unable to substantiate that the aircraft's diversion from its flight plan track was the result of a deliberate action by the flight crew'[29] – but the ANC report left the feeling that perhaps that was the area in which an explanation should be sought. The ANC's report did not make comfortable reading and it received remarkably little press coverage.

## The perfect compromise

With this ICAO, in effect, put the affair of KAL 007 behind it and instead busied itself with the question of how to prevent the use of force against civilian airliners in future. These discussions led to the Extraordinary ICAO Assembly of April 1984.[30]

The Assembly faced three main resolutions: one from the US, which simply sought to prohibit the use of force against civil aircraft; one from Austria and France, which sought the same but also allowed a state to use 'any appropriate means' to prevent violations of the sovereignty of its airspace;[31] and one from the USSR, which sought to ban the use of 'weapons' against such aircraft but insisted that national sovereignty was an absolute right. In debate the USSR argued that if a civilian aircraft intruded over one's territory and refused all requests to land or obey orders, to say that the state thus offended against 'could in practice do nothing about it was to make national sovereignty meaningless. The weight of the Soviet proposal therefore lay in tightening the responsibilities of states to ensure that their national civilian aircraft did not make unauthorised or illegal sorties over the territory of other states. There followed a period of intense bargaining in which it became clear that many Third World states shared Soviet fears of unauthorised intrusions into their airspace – intrusions which they would lack the means to monitor or intercept. (The US, for its part, did not like talk of 'violations' – its delegate found the term 'subjective'.) The so-called North Group of twenty-five pro-Western states, led by the US, pressed hard but in the end unavailingly to overcome these fears.[32] Nobody liked the thought of force being used against civilian airliners, but to legislate its prohibition under all circumstances might mean that henceforth such planes could be used for surveillance or military intrusions with impunity. When they thought about that, the majority liked it even less.

In the end a compromise draft was unanimously agreed and voted as a new Article in the ICAO Convention. As one might have expected, it had something for everyone and resolved nothing. While agreeing that civil aircraft must not be used 'for any purpose inconsistent with the aims of the Convention' (i.e. including surveillance), it also agreed that 'the safety and lives of persons on board civil aircraft must be assured' – but simultaneously recognised the principle of absolute sovereignty of states over their national airspace.[33] Thus everyone agreed not to misuse civil aircraft for surveillance purposes; not to use force against such aircraft if they were nonetheless misused to that purpose; but also to reserve their right to do so if they felt it was absolutely necessary. All the delegates, including those from the US and the USSR, congratulated the Assembly (i.e. themselves) on its wonderful work. In fact the resolution proved little more than that if one can get all 151 states of the world voting unanimously on something, that 'something' is liable to be meaningless. No doubt a motion in praise of motherhood would pass unanimously, provided there was a saving clause conceding that matricide was an occasionally permissible act.

This may seem a harsh attitude to take towards ICAO – a worthy organisation which has done a great deal of valuable work over the years in standardising aviation procedures and has presided over a steady and almost miraculous improvement in aviation safety. But the fact is that if ICAO is to live up to its responsibilities, it will have to display a greater determination to confront military and political sensitivities than it showed in the case of KAL 007. ICAO faced a situation, after all, where both superpowers were making deadly serious accusations that civilian airliners – Aeroflot or KAL – were being used for purposes of military espionage, with consequent terrible dangers for passengers and crew. It is difficult to imagine a more terrifying threat to civil aviation than this: if the superpowers believe this is happening even occasionally, then *all* civil aviation becomes suspect in their eyes, which means that *all* airline passengers and crew have had their margin of safety reduced. This ought to put the issue in the front line of ICAO's concerns.

## The unspeakable issue: military use of civilian transport

There is considerable evidence that the misuse of civilian transport for military purposes has taken place, and such misuse may be growing. The CIA has actually admitted to the past use of civilian airliners for espionage over East Germany[34] and it is a matter of public record that the agency used to own several whole airlines – Air America, Air Asia, Southern Air Transport and Intermountain Aviation;[35] indeed, Air America was at one time the largest airline in the world.[36] It is possible, in addition, to draw up a list of more than another twenty airlines which have, at one time or another, had CIA ties.[37] And while the CIA was forced to sell off its directly owned airlines after Watergate, there is considerable doubt as to how far the links have really been severed – and one is bound to wonder, if the CIA found such prodigious use for civil air transport 'cover' in the pre-Watergate period, how it has been filling that need since. The similar misuse of Aeroflot and other East European airlines is not well documented. Perhaps they are truly more innocent – with no free press in such countries it is harder to tell – but it seems far more probable that they are not. In many cases such airlines enjoy a symbiotic relationship with their military and intelligence establishments where even the boundaries between what is civil and what is military are extremely blurred.

In addition, there is the ever present temptation to use genuine airlines and civil air routes as 'cover'. In the wake of the 007 tragedy, the Lufthansa pilot, Rudolf Braunburg, spoke out feelingly on this issue. It is worth quoting him at length:

Pilots who have flown international routes for more than two decades often notice US military planes using civilian air routes and behaving like civilian planes. Before the Shah of Iran fell, the route linking Istanbul and Tehran was the route where that happened most often. There was one military airport after another along the southern border with the Soviet Union, and there were many US military planes using funny code names flying on civilian routes to deliver cargo to these airfields.

On the North Pacific route one can detect the radio signals of similar planes; in addition, one can see the exhaust trails of other, higher flying planes which are crossing the east–west Pacific routes coming from the north and south. We were never able to detect their signals on the normal civilian radio frequencies; there seemed to be routine traffic crossing international borders.

This air traffic is now being explained: recent statements by the US Administration admit that there are 'routine flights by US reconnaissance planes north of Japan'; one of them took place at the same time as the Korean Boeing was in the area. At times the mixing up of military and civilian planes was purposely provoked by the military.

There are routes all over the world which are very close to strictly forbidden territories. One of the most heavily travelled areas, between Bangkok and Hong Kong, is much closer to Red Chinese territory than the North Pacific route is to the Soviet Union. Not to mention flights over countries at war or landings at Beirut airport. None of the politicians ... including Reagan's staff ... has mentioned that incidents such as the one over the Soviet Union (i.e. KAL 007) have occurred numerous times in the past.

To be precise, if I am evaluating statistics correctly, it has happened thirty-two times since 1947. Thirty-two times a civilian airplane has been shot down for the very same reason as the one over the Soviet Union: violation of foreign airspace. This is where the real political scandal begins. Pilots, and not politicians, have been protesting against regulations which allowed these downings for decades. They would have been grateful had their governments just shed a few tears over these incidents in the past – compared to the many tears they are shedding now that the Soviets are involved.[38]

Braunburg's figures were not quite correct. In September 1983 the UK Civil Aviation Authority listed 33 occasions since 1947 on which an airliner had been shot at or forced down by fighter aircraft. In the last twenty years such cases had increased to an average rate of one a year.[39]

There are signs, moreover, that the notion of using civilian transport as military or intelligence 'cover' has gained ground with the advent of the Reagan Administration. The Administration has made a positive virtue out of 'unshackling' the CIA and encouraging a more gung-ho attitude among the military in general. In such an atmosphere all manner of wild schemes tend to get hatched and some even to get carried out. Thus Japanese public opinion was shocked in 1981 to learn that there were Pentagon plans to place nuclear-armed cruise missiles on the Japanese *Shinkansen* 'bullet trains', with the trains' mobility and high speed making them effectively invulnerable to Soviet attack.[40] This would clearly have made *all* such trains into legitimate military targets. In the ensuing furore such plans were apparently shelved. But how often will such schemes escape without publicity?

To be fair, the US military are by no means always the strongest supporters of such schemes – the danger has lain more in the new breed of Reaganite civilian superhawks who have frequently been willing to push for schemes which have left professional military men aghast. In the eyes of men like Weinberger and Perle, even the Joint Chiefs of Staff were seen as dangerous moderates, willing to make irresponsible concessions to the Russians. Indeed, one of Perle's deputies, clearly echoing his boss's prejudices, referred to the Chiefs as 'has-beens who haven't assimilated the political fact of life that SALT II is *ipso facto* bad'.[41]

This sort of split was evident in an even more hair-raising proposal which gained favour with the superhawks, that of placing MX missiles on randomly flying aircraft which would fly 'at the same altitude as private aircraft'.[42] (If the object is, as it seems to be, to hide a nuclear attack force among civilian planes, one suspects that such 'randomly roving' aircraft would find normal airline routes, as well as altitudes, the best cover.) This idea surfaced in 1981, the brainchild of a panel chaired by the University of California physicist, Charles Townes. The USAF did not like the idea at all and 'tenaciously tried to arrange its demise'. Caspar Weinberger, however, was a strong supporter of the idea and sold it to the always receptive President, so that by October 1981 Reagan was announcing that the proposal was one of 'three promising long-term options for basing the MX' which would be investigated in depth. The USAF has continued to oppose the idea but they have to do so in the face of 'the Defense Secretary's and the President's strong support' for it. What is perhaps even more fantastic is that the original proposal was for unmanned planes to perform this mimicry of civilian aircraft but that Townes's panel had just one suggestion for improving the idea – 'that human beings be put aboard the planes, too'. No one, not even the USAF, seems to have openly queried the scheme on the grounds of the potential dangers it poses for civil aviation.

At the moment, these are just plans, but the mind-set they reveal is – or ought to be – deeply alarming to ICAO. Similarly, there have been a whole series of incidents over and around Nicaragua in which William Casey's CIA seems to have used civilian planes for a variety of 'covert' bombing and intelligence missions.[43]

But it is important to realise that the dangers do not stem simply from one set of politicians or generals in just one country – the problem is more pervasive than that. Thus in July 1985, during the Soviet Summerex '85 exercises in the eastern Atlantic, an RAF Nimrod was quite widely reported as having mimicked a civilian airliner in order to catch the Soviet ships unawares. The Nimrod, piloted by Crew 9 of RAF 42 squadron, based at St Mawgan, Cornwall, had 'flown out ... at 29,000 feet "disguised" as an airliner, chatting with civilian air traffic controllers at Prestwick and Shannon on a dummy civilian call sign'.[44] The controllers, as also, probably, the Russians, were entirely fooled by the call sign and the airliner altitude and had the plane marked down as being on the routine civilian run across the Atlantic.[45] Then, at the last moment, the plane dived low over the Soviet ships. 'The leading Soviet frigate probably knew nothing of their presence until they came hounding out of the northwest haze at 200 feet, camera shutters clattering, to pick out every inch of sophisticated electronics and weaponry.'[46] The *Sunday Times* reporter with the crew gaily commented, 'Going in covertly on such Soviet groups catches the vessels with weapons and electronic systems in operation or uncovered for maintenance . . . For Crew 9 it offered more adrenalin than the routine "tapestry ops" – photographing all the fishing boats in a given area. However, such activities are a peacetime luxury.'[47] The whole tone of the report suggests that this sort of civilian-miming is not that unusual. On this occasion the Nimrod carried out its manoeuvres in radar range of the (enraged) Shannon controllers,[48] but how often does such behaviour occur out of radar range?

No doubt such fun and games do things for a crew's adrenalin, and also for that of the Russians below. As they watched the radar blip streak down from 29,000 feet and disappear from the screen, and saw a jet screaming in at mast-height, the Russians may even have wondered if photography was all it had in mind . . . By the same token, such manoeuvres ought to put up the adrenalin count of all ordinary civilian passengers and crew on the Atlantic run – the busiest in the world. For, quite clearly, such behaviour encourages the Russians to see 'airliners' as potential military or intelligence threats. The consequent jumpiness of the Soviet military could have dire consequences for civilian airliners much further afield than the Atlantic; in the Sea of Japan, for example.

There is no doubt that for ICAO to confront the issue of the dangers posed to civil aviation by military and intelligence activities would bring great problems and pressures for the organisation. What is needed is a thorough, no-holds-barred investigation of the past record and a continuous, tough-minded monitoring of all such activities. This would undoubtedly cause grave embarrassment to a number of states who are leading members of the ICAO Council. But the alternative – to go on averting one's eyes like a Victorian maiden – is to betray the many pilots and passengers for whom Rudolf Braunburg speaks. It is, ultimately, a question of what ICAO is there for.

The ICAO investigation of the KAL 007 tragedy thus fell far short of providing a final, authoritative explanation of what had happened. Indeed the organisation's final position in the wake of the ANC report appeared to be that it was highly unlikely – perhaps even impossible – that 007 had been off course by accident, but that it could not say definitively that it was deliberately off course either.

The major reason why the ICAO exercise was so inconclusive was simply the organisation's inability to require evidence from those who had it. It could not ask the US to provide the radar and radio intercepts of 007's flight which it undoubtedly had; or the radar tapes of the last section of 007's flight; or the tapes of the Soviet ground-to-air conversations. Nor could it interview the pilot of the RC-135 which had crossed paths with 007. It must surely have been a major humiliation for ICAO that it failed to obtain even the explosive information about 007's deception of Narita ground control and its apparent evasive tactics in the last stage of its flight. This data was finally produced to the Japanese Diet, but not to ICAO.[49] Indeed, ICAO had not even known that there *were* radar tapes. When it considered the varying Soviet and Japanese versions of the turn over Sakhalin (where it instinctively chose the Japanese version) it had to assume 'that the radar track information is based on memories of radar observers rather than on recorded radar data'.[50] ICAO must have been stunned to find out that this was not true, especially as those tapes included the crucial turn over Sakhalin. When the Japanese made public the facts about 007's descent when it was reporting an ascent, one of the members of the ICAO inquiry, Marinus Heijl, a technical officer of the Air Navigation Bureau, said, 'We were never aware of any descent in that phase of the flight. We heard about the turn [over Sakhalin] and the different theories about it. But we had no real explanation for any turn or any information on that turn.'[51]

Even so, ICAO was pusillanimous. Why did it make so little of 007's turn over Sakhalin? Even from the little it knew of the turn, it might have done more than simply try to suggest that the Japanese report of it was right and the Russians' wrong: after all, they had only hearsay on both sides.

Why did it fail to notice the mysterious fuel/weight discrepancies on the manifests which it did examine? Why did it not pay any attention to Captain Chun's jottings on the back of his flight plan (reproduced by ICAO), in which he seemed to have been planning the route he actually took?[52] One could go on and on. Clearly, any proper explanation of 007's flight must attempt to take into account many factors which ICAO did not consider at all. It is to that task that we must now turn.

# TWELVE

# Reaching a Verdict on KAL 007

It seems clear enough that once KAL 007 had strayed so disastrously off course a terrible tragedy was in the offing. So explaining why the tragedy took place comes down largely to explaining how the plane came to be so far off course. In the present state of knowledge it is not possible to give a definitive answer to this. All that one can do is to evaluate the various alternative explanations which have been offered and decide which is the most probable. Murray Sayle has suggested a useful criterion for such an evaluation, that of William of Occam: that in seeking an explanatory hypothesis one should not increase the complexity of the argument beyond the call of strict necessity. Given the absence of any proper official enquiry into the KAL tragedy, however, one also has to weigh the odds and probabilities in the manner so famously prescribed by Sherlock Holmes. All told, four theories have been put forward: that 007 strayed off course by accident; that the pilots deliberately attempted to short-cut their route in order to save fuel; that the Russians deliberately attempted to lure the plane off course by electronic interference with its navigation equipment; and that it was on a surveillance mission.

## Accident theories

The main ICAO report considered six possible accident theories but regarded only two as serious candidates.[1] The first of these was that an erroneous ramp (i.e. takeoff) position of 10 degrees too far to the east had been inserted into the controlling inertial navigation system (INS) only, with the other two INS correctly programmed. If this had been done, however, then the triple-mixing system of the three INS would quickly have led to the correction of the controlling INS – so ICAO further supposed that this triple mixing feature had, unaccountably, not been employed. If, somehow, 007 had then followed the resulting course it would have produced a track at least approximately close to that plotted by the Soviet radars for a large part of the flight.

The second accident hypothesis was that 007 had not been flying on its INS at all but that the autopilot mode-selector switch had been inadvertently left in heading mode, harnessed to the magnetic heading of 246 degrees. This was, after all, the heading which 007 would have taken from Anchorage as it flew towards its first 'signpost', Cairn Mountain. If the pilots had then forgotten to move the switch on the autopilot mode-selector in order to hook up the INS, then the plane could have continued on 246 degrees magnetic all the way – and this too would go some way to accounting for the course 007 took.

Those who have argued most powerfully for an accidental explanation – most notably the Australian journalist, Murray Sayle – have fastened exclusively on this second hypothesis. It is not difficult to see why. If one draws out the route implied by the first hypothesis, two things stand out: first, the route would have taken 007 38 nautical miles north of Bethel, not the actual twelve;[2] and second, the route would only just have shaved the very southern tip of Sakhalin and would not have put 007 where it was finally shot down. These errors alone really knock out the theory, for a plane flying on INS will follow the route programmed into it to within a margin of feet: variances of dozens of miles are just not possible. In addition, there would have been significant differences in the times required to reach the various (notional) waypoints and the other two INS would have clearly displayed the plane's increasing cross-track error.[3] But really it is not necessary to add such points: the key one is just that if 007 had been flying on INS at all, one has to find a route which corresponds *exactly* with at least the two certainly known parts of 007's route (past Bethel and at the shoot-down). Since this can't be found, such a hypothesis has to be rejected outright – no doubt why ICAO's Air Navigation Commission was so cutting about it.[4] So if one is looking for an accident hypothesis, one more or less has to go for the 246-degree magnetic-heading mode explanation.

Sayle has argued strongly for this hypothesis,[5] pointing out that it merely required that the autopilot switch should have been a single notch off its right position – something which might, with an inattentive crew, have passed unnoticed. Moreover, although in effect the plane would then have been flying on its magnetic compass, the INS would still have provided the crew with regular indications of waypoints – the INS alert lights going on and off in the normal way as the plane approached each notional waypoint. Although in fact the real waypoints would have been further and further abeam of where the plane really was, the pilots might not have realised this and might have had the impression that they were navigating in the INS mode all the same.

In order to make this case, Sayle has to make several further suppositions. First, there is the problem of how 007 failed to correct itself by checking with the VOR radio beam at Bethel. Sayle suggests that perhaps just at that moment Captain Chun had wandered out of the cabin in order to go and greet his travelling VIP, Congressman Larry McDonald, and perhaps the KAL officers travelling as passengers. He further imagines that the copilot, First Officer Son, though left in the cockpit with the flight engineer, also failed to notice that the INS was uncoupled or to make the VOR check at Bethel. Thereafter, Sayle also imagines that Captain Chun, due to 'excessive confidence', did not use his weather radar in ground-mapping mode (which would have shown up the land contours first of the Alaskan and later of the Soviet coastline below). As to the Soviet attempts to contact 007, Sayle agrees that the evidence of the Soviet fighters' tapes is that they certainly tried and could get no answer. Against this he makes certain further suppositions: that 007 'had no reason' to be guarding the 121.5 MHz frequency; that 007's officers might not have noticed the Soviet tracer bursts because these would have been quite dispersed by the time they passed 007; and that anyway the copilot was chatting to Narita ground control at the time (and the other two officers presumably not looking). Finally, there is the question of 007's turn over Sakhalin. Sayle is emphatic here: if the Soviet radar twice showing a curve in the 007's track is correct then, he avers, there cannot possibly be an innocent explanation of the plane's flight. But he argues that actually there may not have been a curve at all – that if the plane had passed directly over the Soviet radars, this could have distorted the reading through what is known as the 'slant range effect'.

Sayle's is by far the most thoroughly worked-through attempt at an accidental explanation. There are, however, many problems with it. The first and most crushing of these is simply that a course based on 246 degrees magnetic does not produce a track comparable to that which 007 took. Not only does this track take 007 6.5 nautical miles north of Bethel (instead of the actual 12),[6] but, as the ICAO map clearly shows, the course then only cuts the very southernmost edge of Kamchatka and misses Sakhalin altogether – indeed, misses it by a far wider margin than is produced by the other accidental hypothesis, which Sayle rejects (see Map 10 on pp. 232–3). Remarkably, although Sayle has clearly had access to the ICAO maps, he simply produces a map which shows a quite different track and labels it '246° magnetic'.[7] The only explanation we can presume for this variance from ICAO's careful simulation at Boeing and Litton is that Sayle adds that he has made allowance for the prevailing winds on the night in question. This is, in itself, not unreasonable, for a course steered only by magnetic compass will not be subject to the same multitude of instantaneous on-course corrections as an INS produces. Indeed, it would be all but impossible to steer a really straight-line course relying on a magnetic compass alone – gusts of wind would blow the plane well off course and when the gust subsided the plane would simply carry on flying 246 degrees on a laterally displaced course. But this only increases Sayle's problems for, as ICAO's meteorological map plainly shows, all the prevailing winds that night were blowing towards the south and the west – which would have blown 007 further away from the USSR, not nearer to it.[8]

If this were not enough – and probably it should be – the rest of Sayle's case does not stand careful examination either. He rests almost everything on the fact that the INS alert lights would come on at the waypoint stages as if all were normal, provided the plane was not more than 200 miles off track. Yet even Sayle accepts that 007 was 365 miles off track when it was shot down.[9] Thus, even according to his own hypothesis, the INS would have been clearly showing that something was badly wrong long before that. Sayle also offers no explanation of how 007 failed to see its true position from failing to pick up the Shemya VOR beam – a standard precaution on Romeo 20.

It is also not as easy as Sayle suggests to imagine that 007 was not using its weather radar in ground-mapping mode. This is, after all, standard practice both for KAL and most other airlines on this route. For a plane so close to forbidden Soviet airspace and so long out of civilian radar coverage, it is a very obvious precaution. As P. J. R. Reynolds, PanAm's former director of navigation services, put it, 'Kamchatka and the Kurile Islands are high, prominent and rocky – beautiful radar targets.' All a plane had to do to be sure of staying out of trouble, said Reynolds, was to keep the islands 50 miles to his right.[10]

Nor is Sayle right to suggest that 007 had no reason to monitor the 121.5 MHz channel. The ICAO Air Navigation Commission experts were quite emphatic on this point:

KE 007 was equipped for communication on 121.5 MHz and company procedures required that this frequency be monitored throughout the flight. There is no indication that this procedure was not complied with. The aircraft was equipped with three VHF transceivers. Even if VHF set No. 2 had failed to function properly, listening watch on 121.5 MHz could have been maintained on VHF set No. 1, while the air-to-air communications with KE 015 could have been carried out on VHF set No. 3 . . .[11]

Similarly, Sayle's claim that 007 would not have noticed the Soviet tracer bursts due to dispersion of the shells before they passed 007 does not really stand up. It is certainly true that tracer bullets lose their brilliance after travelling around 9000 feet[12] – but Major Kasmin's SU-15 was about two kilometres behind 007 when the tracers were fired, and two kilometres is 6562 feet. From that range the tracers should have been clearly visible.

Then again, Sayle seems to be unaware that ICAO agreed that 007 *had* made a turn over Sakhalin[13] – it is quite incorrect to say, as he does, that there is only Soviet evidence for the turn. The Wakkanai radar reported a (slightly flatter) turn too, and the ICAO technical experts used the argument of 'slant range effects' merely to explain the difference between the Wakkanai and Soviet versions of the turn. Sayle also offers no explanation at all for the way in which 007 was deceiving its Narita ground controller and failing to carry out its ascent to 35,000 feet in the last stages of the flight;[14] nor, indeed, does he have anything to say about the jottings on the flight plan left at Anchorage which suggest that a route plan was being drawn up for the course actually taken.[15] Even without taking all these factors into account, the ICAO Air Navigation Commission found they could not 'validate and endorse' this scenario.[16] Again, one can see why.

Major-General Richard Rohmer, surveying (some of) this evidence, concluded that an accidental explanation was simply impossible:

The answer to the question, 'Did the 747's crew know the aircraft was off course?' is, 'Yes, they knew exactly where they were from the time they left Anchorage through the false waypoint checks that they transmitted past Kamchatka and over Sakhalin Island to their final destruction.' The final, crucial question about the route flown by Captain Chun is: 'Why was he intentionally there?'[17]

Sayle is equally emphatic about the turn over Sakhalin. If the plane really did make changes of course, he concludes,

Then they cannot be explained either by the aircraft's flying in magnetic heading unknown to the crew, or by any conceivable misprogramming of the INS, or 'finger trouble'. Someone must therefore be guilty, in a conspiracy which must include some combination of the CIA, the dead pilots, Korean Air Lines, the NSA, Ronald Reagan, the FAA, the US Air Force, or all of the above.[18]

No doubt Sayle intends this as a humorous shaft against 'conspiracy theorists', but the remark rebounds. If he had bothered to read the ICAO report Sayle would have seen that 007 *did* make changes of course over Sakhalin, and that he was therefore committed to believing a theory quite opposite to that which he was arguing for.

In fact one cannot rule out the possibility of an accidental deviation from course quite as definitively as Rohmer and (logically) Sayle would do, just because neither of the scenarios postulated by ICAO holds water. There is, after all, almost no end to the possibilities of human incompetence, snafus and so on, and it may not always be possible after the event to reconstruct a logical path back into what actually happened. What one can do, though, is to work out the odds applying to *any* accidental explanation, remembering that the odds compound as at a horse race: the odds against picking *two* 20–1 winners are 400–1, not 40–1.

One might start with the testimony of the NASA official, William D. Reynaud, to the subcommittee of Transportation, Aviation and Materials of the US Congressional Committee on Science and Technology on 19 September 1983. Mr Reynaud, who heads a NASA safety reporting unit, told the Committee that he had made a special study of navigational errors by aircraft carrying the same INS as that carried by 007. Over the past five years he had found just twenty-one cases of error – one in every 20,000 flights.[19] 'The equipment itself was reliable,' he said, 'human error in programming was almost always the cause.' The average deviation in these twenty-one cases was well under 100 miles and the maximum ever recorded was 250 miles.[20]

007 was some 365 miles off course when shot down. Thus the one in 20,000 odds against navigational error must be compounded by the at least 21–1 odds against the plane setting a new world record for such deviations – that is, overall odds of 420,000–1 against. After that there were a large number of decision points when 007 inexplicably failed to correct its course via normal checking procedures. Such decision points occurred at Bethel, NABIE, NEEVA and NIPPI, plus the failure to check against the St Paul's radio beacon, the Shemya VOR, the failure to look at the magnetic compass or to use the weather radar. Most pilots would be outraged if the odds against each of these failures were set at less than several thousands to one, but let us be ultraconservative and allot each of these failures odds of a mere 100–1 against. This produces further odds of one quintillion (1 followed by eighteen 'o's) to one, to be compounded with our previous 420,000–1.

This is, however, just the beginning. We must also add in all the odds against a whole series of other factors all being accidents: the unexplained loading with extra fuel and the discrepancy between the weight/fuel manifests at Anchorage; the jotted notes left at Anchorage suggestive of a planned deviation from route; the apparent variations in speed by both KAL 015 and 007; the missing of the Soviet signals, the noise of their planes, and their firing of tracers; KAL 015 failing to notice the discrepancy in the winds reported by 007 and itself; and the final failure to send out a Mayday. Beyond that we have the deliberate deception of Narita ground control over the altitude ascent which did not take place; the coincidence of the close encounter with the RC-135, and the changes of course. It has to be remembered that there must have been a minimum of three of these – two to cause the curve over Sakhalin and one earlier one to take 007 from the line it was on as it passed Bethel into the track it was ultimately following over Kamchatka and Sakhalin. It would be possible to add yet further factors to this list (e.g. the failure to use Distance Measuring Equipment (DME) readings to check position; Captain Chun's 'human computer' reputation being so sharply refuted by the negligence necessary for even a few of these errors to occur; the difficulty in providing reasonable simulations of waypoint times and distances through which 007 was not in fact travelling; and so on). But there really doesn't seem much point in going on. Long before we have finished our calculations we will have arrived at odds expressed in the sort of numbers which would make even astronomers blench: literally billions of trillions to one against. It is, though, in the nature of the 'accidental' explanation that the possibility of all these things occurring simultaneously by accident can never quite be eliminated. Nonetheless, as one looks at those odds one knows that neither William of Occam nor Sherlock Holmes would waste much time in dispensing with this form of explanation.

It is important that one does apply this reckoning-of-odds method through. The key weakness of those who, like Sayle, wish to argue for an accident hypothesis lies not so much in the sheer impossibility of each of their premises, but in the monstrous unlikelihood of every single one of their long-odds-against suppositions being simultaneously true. Each new step in the argument forces such proponents to increase the odds against themselves further and further: thus Sayle would wish to question the reliability of the Japanese radar data on the general principle that both radar and airliner altimeters can be unreliable.[21] And so they can: but if one is to make that point then one must also reckon in the further odds against 007's altimeter, though working well at Anchorage, having gone wrong during the flight; and against the advanced military radars at Wakkanai being not merely grossly unreliable but not consistently unreliable either. While those who wish to argue for an accident hypothesis will certainly continue to do so, surely even they must recognise a point where their position is overwhelmed by the ever accumulating weight of sheer improbability.

A subsidiary form of the accidental hypothesis lies in the possibility of a hijack. This was suggested early on by Kim Chang Kyu, the pilot of the KAL plane which had strayed over Murmansk in 1978. Kim pointed out that 007's INS was far better than the type of navigational equipment on which he had had to rely, and that in any case 'everybody uses weather radar in that area'. Kim found an accidental explanation quite implausible and said the only thing he could come up with was the possibility that a hijacker had taken over the plane and flown it (very badly) himself.[22]

This hypothesis was, however, immediately discounted by one and all – ICAO simply refused to countenance it. It would, after all, have been a pretty funny hijack, given that 007's deviation simply meant that it was short-cutting to its scheduled destination. That is, the motive for a hijack would have to have been just to get the plane where it was going anyway – a bit more quickly and at a horrendous risk. But in any case, 007 carried on talking normally over the radio and gave no indication of a hijack. 007, like most other 747s, had a hidden hijack alert signal but this was not activated.[23] Moreover 007 did have – disguised amongst its passengers or crew – two sky marshals aboard,[24] precisely to thwart hijackers.

Thus Kim Chang Kyu's suggestion can be discounted. Unfortunately Kim did not speculate further – for example, about what looks very much like the evasive tactics adopted by 007 once the SU-15 was on its tail.

One is bound to add, in parenthesis, that Kim's own 1978 excursion still has question marks hanging over it. His plane, KAL 902, was flying in a northwesterly direction on the Paris–Anchorage run when it unaccountably turned in an opposite, southeasterly direction and flew over the biggest and most secret Soviet base of all, Murmansk. The Russians claim they tried repeatedly to contact KAL 902 but were ignored. In the end they fired warning shots past his plane, but these too had no effect. Kim then apparently took evasive action – at which point the Soviet fighter fired at his plane and forced it down.[25] Kim's own story was that he had signalled that he would follow the SU-15 down – but Sampson and Bittorf cite US sources to the effect that Soviet signals were initially ignored as the plane continued on southwards.[26] Given the exceptionally strong Korean ethic of honour and disgrace, and the gross nature of Kim's navigational error it would normally have followed that Kim would have been liable to fairly heavy sanctions. In fact he was welcomed home like a hero and not sanctioned.

Another KAL pilot, Captain S. S. Yang, who had been flying his plane the opposite way to Anchorage and had passed 007 over the Aleutians, said that he had attempted to raise 007 on his radio to swop weather reports but had been unable to get through and had also overheard Anchorage ground control having difficulty in getting through to 007. 'His radio was very garbled,' said Yang. 'They do not understand each other. I tried to relay, but he couldn't hear me. I tried to call him several times.'[27]

The strange thing about this report was the way that it was immediately met with strong denials by US officials that there had ever been any communications problem with 007[28] – though, as we know, there had been and KAL 015 had relayed a large number of 007's messages for it.

It is difficult to see, however, that Captain Yang's evidence makes much difference either way. If 007 had been on a surveillance mission, no doubt it would not have wanted to have casual weather chats with passing planes. And, in any case, we know that 007 had several radios and used them throughout the flight.

Yet another KAL pilot, Choy Tack Yong, made what *Le Monde* described as a 'surprisingly tardy'[29] appearance on 9 September, when he was interviewed for the South Korean paper, *Joong-ang Ilbo*. Captain Choy, who had piloted 007 on its flight from New York to Anchorage, now surfaced to say that he had reported at Anchorage that one of 007's VHF radios was giving trouble and that a warning light on one of the horizontal situation indicators (i.e. part of the navigation system) had been flashing – indicating that it wasn't working properly. But Captain Choy did add that these faults had been reported, repaired and tested at Anchorage.[30]

With Captains Yang, Kim and Choy all helpfully volunteering evidence – albeit some of it a bit belated – the real question was, what about Captain Y. M. Park, the pilot of KAL 015? Quite clearly, he had had more to do with 007 than anyone else. Moreover, it was important that he appear in order to refute allegations that there had been a surveillance mission and that KAL 015 had been involved in the mission as a sort of relay dummy. Captain Park was a key witness and one might have expected him to cut the largest figure of all in the intense media coverage following the shoot-down. But in fact no press or TV journalist managed to interview Captain Park. It is no less surprising that the press and TV made no comment on Captain Park's unavailability.

## Fuel-saving?

Another theory to make an early appearance before being universally discounted was that 007's pilots had deliberately short-cut their route in order to save fuel. The origin of this hypothesis seems to have lain largely in the scuttlebutt of the aviation business in which KAL pilots were sometimes depicted as rule-bending cowboys, and in KAL's reputation for dramatic price-cutting. One early proponent of this hypothesis was Murray Sayle, who calculated that by flying the shorter, cross-Russia route to Seoul 007 would have saved 6.2 tons of fuel costing about £2000 ($2500).[31] Another figure to air such a speculation was Umberto Nordio, the President of Alitalia. The pilot of 007, said Signor Nordio, 'knew perfectly well' that he was off course. It was a 'voluntary deviation' in order to save fuel, and the 'explanation of an involuntary error is by a long way the most unlikely'.[32] Rohmer, too, flirts with this hypothesis in his book.[33]

In fact, the fuel-saving hypothesis won't stand up. ICAO looked at it and found no evidence for it or for previous such short-cutting by KAL.[34] Sayle, having originally propagated this theory (and received a journalism prize for it), later abandoned it altogether. The reasons are not difficult to see. First, if KAL were to try such illegitimate fuel-saving techniques, this would be the last (because most dangerous) route on which it would be tried. Two thousand five hundred dollars is really a very small amount to save if it entails putting not only all one's passengers but oneself at risk. To get pilots to take such risks (even supposing one wished to) one would have to offer them incentives far in excess of $2500. No pilot would risk his neck to save the company – not himself – just $2500. Finally, any pilot who was knowingly short-cutting would, in this region, be like a cat on hot bricks – desperately aware of the risks he was running, knowing that any moment he was likely to be intercepted by Soviet fighters. The idea that such a pilot could possibly miss a fighter interception when it occurred is ludicrous. Beyond that, of course, anyone who argues for such a hypothesis has to admit that a surveillance-mission hypothesis works far better – for then it would be both necessary and possible to offer the pilots incentives far greater than the $2500 thus saved, and this could also account for a (deliberate) ignoring of the Soviet attempts to contact the plane. One can understand why Sayle, having originated such a theory, was, on second thoughts, happy to abandon it.

## Soviet electronic interference?

Another theory to make an early appearance was that the Russians had deliberately lured 007 off course in order to shoot it down, using a special electronic ray to interfere with the airliner's INS and make it think it was somewhere where it was not. This theory was put forward by 'Harry' Cho, the President of KAL,[35] by the John Birch Society in the US, and by the further fringes of the Right in general. It was given a wide currency by the Reverend Jerry Falwell, the Moral Majority leader, and a degree of legitimacy by Professor Richard Pipes,[36] the right-wing Soviet specialist, who had just retired from a tour on the US National Security Council but retained a cordial relationship with the President.

Perhaps the fullest version of the theory was set forward by Hilaire du Berrier, Larry McDonald's adviser on foreign affairs.[37] According to du Berrier, the South Koreans had decided in the late 1970s that in the event of war, the most probable Soviet thrust would be into Scandinavia and that this would be accompanied by a North Korean invasion of the South. Accordingly, the South Korean Ambassador to Denmark, Air Marshal Chang Chi Ryang, had set up a network of listening posts and (presumably KCIA) 'anti-communist agents' to monitor Soviet activity in Scandinavia. This had been the context in which the KAL airliner had flown off course over Murmansk in 1978. Du Berrier had, as it happens, been in Copenhagen at the time and had conferred with Chang Chi Ryang who had told him that the airliner had been deflected off course by Soviet electronic interference. Chang, he claimed, had told the Soviet ambassador that he was aware of this and that it was meant as a warning to the South Koreans to stop 'certain operations' they had mounted in Scandinavia, but that they certainly would not stop. Then in 1979 Chang had returned to South Korea, leaving the surveillance operation he had set up under the command of his most trusted agent, 'Dr John'. However, the Russians had cunningly placed 'a communist lesbian nurse' in Dr John's household and then leaked his activities to the Scandinavian press. Because the 'communist grip' on 'socialist Scandinavia' was already so strong, the Scandinavians objected strongly to this KCIA network and Dr John and his associates had to flee.

Meanwhile, however, Chang became a close friend of both McDonald and du Berrier, and the Birchers had strengthened their links with the South Korean government. From this had stemmed a fruitful cooperation, and McDonald's Western Goals Foundation (WGF) had been set up, with the aim of exposing Soviet activities throughout the West. Finally, with the computerisation of WGF's files, the threat to the USSR became too great and it was decided to assassinate McDonald – particularly since McDonald was bringing to South Korea vital intelligence information from Dr John for Air Marshal Chang and the KCIA. Accordingly, the Russians decided to lure 007 off course and shoot it down. The fact that 268 other people had to die as well was by the way, the Russians being nothing if not callous and thorough in such matters. In answer to correspondence from the author of this book, M du Berrier kindly revealed that the South Koreans with whom McDonald was negotiating were 'bringing two of their best agents home to brief the congressman on that plane, but Larry did not know they were aboard'. (It is only fair to add that M du Berrier, in revealing these facts to me, also told me that he had been asked not to reveal them.)[38]

Nobody beyond the far Right and the President of KAL has taken the Soviet electronic ray theory seriously, but with explanations of why 007 was off course in such short supply, we can hardly afford to leave stones unturned. In any case, we cannot ignore a theory which is supported by a former member of the NSC and by the President of an airline which has not made publicly available the report of any internal investigation it may have ordered on the tragedy.

What is being suggested in the existence, in Russian hands, of a machine which can somehow – and at a range of thousands of miles – not only interfere with the operation of three powerful computers but can actually make them spew out data clean contrary to the programs and factual information inserted into them. That is, the electronic beam can wipe out the existing programs and data, substitute an extremely complex and finely calculated set of new data, and do all this without disturbing the suspicions of those who are operating the computers in front of them. If such a machine existed, it would, of course, enable the Russians to win the Third World War at a stroke, for it would mean that they could, over great distances, interfere with US defence and missile computers – even making them launch their missiles at American targets, presumably. Not the least remarkable capability of this machine would have to be that it could have started affecting 007's flight even before it got to Bethel. Given that even in the far more elementary matter of radar coverage, the Russians have nothing like that range, this would represent a truly stunning achievement.

The problem with this theory is that nothing resembling evidence, even circumstantial evidence, has been offered for it by anyone. Professor Pipes, the Birchers and 'Harry' Cho all assert that the Russians have this devilish equipment, but no reputable scientist seems to do so, or even to believe that it would be technically possible to construct it. No one has suggested that the US, with its immense technological superiority in such matters, could make such a ray-emitting machine – indeed, if it could, there would clearly be no call for the whole Star Wars programme.

However, let us imagine that Professor Pipes, 'Harry' Cho and the Reverend Jerry Falwell have somehow gained special knowledge of this technological miracle and that it exists. There are still grave problems with their theory. Why should the Russians choose to use it against 007 rather than against really important military targets? This is the war-winning weapon, after all. Even supposing they did want to use it against a civilian aircraft, why choose KAL 007 with Larry McDonald aboard, when KAL 015 was just behind with Senators Jesse Helms, Steve Simms and Congressman Carroll Hubbard? And since, apparently, the USSR has had such a weapon at least since 1978 (to account for the KAL deviation over Murmansk), why has it not been used in the interim or received any attention from the US defence establishment? The beam could also hardly have accounted for Captain Chun's margin jottings left at Anchorage in which it seemed as if he was planning the course he took, or the discrepancy in the fuel/weight manifests. The theory also flies in the face of the CIA's conclusion that the Russians did not realise they were shooting down an airliner at all. Moreover, there is no evidence that the USSR has ever seen McDonald and his WGF as a particularly significant threat to its interests. Even if they had, they would have had great difficulty knowing he was on that particular plane. Mrs McDonald claimed that 'we had been told that the Soviets knew he was on the plane' from 'Korean sources'.[39] This seems extremely unlikely: Congressman Hubbard had been scheduled to travel aboard 007 too, but had switched to KAL 015 at a very late stage. McDonald could have done the same. Indeed, afterwards his Congressional colleagues said that had they known McDonald was aboard 007 at Anchorage they would have prevailed on him to join their party on 015 – but, of course, they did not know, for McDonald had elected to stay aboard and sleep rather than stroll through the Anchorage lounge with the other passengers. It was that decision which cost Larry McDonald his life.

One cannot blame Mrs McDonald, a distressed widow, for clinging to such a wild story, but it seems safe to say that the whole story is utter nonsense. All else apart, it assumes the Russians had something to gain from shooting down 007, while in fact it was one of the USSR's greatest diplomatic disasters in the entire Cold War. The real question is how on earth Professor Pipes – formerly the NSC's Soviet specialist – and the President of KAL could support such an absurd, indeed grotesque, notion.

Perhaps the most interesting point to emerge from this episode is that the President of KAL was apparently of the view that 007 could not have been off course by accident.

## Aerial surveillance and passive probes

There are two variants to the surveillance-mission hypothesis, the first being that 007 was on a surveillance mission itself, equipped with cameras or other sensors, the other that it was being used as a passive probe to switch on Soviet radars whose operation could then be monitored by other US listening platforms in the vicinity. Clearly, a large amount of the scenario one can mount for this hypothesis would apply equally to either theory, but in practice it is possible to eliminate as a hypothesis the original Soviet allegation that 007 was carrying surveillance equipment.

This is so for several reasons. First, it is doubtful if the US had any real or urgent need for extra aerial reconnaissance of the Sakhalin–Kamchatka area. True, satellite pictures of the region would frequently find impenetrable clouds in the way, but on a simple basis of having to be lucky at least occasionally with cloud cover, what the US already had by way of such information was probably sufficient. Moreover, the US is able to send high-flying SR-71 Blackbirds shooting over the area at more than three times the speed of sound to complement what its satellites provide. And 007 was flying over the region at night, when only infra-red photography could have been used. From 29,000 feet or more the resolution of such photographs is almost impossibly imprecise.[40] So, with the possible gains of such a mission tiny or nil, it is in the highest degree improbable that anyone could possibly have thought it worth risking an airliner full of people to that end. Beyond that, of course, to place surveillance equipment of any sort aboard 007 would have been to take enormous extra risks of leaks by those who loaded it aboard, the mechanics who serviced the plane at Anchorage, and so on. Moreover, any planning for a surveillance mission would have to accept the possibility that the plane would be forced down to land on Soviet territory, when it would be taken apart almost rivet by rivet (as happened to the KAL plane forced down over Murmansk in 1978). Such equipment could then have been brandished before the world with at least equal effect to the exhibiting of the American U-2 spy plane and its pilot, Gary Powers, in 1960.[41] The U-2 incident not only ruined the 1960 Geneva negotiations but left the US terribly exposed, with President Eisenhower having to admit that his Administration had been lying when it had earlier asserted that the U-2 was merely a weather reconnaissance plane which had lost its way. The incident left a scar on the US intelligence community which would have precluded any willingness to take such a risk of exposure again. (Incidentally, many of the same arguments would suggest that the Reagan Administration claims of Aeroflot airliners carrying out aerial reconnaissance over the continental United States are equally improbable.)

Some of the same reservations must apply to the possibility that 007 was working as a passive probe merely in order to switch on the radars on the southern tips of Sakhalin and Kamchatka. To be sure, this could have been done with 007 acting as a passive probe, carrying no equipment itself. But the fact is, of course, that the US is regularly in the habit of 'tickling' these radars with RC-135s and other military planes, making the Russians turn their devices on, and hurriedly effecting a getaway before the Russians can send up interceptors. The Russians, in turn, know this game perfectly well and are naturally parsimonious with their radars – switching them on just long enough, and using only the fewest possible and already best-known radars – in order to deprive the US of any unnecessary extra electronic information.[42] No doubt the US is always hungry for more and better intelligence about these radars, but by the same token it seems probable that these constant 'tickling' tactics have already given the US most of the information it wants, at least about the radars on the edge of the Kamchatka–Sakhalin promontories. To mount a passive probe to find out more about them, using a civilian airliner, would thus have amounted to taking an irrationally high risk relative to the significance of the new information to be acquired. This does not, of course, rule out the possibility of such a mission being mounted, but it does make it less likely.

There remains the possibility of a passive probe aimed at getting the

Russians to turn on radars further towards the Soviet interior, radars about which previous 'tickling' had failed to provide any information. This hypothesis is far harder to discount. As we have seen, only five weeks before 007's flight the US intelligence establishment had been electrified by the discovery of the vast new Soviet radar being built at Krasnoyarsk.[43] So the US certainly had a particular and strong motive for finding out more about the interior Soviet radar network. There was, moreover, a considerable urgency about getting such information, especially to the Administration's superhawks. Not only was it crucial to know whether the Russians were planning to cheat on the SALT I treaty, but the Administration wanted that information before it was pushed into possible concessions in the arms-control talks – talks which the real hawks didn't want to succeed in the first place. In addition, to have evidence of Soviet treaty violations might well be the crucial lever with which to bolster flagging Congressional support for a whole series of the Administration's weapons programmes. Could the vital nature of this intelligence-gathering task – and the pressing necessity to get the information quickly – have led to a decision to take the terrible risk of using a civilian airliner as a passive probe? Certainly, if a surveillance mission hypothesis is to have any credibility, there needs to have been a motive of this, or comparable, urgency.

Perhaps the best way to evaluate this hypothesis is to rerun the entire sequence of events surrounding the flight *as if* the hypothesis were true, and see how well it fits the facts.

## The surveillance hypothesis: A scenario

Let us begin by asking who would have had to deal with the problem of Krasnoyarsk when news of the new Soviet installation first reached Washington in July 1983. Without much doubt the two men whose concern it would chiefly have been were William Clark, then the unchallenged foreign policy supremo, and William Casey, head of the CIA. It seems certain that the new radar would have been a hot issue for the Senior Arms Control Policy Group:[44] indeed, it is possible that it was discussed at the group's first meeting on 19 July. This group, it will be remembered, was headed by Clark and its members included McFarlane, Perle, Burt, Eagleburger and Casey. It is probable, too, that the issue would have received the consideration of Casey's ultrasecret National Security Planning Group (NSPG),[45] whose membership also included Casey and Clark, but from which most real intelligence experts had been excluded. Let us remember the comments which the NSPG had drawn from such experts: 'There's nobody there to tell these guys what the problems will be and what could go wrong' and 'people at the top of this Administration are fascinated with covert operations and find it easier to approve them than to discuss complicated diplomatic matters.'[46] There is a little doubt that Clark's inexperience and Casey's high-risk buccaneering were a heady mix, especially given that both men were such instinctive hawks.

There is, in a word, some reason to believe that risky schemes could get hatched in a milieu like this – especially since both men could be entirely confident of the President's goodwill, almost regardless of what they did. Between them Clark and Casey undoubtedly had the power to do almost whatever they liked – and might not have felt constrained to tell the President, particularly given the President's tendency to OK more or less whatever they put in front of him. It would, moreover, be difficult to argue that Casey's career suggested that he was a man likely to be held back by over-nice considerations of scruple. One of the oddities of the Reagan White House, indeed, was the way in which the National Security Council was willing to get involved in clearly illegal activities: thus when Congress forbade the CIA to give direct assistance to the Nicaraguan Contras, the NSC simply went gaily ahead and arranged the assistance itself.[47]

As the US national security élite examined the problem of the Krasnoyarsk radar in July 1983, it would have been clear right away that the facility was probably not an ABM radar. But it might still be a SALT violation in the shape of a forbidden early-warning radar. How on earth to tell, though? After all, the new radar would not be completed and operational until 1988, and what was wanted – especially by such opponents of arms control as Casey, Clark and Perle – was immediate verification. There was also the question of how Krasnoyarsk might fit in with the already disputed ABM radar on southern Kamchatka (the Russians claimed that this had been built before the SALT I treaty and was therefore not covered by it[48]) and the already operational radar at Komsomolsk. What was needed, in other words, was a thorough testing of the capabilities of the whole Soviet radar line pointing towards the north Pacific. If there was a gap in the early-warning line which Krasnoyarsk might fill, this would be powerful evidence that the new facility was indeed an early-warning radar.

But how could one test the whole Soviet radar net in this region? The Russians would not obligingly switch on all their facilities at once just to oblige the US: indeed, rather the reverse. Clearly, the normal 'tickling' of the coastal radars by RC-135s would be no solution. So how to make the Russians expose a much larger part – and preferably all – of their radar network?

It is not, perhaps, impossibly difficult to imagine that such discussions might have led to the notion of staging an aerial intrusion across the eastern airspace of the USSR. The more those considering such a notion were themselves anti-arms-control hawks, the greater the motivation would have been.

## A mission plan?

Let us imagine that the aerial-intrusion plan was adopted. Several things would be necessary for such a stratagem to work. First, it would be necessary to jam the known Soviet coastal radars so that, if the Russians wished to track the intruder, they would have no option but to switch on radars not normally exposed by 'tickling', including radars further into the Soviet interior. Second, the intrusion would have to be a lengthy one. As time dragged by and one coastal radar after another confessed failure to track the intruder, the frustrated Russians would at length realise that they had no option but to switch on their interior radars if the intruder was not to slip away. Probably, they would resist making this fateful decision as long as possible – so the intruder might well get clean away overflying its first stage (Kamchatka). But by the time it threatened to overfly Sakhalin too, surely the Russians would act. One had to give time for the elephantine Soviet bureaucracy to take a decision – but in the end Russian careers, perhaps even lives, might be on the line if they did not act. One could even increase the stakes further by getting the intruder to fly over the most sensitive possible Soviet facilities – fighter bases, nuclear-submarine pens and the like. At some point the Russians' nerve would surely crack and they would switch on every radar facility they had in their determination to stop the intruder.

If such an intruder there was to be, which plane? The problem would be that, if the stratagem worked, there was a significant chance that the plane would be intercepted, if not over Kamchatka, then at least over Sakhalin. If one used a military plane and the Russians caught up with it, then the whole operation would be a disaster. Either the USAF plane would have to obey Soviet instructions and be forced down, producing a major propaganda coup for the Russians – a new U-2; or, if it did not obey Soviet instructions to land, it would be shot down. That too would be a propaganda disaster, as well as a lost plane and crew. Anyway, one could hardly ask the crew of such a plane to commit suicide by deliberately ignoring Soviet orders to land (and even if one did, they still might not in the crunch). Well, then, what if the intrusion was made, instead, by an airliner? This would solve both problems. If the Russians did catch up with it, they would see it was an airliner and, clearly, nobody would wittingly shoot down an airliner. But in any case, the airliner pilot would be told to accept Soviet orders to land if necessary – there was no need to put himself or his passengers at risk. If he was forced down, the Russians would search the plane, find nothing, and would quickly have to let the crew and passengers go – as they had in the case of the 1978 KAL intrusion over Murmansk.[49] The pilot could just say he lost his way and the Russians would probably emerge with the greater diplomatic discredit, just as they had in 1978.

Such a plan would have seemed risky, but not impossibly so. After all, as we have seen, US reconnaissance planes have had an astonishing 100 per cent record of success in evading the more than 900 SAM missiles launched at them during 'tickling' operations.[50] So it would have been (rightly) possible to feel that a SAM shoot-down could be avoided. As for fighters, the record there was patchier, but the US did have a hypersensitive real-time capability for tracking all Soviet fighter activity,[51] and extra ECM measures to blind the fighters could certainly be used.

If such measures were effective, a successful interception of the intruder plane might even depend on a sheerly visual sighting by a Soviet fighter. One could make that in turn as difficult as possible by staging such a flight at night – and one with little moon – and rely too on the always heavy cloud formations hanging over Kamchatka and Sakhalin. If the airliner also kept its lights switched off, it might take a very good – or very lucky – Soviet fighter pilot to find it.

If using an airliner as the intruder – the passive probe – had clear and crucial advantages, then the question would be, whose airline? It would have to be an airline running scheduled flights on the Romeo 20 route which had at least a trio of flight-officers willing to co-operate.

## South Korea: The KCIA state

It is not impossible to imagine that US intelligence, faced with this problem, might have hit on the idea of using its undoubted influence in South Korea. It is not just that South Korea is an American client state, or that it is an exceptionally tough dictatorship where secrets can be kept and stay kept; more than that, South Korea is a country in which the CIA has a quite peculiar leverage. This is so because the CIA played the godfather role in setting up the Korean CIA (KCIA) in 1961; because the two agencies retain strong umbilical links; and because, in effect, the KCIA rules South Korea.

Perhaps the easiest way to illustrate the extraordinary extent to which the South Korean state is dominated by the KCIA is just to list the biographical details of the directors of the KCIA since its inception. The first director, Kim Chong Pil, was later accused by the Seoul regime of having peculated $36 million in office,[52] but this did not prevent him from becoming Prime Minister from 1971 to 1975. His successor, Kim Hyung Wook, was sacked as director in 1969 after the revelation of KCIA kidnappings in West Germany.[53] He fled abroad but in 1979 threatened to write his memoirs. He was then kidnapped from Paris by the KCIA, drugged, and brought back to Seoul in a South Korean cargo plane, taken to the cellars of the presidential palace and shot there by President Park.[54] Kim Hyung Wook's successor at the KCIA, Lee Hu Rak (also later accused of massive corruption), was forced to resign after the kidnapping of the Korean opposition leader, Kim Dae Jung, from Tokyo in 1973.[55] Lee's successor, Shin Jik Soo, was forced to resign over revelations of large-scale and systematic bribery of US Congressmen by the KCIA, and the intimidation of Koreans living in the US.[56] (During the Congressional investigation of 'Koreagate', two former KCIA directors were named as unindicted conspirators.[57]) Shin's successor, Kim Jae Kyu, invited President Park to dine in the KCIA dining room in 1979, where he shot the President dead over dinner.[58] Kim Jae Kyu was then arrested on charges of having sought to use the KCIA directorship to capture the presidency for himself, and executed.[59] His successor was General Chun Doo Hwan, head of the Army Security Command. Chun took over as President himself four months later. His nominee to the KCIA directorship, Lo Shin Yung, was, in 1985, made Prime Minister. Thus, at the time of writing, both the presidency and the premiership of South Korea are held by former KCIA heads . . . To put it mildly, the KCIA is no ordinary intelligence organisation (its infamous sixth bureau was charged with Assassinations, Abductions and Sabotage).[60] Despite recurrent promises that the bad old days are over (and the renaming of the KCIA as the Agency for National Security Planning), the fact is that no part of South Korean society is beyond the reach of the KCIA. If, as the CIA does, one has strong links into the KCIA, it is possible to arrange things that would be unimaginable in many countries. Moreover, the KCIA maintains a strong presence in Washington (the Moonies, through whom the KCIA has frequently been accused of operating,[61] own the *Washington Times*), so doing a deal with the KCIA is, for the CIA, a matter of a local phone call.

Thus if the CIA *had* been looking for a civilian airliner to carry out a passive probe, it is hard to imagine that the notion of using the link with the KCIA in order to make an arrangement with a KAL pilot would have taken long to occur. Moreover, as we have seen, William Casey, the CIA head, had a history of previous dealings with the South Korean government – dealings he had originally 'forgotten' to tell Congress about.[62] Finally, KAL would have had the indispensable advantage of running normal scheduled flights which skirted Kamchatka and Sakhalin. None of this, of course, proves that a KAL plane *was* selected for such a mission. All that one can say, if one develops the surveillance mission hypothesis, is that if such a mission were to be mounted, a sufficient nexus of interests and contacts existed which might have made it possible to attract a trio of KAL flight officers. Maximum security would dictate a 'deal' with the minimum number of people, but the pilot, co-pilot and flight engineer would be the irreducible minimum.

What is certain, though, is that if a passive-probe mission using a KAL plane had been planned by the CIA, the two men at whose desks the buck would have been bound to stop would have been William Clark and William Casey. It is interesting, in this respect, to note the sudden and surprise departure for the Middle East of Clark's deputy, McFarlane, in July 1983.[63] One can only speculate if this move could have been related to our hypothesis: but it certainly had the effect of removing McFarlane from all responsibility for whatever his boss, Clark, was up to in August 1983. Equally, of course, Clark, deprived of McFarlane's crucial back-up, would have been more prone to give the go-ahead to initiatives which would never have got off the ground if McFarlane had been in post.

## A possible mission?

Let us then imagine that KAL 007 was selected for such a mission. One would, for such a mission, want nothing less than the very best and most reliable pilots – which is certainly what 007 had. Just to cater for every contingency, one might hope for some reserve pilots and engineers on board (which, in the shape of the dead-heading officers, 007 had).[64] In addition it would be convenient to have another plane flying close to or parallel with 007 to relay its radio messages to ground control as 007's deviation took it out of VHF range – thus preventing ground controllers from smelling a rat. But first, 007's pilot would have to prepare his flight meticulously. Because one could not possibly have up-to-date meteorological information until just before the would-be intruder plane took off, the pilot would need to make last-minute calculations of his (real) flight plan. This would account for the jottings made by Captain Chun on the margins of his computerised flight plan. Chun would also know that if things became difficult he might well want to give 007 a considerable extra turn of speed. To that end he would want to lighten the plane of any cargo he could (which would explain the otherwise inexplicable decision to leave 1800 pounds of profitmaking cargo behind at Anchorage) – and he would also want to load some extra fuel reserves, though he would not wish to advertise this too much. This would then account both for the extra

10,000 pounds of fuel loaded onto 007 – and the discrepancy in the fuel/weight manifests.

On the other hand, there would be no particular need for Chun to worry about leaving these potentially incriminating documents behind at Anchorage. If the mission was a success – or even if 007 were to be forced down onto Sakhalin – they would never receive public scrutiny. And these would have been the only outcomes that Captain Chun needed – or, perhaps, would have been willing – to contemplate: he was a man both determined and accustomed to succeed.

007 would then program into its INS the route it actually intended to take, though with notes of the false waypoint passages it would need to relay back to ground control. The crucial first misreport would come at Bethel, as 007 settled down into the course to take it towards the rendezvous with the RC-135 just short of Kamchatka. Meanwhile, although 007's extra fuel load would allow the plane to use every ounce of speed in the later stages of the flight (especially if a Soviet interception seemed possible), 007 would, at first take care to dawdle over the initial stages of the route, thus narrowing the gap between itself and KAL 015, which had taken off not long afterwards. Given that KAL 015, as Allardyce has shown,[65] was itself striking a cracking pace over the same early stages of the route, the two planes would remain within easy VHF range of one another, allowing 007 to use 015 as its relay post. Once the requisite pattern had been established 007 would cease its own direct transmissions to Anchorage and instead use 015 to clock off steadily its waypoint positions and altitude requests back to ground control.

Not long after 007 took off, an RC-135 would take off from Shemya and establish its normal figure-eight mission orbit off the Kamchatka coast, there to await 007's arrival. It is unlikely that the Russians could have been correct in their assertion that the RC-135 was 007's mission controller – such a role would more likely be played by an EW (electronic warfare) plane continuously aloft throughout 007's flight. Rather, the RC-135 would play a diversionary and 'masking' role. The Russians watching below would know that RC-135s typically operate in pairs, so that as 007 approached the RC-135, it would be a normal assumption that this was the relieving RC-135 taking up station. Finally, the two planes would meet off Kamchatka, 007 having made a further course alteration to achieve this. As the two planes merged into a single blip on the Soviet radar screens, both heading towards Kamchatka, their separate identities would be lost, and as they parted company the Russians would be unsure which plane was now which.

The RC-135 would now break away and head up the Siberian coast back towards Eielson, no doubt listening to Soviet electronic reactions as it went.

But it would not leave 007 alone, for a whole fleet of other EW/ELINT platforms would be standing ready further down 007's route – planes, ships, the satellite and perhaps even the shuttle. These platforms would have three major functions: to jam Soviet coastal radars; to listen to every possible Soviet radio and electronic communication (and radar) triggered by the intrusion; and to provide 007 with such further technical assistance as it needed. The chief need, of course, would be to keep Soviet interceptors and SAM batteries blinded and confused, thus making it as hard as possible for the Russians to locate 007 precisely. To this end the complete range of electronic warfare techniques would be deployed, not just radar-jamming but a whole host of other tricks as well. (And certainly, as we have seen, the Russians did finally admit that two out of three radars were not working on Kamchatka that night. Such measures might also account for the late Soviet scramble over Kamchatka, the difficulties Major Kasmin's ground controllers had with their radars – and why the radar-guided missile apparently missed.)

007 would, though, switch its transponder to 'squawking code' SSR 1300 both to disguise from the Russians the fact that it was an ordinary civilian airliner (using the normal airliner code would have been too much of a give-away). This distinctive code would also enable easy identification of 007 by other US ELINT platforms, which would have been simultaneously monitoring scores of other communications, fighters, KAL 015 and so on. Meanwhile 007 would make life as easy for itself as possible by showing minimum (or no) lights, and changing altitude and speed unpredictably. If all these things were done simultaneously with the great battery of electronic countermeasures being thrown at the Russians by the US ELINT platforms, 007 would probably have no great difficulty in avoiding Soviet fighters as it crossed Kamchatka.

The real test, though, would be Sakhalin. The Russians would be furious, perhaps steeling themselves to switch on hitherto secret radars, and they would be ready. They would, of course, be trying to reach the intruder plane by radio in order to identify it positively and order it down, but 007 would pay no attention. This time, though, the Soviet fighters would scramble early and position themselves to block off 007's presumed course across Sakhalin. To counter this predictable move 007 would, however, make a further course change just as it approached Sakhalin – and would do just the opposite of what the Russians might expect, cutting in northwards, further in over Soviet territory, rather than trying to escape southwards. These manoeuvres might, with luck, mean that 007 could evade the Soviet fighters over Sakhalin just as it had their first wave over Kamchatka. The Russians, though, no doubt had some of their crack pilots in the air and, whether by luck or skill, actually managed to find 007.

At this point 007's flight instructions would require that it not try any heroics. Anyone planning such a mission would have to assume that if and when interception was made, the Russians would realise their mistake and see that 007 was actually a civilian airliner – indeed, it would be sensible for 007 to flash its lights to make sure this was understood. 007's ultimate protection would, of course, simply be that it was an airliner and that the Russians would surely not try to shoot down such a plane. If an interception took place, then it would be 007's duty to accept the orders to land, go down onto a Sakhalin airfield and then indignantly protest that it had somehow flown accidentally off course.

However, let us imagine that Captain Chun now took a gamble, against orders. After several hours of successful evasion, he might have felt utterly committed to getting all the way through: his reputation as a top fighter pilot might even seem to him to be on the line. In any case, the Russians would never dare shoot down an airliner. And 007 was now within minutes of international airspace (at the end, just one minute). What if 007 could throw the Soviet fighters off its tail for just one more minute? As we have seen, just as Major Kasmin's SU-15 closed in behind 007, 007 (or someone 'impersonating' 007) suddenly decided to broadcast its intention to climb to 35,000 feet – a broadcast which the Russians were bound to pick up. If, instead, 007 dived a few thousand feet while steadily claiming over the airwaves that it was climbing, the Soviet fighters might be fooled – or ordered up to 35,000 feet by their anxious ground controllers. It would, in other words, be the standard fighter tactic in aerial combat of feinting a climb and diving instead. No doubt the Soviet fighters would quickly realise their mistake, but by then 007 might be in the clouds – and out of Soviet airspace, effectively home free. Whatever 007's pilots were thinking – and we can only speculate – we know how this tragic sequence ended. For something had happened which would have upset any mission plan: the Russians had failed to see that 007 was an airliner . . .

Meanwhile, however, 007 would, in one sense, have triumphantly fulfilled its mission. With the satellite overhead and the whole array of other ELINT platforms offshore, the US would have garnered an immense intelligence harvest. As Ernest Volkman, the editor of the American journal, *Defence Science*, puts it:

As a result of the KAL incident United States intelligence received a bonanza the likes of which they have never received in their lives. Reason: because of the tragic incident it managed to turn on just about every single Soviet electromagnetic transmission over a period of about four hours and an area of approximately 7000 square miles, and I mean everything. I think the only thing that wasn't turned on, they didn't detect, was somebody's portable radio in the barracks, when everything else was detected – communications back and forth between Moscow, radar systems, computer tracking systems, communication systems, air defence systems, what one person has described to me as a Christmas tree, lit up. Everything you could possibly ever hope for. Now, admittedly that's a cynical statement, but we're talking about a very cynical business here.[66]

Anyone within the intelligence community who might have argued even for a high-risk passive-probe mission in the hope of gaining such information would doubtless have been exultant: such a harvest would keep teams of analysts working for perhaps years ahead. These were truly the crown jewels. But the problem (following such a hypothesis) would have been that while the risk might have paid off in one sense, in another it hadn't: 269 people were dead. What on earth to do about that?

## Dealing with disaster?

If anything like the above hypothesis were true, one can imagine the scene as the news of the tragedy flashed back to the NSA and CIA through the SPINTCOM/CRITICOM network. There would have been utter consternation as it sank in that 007 must have pressed its luck too far and that the long-odds possibility – which policy-makers had been assured could never happen – of a Soviet fighter making a visual sighting of 007 had somehow come off. The news would be flashed on to Clark and Meese at the Biltmore Hotel.[67]

The policy-makers would need time to think as the implications of the ghastly and unexpected tragedy sank in. The first thing would be to check the essential facts – and then to consider how on earth to deal with this catastrophe. A teleconference with the key members of the Senior Arms Control Policy Group and the National Security Planning Group would be essential, this time including Shultz, who would be needed as the front man to present the news.

Time would be crucial for another reason, too. The ghost of the U-2 would walk again. If the US reacted too quickly, it might be only to find that the Russians were holding back some crucial piece of evidence – a tape of 007's conversations with its mission controller, for example – which could then be surfaced with the same dreadful éclat with which, in 1960, the Russians had suddenly produced Gary Powers. So delay was crucial while Soviet communications were monitored for a few further hours in order to work out what they did know. To effect this delay, one would need to get hold of Nakasone quickly by backchannel and stop the story leaking out in Japan. But to hold off the hungry press, something more – a cover story – would be needed. What simpler than to fall back on the already prepared contingency plan of a forced landing on Sakhalin? Meanwhile, it would be essential to prepare a version of events to explain this delay more plausibly – hence the elaborate version produced for the press by Burt a few days later.

Once the monitoring of Soviet communications showed that the Russians were still bewildered and at sixes and sevens over the whole affair, one's course of action would be obvious: an all-out propaganda barrage against the Russians, putting them squarely in the dock and getting the US version of events worldwide splash coverage before the Russians could even begin to put their story together. Since the circle of those who knew the truth about the mission had been kept to the barest minimum, one could safely delegate the major propaganda roles to people like Shultz and Mrs Kirkpatrick, who hadn't known what was going on. Their indignation would be quite genuine, spontaneous – and convincing. In the end the disaster could serve all the same ends that a successful verification of Soviet SALT violations would have done – indeed, far more so. With really blitzkrieg news-management tactics, one could even news-manage and package the deaths of 269 people in a politically effective way – the greatest news-management challenge the Reagan Administration had ever faced.

Meanwhile, it would be essential to ensure that 007's black boxes were recovered as quickly as possible – by the US. A maximum-security blanket would have to be thrown over the search operation and the press kept away. In case the Russians did recover the boxes first, it would be necessary to precondition public opinion against the surfacing of black boxes which did suggest a surveillance mission. Once the boxes had been recovered – or once it seemed certain that they had been destroyed – one would need one final cover story, that they were unfindable. No one, doubtless, could have been cynical enough to plan things this way before the mission, but once the disaster took place, the options of how to deal with it would have seemed very limited indeed. Men who were hardly happy with the outcome would find themselves swept inexorably along by the tide of events and the exigencies of the media war. Those who could would simply keep quiet and keep their heads down.

For Clark such a scenario would surely have created a considerable moral dilemma. While he might be inclined to argue that perhaps some good had, after all, come of the 007 mission,[68] he would not have been a man to be able to cope at all easily with the affair. Such doubts as he might have had earlier of his own expertise in his foreign policy role would have been strongly reinforced. And, moreover, the awful possibility might loom that the Russians, having made their own calculations, would blame him openly and personally for the tragedy. Everything would point to getting out of his job as National Security Adviser. But the problem would be: what if sequels and dribs and drabs of information about the 007 affair were to continue to come to light? If so, they would arrive first on the desk of the National Security Adviser. So if he was to go, it would be essential that someone he could trust utterly would fill that job, someone who would know that they owed their position to Clark and Clark alone. McFarlane . . . And if others wanted the job – there was bound to be fearsome competition: well, then Clark would have to turn to the other person with him on that awful day at the Biltmore Hotel when news of the tragedy first came through: Ed Meese. When James Watt put his foot in his mouth one more time, the inkling of opportunity would dawn: why not go into quiet retirement at Interior? To resign completely from the Administration would cause an explosion of speculation. Going to Interior would be peculiar enough, but one might just get away with it, particularly since one could live a quiet and blameless life there, finally slipping out of the government altogether without further comment. It might work. So: tell Reagan that Watt had to go, volunteer for his job, and combine with Meese to shut out all contenders other than McFarlane for the National Security Adviser job. Some former colleagues – like Jeane Kirkpatrick – might be hurt and mystified by such behaviour, but more important things would be at stake.

## Mission fruits?

There seems little doubt that 007's intrusion did furnish the US with an intelligence bonanza. Volkman's assessment was confirmed by the American intelligence writer, James Bamford: 'In terms of electronic intelligence the violation was an intelligence treasure chest.'[69] It is, of course, impossible to say whether the flight added anything to US knowledge of, specifically, the Krasnoyarsk and southern Kamchatka radars. It did emerge, however, that there *was* a gap in the Soviet early warning network facing the north Pacific and that Krasnoyarsk would plug it, albeit somewhat awkwardly.[70] It looked as if the Russians had faced a problem gap which needed to be filled by two or more peripheral radars, but had balked at the construction costs and difficulties – for they would have needed to be built in the most remote, inaccessible and climatically horrible parts of Siberia. Instead they had chosen to build a single large radar, with a vector covering Kamchatka and Sakhalin, further inland in a somewhat easier location. If this was indeed the intention, then the radar would constitute a (minor) violation of SALT – but it would leave the Russians still needing a different type of radar to handle the engagement phase of a missile attack. This, at least, was the conclusion the CIA finally came to. This made the new radar a lot less alarming than had been feared. As one congressional expert put it, 'If they had spent a few more bucks, they could have built the facilities [i.e. on the periphery] and have been fully in compliance.'[71] All that one can say is that, given the gap to be filled lay somewhere between Kamchatka and Sakhalin, 007's flight path would have been perfectly on track to reveal it: indeed, if the overflight did cause the Russians to turn on *all* their radars, the listening US ELINT platforms could hardly have failed to spot the crucial gap. There certainly seems no doubt that 007's intrusion caused the Russians to switch on a good deal – and there also seems fairly solid support for the fact of 'a large gap in Soviet radar coverage of its northern airspace in East Asia'.[72]

Moreover, as we have seen, it was immediately after 007's flight that the US, while giving no explanation, suddenly reneged on a previously reached agreement regulating 'concurrent' use of air-defence radars.[73] One cannot but wonder whether that decision was not affected by intelligence made available as a by-product of 007's flight.

There is another oddity, too. As we observed above,[74] the Pentagon maintained a remarkable silence over the early discovery of the Krasnoyarsk radar, so that the news leaked out more informally through the columnists, Evans and Novak. It was only on 4 October – five weeks after the 007 shoot-down – that the Pentagon gave its first official briefing on the new radar. At this briefing reporters were informed that a US satellite had first observed the radar 'about 10 August'.[75] This went unchallenged by the press, but it was manifestly untrue – the Evans–Novak story had broken on 27 July and by 3 August the White House was telling the Senate hawks that the issue of the new radar had already been raised with the Russians.[76] It is tempting to wonder whether this attempt to move back the sighting by at least two weeks might not have been linked to a concern to conceal the means by which the US had gathered its information about the new radar.

It goes almost without saying that the discovery that Krasnoyarsk could not really be an ABM radar in no way stilled the Right's furious assertions that it was – indeed, in the torrid atmosphere engendered by the 007 tragedy such accusations reached fever pitch. Yet as the Director of the US Arms Control and Disarmament Agency, Kenneth Adelman, put it, reviewing the Reagan Administration's list of alleged Soviet SALT violations, 'You could say that none of these violations in and of themselves have immediate and profound military significance.'[77] Indeed, Adelman – no mean hawk himself – compared the violations in gravity to 'a taxpayer violating income-tax laws'.[78]

Ironically, this question of alleged Soviet SALT violations was to dog the Administration. As the 1984 election neared, the Senate conservatives furiously demanded that the Administration publish its whole list of alleged violations, but the Administration tried its best to hold back, as if embarrassed.[79] In the end the Administration was forced to publish its list in October 1984, replete with references to the radars at Krasnoyarsk and on southern Kamchatka. The former US chief arms-control negotiator, Gerard C. Smith, was one of a number who found the list deeply unimpressive. 'How low they have stooped,' said Smith. The list was, he said, 'a lunge into the dark', full of 'largely stale' accusations. 'We are seeing a phenomenon which may be a precursor to getting out of the treaties themselves.'[80] In fact it was only after the election was safely out of the way that the Administration began to drop its charges that Krasnoyarsk was an ABM radar with allegations that it was, instead, an (illegal) early-warning facility. The Russians continued, officially, to insist that it was for space-tracking only and even invited US scientists to come and examine the installation when it was completed. Unofficially, some Soviet officials were reported to have admitted that the radar might still be able to serve military purposes.[81]

## Assessment

It will be apparent that with this version of the surveillance hypothesis we have a theory which fits – or can be made to fit – just about all the known facts about the 007 tragedy. Indeed, the hypothesis can even fit a whole series of further facts about the political context of the event, the delay in releasing the news, the false 'safe-on-Sakhalin' story, the oddities in the search for the black boxes, and so on. Indeed, it is because the theory fits at so many different points that its exposition takes longer than those of the rival hypotheses. It is important to say that this still does not prove that the theory is true. What are the major criticisms such a theory has to face?

A first and obvious criticism is that the theory involves making a very large number of different suppositions. While these may be supported by circumstantial evidence in every case, any long chain is bound to have some weak links. For example, even if one made the supposition that 007 was on a surveillance mission, there would be no certainty that intelligence relating to Krasnoyarsk was the objective, or that Clark's resignation was connected to the subsequent tragedy. This is perfectly true: it would be possible to discard quite a lot of the circumstantial suppositions relating to such matters and present a slimmed-down theory dealing strictly and only with 007's flight. But if one does this, one discovers that the parts of the hypothesis which apply only to the flight itself are quite self-contained: the surveillance hypothesis itself would not be damaged. But one important reason for the investigation of the wider background is that it provides the hypothesis with a plausible motive and suggests a political context within which such a decision might have been taken. If one were to uphold the surveillance hypothesis at all, these are simply the next set of questions one would have to try to answer anyway.

A more frequent objection would be that, if the surveillance hypothesis were correct, it would have involved too large a number of people being in on the secret. The US is an exceptionally open society, everyone talks, and no one could plan an operation of this sort with any hope that secrecy could be long maintained.

There is some force to this objection, but only some: most of the covert operations launched under Carter have remained secret, after all. Stansfield Turner, Carter's chief of CIA, explains that normally he would take proposals for such operations to the NSC, but 'if it was very sensitive, I'd limit it to Zbig Brzezinski, [Defence Secretary] Harold Brown, and [Secretary of State] Cy Vance to minimise the risks from a formal meeting. If they agreed, Brzezinski would take the written proposal to the President for his approval and signature. It then was returned to the CIA, and we hand-delivered it to the appropriate congressional committees.'[82] Often, though, Turner recalls, it was the National Security Advisor, Brzezinski, who originated such ideas; sometimes Brown; more rarely Vance.

Under Reagan the circle of top decision-makers would certainly have been narrower than this: Vance might have been consulted but Shultz wouldn't, and Casey was extremely unwilling to tell congressional committees about all he was doing. Whether or not Presidential authorisation for covert operations is still required in the Reagan White House is not known. Quite possibly, as in other areas, Reagan allows a large measure of delegation and doesn't know much himself.

What one can say with some certainty is that if a surveillance mission had been mounted across Kamchatka–Sakhalin, those in the know would *have* to have included at least a few top actors within the CIA, the National Security Agency, the office of the National Security Adviser, the Defence Department and the Joint Chiefs of Staff (or at least the USAF) – though in the case of Defence all that would need to be known was that an intelligence operation was being mounted such that unusual sightings on radar screens should not be allowed to trigger the normal responses. Finally, the staffs of a number of US ELINT platforms around the Sea of Japan and at least some of the US Navy personnel involved in the search for the black boxes would have had to know enough to smell a sizeable rat. No doubt such an operation would be handled on the barest minimum 'need-to-know' basis, so most of these people would only know of a specific part of the operation. But that is still quite a lot of people: maybe a hundred, maybe even more. Surely no one could plan such an operation knowing that they were placing themselves at the mercy of the discretion of so many talkatively American people?

There are a number of answers to this. First, of course, it already is the case that within a short time of the 007 tragedy enough information *has* indeed come to light to show that the Reagan Administration was lying about many aspects of the affair and, indeed, for one to be able to construct a possible surveillance hypothesis.

Secondly, and more importantly, one has to think of the situation, following this hypothesis, if Captain Chun had either taken 007 down to a landing on Sakhalin or if he had succeeded in piloting the plane into international airspace, beyond the reach of Soviet fighters. Had 007 gone down on Sakhalin, there would, perhaps, have been a minor row but no more; after the 1978 incident President Park actually thanked Brezhnev for the considerate and expeditious Soviet handling of the affair – despite the fact that Soviet fighters had fired on the KAL plane and life had been lost.[83] In such a case, there would not have been a major international tragedy and *cause célèbre*: there was no great inquest into the 1978 incident. In other words, anyone who planned a surveillance role for 007 might well have felt that even the worst eventuality – a forced landing on Sakhalin – did not carry particular terrors.

If, on the other hand, 007 was on a surveillance mission and had successfully completed it, there would also have been minimal fuss. The Russians might well not even have complained – to do so would only have been to demonstrate their impotence. There would have been no sailors fishing for a black box to keep quiet and the personnel manning the ELINT platforms could have been told that the intruder *was* an RC-135 and might never have known it was an airliner that they were tracking. In either of these eventualities, a very much smaller number of people would have been privy to any secret about the incident, particularly since there would have been no blaze of media publicity, with dozens of reporters asking leading questions of half-informed official sources, with all the embarrassing snippets of information that might produce. There would have been no tapes of the Soviet fighters, of 007's conversations with ground control, no ICAO inquiry. In other words, had such an operation been planned on the assumption that it would be a success or that the worst possibility was a forced landing on Sakhalin, then the dangers of leakage would probably have seemed – and been – acceptably small.

Then again, it is possible to overplay the inability of the US government to keep secrets. Many US military and national security secrets have been kept for a very long time. Moreover, one of Casey's principal concerns since taking over the CIA has been to tighten security in a host of ways. In this he has been extremely successful and Congress notably compliant. It was, by 1983, very, very much harder to learn about CIA activities than it had been before 1981 – and since 1983 it has become harder still.

It is worth recalling, as a case in point, the history of US military spy flights into Soviet airspace in the decade following World War II. Although a considerable number of the USAF planes involved in such missions were shot down with substantial loss of life,[84] the entire programme remained a well guarded secret. The first real breach in security did not come until 1960 with the U-2 incident and the Mitchell–Martin affair. The latter is perhaps the more revealing.

Bernon Mitchell and William Martin were two NSA employees who, though aware for many years of the US flights skirting into Soviet airspace, were shocked to discover, in 1959, that some of these flights were actually trespassing far into Soviet territory.[85] In September 1958 a USAF EC-130 was shot down by MIGs over Soviet Armenia with the loss of all seventeen crew (according to the US it had made a navigational error and flown off course). Martin and Mitchell felt that such flights were a major danger to peace and, despite the COMINT statute providing for a ten-year jail sentence for such indiscretions, they attempted to brief Congressmen on the affair but found no one willing to listen (the US was meanwhile angrily haranguing the Russians, playing them tapes of their own MIG pilots talking during the shoot-down, and accusing the USSR of a murderous attack on an unarmed aircraft). Ultimately, unable to get themselves taken seriously in the US, Mitchell and Martin defected to the USSR in 1960 where they held a public press conference describing the EC-130 spy flight in detail. As Bamford says, 'in the United States the reaction to the press conference ranged from disbelief to outrage.'[86] Eisenhower furiously dismissed the case as being about 'self-confessed traitors',[87] while ex-President Truman simply said 'they ought to be shot'.[88] A Congressional inquiry sat for thirteen months on the affair and finally concluded that the reason for the men's defection was that they were probably homosexuals. Yet Martin and Mitchell were telling the entire truth – it was impossible to deny it and no one did, but in effect there was an enormous act of collective suppression of the news. The men had tried to use legitimate US channels to get the news out and failed. Nothing less than the extreme act of defection to the other side did the trick – a defection which both were bitterly to regret. Those who argue that the US is not a country in which spy flights could be kept secret are not much prone to quote the Martin–Mitchell case.

The Martin–Mitchell case raises several other points of relevance to the 007 surveillance hypothesis. One is simply that to bring up information which, whatever its truth, has the effect of embarrassing the US side in the Cold War is commonly regarded as deeply unpatriotic. Television producers and newspaper editors as well as Congressmen are quite powerfully reluctant to pay attention to such matters for fear of being termed pro-Soviet, un-American and the like. This is hardly less true in Reagan's America than it was in Eisenhower's, despite the intervening Watergate era. Secondly, one has to realise that cases where there has been large-scale loss of life are, in a paradoxical sense, much harder to talk or write about openly than those involving more trivial events. For Martin and Mitchell were in effect pointing a finger at those who had sent the EC-130 (and other planes before it) on a mission over the USSR where, to their certain knowledge, the Russians would attempt to shoot the plane down: it was, in that sense, the mission controllers who were responsible for those seventeen deaths and who might be endangering many more lives besides. To accuse someone of responsibility for taking life is to up the stakes considerably and the pressures exerted by those who stand to be thus accused are correspondingly much fiercer.

This undoubtedly applies to the 007 case as well. If the surveillance hypothesis were indeed to be proved true, then at least some top figures in the Reagan Administration would have taken a decision which had led indirectly to the deaths of 269 people, most of them hapless passengers and including many women and children. The scandal and dénouement which such a scenario would present would be far, far greater than Watergate. And just as the Nixon Administration attempted every manner of cover-up and pressure tactics against the media to prevent Watergate coming to light, so the Reagan Administration could be expected to apply at least equivalent pressures – from a far stronger initial position with the media – to prevent a scandal involving 269 deaths hitting the surface. Those who uncovered Watergate had the advantage that all they were accusing the Administration of was burglary and that they were not damaging the US side in the Cold War.

Nonetheless, it is important to reiterate that the surveillance hypothesis remains just that – a hypothesis. There is an enormous accumulation of circumstantial evidence in favour of such a hypothesis, but there is no 'smoking gun'. And, most of all, the hypothesis gains its strength not just from the way it fits – or can be made to fit – a very large number of disparate facts, but by the sheer inadequacies of all the other possible hypotheses. That is, even if one did not consider the surveillance hypothesis on its own merits, one

would be impelled towards it by the simple elimination of possible alternatives.

There is no doubt, too, that the surveillance hypothesis gains strength from
the failure – indeed, the refusal – of most of the governments concerned to
institute a thorough, convincing and detailed inquiry into the tragedy. To
date only the USSR has carried out an investigation of its own: the US, the
South Koreans and Japanese have not. The ICAO Report is no real answer to
this, and nor is the US court case over the affair in which all considerations
relating to 'national security' have been ruled *ultra vires*. Unless and until
there is a really full, thorough, and honest investigation which can satisfactorily resolve all the many mysteries of the affair, the belief that KAL 007 was
indeed involved in a surveillance mission is likely only to gain wider credence,
*faute de mieux*. Without doubt such an investigation would create considerable
embarrassment, but if there is indeed an innocent explanation, establishing it
conclusively is surely worth such a price.

At about this point the objection is, indeed, frequently made: well, OK,
whose side are you on? Are you trying to incriminate the President himself?
Would you rather help score a propaganda triumph for the Russians over the
US? What motives do you have for doing that? You're not suggesting that
Martin and Mitchell did the right thing, are you? This form of objection –
which often seems almost to concede the surveillance hypothesis – is often
passionately put. In essence it is a sign of the deep discomfort which the
surveillance hypothesis inflicts on many people, who very much do not wish to
believe that their leaders, or those of their allies, could even be capable of
such a thing and, if they were, would almost rather not know. The real
objection here is not that the surveillance hypothesis is wrong; it is that it is
unthinkable, even if right. This objection is so widely held that, though it is
essentially political rather than technical, it is best to confront it openly.

Our main concern has to be simply to find out the facts. There is no doubt
that the Soviet, American, South Korean and Japanese governments could all
provide us with more facts if they wanted to. The US alone must have enough
information on its radar and recording tapes to settle the whole matter beyond
reasonable dispute. We don't have that data and we therefore have to
hypothesise. If the US wishes to end such speculation, it has the entire power
to do so by publishing the full and honest record. As for the President, even if
the surveillance hypothesis were true, there is nothing to suggest that he
would have had to know about it. Even the White House staff describe
President Reagan, somewhat euphemistically, as having 'a limited attention
span'.[89] It might seem extraordinary to imagine that top Administration
officials could initiate something like the 007 affair without telling the

President, but in the Reagan White House it would indeed have been possible.

But the key thing is surely just that the death of the 269 people aboard 007 was, in President Reagan's words, 'a crime against humanity [which] must never be forgotten'.[90] One owes it to those 269, their friends and relatives, and indeed, to civil air crew and passengers in general, to try to establish the truth, irrespective of the direction in which the political fallout might go. To argue, in effect, that one's top priority ought to be to protect one side or another in the Cold War is simply to echo the argument of the anti-Dreyfusards: what did it matter whether the Jew, Dreyfus, was innocent or not; to find him not guilty would be to damage the honour of the French army: therefore he *must* be guilty, even if the evidence wouldn't add up. No, Martin and Mitchell did not do the right thing: they should have stayed in the US and fought longer and harder for the truth there. One does not have to take or change sides in the Cold War; indeed, it is a vindication of the supreme virtues of western democracy that one can ask even the most awkward and embarrassing questions about one's leaders. And finally, of course, no matter whether the surveillance theory is true or not, this does not exculpate the Russians. They should not have shot down an airliner whatever it was doing; and they should not have shot down a plane that they could not identify. Two kilometres below and behind 007, no doubt Major Kasmin could not easily see through a murky night that he was pursuing an airliner: in that case he should simply have gone closer before shooting. No excuse is good enough.

Such, then, are the major theories as to how 007 came to be so dangerously far off course. It is no good saying, as some do, that they always prefer 'the cock-up theory of history to the conspiracy theory of history', as if this solves anything. One cannot reject any of the hypotheses we have examined unless one has a viable theory to put in its place. On the available information, the choice is for one out of only four theories. On our present state of knowledge the odds heavily favour the surveillance hypothesis, but it is still only a hypothesis. Readers must decide for themselves which theory they choose to believe, but if the surveillance hypothesis is not to carry the day it has to be because an explanation is found which carries a great deal more substance than any of the alternatives presently on offer. There seems little doubt as to which theory William of Occam – or Sherlock Holmes – would choose.

# THIRTEEN

# Strange Sequels

The first and immediate reaction of aviation administrators to the 007 tragedy was to consider whether Romeo 20, the course from which 007 had strayed, was not a dangerous route. The Federal Aviation Administration summarily closed the route on 2 September – while insisting that safety was not the reason. 'This is a precautionary measure that we are taking pending the results of our investigation,' said an FAA official. 'Past operating experience has shown this route to be both safe and efficient.'[1] As much as anything the move simply reflected shock, and a need to reassure public opinion. Although Romeo 20 comes, at its nearest point, as close as 17 miles from Soviet airspace, with each route band being 50 miles wide and with the help of the modern INS, pilots do not regard it as intrinsically unsafe.

The closure quickly met with fierce resistance from airlines and pilots alike, as they faced the resultant queues and delays. The US Airline Pilots' Association insisted that 'safety is not a major factor' on the route, while Pan-Am wanted the route 'restored immediately'.[2] In the end the route was reopened on 2 October.

The Russians were more cautious. Immediately after the 007 shoot-down they suspended the 'Vietnam Express', the twice weekly Ilyushin IL-62 service from Siberia to Hanoi. Almost as if fearing a reprisal, the Russians maintained the suspension for a full seven months.[3]

Far more significant was the decision to utilise the US military radars at King Salmon, Cape Newenham and Shemya to extend the radar coverage available to civilian ground controllers. From the beginning of January 1984, tracking data from King Salmon was fed directly onto screens at Anchorage, while Cape Newenham and Shemya committed themselves to monitor civilian flights and call Anchorage if such planes deviated more than 10 miles off course.[4] In effect this extended the radar coverage from Anchorage from its previous 200 miles to over 1200 miles. Such a system would clearly have made the 007 tragedy impossible – though, as the 1968 deviation of the Seaboard World Airlines DC-8 shows,[5] this should have been little more than the codification of previous practice: the question of why these radars were not used to alert 007 remains. The traffic on Romeo 20 is exceptionally heavy – it is one of the most heavily used air routes in the world – but after a whole year of operating this new radar coverage the FAA found that just two planes had wandered as far as 25 miles off course – less than one fourteenth as far as 007.[6]

Nonetheless, the international public remained keenly sensitive to the question of unscheduled route deviations and each new case was seized on as 'another possible KAL 007' (though there was no case of a similarly huge deviation). Perhaps the most ironic case was that of the Soviet Tupolev TU-54 flight from Leningrad to Athens on 10 April 1985, which strayed 35 miles off course in a way which took it over the principal Greek Air Force base at Tanagra. (The Russian pilot, who appeared to lack the English to understand the queries of air-traffic controllers, admitted he had made an error.) Greek fighters did not scramble.[7] The incident was a considerable embarrassment to the Papandreou government. In October 1984 Mr Papandreou had infuriated the US with his declaration: 'The world is now convinced the jumbo jet [i.e. KAL 007] was on a spy mission for the CIA and that it really did violate Soviet airspace for intelligence-gathering purposes.'[8] He had followed this up, in an interview with American television in January 1985, by asserting: 'If such a plane entered Greek airspace, we too would have shot it down. So would the United States, I am sure. These are the rules of the game.'[9] Happily, Mr Papandreou's bark was worse than his bite.

## Trauma at KAL

The tragedy of 007 caught KAL in the middle of an advertising campaign (which could not be immediately stopped) whose slogan ran: 'Our flights not only seem shorter, they are shorter.'[10] It did not need this macabre touch for KAL to face a thorough-going crisis. Any large plane crash tends to be a commercial as well as a human disaster for the airline which suffers it – but in this case the situation was made far worse by the fact that the airline found itself the centre of a major international political storm. No air disaster in history has received such prolonged publicity as the KAL 007 tragedy, with angry allegations and counter-allegations echoing for months through the UN, ICAO and the headlines of the world's media. Only seven months after the shoot-down was the airline willing to admit that it had suffered a considerable (though undisclosed) fall-off in business following the disaster.[11]

The 007 disaster was, moreover, followed by another incident in December 1983 when a KAL DC-10 went down a wrong runway at Anchorage, colliding with a light plane and injuring seven people. A month later another

KAL plane skidded off the runway on landing at Seoul – though this time no one was hurt.[12]

At the beginning of December 1983 it was announced that the President of KAL, Cho Choong Hoon ('Harry' Cho), would resign in order 'to take responsibility'[13] for the 007 tragedy, and that he would also retire from other front-line business positions. In fact his resignation did not become effective for another three months, when Cho's younger brother, Cho Choong Kun, succeeded him. According to the *International Herald Tribune*, a considerable re-organisation followed, with a number of senior executives shifted to other jobs, fourteen pilots forced to resign, and all 582 cockpit crew members subjected to tighter screening procedures, producing a number of further demotions and transfers. Two new 747s were bought, one of which replaced the ill-fated 007, though the '007' designation was dropped for good and replaced with '017'.[14] Finally, in September 1984, the airline attempted a wholesale relaunch under the slogan: 'Announcing the departure of Korean Air Lines. And the Arrival of Korean Air.' Not only did the airline change its name but also its colours and logo. The planes were now to be blue 'like the sky, representing the eternal future of the airline'. 'Sixteen years of experiences,' the blurb ran on, 'have enabled Korean Air to explore limitless possibilities.' It was, though, hard to know how thorough-going the shake-up had been, especially since 'Harry' Cho remained chairman of the Hanjin Group which controlled KAL.

KAL now faced several major challenges. On the one hand, it had been named as the designated carrier to the Asian Games to be held in Seoul in 1986 and, more important, for the Olympic Games there in 1988. Both of these events promised great commercial opportunities. Moreover, the 007 case would not quite lie down. Speculation continued as to how the airliner had come to be so far off course. In addition, the airline faced a major lawsuit on behalf of the relatives of the dead passengers.

The numbers involved in this lawsuit were enormous. Only the day after the shoot-down the California attorney, Melvin Belli, filed claim for $52 million on behalf of just one of the passengers.[15] The widow of another passenger brought suit against KAL, Boeing, Litton, and the US and South Korean governments for $2 billion.[16] KAL's initial estimate of the insurance claim for the plane and its passengers was initially set at $435 million,[17] but it was soon clear that this was a wild underestimate.

The situation was extremely complex. The aggrieved relatives quickly learned that the USSR would refuse absolutely to countenance their claims. Similarly, the claims against Boeing and Litton were dismissed in a US court. This left the relatives suing KAL, the US government and the South Korean government on a variety of grounds, including that of a possible surveillance mission. But however the case narrowed, KAL was always bound to be at the centre of it. And while KAL had received $26,824,000 immediately from Stewart Wrightson, the Lloyds syndicate insuring the plane[18] (the claim was paid out under the 'war damage' clause), the claims on the lives lost were clearly the heart of the matter.

The situation is also complicated by the fact that, as of late 1983, KAL had still not settled all claims outstanding from the 1978 incident over Murmansk – it was offering 5 million yen to the bereaved family of one Japanese passenger who were claiming 187 million yen.[19] In the 1983 case, KAL initially estimated that it would pay out $40,000 for every dead passenger,[20] somewhat less than the internationally agreed minimum figure of $75,000.[21] This figure was then upped to $100,000 as the clamour of the relatives grew. But while KAL was able to satisfy some relatives with such a sum,[22] it could not satisfy all, certainly not in Japan – where twenty-eight of the victims came from, and where $285,000 is paid out immediately to the family of any road-accident victim. In the Washington courts the stakes were similarly astronomical. Happily for the airline, it did not face similar suits in South Korea – 'the gentleman's country in the Orient', as the KAL brochures call it – even though most of the passengers came from there. But since the US and Japan are easily KAL's most important markets abroad, the growing agitation of the passengers' relatives there could not but disquiet the airline.

## South Korea: The apotheosis of General Chun

It is difficult not to feel that the 007 tragedy was of considerable political benefit to General Chun's regime. Although he had been 'legitimised' to a degree by being accorded an official visit to Washington in 1981, the bloody coup which had brought him to power and South Korea's appalling human-rights record had not won Chun many friends, at home or abroad. He had clamped down with particular ferocity on students and religious critics and banned over 400 journalists from practising their profession.[23] He had, moreover, begun to lose the confidence of both businessmen and foreign investors as the economy slowed down and corruption, which, on taking power, Chun had pledged to stamp out, soared.

On the eve of the 007 tragedy, Chun's regime had begun to look extremely vulnerable. Especially damaging were a series of corruption scandals which had involved the President's own associates. Yoon Ja Joong, one of the generals who had helped Chun into power in 1980 and had been rewarded with the Ministry of Transportation, had been jailed in 1981 for accepting

$109,000 in bribes. In 1982 a $959 million loan-manipulation scandal broke, this time involving a relative of Chun's wife, while only days before the 007 shoot-down another large scandal involving over $150 million had led to the arrest of nine government officials and five bankers.[24] Chun had never had a real popular base and by September 1983 he was in serious trouble.

The 007 affair immediately overshadowed all these problems and Chun was quick to exploit the great wave of rage and grief which now swept South Korea, ordering major anti-Communist rallies throughout the country. The images of these rallies (Seoul's attracted 100,000 people) and of the grieving relatives throwing garlands on the waters west of Moneron Island went round the world, engendering a natural wave of sympathy for South Korea and harmonising with similar, if smaller, rallies in the US and elsewhere.

Two months later Chun was paid the supreme compliment of an official visit by President Reagan. What made the visit all the more impressive was that the Aquino assassination had led Reagan's advisers to cancel the scheduled visit to the Philippines and similar queasiness had also led to the elimination of Indonesia and Thailand from the itinerary. The fact that Reagan thus visited only Japan and South Korea made the impressive point that the US posture in the area was now based on a central alliance with these two countries above all others.

The visit to Japan was routine enough.[25] Japan might recently have declared that it 'deplored but understood' the US invasion of Grenada, but given the close relationship between the Nakasone and Reagan governments ('Ron and Yasu'), there were few surprises. South Korea was a different matter: the question here was how far Reagan would go in public support of what was still unmistakably a brutal military dictatorship with limited popular support. If General Chun had had any worries on this score, they were soon laid at rest. Still flushed with his rhetorical triumphs over the 007 affair (which he frequently evoked), President Reagan made repeated references to South Korea as part of the 'free world', and spoke of the Chun regime's aim of 'strengthening respect for human rights'.

The tour was, of course, the typical Reagan 'show', replete with 'photo opportunities', televised minidramas, and the striking of postures for 'history'. The inevitable high point was the President's visit to the demilitarised zone to meet the 40,000 US troops stationed nearby. Here, Reagan's rhetoric must have particularly delighted Chun: 'Peace,' he declared, 'cannot be obtained simply by weeping or crying its name. It can only be maintained if it rests on adequate strength . . . even if that means the temporary sacrifice of individual interests.' This is more or less the rationalisation which the Chun regime makes for its own suppression of opposition. The Reagan party were later considerably embarrassed to be questioned about the more than one thousand opposition and human rights campaigners placed under house arrest or other restraint by the KCIA to ensure security during the visit. It was of little import to Chun, for whom the visit was a sort of consecration. He had already declared his belief in South Korea's future in civil aviation by announcing the construction of a giant new airport for Seoul, capable of handling 10.2 million passengers a year.[26] Soon after, it was announced that Chun would make the first ever visit by a Korean head of state to Japan. It was not until the end of 1984, with the international outcry that resulted from the maltreatment accorded to the returning South Korean opposition leader, Kim Dae Jung, that life returned to anything like normal.

The only real fly in the ointment was that, prior to the 007 tragedy, South Korea had been bent on improving its relations with the Soviet bloc, particularly the USSR. The long-term objective was the stabilisation of the regime which separate recognition of two Koreas from the Communist bloc would bring; but short of that, Seoul was anxious that the Communist bloc should not boycott the 1988 Olympics. Ironically, the presence of Soviet delegates to the Inter-Parliamentary Union meeting to be held in Seoul at the time of the tragedy (to which McDonald, Helms and other US legislators were travelling) was to have been a major seal on that rapprochement. (One of Chun's associates most linked with this policy, Kwon Chong Dal, lost a daughter aboard 007.)[27] In the wake of the tragedy all such links with the USSR were, naturally, swept away. But only three months after the shootdown Seoul announced that it was keen to return to its previous policy[28] and non-political links were indeed restored in August 1984.[29] Two months later, Chun himself declared that he would like the rapprochement to go much further.[30] Less than a year after the 007 tragedy it was already clear that Seoul wanted the affair to become no more than a forgotten hiccup in this overall diplomatic campaign.

Viewed in the more general strategic context, this slight improvement in relations between Seoul and Moscow was a minor motif. In the much more important relationship between the USSR and Japan, the 007 tragedy was another step towards escalation. The already tense situation in the Sea of Japan worsened noticeably in June 1984 with Mr Nakasone's declaration that Japan was willing, if necessary, to blockade the straits which give the Red Navy its only route into the Pacific. The USSR responded by calling this 'a declaration of war'.[31] Meanwhile the USSR moved launchers for 135 SS-20s – a third of all such missiles – into the Far Eastern region and Japan gave the go-ahead for the deployment of cruise missiles on US warships operating out of Japan. In September the Japanese reacted with anger to the doubling (from

20 to 40) of the Soviet MIG-23s based on Iturup, in the Kuriles.[32] Needless to say, the fishermen of Hokkaido were caught in the middle, as they had been in the 007 affair: the Russians announced in June 1984 that they were terminating the agreement whereby the Japanese fished for salmon in Soviet waters.[33] More and more, the craft swimming in and around these waters were iron-clad and nuclear-armed.

## Soviet second thoughts

The 007 affair continued to reverberate in Russia for a considerable time. The apocryphal story made the rounds that a PVO officer from the Soviet Far East Regional Command (Major Kasmin?) had been seen drinking alone and crying into his vodka in Moscow's closed hotel for military personnel. The original untruthful phrase that the plane had disappeared 'in the direction of the Sea of Japan' became a sort of standing joke. More generally, some commentators noted a gathering air of doubt, embarrassment and guilt, as the point sank in that even if 007 had been on a surveillance mission, this would not have exonerated the Soviet action.[34]

There was considerable speculation as to who had ordered the shoot-down. Some believed that the decision had been made by Colonel-General Semyon Romanov, the PVO chief of staff, while others insisted that he had referred the decision up to Marshal Alexander Koldunov, the head of the PVO and First Deputy Defence Minister.[35] It seems certain that Koldunov was involved in the decision – certainly if Ogarkov's claim that the whole military high command was contacted is to be believed. After the 1978 KAL incursion into Soviet airspace, the ten PVO Commands had been regrouped into just five, each relating directly to Moscow. In the case of the Far Eastern Command, this would have meant that the Kamchatka/Sakhalin commanders would have referred to Far Eastern Command headquarters at Tschita, which would in turn have contacted the Operations Directorate in Moscow.[36] Certainly, in the case of the 1978 incident the head of the PVO, Marshal Pavel Batizki, had been held responsible and dismissed. This was how Koldunov had become the head of the PVO.[37] No doubt Koldunov was keenly aware that the 1978 KAL incident had cost his predecessor his job, and would have been determined not to be the second PVO head in five years to be toppled by a wandering KAL plane. Koldunov had a lot on the line and his comments on the incident should be seen in that light.

This time too there was continuous rumour of sweeping sanctions being operated within the PVO's Far Eastern Command, and General Romanov's move to a liaison post in East Germany was widely interpreted as a demotion.[38] Meanwhile, by the end of 1983 the Politburo had announced a new, unified air-traffic-control system to replace the old regional structure – with Moscow as the nerve centre. Some analysts claimed such a system might have helped to avoid the 007 tragedy (though it is difficult to see how). The Aviation Minister, Boris Bugayev, also announced a shake-up within Aeroflot. The high number of Aeroflot's (mainly unannounced) crashes was, he said, damaging morale: Bugayev's own deputy was sacked and a new civil air-transport code announced.[39]

There were also signs of a limited debate on the 007 affair. In early December 1983 *Krasnaya Zvezda* first brought up a topic that was to occupy much space in Soviet military journals – the possibility of fighters using ramming tactics as a last resort against aerial intruders.[40] The newspaper described a training session for PVO pilots which seemed designed to simulate the 007 interception – the emphasis was placed on slow-flying intruders, and on destroying such intruders at all costs. The USSR had to protect its airspace round a gigantic 42,000-mile border, it was argued, and this border was under continuous threat of US aerial penetration. The (suicidal) tactic of ramming – first used by Soviet pilots against the Luftwaffe – was described in one journal as 'the weapon of the brave', but Western analysts were quick to note that such a tactic would also allow the ending of an intrusion to be excused as a mere midair collision – thus avoiding all the embarrassment of an 007-type shoot-down. This thought was prompted by the revelation in one military journal that one PVO pilot had died a few years before after ramming at full speed an intruder which was on the point of escaping back out of Soviet airspace. Observers wondered if this could provide the explanation for the 'midair collision' (as it was reported at the time) which had ended the flight of an Argentinian cargo plane which had unaccountably strayed over Soviet Armenia in August 1981, on a flight from Turkey. (Turkey, with its strong US military presence, is certainly viewed by the USSR as a prime source of CIA activity.)

It was difficult to imagine a more gung-ho way of justifying the 007 shoot-down than to talk in this fashion. But such articles were immediately countered by an article by Colonel-General Sergei V. Golubiev, a PVO deputy commander for combat training, in *Aviatsiya i Kosmonavtika* of 9 January 1984.[41] While Golubiev was careful to justify the necessity of taking 'resolute measures' against intruders such as 007, the tone of his article was implicitly critical. His whole stress was on the need for 'correct acts', 'strict conformity to the rules', and 'maturity' in the PVO pilot, who 'must do all he possibly can to force the intruding plane to land at the nearest aerodrome'. In the end, he stressed, responsibility rested with the pilot, and the pilot alone –

and he criticised ground commanders who tried to hide behind others.

As if stung by the implications of this widely noted article, General Romanov replied in April 1984 with a strong statement, which spoke of the PVO's formidable strength and combat-readiness and its utter determination to destroy all Western aircraft which came 'anywhere near their range'.[42] He also spoke of PVO pilots and commanders who had received high decorations for heroism in recent months (it is not known if Major Kasmin was one of these).[43] Romanov was quickly backed up by his superior, Marshal Koldunov, writing in *Pravda* to mark PVO Air Defence Day (8 April). Koldunov specifically referred to the 007 shoot-down as a historic example of the PVO's 'high level of readiness to perform their military duty'.[44] It was clear that this was the official line – indeed the Soviet press attacked as 'anti-Soviet' those who had portrayed Golubiev's article as a criticism of the 007 shoot-down.[45] This was clearly a public reprimand for Golubiev: writing articles which can be turned to 'anti-Soviet' uses is a grave misdemeanour indeed. As if to emphasise the point, *Trud* carried interviews with PVO pilots at a northern base who complained of repeated US and other NATO patrols along the edge of Soviet Arctic airspace.[46] When General Romanov died in May 1984 (of an undisclosed cause), there was certainly no hint of any disgrace. His obituary, signed by Marshals Ustinov and Ogarkov, spoke of him as a 'true son of the Party and people' whose memory would live in the hearts of the Soviet nation.[47] Koldunov, for all the rumours that he might be sacked or demoted, kept his job as head of the PVO. Oddly, Marshal Ogarkov, who had captured most publicity in the presentation of the Soviet case, may have suffered as a result. When he was demoted as head of the Soviet Armed Forces in September 1984, there was considerable muttering about his 'un-Party-like tendencies' and of his 'getting too big for his breeches'.[48] Ogarkov's flamboyant style had been displayed on many topics – but never to a greater audience than over 007. (His eclipse was short: he was just the man to appeal to Gorbachev, who promoted him back to prominence soon after taking power.)

In general, though, the Western correspondents who watched for some sign of a real Soviet change of heart over 007 watched in vain. Indeed, it was striking how Soviet journals and newspapers returned again and again to the affair – including a whole barrage of articles on the first anniversary of the shoot-down. Whatever doubts and regrets had surfaced privately, the resentments over the incident remained strong and genuine. Indeed, with the growing reconsideration in the West of the many odd and suspicious elements in the affair, Soviet self-righteousness grew rather than diminished.

## The US: diminishing returns

On the first anniversary of the 007 shoot-down, several officials of the Reagan Administration gave their view of the effects of the tragedy. 'When you look back on the KAL affair,' said a senior White House staffer, 'there is a temptation to say it worsened relations [with the USSR]. That's not the real significance. The real significance is that it provided a groundswell of criticism of the Russians here and everywhere that put them on the defensive and gave us some flexibility.' Others put the position more strongly. 'It was a black eye of colossal proportions to the Soviets,' said a senior State Department official. 'It provided a political boon' for Reagan, said another. 'The way the Russians handled it, they took the heat off Reagan.' 'I'd almost go so far as to say it created a consensus in this country about the Soviets,' was another comment. 'A basic kind of anti-Soviet mood was created that is fairly supportive of the President. Until the KAL, Reagan was blamed for the bad relations. Everyone remembered he had called them "liars and cheats". But after the KAL shooting-down, the President seemed to make sense to a lot of people.'[49]

It is certainly true that after the 007 affair Reagan never really looked back. With Congress and the electorate now at one with him on the Right's basic attitude to the USSR, his 'window of vulnerability' over never having had a summit, having made no progress with arms control, was closed. In 1984 the Democrats tried in vain to use these issues, but after 007, they wouldn't work. In that sense, the affair did much to help Reagan win re-election.

But there was a negative side too. As reconsideration of the affair proceeded, it was increasingly recognised that many of the things the Administration had said at the time had been untrue. Moreover, the surfacing of critical articles, focusing on the mysteries of the affair which still could not be explained, threw some Administration spokesmen onto the defensive. Thus Richard Burt, who had been close to the centre of the affair, when asked to give his thoughts on the anniversary of the tragedy, spent much of his time heavily on the defensive, attacking those who had begun to suggest that perhaps 007 *had* been on a surveillance mission after all. Such people were, he suggested, Soviet dupes or worse.[50] Increasingly, too, one could find people who argued merely that, 'OK, maybe it was a surveillance mission, but . . .'. It is possible that this may help explain why, in the longer run, US voters were little disposed to see the affair as a plus for the Administration. When voters were asked, in March 1985, to score Washington's handling of foreign-policy situations on a score of 1 to 10, it was Carter who topped the poll for his Middle East peace agreement (6.45), with the 007 affair coming absolute bottom with 3.96.[51] (Many, though, would have been critical because Reagan was not anti-Soviet enough.)

## A cover-up?

Increasingly, indeed, the sort of mentions that the 007 affair did get in the press were unwelcome to the Administration, for they suggested something which seemed very like a cover-up.

The evidence for a cover-up starts, of course, with the blocking of the normal inquiry by the US National Transportation Safety Board (NTSB). The Alaskan section of the NTSB was notified by the Anchorage airport authorities when 007 was just two and a half hours overdue at Seoul. An NTSB investigator went to the airport and picked up the passenger list, crew list and other documents. Just as their inquiry was about to begin, however, the State Department telephoned to say that the 007 affair was not an accident and therefore no concern of the NTSB. The Anchorage chief investigator, James Michaelangelo, described the order he received to call off the investigation as 'unprecedented'. The State Department, to which Michaelangelo was made to hand over his documents, never carried out an inquiry. Almost certainly, this was a breach of US law. Normally, the NTSB would routinely have investigated every crash involving US citizens and where a plane has taken off from a US airport. In this case, uniquely, it has been prevented from doing so.[52]

There was, too, a fairly clear cover-up of the truth over revealing when the news of the shoot-down was received in both the US and Japan.[53] This we have already described. Then again, there was the unmistakable evidence of evasion and deception by both the Defence and State Departments reported by the Munich TV journalist, André Libik.[54] Or, again, there is the curious case of Bernard and Eskelson, the two RC-135 pilots who challenged the Administration's version of the RC-135 mission which 'rendezvoused' with 007. They published their protest shortly after the disaster, on 13 September. For three and a half months they were ignored. Then, in early February 1984, they were cautioned by an FBI agent, on behalf of the NSA, that they had 'technically' violated US espionage laws and that any future statements by them should be viewed in that light. The two men said that if this had been an attempt to intimidate them, it had indeed succeeded. They had, they said, no intention of compromising national security – they had just found the Administration's version of the tragedy 'incomplete and misleading'.[55] If, indeed, they were infringing the Espionage Act, it is curious that it took the

NSA and FBI three and a half months to notice it. It seems more probable that a calculated – but much later – decision was taken to clamp down hard on all such critical speculation about the tragedy.

Meanwhile, the bereaved relatives of 007's passengers fastened increasingly on the notion that the plane might have been on a surveillance mission. Shozo Takemoto, a spokesman for the relatives of the Japanese victims, issued a statement in early September 1984 saying that 007 might have been part of 'an elaborately schemed plot on the part of a government agent of a certain country'. Accusing the US of deliberately witholding information about how the plane came to stray, Takemoto appealed for full disclosure[56] – in vain, of course. Similarly, speculation that the US had actually found 007's black box grew: indeed *TV Eye* journalists found that the editor of an American technical magazine, Alexander Braun, had been tipped off by a State Department contact that the box had been found and would shortly be publicly revealed. Then, at the last moment, it was decided the box should be kept secret.[57]

Doubts also surfaced over the quite remarkable number of coincidences which had combined to prevent Anchorage knowing 007 was off course. First, there was the fact that the Anchorage VOR had been shut down for maintenance purposes only an hour or so before 007's take off: had that VOR been on, 007 could have had no possible reason for being off course even initially. Second, there was the fact that virtually all air controller services at Anchorage – flight data, clearance delivery, ground-control position, local control and approach control – had been combined that night: the reason given was the light traffic at night.[58] Then again, ICAO found that the Anchorage radar approach-control unit was also not operating that night, and that instead radar information was being displayed on a VDU in the control tower – where all the other services had been concentrated.[59] Initially, the radar information on 007 came from the radar at Kenai – but this radar was shut down at 13.27 while 007 was still (just) within its coverage – even though there was no other radar to hand the plane on to.[60] And – yet again – there were vexed questions about the availability of the findings of the US military radar at King Salmon to Anchorage ground control. King Salmon's radar (which showed 007 deviating further and further off course) was fed onto a VDU in Anchorage control tower, but, according to ICAO, this VDU was in the basement of the tower and would not have been visible to controllers upstairs. But *TV Eye* journalists claimed that they had discovered two screens in the main control room tuned to take the King Salmon radar feed. On the night of the tragedy one of these had been out of sight of the controllers and the other one might have been switched off.[61] All these coincidences were separately plausible, but their combination on the same night that so many other oddities occurred did not escape critical comment.

The relatives of the dead passengers naturally wished to clarify whether US radar capabilities could not have been used to alert 007 that it was off track. In the court case being held before the US District Court judge, Aubrey E. Robinson Jr, in Washington, the US government attempted to have itself dismissed as a defendant. This Judge Robinson would not allow, but his ruling was helpfully narrow: legal discovery proceedings against the US government would be limited to 'facts tending to prove the existence or nonexistence of a legal duty to warn or advise civilian aircraft in peril or off course'. Judge Robinson specifically ruled out of order any attempt to pursue the question of whether USAF planes in the vicinity of 007 could have confused the Russians about the identity of 007, and also warned the plaintiffs away from other such 'national security' issues.[62] (This produced renewed complaint about the fact that the trial was being held in Washington at all – notoriously 'the Administration's town' – rather than – as the law implies – in New York, where the plane started from.) Nonetheless, Judge Robinson's ruling still left open the question of USAF radar tapes of 007's flight, and these the attorneys representing the relatives petitioned to see.

In February 1985 came the bombshell: the USAF Regional Operations Command Center (ROCC) at Anchorage had, according to the US Justice Department attorney, Jan K. Von Flatern, destroyed the key tapes. This was extremely peculiar: the USAF customarily impounds all data relating to an air disaster, precisely for the sort of reasons the relatives had in mind. On this occasion, said Von Flatern, the Anchorage ROCC 'had no idea that it was going to be involved or that that data would be useful in the litigation at any point'.[63] The tape was, he said, kept for just fifteen days and then routinely recycled (i.e. wiped). Unfortunately for Von Flatern, the fifteen-day period made the argument absurd – long before such a period had elapsed it would have been quite apparent that the radar tapes were bound to be a key exhibit for the impending inquiry. Von Flatern then claimed that actually the USAF kept its tapes for only 30 hours and that the relevant tape had been destroyed after that period.[64] This does not, however, answer the question: such an interval would not always be sufficient to know whether the tapes might be required for an inquiry – though, of course, in the 007 case it still would have been. Once George Shultz had announced the news of the disaster 18 hours after it happened, it would have been obvious that the tape would be needed – and still plenty of time to ensure it was retained, even within a 30-hour framework.

Attorneys representing the bereaved families were insistent that the full story of the tape's destruction had not been told and said they wanted to talk to more USAF officials. The trouble was that talking to such possibly helpful contacts was not easy, given the quite extraordinary width of the 'gag orders' placed by the court on all employees of the FAA, those party to the damage suit, and the lawyers acting on behalf of the bereaved. The notion that the radar tape had been deliberately destroyed to prevent embarrassment to the US government was hardly beyond question, particularly since the USAF seems to have developed this sort of habit under the Reagan Administration. In another court case NBC had filed suit to obtain a videotape of the fatal crashes of four USAF Thunderbirds in 1982, only to find that the USAF had erased part of the tape. Similarly, in March 1984 a Washington District Court found that the USAF had 'intentionally destroyed' pictures 'along with other voluminous evidence' relating to the crash of a USAF C-5 carrying Vietnamese children out of Saigon in 1975.[65]

There was a certain irony in the fact that the chief defendant in the case should have been the US Justice Department, for that department was, of course, headed by the Attorney-General, Edwin Meese III. Meese – one of the President's oldest and closest associates – had achieved wide fame for his bad memory. Repeatedly, and under oath, Meese had 'forgotten' to mention sundry of his stock-market transactions and a number of personal loans to him and his wife from benefactors who had received federal jobs after making these loans. He was famous, too, for such *bons mots* as labelling the American Civil Liberties Union 'a criminals' lobby', investigative journalists as the receivers of 'stolen property', and Scrooge as the victim of a 'bad Press'.[66] But the irony lay not there but in the fact that Meese had been in on the 007 affair almost from the start. A close friend of William Clark's (the two men go back almost twenty years in Reagan's 'California mafia'), he had been with Clark at the Biltmore Hotel when the news of the shoot-down first broke and had been one of the highly select participants in the secret early teleconference on how to handle the affair.[67] No doubt Meese showed a friendly interest in his department's role in the case being heard not many blocks away.

In late August 1985 the Justice Department applied to Judge Robinson to dismiss all civil charges against the US government in the case. At this the lawyers representing the bereaved filed an affidavit sworn by Raymond Yeager, the former head of the FAA's accident-analysis branch. The affidavit testified that 'I heard a statement at 14.34:04 GMT [i.e. four hours before the shoot-down] which included the words . . . "We should warn him".' The plaintiff's attorneys said that the words were part of the background noise picked up on the microphone near the air-traffic controller's position at Anchorage: they had been spoken by an FAA supervisor or controller or by a military radar operator at Elmendorf USAF Base (Alaska).[68] They had not made their way into the official tape transcript, but that tape was again produced. The Justice Department produced a countering affidavit from an FBI expert saying that no intelligible words could be made out.[69] With two experts in disagreement this meant that the final decision on the tape would have to rely on the entirely lay opinion of Judge Robinson . . .

There was no doubt that the whole drift of the case was going against the plaintiffs. Already, in October 1984, they had received a sensational setback in their attempt to secure testimony from both Captain Choy Tack Yong (who had flown 007 from New York to Anchorage) and Captain Y. M. Park, the pilot of KAL 015.[70] KAL's lawyer, George N. Tompkins, attempted to curtail the deposition which Captain Yong was to give – though of course, Captain Park's testimony was awaited with far greater anticipation (somewhat oddly, it was ruled that Captain Park's testimony would be taken in private). In the middle of the dispute over curtailment, Tompkins announced that Captain Park would not be coming to testify after all. In spring 1984, he said, Park had been given a desk job by KAL and had been very discontent, threatening that unless his flight status was restored, he would not go to Washington to give testimony. KAL had turned him down, and Captain Park had resigned from the company. Captain Park's resignation, as it had happened, had occurred just the week before, with Park due to testify shortly. Now that Park was no longer a KAL employee, it was not the company's business to produce him as a witness. It would now be virtually impossible to make Park come to Washington, unless, of course, the US State Department and the South Korean Foreign Ministry worked hard together to secure such a result – a most unlikely eventuality.

This was a tremendous blow to the plaintiffs and, indeed, to anyone who wanted the truth about KAL 007 out in the open. There would, after all, have been many questions which any investigator would have wanted to put to Captain Park. Why had he apparently flown KAL 015 at such extraordinary speeds over the early parts of the route? Had he been aware that 007 was actually doing the very opposite – flying more slowly than planned – and had he realised that, as a result, he had come close to catching up with 007? Given that 007 had delayed its departure time from Anchorage because there was, reportedly, no point in arriving early at Seoul, why had KAL 015 been in such a hurry? And what about KAL 015's Mach buzzer? Had Captain Park switched the buzzer off, and if so why?

Even more important were all the questions for Captain Park about his role as relay post for KAL 007. Captain Park had, after all, been the only man in the world to have had close, continuous and easy communication with 007 once its fateful flight had begun. Had Captain Park never thought it odd that the weather conditions being reported by 007 were clearly different from those KAL 015 was encountering, although they were supposed to be on the same route – and, given 015's turn of speed, were also quite close together? Or again, Anchorage ground control had asked Captain Park to relay to KAL 007 a firm instruction to make its next report after NABIE direct to ground control on VHF (i.e. and not use KAL 015 as a relay post). Had Captain Park passed this order on? If so, had he not been surprised when KAL 007 did not comply with this command but had continued to use KAL 015 as a relay? Had Captain Park not queried Captain Chun about this, and if so what reasons had Chun given? And if Park was hearing Chun loud and clear on VHF, why did he think that Chun was not using VHF to contact Anchorage? Then again, why had Park only volunteered a position report for 007 at NEEVA when Anchorage had called up KAL 015 on the radio? Why had he not transmitted that position report automatically, without waiting for Anchorage to make a move? Moreover, the same thing seemed to have happened all over again over 007's request for an altitude change: when Anchorage had called KAL 015 at 16.06 Park had only then revealed that 007 had earlier passed on to him a request to ground control for an altitude change. So why had Park not passed this request on right away instead of waiting for Anchorage to call up? And had 007 later said anything to KAL 015 which betrayed any knowledge that it was off course?

There were other questions even beyond that. Had KAL 015 picked up any interrogatory messages from Soviet ground control or aircraft directed towards 007 – after all, 015 had had an open, working radio channel to 007. Had 015 itself been quizzed by Soviet aircraft or ground controllers once Soviet air defences on the Kuriles had gone into action? Had Park observed a higher than usual level of Soviet radio activity? And what of KAL 015's weather radar: had it picked up any sign of Soviet fighters – or of the RC-135? And had it picked up the signals or presence of any other US surveillance aircraft operating in the area – according to the Soviet maps, after all, there had been at least one P-3C Orion not far from the correct Romeo 20 route, and according to the US version of the RC-135's flight that plane had broken away and flown towards Shemya – that is, in the direction of Romeo 20 – just as KAL 015 was following up behind 007.

There was, indeed, almost no end to the leading questions which could have been put to Captain Park. Why had he alone had nothing to say about the KAL 007 tragedy at a time when everyone with even half an idea was holding forth about it – when he had known more than anyone else? Why had he been so completely unavailable for interview? What was the exact nature of the dispute which reportedly existed between KAL and himself, which had resulted in an expensively trained pilot being summarily told that he had to stop flying? But with the news that Captain Park would not, after all, be available both the legal process and the general hope of a fuller investigation had suffered a shattering setback. Given that the issues at stake were the deaths of 269 people, a major escalation in the Cold War and, not least, the loss of a multi-million dollar aircraft, it is not surprising that many of the passengers' relatives were acutely dissatisfied that a relatively minor personnel matter should have been enough to prevent Park's testimony from being heard.

There is no doubt that the plaintiffs had been heavily handicapped by Judge Robinson's ruling in February 1984: 'We don't want to open up that can of worms as to whether this is ... military intelligence, whether it is foreign surveillance, what are the capabilities of NASA, what satellites you have got up there and what they are doing. This is out of the case once and for all.'[71] The gag order covering all 50,000 FAA employees was another considerable handicap. But beyond such legal obstacles were a whole host of others. It was quite clear that neither KAL nor the Reagan Administration wanted to hear more discussion of the 007 case, and this generated strong pressures against further investigation.

Thus a partner in one firm investigating a technical aspect of the case was strongly warned off by a Pentagon official who told him his firm was 'walking on eggshells', reminded him that the government was an important client of the firm, and warned him to hand over immediately to US intelligence any sensitive material he came across. 'I got scared,' the partner frankly admitted. Similarly, a State Department official approached about the immediate post-shoot-down teleconference replied, 'I could find out if this happened, but I would lose my job for asking.' Steve Jorgensen, an air-traffic controller at Anchorage, when asked about the military radar feed, replied, 'We've been told not to talk about that. Listen, buddy, I got to keep on making money. I can't talk to you. Sorry.' Another air controller had to call off a meeting on the 007 case when he was warned off by the Anchorage FAA.[72]

Similarly, attempts to use the US Freedom of Information Act to see material relating to the 007 case have met with systematic obstruction. The State Department has announced that it is reviewing all the documents to do with the case in order to see what can be made public – and meanwhile nothing will be made public. This was an unprecedented restriction under the Act. When the State Department was asked for a list of the documents it had supplied to ICAO, it claimed – quite incredibly – that it could not find such a list. Even more remarkably, ICAO too claimed it could not find such a list. Moreover, although ICAO has a formal standing request for further data about the 007 case, three months after the Japanese published their data showing 007's altitude changes and deception of ground control in the last minutes of the flight, ICAO still claimed that it had not received such data. The American head of ICAO's Air Navigation Commission, Duane Freer, professed himself quite unworried about that – if the Japanese did not want to give such data to ICAO, that was their business.[73] Yet the data was publicly available in the official Japanese Diet proceedings.

To these obstructions one could add an almost infinite list of others. As Donald Madole, the plaintiffs' attorney in Washington, complained, 'This is the only accident investigation that I have ever been involved in . . . where the release of information is . . . apparently controlled by the Department of State.'[74] Other investigators found that aviation companies they turned to for technical advice were likely to tell them that they could not afford to annoy their principal customer, the Pentagon.[75] At least one magazine which carried a critical article on the case was warned by defence contractors that they would withdraw their advertising if such coverage continued.[76] An article on the affair by the present author resulted in a letter from a Conservative MP to the head of my college, suggesting I was no longer a fit person to hold a job there. One could go on.

There is no doubt that the manner in which the 007 investigation has been had to be conducted does not reflect well on the US government. Normal procedures have been flouted in order to shut down the NTSB's inquiry and the principal legal case is being heard in the wrong city. The State Department, having confiscated the NTSB's documents, failed to hold any investigation of its own. Although the Administration earlier boasted that it had made great efforts to recover all relevant tapes recorded at US listening posts which might assist the inquiry, the key radar tapes have been destroyed. The Freedom of Information Act is being virtually ignored. Ludicrously extensive gag orders have been used to inhibit discussion of the case. There is a clear pattern of Administration intimidation of those close to the case. The two inquiries into the affair held by the House and Senate intelligence committees were held in private and only US State Department and intelligence officials were called to testify before them. Even so, neither committee will release the names of the officials they saw or any summary of the material on which they based their findings (which wholly exonerated the US Administration).[77] The Administration is unwilling even to supply a list of the documents it tendered to an international organisation. To this one is tempted to add the decidedly thin and patchy coverage of the case in much of the US media. It is utterly unprecedented for the investigation of a disaster affecting a civilian airliner to face such obstacles.

## New evidence?

Despite these pressures, other titbits of possible evidence did dribble out, none of them conclusive. Some came from the irrepressible Melvin Belli, representing a number of the bereaved families. As early as November 1983 Belli claimed to have a sworn affidavit from a woman in Seoul alleging that KAL pilots had been secretly paid to fly over Soviet territory.[78]

Belli (the man who had earlier pioneered the concept of the high damages 'palimony' suit for his Hollywood clients) later added detail to his charges. On 23 August 1984 Belli told the West German ARD television station that he had conducted interviews in Seoul with the widows of both the pilot and co-pilot of KAL 007. According to Belli both women – speaking in the presence of three other American attorneys and thirty other people bereaved by the tragedy – had said that a number of its pilots had been paid to fly over Soviet territory. The two widows, said Belli, had said that their husbands had become very afraid of these flights and had wanted to discontinue them; Captain Chun had, reportedly, been particularly nervous about his last flight, which he had regarded as a specially dangerous mission.[79]

Belli has not since publicly produced any supporting evidence for his charges, which have to be viewed against the background of his own colourful high-profile style and in the context of pre-trial manoeuvres. If KAL over-flights of the USSR had indeed been a regular occurrence it is surprising, to say the least, that the Russians have not lodged protests about them before.

Another potentially explosive item of information was revealed on the American Broadcasting Corporation's television news show, *Twenty-Twenty*, on 30 August 1984 in the shape of a tape ABC had acquired from a Japanese news agency of KAL 007's last few minutes. The tape was matched against the voice-prints of the earlier transmissions from 007 and the voice verified as that of First Officer Son. The tape is extremely fuzzy, with a good deal of static, but it is possible to make out snatches of conversation which do not seem to correspond at all with the ICAO version or indeed with the secondary Japanese version of what was said in these last few vital moments.

Robert Allardyce and his associate, James Gollin, have spent a great deal of effort on trying to elucidate and enhance this last fragment of tape. There is room for dispute as to what some of the words spoken actually were, but they have arrived at a version which is reproduced below:[80]

*007:* . . . first, for South Korean director, zero zero seven.
*Tokyo (Narita ATC):* . . . Korean Air zero zero seven, Tokyo.

*007:* For South Korean director . . . repeating instructions. Hold your bogey (or 'bogies') north (or 'course') . . . repeat conditions. Gonna be a bloodbath . . . you bet.

The significance of the tape lies partly in the words 'director' and 'bogey'. Both are military, not civilian aviation terms. A military or surveillance mission has a mission director, while a bogey is an enemy aircraft. The implication appears to be that, thirty-eight seconds after the missile hit 007, First Officer Son Dong-Hui was in touch with the mission director of what could only have been a surveillance mission. The reference to 'hold your bogey north' suggests a possible reference to electronic warfare techniques aimed at deceiving enemy planes into maintaining a false position.

The tape has a number of problems. First and foremost there is the question of interpretation. Robert Allardyce has kindly supplied me with a copy of the tape. I have listened to it many, many times. All I can say – for what it is worth – is that my own reading of it tallies with the version supplied by Allardyce and Gollin.

Second, there is the question of how such a wholly different version of the tape has come to be reproduced both by ICAO and the Japanese. The words on the tape are so different from those publicly reported that one cannot but wonder whether one is really talking about the same tape – but the voice-prints do match those of First Officer Son on the earlier portions of 007's conversations with ground control.

But there is also the same worrying fact that this tape relates to a period up to thirty-eight seconds after missile impact – and, as we have seen,[81] there is a great deal of circumstantial evidence to suggest that 007 may have blown up and crashed only three minutes after missile impact. If so, it is hard to understand the sheer coolness of Son's voice and his words. It is hard to imagine a copilot, shortly after his plane has been hit by a missile and is beginning its death-plunge, reporting coolly: 'gonna be a bloodbath . . . you bet.' The conversation sounds far more like that of an (extremely hard-boiled) observer. Could the voice actually have been that of someone in another plane, closely monitoring 007's flight? After all, if 007 did plunge six miles down in just three minutes, it is simply impossible that anyone could have been broadcasting – calmly at that – from 007 itself at that point. But if so, then the only possible conclusion is that the voice heard on the tape is not that of First Officer Son but of someone who was impersonating Son throughout the flight (for the voice-prints match). The tape, in other words, raises more questions than it answers.

At the time of writing, the case of KAL 007 has already dragged on for two years. We are still in a position where we have no absolutely definite answers, merely a vast pile of circumstantial evidence. It is frustrating to leave the case on a hypothetical basis, but that is still the only honest way to do it. Readers will have to decide for themselves what to believe: what evidence there is to date, is here. In the end the truth has to – and surely will – come out, however explosive it may be. Certainly, the quest for the truth cannot be abandoned. That is the least we owe to those 269 hapless people, lying in their unquiet grave on the floor of the Sea of Japan.

# Appendix

*Opposite:* Computerised Flight Plan
Captain Chun's Computerised Flight Plan, showing how he has simply crossed through the computer's indication of his fuel needs, and then made a series of marginal notes which more exactly correspond to the route he actually took than the Romeo 20 course he was meant to be taking.

*Page 300:* Flight Release Sheet
KAL 007's Flight Release Sheet, showing how 1800 lbs of payload have been rather oddly left behind at Anchorage, and indicating a fuel figure of 4100 lbs less than the computer had indicated would be required.

*Page 301:* Weight and Balance Manifest
KAL 007's Weight and Balance Manifest, showing that in fact Captain Chun disregarded his own Flight Release Sheet and actually loaded 10,000 lbs more fuel than he had said he had done on the Flight Release Sheet and 7900 lbs more than even the initial figure provided by the computer.

FLT/DRT ORG/DEST RLTN/DIST EQPT/NO. CRZ DIST NRM  AUG WIND/ORT
KE007/31 HNC/SEL  PLS/   8747/442 N54 3556 3776   A026/N45

ETP TIME/DIST SEL ROUTE SOW     RO /TO /LJ /RI
HNC SID CRN J501 BET R20 NOM RTS IFM DTR1 AX RTS GTC FIX KAE

JCAP
GXQ

697 SEL DCT SEL

|  | TIME | FUEL |  |  |
|---|---|---|---|---|
| TRIP FUEL | 07.53 | 2064 | TOW 7185 | ACT TOW |
| CONTINGENCY |  | 0175 | LOW 5121 | PCT LOA |
| ALTERNATE |  | 0178 | ROL 0907 | ACT FLJ |
| HOLDING |  | 7420 |  | FHA / |
| TTL RSV |  | 0454 |  | CGO |
| FOB |  | 2568 |  |  |

GTP 1501 NM
3HR 22 min

| TO / COORD | NM | AC | RM | ETR | FL | ATH | REMAIN PLN/ACT | OR ACT WIND | WIND/COMP | SR AX | TAS GS | ZT ACTA | B/O ACBO |
|---|---|---|---|---|---|---|---|---|---|---|---|---|---|
| CRN | 162 | 2449 | 243 | CL |  |  | / |  | 25/033/A032 |  | 23 |  |  |
| N61 05.0 A155 33.0 |  |  |  |  |  |  |  |  |  |  |  | 0023 |  |
| TUC | 012 | 2438 | 244 | CL |  |  | / |  | 26/034/M034 |  | 02 | 224 |  |
|  |  |  |  |  |  |  |  |  |  |  | 0039 | 0224 |  |
| BET | 174 | 2438 | 242 | 31 |  | 2227/ | 46 | 16/034/N033 | 01 493 | 23 | 197 |  |  |
| N60 47.1 W161 49.3 |  |  |  |  |  |  |  |  |  | 35 450 | 0053 | 0331 |  |
| NASIE | 312 | 2381 | 237 | 31 |  | 2040/ | 46 | 24/029/N028 | 01 452 | 40 | 167 |  |  |
| N59 18.0 W171 45.4 |  |  |  |  |  |  |  |  |  | 24 464 | 0133 | 0516 |  |
| NUKKS | 296 | 2362 | 235 | 31 |  | 1871/ | 45 | 24/018/N017 | 01 493 | 38 | 169 |  |  |
| N57 15.1 E179 44.3 |  |  |  |  |  |  |  |  |  | 35 476 | 0211 | 0687 |  |
| NEEVA | 297 | 2345 | 235 | 33 |  | 1697/ | 50 | 24/033/N033 | 00 488 | 39 | 174 |  |  |
| N54 40.7 E172 11.8 |  |  |  |  |  |  |  |  |  | 35 455 | 0250 | 0861 |  |
| NINNO | 281 | 2403 | 243 | 33 |  | 1543/ | 43 | 29/036/N024 | 01 483 | 36 | 74 |  |  |
| N52 21.5 E165 22.8 |  |  |  |  |  |  |  |  |  | 36 465 | 0326 | 1015 |  |
| NIPPI | 279 | 2383 | 242 | 33 |  | 1399/ | 50 | 32/032/N003 | 00 485 | 36 | 401 | 1159 |  |
| N49 41.9 E159 19.3 |  |  |  |  |  |  |  |  |  | 36 485 |  |  |  |
| NYTIM | 330 | 2360 | 237 | 35 |  | 1235/ | 48 | 36/018/P010 | 02 485 | 39 | 164 |  |  |
| N46 11.9 E153 00.5 |  |  |  |  |  |  |  |  |  | 39 499 | 0440 | 1323 |  |
| NOKKA | 330 | 2337 | 236 | 35 |  | 1075/ | 45 | 32/028/P001 | 00 492 | 40 | 160 |  |  |
| N42 23.3 E147 23.8 |  |  |  |  |  |  |  |  |  | 44 493 | 0320 | 1443 |  |
| NOM | 163 | 2306 | 238 | 35 |  | 0994/ | 43 | 30/066/M021 | 02 485 | 21 | 081 |  |  |
| N40 25.0 E145 00.0 |  |  |  |  |  |  |  |  |  | 46 474 | 0541 | 1504 |  |
| IFM | 117 | 2493 | 255 | 35 |  | 0932/ | 42 | 29/071/M050 | 00 495 | 16 | 052 |  |  |
| N39 30.0 E142 45.0 |  |  |  |  |  |  |  |  |  | 49 445 | 0557 | 1526 |  |
| AX | 101 | 2347 | 240 | 35 |  | 0880/ | 43 | 29/065/N043 | 00 494 | 13 | 052 |  |  |
| N38 21.5 E141 09.3 |  |  |  |  |  |  |  |  |  | 48 445 | 0617 | 1578 |  |
| GTC | 100 | 2631 | 265- | 35 |  | 0828/ | 42 | 28/057/N052 | 00 495 | 14 | 052 |  |  |
| N37 57.1 E139 06.7 |  |  |  |  |  |  |  |  |  | 48 443 | 0629 | 1730 |  |
| FIR | 317 | 2689 | 269 | 35 |  | 0660/ | 42 | 26/065/N065 | 00 485 | 44 | 165 |  |  |
| N37 10.0 E132 32.0 |  |  |  |  |  |  |  |  |  | 48 430 | 0708 | 1898 |  |
| KAE | 163 | 2875 | 282 | 35 |  | 0557/ | 44 | 24/068/N053 | 01 493 | 23 | 093 |  |  |
| N37 41.9 E128 45.3 |  |  |  |  |  |  |  |  |  | 48 440 | 0733 | 1991 |  |
| TOO | 007 | 2661 | 263 | 35 |  | 0554/ | 44 | 24/068/N064 | 01 493 | 01 | 003 |  |  |
|  |  |  |  |  |  |  |  |  |  | 48 429 | 0734 | 1994 |  |
| SEL | 082 | 2661 | 264 | 30 |  | / |  | 24/038/N036 |  | 15 |  |  |  |
| N37 24.7 E126 55.3 |  |  |  |  |  |  |  |  |  |  | 0749 |  |  |
| SEL | 025 | 3310 | 326 | 30 |  | / |  | 25/035/N017 |  | 04 | 070 |  |  |
| N37 33.3 E126 45.0 |  |  |  |  |  |  |  |  |  |  | 0753 | 2064 |  |

2852

-J FL 26 31 33 35 50  B/O 2L82 CRZ 184 AT J145

# (REFILE) FLIGHT RELEASE SHEET

KOREAN AIR LINES

DAY _21_   MONTH _March_   YEAR _77_

## 1) GENERAL

| FROM | KE 2 | HL 7_ _ _ | TO | SEL |
|------|------|-----------|----|-----|

| | | |
|---|---|---|
| FROM | ANC | TO SEL |
| ETD | | ETA |
| ETD | | ETA |

## 3) TAKE OFF DATA

| WX FCST | TEMP | 52 | °F ( ) |
| | WIND | 17004 | QNH |

| | | | |
|---|---|---|---|
| 1 MAX STRCT T/O WT | | 7 2 6 0 0 0 | |
| R/w 06R F10 | | 7 8 9 0 0 0 | − 2 575 |
| 2 R/W LIMIT T/O WT | | | |
| R/w 32 F20 | | 7 4 4 1 0 0 | |
| MAX L/D WT | | 6 6 0 0 0 0 | |
| 3 B/O FUEL | + | 2 0 6 4 0 0 | |
| MAX L/D LIMITD WT | = | 7 9 1 6 0 0 | |
| MAX Z/F WT | | 6 2 6 6 0 0 | |
| 4 GATO | + | 2 5 1 2 0 0 | |
| MAX Z/F LIMITD WT | = | 7 7 1 3 2 0 0 | |
| AGTOW | | 7 8 9 0 0 0 | |
| OEW | − | 2 7 3 2 0 0 | |
| GATO | − | 2 5 1 7 0 0 | |
| ACL | = | 1 3 4 1 0 0 | |
| EST T/O WT | | 7 1 2 6 0 0 | |
| B/O FUEL | − | 2 0 6 4 0 0 | |
| EST L/D WT | = | 5 0 6 2 6 0 | |

## 2) PAY LOAD

| | | | |
|---|---|---|---|
| PAX | 12/335 | | |
| BAG | | | |
| CGO/MAIL | | +2 0 0 | |
| V.L.D | | | |
| TOTAL | | 8 7 7 6 7 | |
| SOW | 3 7 2 0 0 0 | | |
| CORR | | 1 2 6 0 | |
| OEW | | | |
| Z/F WT | | | |

## 4) FUEL CALCULATION

460947

| | PORTION | ANC / SEL | | | | | / | | | | / | |
|---|---------|-----------|---|---|---|---|---|---|---|---|---|---|
| RSV | ALTN | :40 PUS 1 7 3 0 0 | | | | | | | | | | |
| | HOLD | : 30 1 1 0 0 0 | | | | | | | | | | |
| | 10% CONT | : 47 1 7 0 0 0 | | | | | | | | | | |
| | TOTAL | 01:57 4 5 3 0 0 | | | | | | | | | | |
| | EXTRA | : | | | | | | | | | | |
| | FOD | : 3 5 1 3 0 0 | | | | | | | | | | |
| | B/O FUEL | 07:53 2 0 6 4 0 0 | | | | | | | | | | |
| | GATO | 09:50 2 5 1 7 0 0 | | | | | | | | | | |
| | TAXI | 2 0 0 0 | | | | | | | | | | |
| | RAMP FUEL | 2 5 3 7 0 0 | | | | | | | | | | |
| | USABLE FUEL | − 8 0 0 0 | | | | | | | | | | |
| | SUPPLIED FUEL | 2 5 2 9 0 0 | | | | | | | | | | |
| | RQRD FUEL | : | | | | | | | | | | |

## 5) NOTAM: AS ATTACHED

## 6) WX : AS ATTACHED

ANC VOR/DME o/s

## 7) OTHER SPECIAL INFO

I hereby release the above flight in full compliance with
CIVIL AVIATION LAW and/or COMPANY OPERATIONS MANUAL

_Bang Hwa_    DISPATCHER

I hereby acknowledge to conduct flight in accordance with
Regulations and Procedures Outlined in CIVIL AVIATION LAW
and/or COMPANY OPERATIONS MANUAL

CAPTAIN

AL.–OP–4
974. 9. 1 6 4

210 mm × 334mm V. P. 70g/
163. 7. 1 / 26, 1831–4

# KAL B747-200B WEIGHT AND BALANCE MANIFEST

| FLIGHT NO. | DATE | FROM | TO | AIRCRAFT NO |
|---|---|---|---|---|
| KE- 007 | 8-31-1183 | NRC | SEL | HL- 7442 |

| NO. | ITEM | | WEIGHT (LBS) | I.U | CORRECTION WEIGHT |
|---|---|---|---|---|---|
| 1 | STD. OPERATING WEIGHT | | 3 7 2 0 0 0 | 648 | |
| 2 | ADDITIONAL ITEM | 2/4 DH | 1 2 0 0 | | |
| 3 | OPERATING WEIGHT | (1+2) | 3 7 3 2 0 0 | | |
| 4 | FWD HOLD ① | ALLOWABLE (18,500 LBS) MAXIMUM (21,000 LBS) | | | |
| 5 | FWD HOLD ② | (28,800 LBS) (35,000 LBS) | | | |
| 6 | AFT HOLD ③ | (23,070 LBS) (28,000 LBS) | | | |
| 7 | AFT HOLD ④ | (17,900 LBS) (21,000 LBS) | | | |
| 8 | BULK HOLD ⑤ | (14,880 LBS) (14,880 LBS) | | | |
| 9 | MAIN DECK CARGO⑥ | (19,250 LBS) (19,250 LBS) | | | |
| 10 | PASS - ZONE A | (NO. ) | | PASS NO. | |
| 11 | PASS - ZONE B | (NO. ) | | PASS NO. | |
| 12 | PASS - ZONE C | (NO. ) | | PASS NO. | |
| 13 | PASS - ZONE D | (NO. ) | | PASS NO. | |
| 14 | PASS - ZONE E | (NO. ) | | PASS NO. | |
| 15 | TOTAL PAYLOAD | | 8 7 7 6 7 | | |
| 16 | ZERO FUEL WEIGHT | (3+4 THRU 14) | 4 6 0 9 6 7 | 55 75 | |
| 17 | FUEL EXCEPT R, & R, Reserve Tank2 & 3 | | | | |
| 18 | TOTAL FUEL | | 2 6 3 7 0 0 | | |
| 19 | TAXI WEIGHT | (16 + 18) | 7 2 4 6 6 7 | | |
| 20 | START/TAXI FUEL | | 2 0 0 0 | | |
| 21 | TAKEOFF WEIGHT | (19-20) | 7 2 2 6 6 7 | 37.05 | |
| 22 | EST. BURN-OFF FUEL | | 2 0 6 4 0 0 | | |
| 23 | EST. LANDING WEIGHT | (21-22) | 5 1 6 2 6 7 | 58.9 | |

A.G.T.O.W. = 759000 LBS

A.C.L. = 134100 LBS

REMARKS: ZWF1 JRKLINE

FAT

f/. c/12 4/225

STAB TRIM SETTING-7A HL 749 (67, 63 4) ?

## BALANCE CONDITIONS

T.O. = 16.6 M.! % MAC

Z.F. = 23.4 % MAC

L.W. = 22.1 % MAC

TRIM = 7.0 UNITS

SIGNATURE DISP. OR AGENT

SIGNATURE CAPTAIN

| GROSS WEIGHT 1000 LB | C G % M A C STABILIZER TRIM UNITS FOR TAKEOFF | | | | | | | | | | | | | |
|---|---|---|---|---|---|---|---|---|---|---|---|---|---|
| | 9 | 10 | 11 | 12 | 13 | 15 | 17 | 19 | 21 | 23 | 25 | 27 | |
| 800 | | | | | | | | 7 | 7 | 6 | 5 | 5 | 4 |
| 750 | 9 | 9 | 8 | 8 | 7 | 7 | 7 | 6 | 5 | 5 | 4 | | |
| 700 | 9 | 8 | 8 | 8 | 7 | 7 | 6 | 6 | 5 | 5 | 4 | | |
| 650 | 9 | 8 | 8 | 8 | 7 | 7 | 6 | 6 | 5 | 5 | 4 | | |
| 600 | 9 | 8 | 8 | 7 | 7 | 7 | 6 | 6 | 5 | 5 | 4 | | |
| 500 | | | 8 | 7 | 7 | 6 | 6 | 5 | 5 | 4 | | | |
| 400 | | | 8 | 7 | 7 | 6 | 6 | 5 | 5 | 4 | | | |

# Postscript

*Shootdown: The Verdict on KAL 007* was first published in May 1986. The book had a curious reception. Advance expressions of interest were very great – the rights were sold for American and Japanese versions of the book and it was chosen by one Australian and two UK bookclubs, as also by the US Book of the Month Club. I found myself much in demand on radio and TV programmes in the US, Japan, Australia and Canada. In the UK BBC radio and TV both booked me for programmes to coincide with the book's launch, and excerpts of the book were run in *The Sunday Telegraph*.

Shortly before publication I received a strongly denunciatory letter from a US State Department official, Mr Tom Maertens. Mr Maertens's letter suggested that the book had been available to the State Department for some time, for he claimed that analysis had shown there to be literally several hundreds of errors in the book (though he declined to list these). Neither my UK nor US publishers had supplied the State Department with an advance copy: quite how Mr Maertens had acquired a copy so long before publication I never discovered. I replied to Mr Maertens saying that I had no interest in being wrong and that I would be grateful if he could send me his list of these hundreds of errors so I could correct them. I never received such a list, though on TV and radio both Mr Maertens and several others (with whom, it emerged, Mr Maertens had been in touch) returned repeatedly to this charge. I in turn repeatedly asked for a list and finally I did acquire a list of some thirty alleged errors. Most of these, however, turned out to be mere differences of interpretation, nit-picking over such points as the correct spelling of *Marie (Mary) Celeste* and so forth. Any author knows he is bound to make some mistakes (hence the advance excuses always offered in prefaces) and I have taken advantage of this paperback edition to correct those I have found. I have not, however, found that it was necessary to alter the book in any substantial way. Naturally I am grateful to those who have taken the trouble to point errors out and apologise to the reader for any that may still remain.

Given the book's newsworthy nature and the large amount of advance interest, what happened next was curious. At the last minute both BBC TV and radio cancelled arrangements for a discussion of the book on the air. To my certain knowledge reviews were commissioned by several British papers which never appeared, but in the main the book was wholly ignored: only one British weekly and one quality paper carried reviews. *The Sunday Telegraph*, which had carried excerpts from the book, immediately received an angry letter from the US Ambassador to Britain. Ambassadors to foreign countries do not normally involve themselves in disputes in the book pages of the press, so I took it that this betokened official disapproval at a fairly high level.

There is, of course, no such thing as a right to be reviewed, and authors complaining about the treatment their books have received are at once one of publishing's most common and least attractive sights. Yet all my previous books – none of them remotely as newsworthy as *Shootdown* – received far, far wider reviewer attention. Where mention was made of the book, hostile reviewers made virtually no attempt to grapple with its argument which was simply dismissed in a cloud of invective and angry adjectives. Not atypical was a brief dismissal of *Shootdown* by Christopher Andrew in *The Times*: 'Significantly, the *Shootdown* index contains numerous references to the CIA but not one for the KGB.' In fact, as readers will see, the Index does contain references to the KGB (Komitet Gosudarstvennoy Bezopasnosti), which is also explained in the List of Acronyms.

In the US the situation was often similar, particularly in the more important review spots, though the book was more fairly treated on radio and in second-level newspapers than had been the case in the UK. True, the Director of the CIA did at one point say, somewhat menacingly, that he was looking into the book, and the CIA apparently carried out an investigation of those responsible for disseminating the notion that KAL 007 might not have been off-course by accident in order to see whether they were part of a KGB disinformation exercise. I take it this included me. I am happy to report that the CIA reported negatively on this proposition.[1] Despite all this the book did well – it was, I was told, the US Book of the Month Club's best-selling alternative selection of the year, for example – but generally it had to achieve what it did despite wildly hostile reviews or a blanket of silence. How far such treatment resulted from the exertion of official pressures and how far it merely reflected the predilections of review editors I am unable to say.

Several events have occurred since *Shootdown* was published. The happiest of these was the conclusion of a Soviet-American accord to create a Pacific hotline to ensure that there could be no repetition of the KAL 007 tragedy. Negotiations towards such an accord had begun in February 1985 in Tokyo under conditions of some secrecy, for the Russians, while keen to take steps to prevent accidental incursions into their airspace, wished to avoid any implication (which American publicity about the talks could hardly have helped giving) that they were accepting that the KAL 007 incursion had itself been accidental. The agreement was finally signed at the first Reagan-Gorbachev summit and inaugurated on 15 August 1986. Essentially the new arrangement provided for links between air controllers in Anchorage and Khabarovsk via Tokyo.[2] It was no small measure of the frigid Cold War temperature that it took a major tragedy for such an obvious and technically simple adjustment to be made – but the agreement is valuable, nonetheless.

Korean Air (KA) – the successor to KAL – had meanwhile managed so successfully to put the 1983 tragedy behind it that by 1985 it was carrying more than 6 million passengers a year and had entered the select league of the world's ten biggest airlines. This headlong growth, however, continued to be earned at the cost of severe operating losses on many routes, particularly since a fresh rate-cutting war broke out on routes to Seoul.[3] Meanwhile the fall in the oil price led to the collapse of construction activity in the Middle East, in which South Korean companies had played a major role. The result was a sudden and steep loss of profitability on what had hitherto been one of KA's few really lucrative routes.

Moreover, KA found itself locked into an increasingly bitter dispute with US airlines. The trouble went back to an agreement reached between the US and South Korea in 1978 which had allowed the then KAL landing rights in New York in return for the granting to US carriers rights to handle their own cargo at Kimpo Airport, Seoul: indeed, Seoul committed itself to build a cargo facility at Kimpo by March 1981 to facilitate self-handling of all inbound and outbound cargoes by US carriers. By a further 1980 Memorandum KAL was also promised full landing rights at Anchorage, Oakland and Chicago and rights to fly on to other countries across the US, all in return for the already promised cargo facility at Kimpo. In fact the cargo facility did not get built – although KAL meanwhile built itself a large new cargo facility at Los Angeles and mopped up enough cargo traffic to keep the airline in the black despite the losses on many of its passenger routes. What this meant was that from March 1981 on KAL had been relying on a wholly one-sided benevolence on the part of the US. (No doubt this was the situation the Soviets had in mind when they alleged that KAL had been too dependent on the US to resist demands for special favours.) US airlines themselves became increasingly bitter as they watched KA capture three-quarters of all cargo and passenger traffic between the US and South Korea, and their ire only increased when the construction of a new cargo facility was at last begun at Kimpo, for the hint was dropped that US carriers would be denied access to it until KA was given yet further landing rights in the US.[4] KAL had, after all, never been a particularly popular airline within the aviation community – apart from the criticism of its commercial practices alluded to earlier, there were memories of the allegations of a large-scale bribery racket connecting KAL officials and the McDonnell Douglas Corporation, aired in the 1979 United States v. McDonnell Douglas case.[5]

By August 1986, US carriers had become sufficiently incensed at the non-fulfilment of the Korean promises of 1978 to draw up a list of no less than 16 outstanding issues on which they were dissatisfied. US officials made it clear that there was no chance of KA obtaining further landing rights in the US until the 1978 agreement was honoured. Meanwhile the 1980 Memorandum extending KA further landing rights was declared a dead letter.[6] A full-scale clash seemed in prospect for the issue had become a matter of major public dispute – and national pride – in South Korea. KA might advertise itself as a new and quite different airline from KAL but within the aviation community the cloud of acrimony surrounding some of KAL's activities seemed to have settled just as firmly on KA.

A certain amount of fresh light on the KAL 007 case was shed by the publication in September 1986 of Seymour Hersh's '*The Target is Destroyed*'.[7] Hersh's book received wide publicity, encountering, for example, none of the difficulties in gaining TV and radio coverage in Britain that *Shootdown* had experienced.[8] No doubt Hersh's undoubted fame and distinction accounted for some of the difference, but there was a certain irony in the situation nonetheless. Hersh's book, which argued in favour of the official view that 007's deviation from course had been accidental, was thought sufficiently newsworthy to merit mass coverage, while *Shootdown*, which had questioned the official view, was not. I have found myself so frequently asked to respond to the Hersh view of events – the new conventional wisdom, as it were – that it is worth dealing with it at some length.

Throughout the time I was working on *Shootdown* I was aware that Seymour Hersh was working on a parallel book, and I looked forward to it keenly. Ever since he achieved journalistic superstar status with his exposure of the My Lai massacre in 1969, I have read Hersh's writings with respect, sometimes with admiration. Some, at least, of his undoubted talents are displayed in *The Target is Destroyed*: Hersh has few equals in the culling of Washington gossip; his fame and pertinacity mean that many will talk to him who will not talk to others; and his book contains much fascinating material on the technology and internal rivalries of the US intelligence world. For all those reasons his book is well worth reading. But, that said, I must admit I was severely disappointed by it. It is poorly organised; it omits a great deal of pertinent evidence; and, above all, Hersh has accepted lock, stock and barrel a quite absurd explanation of how KAL 007 came to be so far off course.

In essence, what Hersh has done is to rely heavily on one particular source, Jim Pfautz, the now retired head of USAF Intelligence (AFIN). Pfautz is, indeed, very much the hero of Hersh's book and the story that emerges often verges on a praise-song to Pfautz. That story – and for Hersh it is very much the story – is that AFIN concluded almost immediately that the Russians had mis-identified KAL 007 as a military reconnaissance plane, and had not realised that they were shooting down a civilian airliner. In this AFIN differed sharply from the other three intelligence agencies involved – the CIA, NSA and DIA (Defence Intelligence Agency). Largely due to the urgings of William Casey, who, as Director of Central Intelligence, is in command of all three, these agencies lent themselves to the story favoured on purely ideological grounds by the leading Administration hawks, that the Russians had deliberately shot down what they had known to be a civilian airliner. Thus the scandal is, for Hersh, that this version of events was propagated despite the existence of firm intelligence evidence that it was untrue.

This is rather a curious emphasis. Although it was trumpeted as the sensational finding of Hersh's book, the fact was, as I had pointed out in *Shootdown*, that it was known fairly early on that the Reagan Administration had been ignoring its own intelligence findings on this score (see above, pp. 186–8). But, of course, this presentational matter was a relatively minor question compared to that of how KAL

007 came to be so far off course in the first place.

To answer this question Hersh puts forward the theory of Captain Harold Ewing of Flying Tiger airlines. By his own admission, Ewing set out to find a way of proving that 007's deviation from course had to have been accidental. Fairly quickly he realised that none of the accidental scenarios posited by the ICAO Report would do, so these he (rightly) abandoned. He then began devising ever more elaborate scenarios of his own to 'prove' the deviation accidental. His work became known to those of us who were working on the same problem. But it was immediately clear that Ewing's speculations demanded that one accept far too many long-odds assumptions to be at all credible. It was with little short of amazement that I discovered that Hersh had apparently swallowed whole a scenario I had abandoned long before. Nothing in Hersh's account persuades me that I was wrong to do so.

The version of events according to Ewing/Hersh is as follows. First we have to assume that 007's pilot, for reasons of his own, decided to scrap his computerised flight plan (the fact that his scribbles on that plan suggest that he then planned the route he actually took is ignored). Then, because that meant he was rushed, we assume he made 'a monumental error' about his fuel, taking on five extra tons of the stuff – enough to crash the plane had it been fully loaded. (But there was no rush – take-off was actually delayed for forty minutes – and the pilot filled in one set of papers correctly, one incorrectly.) We then assume that the crew decided not to use the preprogrammed flight cassette with which they had been issued, instead opting to program their computers manually. We further assume that one of these computers was then programmed wrongly with a 10 degree error (we're not just assuming a mistake but one very specific mistake – a 9 degree or an 11 degree error won't do), and when the other computers threw up their inevitable warning of this error, that the error was resolved by switching off the warning light and leaving the error intact. We then assume that the pilot, despite his reputation as probably KAL's No. 1 and a 'human computer', disregarded the obligatory checking procedure designed to ensure that the computers had been correctly programmed. Then we assume that the pilot, once aloft, made a further decision to switch over to control by his INS without checking, as he should have done, that he was on the right course.

Thereafter our assumptions grow exponentially. The rule book says that a pilot may not connect his INS to autopilot without a fix on a VOR, but we assume that this rule too was disregarded. We now assume that the pilot made a further off-the-cuff decision to disregard even his own self-devised flight plan and to make a minor cross-cut to save fuel. (The fact that this would, as Hersh admits, have saved negligible fuel, we ignore.) This means that we also have to assume that the pilot deliberately lied to his ground control in reporting that he was at Bethel, for he had decided to skip Bethel altogether and knew he was never there. We now further assume that the pilot was somehow interrupted while entering the next set of figures into his computer, putting in latitude co-ordinates but failing to enter longitude coordinates. (Again, it has to be this very specific mistake he makes, and he has to be interrupted at this particular point and no other.)

We now assume that the pilot left the cabin and stayed out of it for the next five hours – something unheard of in international aviation circles.[9] We also assume that the pilot did all of this without bothering to explain what was in his mind to the two other officers sharing the flight cabin with him. The two other officers left in the cabin would have been confronted by ever-increasing evidence of the plane's gross error, but we further assume that they were so bound by an Asian sense of discipline and hierarchy that they did not dare to question their captain's presumed intent. We also assume that they broke company rules by not using their ground-mapping weather radar (which would have shown them they were verging over land, not sea, as they entered Soviet airspace); that they disregarded the ever-increasing evidence of cross-track error plainly displayed on the screens in front of them; and that they ignored the fact that the INS was displaying route distances which did not correspond with what they expected. We then assume that the flight officers chose the precise moment after the Soviet fighter zeroed in on 007 (again, it has to be that moment and no other) to re-program their computer. This was now so hopelessly fouled up that it made the plane go into a steep turn, though (we assume) the flight officers corrected it quickly; this, we have to imagine, would explain the large turn 007 made as it approached Sakhalin, even though the turn the plane made was far bigger than could be explained by such a manoeuvre. Finally, we have to assume that even after the Soviet missile hit the plane the flight officers still did not realise that they were in sufficient trouble to warrant the mandatory Mayday call. This despite the fact that they were experiencing terrifying decompression and were conducting a rapid descent.

To accept the Ewing/Hersh scenario one has to accept every single one of these assumptions, despite the fact that the cumulative odds against every one of them being true (and in the right sequence) is astronomical. Anyone who accepts such hostile odds has to be either exceptionally gullible or guided by blind faith. Moreover, these odds can easily be further increased. For example, we know that during the 1978 incident over the Kola peninsula a KAL airliner deviated, 1,000 miles off track and overflew the vicinity of the biggest Soviet nuclear submarine base at Murmansk. By accident, apparently, and despite the vocal alarm of the passengers, who noticed such details as the sun having swung over to be on the wrong side of the plane and Soviet fighters buzzing the plane. What were the odds against another KAL airliner veering accidentally off-track in 1983 and overflying the vicinity of the second biggest Soviet nuclear submarine base (at Petropavolsk)? Accidents will happen, no doubt: but what is it about Soviet nuclear submarine bases which cause the same airline to make repeated accidental deviations over them? One could go on, piling improbability on improbability, but it seems almost like bullying to do so.

Hersh is careful to label Ewing's scenario as 'highly speculative', but in practice he adopts it wholesale, writing quite confidently about the actions of the flight officers ('in the cockpit of the Korean airliner it was yawn-and-stretch time') and even about what 'they undoubtedly thought'. Moreover, Hersh simply dismisses all other possible explanations, arguing that the Ewing scenario 'melds perfectly' with all the known facts.

But it doesn't. Even if, for the sake of argument, one were to accept the truly astronomical odds against the Ewing hypothesis, there are still a number of facts it doesn't explain. There is the mystery of why KAL 007 apparently left paying cargo behind at Anchorage. There is the small matter that it wasn't using the correct transponder code. There is the fact that the plane must have made at least one other (conscious) turn besides the one at Sakhalin. There are several unexplained oddities in the way 007 reported back – or failed to do so – to ground control. There are all the problems about the plane's unusual speed pattern. There is the question of why the pilot did not check his position against the Shemya VOR. There are all the oddities about the search operation. Again, one could go on.

Most remarkable of all, though, is Hersh's attitude to several key episodes. We know, from the data provided to the Japanese Diet by the Japanese Self-Defence Agency, that as the Soviet fighter settled on its tail 007 signalled to ground control that it wished to climb, then that it was climbing, and then that it had completed its climb; but that in fact the plane had made a descent – and that the pilot was thus lying to ground control. Hersh must be familiar with this data: it is public property, and he cites works in his bibliography which contain charts and accounts of this startling event. Yet he simply omits all mention of it, calmly asserting that 007 did indeed carry out a routine climb at this point, without even citing the fact that hard evidence exists to the contrary. During a brief radio debate with Mr Hersh I raised this problem with him. His reply was that it was well known that radar was inaccurate, particularly at extreme range, in giving correct altitude readings and that the Japanese radar data could therefore be disregarded. (This still hardly explains why Hersh omitted all mention of this data in his book[10].) This is the same objection invariably made by all those who wish to argue that this particularly key piece of evidence be disregarded. Sometimes possible altitude error by radar is given as 2,000 ft, sometimes at as much as 6,000 ft. It is worth pausing to consider this point in some detail.

For a start the Japanese radar data was gleaned from three separate radars. One of them was 270 miles away from 007, one 220 miles, one only 160 miles. Thus, at the least, two of these radars were hardly operating at the extremity of their range. (It is worth mentioning, *en passant*, that those who wish to minimise the abilities of either Japanese or US radars to follow 007's flight almost invariably speak of radar as if it were still in its infancy of the 1940s, ignoring the immense advances in radar made by computer enhancement in recent years. Happily, for the sake of civil aviation safety, modern radars are not as likely as is being suggested to make quite casual errors of more than a mile up or down in showing altitudes. Nor are they as strictly bounded by line-of-sight limitations (as one is sometimes asked to believe[11].) Secondly, there can be little doubt that the Japanese SDA must have realised full well just how explosive this data was when it was decided to release it. Thus it is being seriously suggested that the SDA did this while knowingly basing itself on unreliable data and without any warning that this data might be unreliable. This seems in the highest degree improbable, particularly since the SDA must have realised just how much embarrassment it was creating for Washington. Such objections are typically just brushed aside by those who wish to ignore the Japanese radar data. Similarly, all the arguments about radar inaccuracy are used to suggest that the Japanese data must be wrong and the American data right – though, of course, the argument could just as easily be turned around to suggest that the Japanese data must be right and the American data wrong. Given that the US has never released radar tapes of its own or told us which radars its own data is drawn from[12] – which the Japanese, in both cases, have – the burden of proof is surely on the US, not the Japanese side.

But in any case, the objection based on radar inaccuracy simply will not do. Let us, for argument's sake, grant that all the radars in use were maximally inaccurate – that they got altitudes a whole 6,000 ft wrong. A quick glance at the two versions of KAL 007's manoeuvres in these last minutes (reproduced on p.25) shows that the US version has 007 flying level at 32,000 ft. from 18.12 to 18.21, while the Japanese radar tapes show it as having descended to 29,000 ft. by 18.15 and then flying level at that height till 18.21. It really does not matter if the Japanese radars were all 6,000 ft. out, either up or down: they still show an entirely different configuration – as well as different altitudes – from the US version. No amount of long-odds allowances about radar inaccuracy will get rid of that difference in configuration. That is, whether the Japanese radars had shown 007 at 20,000 ft. or 40,000 ft., it really doesn't matter. What matters is that they show the plane conducting a 3,000 ft. descent at a point when the US insists it was flying level preparatory to a climb. Neither Hersh nor anyone else who wishes to ignore the Japanese data has any answer to this point.

This is only one of several points where Hersh's account simply omits all mention of important pieces of evidence. Thus Hersh never mentions at all the fact that 007 was mysteriously using the wrong transponder code. Similarly, he passes over without mention the many very curious features of the abortive search for the black boxes. Faced with the fact that the radio bleeps from these boxes were several times picked up – which should have made recovery almost automatic – he rather lamely repeats the suggestion made by Reaganite ultras that perhaps the Russians had deliberately dropped a false bleeper in the water to confuse the US search. A moment's reflection would suggest that any bleeper, true or false, would then have been recovered. . . .

Quite extraordinary, too, is the fact that Hersh makes no reference at all to the fact that a US reconnaissance satellite was making passes overhead while 007's excursion was in progress, that an Orion P-3C was in the vicinity, or that an electronic reconnaissance ship was on station nearby. (Hersh also, of course, makes no mention of the controversy over the Shuttle.) This is very curious, for Hersh writes most interestingly of the bonanza of electronic intelligence harvested by the US from the 1978 KAL deviation.[13] Yet for all Hersh's inside track with the intelligence community he makes no mention of the fact that comparable data must have been obtained from the 1983 deviation. Hersh fails altogether to mention, too, the fact that the USAF has destroyed some of the key radar tapes of 007's flight. Finally, Hersh mentions without comment the fact that six days after the tragedy US Intelligence was still putting out maps showing 007 as having flown an entirely straight line course. It surely must have occurred to him that those publishing such maps had long had the information which falsified any notion of such a course. If so, Hersh has remained silent on this, as on so much else.

This is quite a list of omissions – and that is what they are, pure and simple. It is not a matter of interpretation, but of fact, that the Japanese did put out the radar data they did, that there was a satellite overhead, that the US knowingly disseminated disinformation about 007's course and so on. As one reflects on this list of omissions one cannot but be struck that all the items on it involve data which the Reagan Administration would prefer simply not to have discussed. What we have, in fact, is an account of the event which is wholly reliant on US intelligence sources; which champions the heroic role of one of those sources; and which omits almost anything which might discomfort those sources. Not surprisingly, Hersh's book has been eagerly seized upon by all those who wish to inter the case of KAL 007 once and for all.

On 31 August, 1986, at the invitation of relatives of the 63 Americans who died aboard KAL 007, I attended a memorial service for the victims in New York. It was an intensely moving occasion. Some there had lost their spouses, others one or both their parents, brothers, sisters; there were parents who had lost all their children. Many of them spoke with, I thought, great courage about the awfulness of their loss – for all of them made worse by the fact that there had been no bodies to grieve over and bury. (Many confessed that this alone made it peculiarly hard to believe that their loved ones were indeed dead.) One moment I shall never forget: a beautiful little Korean girl, perhaps two years old, escaped her mother's clutches during the service and, resisting her urgent summons, stood like a picture of mischief and fun, framed by her grieving elders around the foot of the altar. For many of those elders she was, no doubt, a painful reminder of the many children lost aboard 007. But at the same time the little girl, wonderfully unaware of the sadness of the occasion, was the very picture of youthful renewal, of the life that must and will go on.

But the air was charged with political tension as well as the most elemental grief. Posters in the vestry of the cathedral, headed 'Flight 007 – the Silence is Deafening', referred to the many mysteries still surrounding the affair, the pattern of obstruction which inquiries have met, and ended with the challenge 'When will those who know speak?'

This despite the fact that the relatives are hardly a left-wing group. Even in the US it is still true that the clientele who enjoy international air travel – and thus their relatives – have an upper-income bias, which in turn meant that most of the relatives tended to come from apolitical, centrist or frankly conservative backgrounds. Nonetheless, I did not meet a single relative who believed that KAL 007 had been off-course by accident. They have, naturally, followed the development of the case closely and many are intensely bitter at the systematic obstruction to which they feel the Reagan Administration has subjected them in their quest for more and truthful information about the tragedy. Many of them expressed considerable cynicism about the Hersh book[14] and its dismissal – in a footnote – of any notion that 007 might have been on a planned mission with the statement 'in all my reporting inside the NSA and military intelligence I found no evidence of any advance word on the Korean flight, and advance notice to such units would have been essential'. Apart from the fact that no advance notice would have been necessary to activate electronic intelligence-gathering by the satellite overhead, the electronic reconnaissance ship on station or the round-the-clock monitoring base at Misawa, this statement effectively just asks that Hersh's journalistic reputation itself be regarded as a major argument for the conclusions he reaches. All one can say is that that reputation is unlikely to be enhanced by so large and uncritical an acceptance of a scenario as patently threadbare as that provided by Ewing.

Meanwhile, the questions surrounding the tragedy will not go away. The Californian attorney, Melvin Belli, acting for some of the American relatives, announced on 15 August 1986 that he had definite proof that KAL 007's pilot knew he had flying over Soviet airspace. Specifically, Belli said that he had videotape evidence from the pilot of KAL 015 to the effect that 007's crew had known they were off-course over Soviet territory. Belli also claimed that he had been told by the widows of 007's pilot and co-pilot that 'their husbands knew that they were flying over Soviet territory, and that they had brought home cash – cash under the table'. Indeed, Mr Belli reported Captain Chun as having told his wife before the flight, 'Never again, this is the last trip, it's too dangerous'. Mr Belli declared his intention of appealing the case all the way to the US Supreme Court.[15] Once again, one must caution a certain reserve about such statements. All one can say is that if Mr Belli does not have the evidence he claims he is risking both great damage to his reputation and extreme callousness to those he represents. We shall see.

In Japan, too, an Association of KAL Incident Victims has been founded. Its members too have come to the conclusion that 007's incursion into Soviet airspace was intentional and are bitterly critical of the Nakasone government for, they claim, collaborating with Washington and Seoul in a cover-up, despite a resolution of the Japanese Diet that the government should seek to discover the truth of the incident.[16] Thus, for example, when Diet Member Hata Yutaka demanded that Tokyo ask Washington for the release of radar data of 007's flight recorded at the US base on Shemya Island, the government replied that it would 'not consider your request that we demand the data to which you refer', because it had been told by Washington that the Shemya radar 'is not charged with covering the flights of civilian aircraft on international routes'. Similarly, the victims' relatives are deeply discontented at Foreign Minister Shintaro Abe's repeated insistence that 007 must have been off-course through human error despite the lack of support for such a notion from any of the available data.[17] The relatives draw attention to a report in a Seoul newspaper, *Hanguk Ilbo* (*Korea Daily News*), just three days after the tragedy, that on 30 August 1983 – that is, the day before the flight – Captain Chun's wife had taken out a new life insurance policy on her husband with the Dong Bang Life Insurance Company. The policy, designated as educational insurance for the couple's eldest son in the event of Captain Chun's death, was for 30 million won (US $34,364), paid for with a premium of 106,740 won (US $122) on the day before 007's flight.[18] The Japanese relatives also report that the pilot of KAL 015, Captain Park, whose testimony about the 007 flight has been so signally missing, has had his South Korean passport confiscated and has withdrawn into his house in a

Seoul suburb. (Other reports have it that he has been placed under house arrest. At any event, he is clearly incommunicado.)

Further bits and pieces of evidence continue to dribble out in a tantalising manner. At the time of writing it was still not possible to secure a final report on the analysis of the tapes of KAL 007's conversations with Narita ground control being carried out in the University of Washington's sound laboratories. Initial reports suggested that the tapes revealed a change in voice tone on the part of the officers in 007's flight cabin as the plane veered towards Sakhalin, suggesting that from that point on they were speaking through their oxygen masks. It is, of course, standard military practice to don oxygen masks in any plane flying at high altitude when the plane is thought to be entering a danger or combat zone, for the initial danger encountered is always likely to be that of decompression and oxygen loss. It is important to say that this impression is derived from initial and as yet unconfirmed reports. If, however, it were to be established that 007's flight officers had thus donned their masks it would strongly suggest that they knew they were flying into a danger zone, thus adding further to the case for an intentional incursion.

Naturally enough, in the face of the very large number of pieces of circumstantial evidence all pointing towards the notion of an intentional incursion, the victims' relatives are in no mood to be easily placated. What they want is a full, proper, and searching inquiry into the whole affair. This, at least, they surely deserve. They are, though, up against powerful forces that would deny them this: even to accept the case for an inquiry is, after all, to admit that the official Reagan Administration version of the affair may leave something to be desired. This is hardly something which the Administration is going to concede if it can possibly help it, and the formidable popularity of the President himself has been a quite sufficient shield to deflect all demands for an inquiry to date. Indeed, it has been difficult to find any single US Congressman willing to stick his head above the parapet on this issue, while even the liberal bastions of the American media have been extremely reluctant (to put it mildly) to print stories on the case which question the official view.

In the face of this formidable shut-out it is not surprising that some of the victims' relatives – often facing severe financial pressures through the loss of a breadwinner in the tragedy – have swallowed their reservations and accepted an out-of-court settlement with KAL rather than pursue their court action. It must be assumed that they will be joined by at least a trickle of others over time. Realistically, there is little prospect of a proper inquiry being held without a change of Administration in the US and should the Republican nominee win the 1988 presidential contest that prospect could recede further still. Accordingly, a great deal rests on the legal action being pursued in the courts and on the determination of the relatives to hold out against the pressures for a settlement. At least some of the relatives seem to be both sufficiently determined and financially sufficiently well buttressed to go all the way. Again, we shall see.

At the time of writing it was still unclear how far the Iranian arms/Contra funding scandal had changed the environment within which the KAL 007 case will be viewed. Certainly, the discovery of an international gun-running operation being carried out from the basement of the White House has made it far harder for sceptics to pooh-pooh the notion that all manner of wild and irresponsible covert actions have been possible under the Reagan Administration. Meanwhile, evidence has come to light that KAL may also have been involved in some of the transactions under inquiry. Certainly, KAL had, in 1982-83, bought at least 25 M65 TOW missile systems from Hughes Aircraft. It seems that these missiles may have made their way to a destination other than South Korea – and already information had appeared suggesting that earlier purchases of Hawk missiles by KAL had ended up in Iran. One notes, too, that alongside KAL on the sales contract one finds the state of Israel – which has also emerged as a key intermediary in the arms-to-Iran operation. KAL is registered with the State Department as a licensed arms exporter (a fairly extraordinary thing for an airline to be), but it would, of course, have been subject to the normal strict rules about which third countries it could sell on to. Given this; given the fact that KAL would have a great deal to lose by antagonising the US government by selling arms on to countries not authorised by the US to receive them; and given that arms sold through KAL would escape normal Congressional scrutiny, it is hard to avoid the conclusion that KAL was being used as a covert conduit for US policy in this matter. If this were indeed the case it would raise yet again the spectre that the airline might have been a medium for other US covert activities over time. It is impossible at the time of writing to know how far this trail will lead – or how far President Reagan's much diminished prestige and credibility will at last embolden the media to launch more searching inquiries into the KAL 007 affair.

Whatever the outcome of the legal actions by the relatives of the KAL 007 victims, it seems certain that the case of KAL 007 is not going to 'lie down' until there has been a proper inquiry, or until some of the evidence currently being held back is released. It would, in that sense, be idle to pretend that either Hersh's book or this one is going to be the last word on the matter. One is, indeed, reminded ineluctably of the *Lusitania* tragedy. Those who questioned the official Anglo-American version of the affair – that the Germans had wantonly and without provocation killed 1,201 civilians by attacking a wholly innocent ship – immediately ran into the accusation that even to ask questions was to give implicit support to the German version of events (which was that civilian ships were being used for the transport of war materiel). And there was certainly no doubt that those 1,201 people were dead and that the Germans had killed them. It was not until 1972, when Colin Simpson showed that the *Lusitania* had in fact been loaded with contraband munitions (which may be why it sank so quickly), that a more just appreciation became possible.[19] The issues in the KAL 007 case are the same – the possible misuse of civilian transport for military purposes – and so are the Cold War (Anglo-German, US-Soviet) constraints against asking those awkward questions. In the case of the *Lusitania*, it took 57 years for the truth to come to light. It would be intolerable if we had to wait that long to know the full truth about the KAL 007 tragedy. It is also somewhat unlikely. The official version of the *Lusitania* tragedy was, after all, accepted almost without question for decades after the event. We are already far from that situation in the case of KAL 007. The questions are already out in the open. They will not go away until and unless they are dispelled by a truly comprehensive inquiry. The question which has to be asked about the KAL 007 tragedy is no longer what this or that writer or other individual believes to be the truth. The question is merely does one support or oppose the demand for that full inquiry.

*Magdalen College,*
*Oxford.*
*1 November 1986*

# Notes

CHAPTER ONE

1 – ICAO, *Final Report of Investigation as Required in the Council Resolution of 16 September 1983* (Roneo, Montreal, December 1983), p. 56. The ICAO *Final Report* (as I shall hereafter refer to it) contains a mass of useful data. I have given references only for direct quotes from the *Report*, but unless otherwise specified the account of the flight of 007 in this chapter derives from data in that report.

2 – See, for example, J. St. John, *Day of the Cobra* (Nashville, 1984, foreword by Senator Jesse Helms). St. John's book – an uncritical praise-song to Larry McDonald – takes its title from McDonald's assertion that 'Andropov is a deadly cobra who mesmerises his victims before striking'.

3 – M. Sayle, 'Flightpath to Disaster', *Sunday Times*, 20 May 1984.

4 – ICAO, *Final Report*, p. 12.

5 – Sayle, op. cit.

6 – Much of the information in this paragraph is derived from S. Lohr, 'South Korea's Airline and its Pilots have Reputation for being Aggressive', *New York Times*, 13 September 1983.

7 – F. Kaplan, 'Korean Air Lines linked to nation's intelligence agency', *Boston Globe*, 19 September 1983.

8 – R. Rohmer, *Massacre 007. The Story of the Korean Air Lines Flight 007* (1984), p. 68.

9 – Rohmer, op. cit., p. 67.

10 – A. Sampson, *Empires of the Sky. The Politics, Contests and Cartels of World Airlines* (1984), p. 195.

11 – See, for example, *Aviation Week and Space Technology*, 4 July 1983.

12 – *Boston Globe*, 19 September 1983. See also J. McConnell, 'The CIA and the Airlines. A 36 Year History', *Counterspy*, vol. 8, No. 2, December 1983–February 1984.

13 – *New York Times*, 13 September 1983.

14 – Rohmer, op. cit., p. 25.

15 – *New York Times*, 6 September 1983.

16 – Rohmer, op. cit., p. 25.

17 – St. John, op. cit., p. 81.

18 – Sayle, op. cit.

19 – St. John, op. cit., p. 81.

20 – *New York Times*, 8 September 1983.

21 – Ibid.

22 – *Mainichi Daily News*, 11 September 1983.

23 – St. John, op. cit., pp. 225–6.

24. – The data in this paragraph is to be found in ICAO, *Final Report*, pp. A10–14. I am grateful to Bob Allardyce for guiding me through its complexities.

25 – *Newsweek*, 19 September 1983.

26 – R. and L. Hurst, *Pilot Error. The Human Factors* (2nd edn., 1983), p. 24.

27 – A. Sampson and W. Bittorf, 'Der Todesflug des Korea-Jumbo', *Der Spiegel*, 24 September 1984. This was a four-part series of articles. References are made to the relevant part in each case.

28 – *Los Angeles Weekly*, 26 October–1 November 1984.

29 – Ibid. See also R. W. Allardyce and J. Gollin, 'The Final Moments of KAL 007: New Evidence Considered', *Berkshire Eagle*, 23 May 1985.

30 – ICAO, *1818th Report to Council by the President of the Air Navigation Commission* (Roneo, Montreal, 17 February 1984), p. 5. Hereafter I shall refer to this as ICAO, *ANC Report*.

31 – This point is well explained in Sampson and Bittorf, op. cit., 1 October 1984.

32 – See Allardyce and Gollin, op. cit. In addition I am grateful – yet again – to Bob Allardyce's personal explanation of these points.

33 – Private communication from R. W. Allardyce.

34 – D. Pearson, 'KAL 007. What the US Knew and When We Knew It', *Nation*, 18–25 August, 1984, p. 107.

35 – Rohmer, op. cit., p. 37.

36 – See ICAO, *Final Report*, and *New York Times*, 8 September 1983.

37 – It must have given the Russians some embarrassment to admit to this time in their submission to ICAO. Some (unconfirmed) reports suggest that six Soviet fighters scrambled.

38 – Cited in *New York Times*, 11 September 1983.

39 – Cited in *Washington Post*, 14 September 1983.

40 – Pearson, op. cit., pp. 118–9.

41 – Ibid.

42 – M. Sayle, 'The Inevitable Shootdown', *Sunday Times*, 27 May 1984. See also Sampson and Bittorf, op. cit.

43 – Pearson, op. cit., p. 119.

44 – ICAO, *Final Report*, p. 43.

45 – ICAO, *Final Report*, Appendix F, p. 4. Again, the times are those provided by the Russians themselves.

46 – See Allardyce and Gollin, op. cit.

47 – Pearson, op. cit., p. 119.

48 – Cited in *New York Times*, 11 September 1983.

49 – *Washington Post*, 13 September 1983.

50 – *Mainichi Daily News*, 3 September 1983; *New York Times*, 3 September 1983.

51 – M. Sayle, 'The Sakhalin Crisis. Charge and Countercharge', *Far Eastern Economic Review*, 20 September 1983.

52 – See Mr Mutsuo Kimura, President of the House of Councillors, question No. 35: 'Interpellation Prospectus on the Subsequent Truth Finding of the KAL Downing Case', 20 April 1985; and 'Reply to the Interpellation submitted by Mr Yutaka Hata, Member of the House of Councillors', 14 May 1985 (Roneo).

53 – Cited in *International Herald Tribune*, 14 September 1983.

54 – ICAO, *Final Report*, Appendix F, p. 1.

55 – B. Gunston, *An Illustrated Guide to Modern Airborne Missiles* (1983), pp. 10–11.

56 – Rohmer, op. cit., p. 48.

57 – *New York Times*, 2 September 1983.

58 – Sayle, 'The Inevitable Shootdown'. Sayle has made his own measurement of this distance and I have used his figure. Other sources are vaguer, saying 'over 300' or 'about 350' miles.

59 – See below, pp. 190–2.

60 – But see below, pp. 164–5, 295–6 for alternative versions of this tape.

61 – St. John, op. cit., p. 94.

62 – Sayle, 'The Sakhalin Crisis'.

63 – *Mainichi Daily News*, 10 September 1983.

64 – ICAO, *Final Report*, Appendix A, p. 10.

CHAPTER TWO

1 – H. Seton-Watson, *The Russian Empire 1801–1917* (1967), p. 297.

2 – Seton-Watson, op. cit., p. 445.

3 – Cited in J. Halliday, *A Political History of Japanese Capitalism* (1975), p. 86.

4 – Halliday, op. cit., p. 97.

5 – J. Erickson, *The Road to Berlin* (1983), pp. 500–01.

6 – M. Klare, 'Asia: Theatre of Nuclear War', *South*, November 1983, p. 11.

7 – L. Freedman, 'The Military Dimension of Soviet Policy', in G. Segal (ed.), *The Soviet Union in East Asia. Predicaments of Power* (1983), p. 93.

8 – P. F. Langer, 'Soviet Military Power in Asia', in D. S. Zagoria (ed.), *Soviet Policy in East Asia* (1982), p. 269.

9 – D. Jenkins, 'Close to Confrontation', *Far Eastern Economic Review*, 15 December 1983, p. 29. Confusingly, the NATO designation of the 'Backfire' is a TU-26; the Soviet designation is a TU-22M.

10 – Langer, op. cit., pp. 269–70.

11 – See, for example, the article by Goro Takeda, former chairman of the Japanese Joint Chiefs of Staff, 'Keeping the Russians out of Japan's Air Space', in *Gendai* (Tokyo), November 1983.

12 – R. Bonds (ed.), *Soviet War Power* (1982), pp. 140–1.

13 – Langer – whose estimates of Soviet strength considerably surpass those of some other authorities – suggests a Soviet inferiority in such ships of 70 to 79; op. cit., p. 269.

14 – See Klare, op. cit., and also his article, 'Une zone d'intérêt vital pour l'Union Soviétique', *Le Monde Diplomatique*, October 1983.

15 – 'The North Korean air force is pretty old and has only a limited range . . . We think we could wipe it out quickly enough.' Thus the commander of the USAF Fifth Air Force in early 1983, cited by W. Bello, P. Hayes and L. Zarsky, 'Les Américains consolident leur avantage stratégique', *Le Monde Diplomatique*, October 1983.

16 – Ibid.

17 – 'Guns vs. Butter', *Business Week*, 29 November 1982.

18 – *New York Times*, 19 November 1983.

19 – 'The Defense Buildup Doesn't Have to Happen All at Once', *Business Week*, 26 March 1984.

20 – Bello et al., op. cit.

21 – Ibid.

22 – Ibid.

23 – Ibid.

24 – Ibid.

25 – *Aviation Week and Space Technology*, 28 February 1983.

26 – *Mainichi Daily News*, 3 October 1983.

27 – Ibid.

28 – *Mainichi Daily News*, 4 October 1983.

29 – This was related to me by Murray Sayle.

30 – Bello et al., op. cit.

31 – Ibid.

32 – Ibid.

33 – Ibid.

34 – Ibid.

35 – Ibid.

36 – Ibid.

37 – 'Is America Strong Enough?', *Newsweek*, 27 October 1980.

38 – Bello et al., op. cit.

39 – M. Klare, 'Une zone d'intérêt vital'.

40 – M. Klare, 'Asia: Theatre of Nuclear War'.

41 – Ibid.

42 – Ibid.

43 – 'The Siberian Cruise of the USS Enterprise', *Far Eastern Economic Review*, 16 June 1983.

44 – Cited in Klare, 'Asia: Theatre of Nuclear War'.

45 – Cited in Bello et al., op. cit. See also 'Focus – Japan '83', *Far Eastern Economic Review*, 15 June 1983.

46 – Pearson, op. cit.

47 – *New York Times*, 2 September 1983.

48 – Bello et al., op. cit.

49 – Ibid.

50 – 'Eyes over the Horizon', *Asian Defence Journal*, December 1983.

51 – *New York Times*, 11 September 1983.

52 – On the structure of the US Command, Communications and Control (C3) network, see P. Bracken, *The Command and Control of Nuclear Forces* (1983), and P. Pringle and W. Arkin, *SIOP: the West's Single Integrated Operational Plan for Waging Nuclear War Against the Soviet Union* (1983).

53 – *New York Times*, 5 July 1983.

54 – On the complexities of the radar/ECM world, *Aviation Week and Space Technology* is the best guide, but see also the excellent article by S. Geisenheyner, 'Is Air Defence Unbeatable?', *Asian Defence Journal*, August and November 1983.

55 – *New York Times*, 2 September 1983.

56 – J. Bamford, *The Puzzle Palace. America's National Security Agency and its Special Relationship with Britain's GCHQ* (1982), p. 137.

57 – *Time*, 12 September 1983.

58 – ABC News, *20/20*, 'Cold War, Cold Blood'. Transcript of broadcast of 30 August 1984.

59 – Bamford, op. cit., p. 138.

60 – Bamford, op. cit., p. 139.

61 – Bamford, op. cit., p. 184.

62 – B. Gunston, *An Illustrated Guide to Spyplanes and Electronic Warfare Aircraft* (1983), p. 26.

63 – S. Hersh, *The Price of Power. Kissinger in the Nixon White House* (1983), pp. 73–4.

64 – Ibid.

65 – *Asian Defence Journal*, March 1983.

CHAPTER THREE

1 – Incomparably the best guide to the byzantine intrigues within the Reagan Administration over arms control is S. Talbott, *Deadly Gambits. The Reagan Administration and the Stalemate in Nuclear Arms Control* (1984).

2 – Talbott, op. cit., pp. 45–6.

3 – *Washington Post*, 11 August 1983.

4 – *New York Times*, 14 July 1983.

5 – *Washington Post*, 30 August 1983.

6 – See T. Wicker, 'Why a Missile Accord Would Benefit Both Leaders', *International Herald Tribune*, 16–17 July 1983.

7 – *Washington Post*, 18 July 1983.

8 – See *International Herald Tribune*, 19 August 1983 and 22 August 1983.

9 – For a telling portrait of the remarkable Rowny, see Talbott, op. cit., esp. pp. 277–8.

10 – *International Herald Tribune*, 22 August 1983.

11 – *International Herald Tribune*, 30–31 July 1983.

12 – Ibid.

13 – *International Herald Tribune*, 26 August 1983.

14 – *Washington Post*, 18 July 1983.

15 – Ibid.

16 – *International Herald Tribune*, 22 August 1983.

17 – *Washington Post*, 18 July 1983.

18 – *Financial Times*, 7 September 1983.

19 – *International Herald Tribune*, 30 September 1983.

20 – The following account is drawn from C. H. Farnsworth, 'White House Orders a Review of Controls on Exports to Russia', *International Herald Tribune*, 19 August 1983. See also the *IHT* for 21 and 23 September and 6 October.

21 – Talbott, op. cit., p. 227.

22 – Talbott, op. cit., pp. 227–8.

23 – Talbott, op. cit., p. 273.

24 – Talbott, op. cit., p. 227.

25 – Talbott, op. cit., p. 273.

26 – Talbott, op. cit., p. 274.

27 – On just how difficult it would be for the USSR to violate the SALT treaties without US knowledge, see D. Hafemeister, J. J. Romm and K. Tsipis, 'The Verification of Compliance with Arms Control Agreements', *Scientific American*, vol. 252, No. 3, March 1985, pp. 29–35.

28 – P. J. Klass, 'US Scrutinizing New Radar', *Aviation Week and Space Technology*, 22 August 1983; *Guardian*, 19 December 1984. US satellite launches are secret but it is possible to deduce their timing retrospectively from published details of international space activity.

29 – Bamford, op. cit., p. 201.

30 – Klass, op. cit.

31 – Ibid. See also C. A. Robinson, Jr, 'Soviets Accelerate Missile Defense Efforts', *Aviation Week and Space Technology*, 16 January 1984.

32 – Klass, op. cit.

33 – See, e.g., *Chicago Sun-Times*, 27 July 1983.

34 – *Washington Post*, 12 August 1983.

35 – For an excellent account of phased-array radars, see E. Brookner, 'Phased-Array Radars', *Scientific American*, vol. 252, No. 2, February 1985, pp. 76–84.

36 – M. R. Gordon, 'CIA is Skeptical that New Soviet Radar is Part of an ABM Defense System', *National Journal*, 3 September 1985, pp. 523–6.

37 – *International Herald Tribune*, 22 April 1985.

38 – *New York Times*, 5 October 1983.

39 – Gordon, op. cit., p. 523.

40 – Y. Bodansky, 'What the Soviets are So Anxious to Conceal', *Business Week*, 19 September 1983.

41 – Gordon, op. cit., p. 524.

42 – Gordon, op. cit., p. 526.

43 – Ibid.

44 – *New York Times*, 20 July 1983.

45 – *New York Times*, 12 August 1983.

46 – Gordon, op. cit., p. 524.

47 – *New York Times*, 12 August 1983.

48 – Ibid. See also *Washington Post*, 13 August 1983.

49 – *New York Times*, 12 August 1983.

50 – *Washington Post*, 4 September 1983.

51 – Gordon, op. cit., pp. 525–6.

52 – Gordon, op. cit., p. 524.

53 – Ibid.

CHAPTER FOUR

1 – *New York Times*, 8 September 1983. 007 was about 300 miles from Hakodate at shoot-down. Hakodate's radar range was about 230 miles, so 007 would have come into the range of this radar at about 18.34, if one assumes that it was travelling at about 10 miles a minute.

2 – The account which follows relies on ICAO, *Final Report*, and *New York Times*, 8 September 1983.

3 – *Mainichi Daily News*, 2 September 1983.

4 – *New York Times*, 8 September 1983.

5 – Ibid.

6 – *Mainichi Daily News*, 2 September 1983.

7 – *Washington Post*, 1 September 1983.

8 – *Aviation Week and Space Technology*, 5 September 1983.

9 – *Washington Post*, 1 September 1983.

10 – *New York Times*, 1 September 1983.

11 – Ibid.

12 – Sayle, 'The Inevitable Shootdown'; see also *Washington Post*, 17 September 1983.
13 – *New York Times*, 8 September 1983.
14 – This account of the search and rescue operation relies on ICAO, *Final Report*, pp. 32–3.
15 – Sampson and Bittorf, op. cit., 8 October 1984.
16 – Pearson, op. cit., p. 116. On Cobra Dane see P. J. Klass, 'USAF Tracking Radar Details Disclosed', *Aviation Week and Space Technology*, 25 October 1976, pp. 41–6.
17 – See Pearson, op. cit., and also Klass, 'USAF Tracking Radar'.
18 – See below, pp. 197–9.
19 – J. Bamford, 'The Last Flight of KAL 007. How the US knew so much about what happened', *Washington Post Magazine*, 7 January 1984.
20 – Thames TV, *TV Eye*, '007 – Licensed to Spy?'. Transcript of broadcast 19 July 1984.
21 – Bamford, 'The Last Flight'.
22 – Sampson and Bittorf, op. cit., 1 October 1984.
23 – Cited in Bamford, 'The Last Flight'.
24 – D. Pearson, op. cit., p. 116.
25 – *Washington Post* and *New York Times*, both 2 September 1983.
26 – See below, pp. 167–9.
27 – Cited in *Los Angeles Times*, 1 September 1983.
28 – *Washington Post*, 2 September 1983.


CHAPTER FIVE
1 – This portrait is largely based on material in the *New York Times* and *Washington Post* for 14–18 October 1983; see also *Time*, 1 August 1983.
2 – A. Haig, *Caveat. Realism, Reagan and Foreign Policy* (1984), p. 66.
3 – Ibid.
4 – Haig, op. cit., p. 357.
5 – Haig, op. cit., p. 78.
6 – *Keesings' Contemporary Archives*, 1982, p. 31387.
7 – Haig, op. cit., p. 306.
8 – Haig, op. cit., p. 307.
9 – *Washington Post*, 17 October 1983.
10 – *Washington Post*, 15 October 1983.
11 – J. Kraft, 'After the Clark Takeover, Opportunity for Shultz', *International Herald Tribune*, 8 August 1983.
12 – M. Getler, 'Reagan and Soviet: The Tone Shifts', *International Herald Tribune*, 18 January 1984.
13 – I. Davidson, 'The Power of Two Men', *Financial Times*, 22 August 1983.
14 – *Time*, 11 March 1985.
15 – *Washington Post*, 23 October 1983.
16 – Ibid.
17 – *Business Week*, 21 May 1984.
18 – Ibid. On Perle in general see S. Talbott, op. cit., esp. pp. 15–18, though in a sense Talbott's whole book is about him.
19 – *Business Week*, 21 May 1984.
20 – *New Republic*, 16 April 1984.
21 – *International Herald Tribune*, 9 May 1985.
22 – *Washington Post*, 6 September 1983.
23 – Ibid.
24 – *Newsweek*, 10 October 1983.
25 – Ibid.
26 – *Washington Post*, 7 September 1983.
27 – Ibid.

28 – Ibid.

29 – *Newsweek*, 10 October 1983.

30 – Ibid.

31 – *Washington Post*, 7 July 1983.

32 – Turner describes a situation where, in effect, the CIA Director had largely lost control of the organisation, with subordinates taking independent initiatives almost at will. See S. Turner, *Secrecy and Democracy. The CIA in Transition* (1985), esp. pp. 183–194.

33 – *Washington Post*, 19 July 1983.

34 – *Washington Post*, 1 July 1983.

35 – Ibid. See also *Washington Post*, 10 and 19 October 1983.

36 – *Washington Post*, 10 July 1983.

37 – *Washington Post*, 7 September 1983.

38 – *Newsweek*, 10 October 1983.

39 – Ibid.

40 – *International Herald Tribune*, 29 March 1983.

41 – Ibid.

42 – *The Economist*, 28 April 1984.

43 – *Washington Post*, 7 September 1983.

44 – *Sunday Times*, 15 April 1984.

45 – *Newsweek*, 10 October 1983.

46 – *US News and World Report*, 25 June 1984.

47 – *Washington Post*, 7 September 1983.

48 – *Guardian*, 12 June 1984.

49 – *Newsweek*, 10 October 1983.

50 – *US News and World Report*, 25 June 1984.

51 – *Guardian*, 12 June 1984.

52 – S. Turner, op. cit., pp. 173, 278.

53 – *New York Times*, 31 August 1983.

54 – *Newsweek*, 10 October 1983.

55 – Ibid.

56 – *Guardian*, 12 June 1984.

57 – *New York Times*, 6 September 1983.

58 – *New York Times*, 17 August 1983.

59 – *Washington Post*, 4 September 1983.

60 – Ibid.

61 – Ibid.

62 – Ibid.

63 – Ibid.

64 – Ibid.

65 – *Washington Post*, 2 September 1983.

66 – *Washington Post*, 4 September 1983.

67 – *Los Angeles Times*, 1 September 1983.

68 – Ibid.

69 – *New York Times*, 2 September 1983.

70 – *Washington Post*, 4 September 1983.

71 – *Washington Post*, 3 September 1983.

72 – See, for example, Sampson and Bittorf, op. cit., 24 September 1984.

73 – Sampson and Bittorf, op. cit., 15 October 1984.

74 – *New York*, 12 November 1984.

75 – I am grateful to David Pearson for this information.

76 – Sampson and Bittorf, op. cit., 8 October 1984. See also *Los Angeles Times*, 19 September 1983.

77 – M. Katayama, 'Truth and Falsehood about the Shooting Down of the Korean Airliner', *Sekai*,

No. 3, 1984. I am grateful to Kunihiko Miyoshi for translating this article from the Japanese for me.

78 – Sampson and Bittorf, op. cit., 8 October 1984.

79 – Material in the following paragraph is from M. Katayama, op. cit. and *Los Angeles Times*, 19 September 1983.

80 – While this makes for top security, the reason for this structure derives from the general antimilitarist line prevalent in Japan after 1945, which dictated that there should be no defence ministry as such. Instead the SDA (i.e. in effect the ministry) is a subordinate agency directly under the premier. The SDA is thus the political/bureaucratic controller of the SDF.

81 – Cited in *Los Angeles Times*, 19 September 1983.

82 – The paragraph above and the two following paragraphs rely on M. Katayama, op. cit., and Sampson and Bittorf, op. cit., 8 October 1984.

83 – *Washington Post*, 1 November 1983.

84 – *Washington Post*, 3 September 1983.

85 – Ibid.

86 – *Washington Post*, 4 September 1983.

87 – *New York Times*, 25 October 1983.

CHAPTER SIX

1 – *New York Times*, 2 September 1983.

2 – *Mainichi Daily News*, 3 September 1983.

3 – *New York Times*, 3 September 1983.

4 – *New York Times*, 4 September 1983.

5 – Ibid.

6 – *Washington Post*, 5 September 1983.

7 – *New York Times*, 3 September 1983.

8 – *Washington Post*, 13 July 1983. On Wick, see also C. Maddison, 'Under Wick, the USIA has a Bigger Budget, New Digs and an Image Problem', *National Journal*, 6 September 1984, pp. 1134–8; and *Observer*, 14 April 1985.

9 – *Washington Post*, 13 July 1983.

10 – Ibid.

11 – Ibid.

12 – Ibid. and see Maddison, op. cit.

13 – *International Herald Tribune*, 2 January 1984.

14 – *International Herald Tribune*, 13 January 1984.

15 – *Washington Post*, 13 July 1983; and see Maddison, op. cit.

16 – *New York Times*, 19 September 1983.

17 – *Washington Post*, 13 July 1983.

18 – *New York Times*, 5 and 7 September 1983.

19 – *New York Times*, 3 September 1983; *Mainichi Daily News*, 4 September 1983.

20 – Ibid.

21 – *New York Times*, 3 September 1983.

22 – *Mainichi Daily News*, 4 September 1983.

23 – *Mainichi Daily News*, 9 September 1983.

24 – *New York Times*, 5 September 1983.

25 – Ibid.

26 – Ibid.

27 – Ibid.

28 – Ibid.

29 – Ibid.

30 – Ibid.

31 – *New York Times*, 6 September 1983.

32 – Ibid.

33 – *New York Times*, 7 September 1983.

34 – Charles Z. Wick, 'Public Diplomacy and Private Initiatives: Teammates for Building Peace' (official text of speech to the Israel–America Chamber of Commerce and Industry, Tel Aviv, 13 October 1983), USIS, Tel Aviv (Roneo).

35 – *Washington Post*, 4 November 1983.

36 – *New York Times*, 7 September 1983.

37 – *New York Times*, 3 September 1983.

38 – Admiral Carroll interviewed by David Pearson, 11 December 1984. I am grateful to David Pearson for showing me the transcript of this interview. See also Admiral Carroll's interview with *New York*, 12 November 1984, p. 16.

39 – *New York Times*, 9 September 1983.

40 – Ibid.

41 – Ibid.

42 – *International Herald Tribune*, 19 October 1983.

43 – *International Herald Tribune*, 31 October 1983.

44 – *New York Times*, 11 September 1983.

45 – Ibid.

46 – Ibid.

47 – Ibid.

48 – *New York Times*, 13 September 1983.

49 – *New York Times*, 2 September 1983.

50 – *New York Times*, 15 September 1983.

51 – *New York Times*, 16 September 1983.

52 – The Moonies also own newspapers in New York, Japan, Uruguay and Cyprus, but had by 1985 pumped $150 million into the *Washington Times*, the flagship of the Reverend Moon's worldwide empire. See 'Moon's Global Empire', *Newsweek*, 2 September 1985 – published on the occasion of the Reverend Moon's release from jail after serving 18 months for tax evasion.

53 – The KKK held protest demonstrations near McDonald's home after the shoot-down.

54 – *New York Times*, 2 September 1983.

55 – See S. Fry, *The Great Silver Bubble* (1982).

56 – *Washington Post*, 13 October 1983.

57 – *Washington Post*, 3 September 1983.

58 – *New York Times*, 23 September 1983.

59 – *New York Times*, 7 September 1983.

60 – *New York Times*, 8 September 1983.

61 – A remark made by Howard Phillips, chairman of the Conservative Caucus. *Los Angeles Times*, 4 September 1983.

62 – *Time*, 12 September 1983.

63 – *New York Times*, 12 September 1983.

64 – Ibid.

65 – *Los Angeles Times*, 12 September 1983.

66 – *New York Times*, 8 September 1983.

67 – *Washington Post*, 11 September 1983.

68 – *New York Times*, 10 September 1983.

69 – Ibid.

70 – *New York Times*, 11 September 1983.

71 – *New York Times*, 15 September 1983.

72 – Ibid.

73 – *New York Times*, 19 and 20 September 1983.

74 – *New York Times*, 25 September 1983.

75 – *Mainichi Daily News*, 7 September 1983.

76 – *Aviation Week and Space Technology*, 19 September 1983.

77 – *Japan Times Weekly*, 10 September 1983.
78 – *New York Times*, 18 September 1983.
79 – Ibid.
80 – *New York Times*, 1 October 1983.
81 – *New York Times*, 2 October 1983.
82 – *Mainichi Daily News*, 5 September 1983.
83 – *New York Times*, 4 September 1983.
84 – *New York Times*, 19 September 1983.
85 – *International Herald Tribune*, 13 September 1983.
86 – *Financial Times*, 7 and 13 September 1983.
87 – *Mainichi Daily News*, 11 September 1983.
88 – *New York Times*, 13 September 1983.
89 – Ibid. In that period the USSR had cast 3 vetoes, the US 15.
90 – *New York Times* and *Washington Post*, 18 September 1983.
91 – *New York Times*, 17 September 1983.
92 – *New York Times*, 18 September 1983.
93 – *Los Angeles Times*, 19 September 1983.
94 – *Sunday Telegraph*, 4 March 1984.
95 – *New York Times*, 20 September 1983.
96 – *New York Times*, 24 September 1983.
97 – *New York Times*, 26 September 1983.
98 – *New York Times*, 27 September 1983.
99 – Ibid.
100 – *Le Monde*, 22 September 1983.
101 – *New York Times*, 27 September 1983.
102 – *New York Times*, 30 September 1983.
103 – Ibid.
104 – *New York Times* and *Washington Post*, 10 September 1983. The following account is based on these two sources.
105 – *New York Times*, 19 September 1983.
106 – *New York Times*, 22 and 24 September 1983.
107 – *Washington Post*, 7 October 1983.
108 – *International Herald Tribune*, 26 September 1983.
109 – See below, pp. 150–60.
110 – *New York Times*, 16 September 1983.
111 – *New York Times*, 20 September 1983.
112 – *New York Times*, 29 September 1983.
113 – Cited in *Daily Telegraph*, 5 December 1983; see also *Observer*, 4 December 1983.
114 – *International Herald Tribune*, 6 September 1983.
115 – *International Herald Tribune*, 25 January 1984.
116 – *Le Monde*, 14 October 1983.
117 – *Washington Post*, 8 September 1983.
118 – *Washington Post*, 16 October 1983.
119 – *Washington Post*, 13 October 1983.
120 – Ibid.
121 – *New York Times*, 9 November 1983.

CHAPTER SEVEN
1 – *New York Times*, 5 September 1983.
2 – Ibid.
3 – *New York Times*, 6 September 1983.
4 – Ibid.

5 – Ibid.

6 – *Mainichi Daily News*, 8 September 1983.

7 – *New York Times*, 7 September 1983.

8 – *New York Times*, 10 September 1983; *Soviet Weekly*, 17 September 1983. Material for the whole of Ogarkov's press conference is drawn from these two sources.

9 – *Los Angeles Times*, 9 September 1983.

10 – *Los Angeles Times*, 10 September 1983.

11 – See above, pp. 17–18.

12 – *Washington Post*, 13 and 18 September 1983.

13 – *New York Times*, 13 September 1983.

14 – See W. Green and G. Swanborough, *An Illustrated Guide to the World's Civil Airliners* (1982), pp. 54–7, 40–5, and B. Gunston, *An Illustrated Guide to Spyplanes and Electronic Warfare Aircraft* (1983), pp. 70–7.

15 – *New York Times*, 3 October 1983.

16 – Sampson, *Empires of the Sky*, p. 208.

17 – *Newsweek*, 19 September 1983.

18 – *New York Times* and *Washington Post*, 8 October 1983.

19 – Sampson, op. cit., p. 208.

20 – *New York Times*, 14 September 1983.

21 – This account of the *Krasnaya Zvezda* story relies on *New York Times*, 17 September 1983, and *International Herald Tribune*, 17–18 September 1983.

22 – *Washington Post*, 20 September 1983; *Mainichi Daily News*, 21 September 1983.

23 – See J. Oberg, 'Sakhalin: Sense and Nonsense', *Defence Attaché*, No. 1, 1985, pp. 37–47.

24 – It is difficult to achieve consensus about the satellite track – two independent enquiries which astronomer friends of the author put in hand both had somewhat inconclusive results, though were close to Jasani's version. I have taken Jasani to be the authoritative source. See B. Jasani and G. E. Perry, 'The Military Use of Outer Space', esp. their section on the KAL incident, in SIPRI, *World Armaments and Disarmament, SIPRI Yearbook 1985* (1985), pp. 137–9.

25 – Jasani and Perry, op. cit., p. 137.

26 – On 'Ferrets' see Bamford, *The Puzzle Palace*, pp. 188, 195–204, 207, 211.

27 – I am grateful to Dr John Ponsonby of Jodrell Bank Observatory for pointing this out to me.

28 – Interview with Volkman on Thames TV, *TV Eye*, '007 – Licensed to Spy?'

29 – The 1982–41C was launched into a circular orbit 700 km high, inclined at 96°, and with an original orbital period of 98.87 minutes. By the night of 31 August 1983, however, this orbit had decayed to produce an orbital period of 98.8 minutes. I am grateful to Dr Russell Eberst, of the Royal Scottish Observatory, Edinburgh, for this information.

30 – Cited in D. Pearson and J. Keppel, 'New Pieces in the Puzzle of Flight 007', *Nation*, vol. 241, No. 4, 17–24 August 1985.

31 – P. Q. Mann, 'Re-Assessing the Sakhalin Incident', *Defence Attaché*, No. 3, 1984, pp. 41–56.

32 – Oberg, op. cit.

33 – C. Covault, 'Military to Withold Shuttle Liftoff Time', *Aviation Week and Space Technology*, 5 November 1984.

34 – On the 'Keyhole' see Bamford, *The Puzzle Palace*, pp. 201–2, 208.

35 – *New York Times*, 28 August 1983.

36 – Ibid.

37 – The material in this paragraph is drawn from the *Washington Post*, 3 September 1983.

38 – *Washington Post*, 4 September 1983.

39 – Covault, op. cit.

40 – One of the author's own articles on the KAL 007 affair was reprinted in such circumstances by the *Soviet Literary Gazette*. All critical references to Soviet behaviour disappeared in this 'new' version.

41 – *Guardian*, 28 August 1984.

CHAPTER EIGHT

1 – *New York Times*, 8 September 1983.

2 – ICAO, *Final Report*, p. 43, and ICAO, *1818th Report to Council by the President of the Air Navigation Commission*, p. 8. Henceforth I shall refer to this latter as ICAO, *ANC Report*.

3 – *New York Times*, 4 September 1983.

4 – *New York Times*, 17 September 1983.

5 – I am grateful to John Keppel for his account of his interview with Dr Suzuki.

6 – Bamford, *The Puzzle Palace*, p. 201.

7 – F. G. Powers, *Operation Overflight. The U-2 Spy Pilot Tells his Story for the First Time* (1970), p. 95.

8 – *Washington Post*, 18 September 1983.

9 – *New York Times*, 4 September 1983.

10 – Ibid.

11 – Ibid.

12 – *New York Times*, 11 September 1983.

13 – Sampson and Bittorf, op. cit., 8 October 1984.

14 – *Washington Post*, 8 September 1983.

15 – A. Sampson, 'Whatever Happened to 007?', *Parade*, 20 April 1984.

16 – *Mainichi Daily News*, 7 September 1983.

17 – *Mainichi Daily News*, 26 September 1983.

18 – See above, pp. 118–9.

19 – Indeed, this was stated quite flatly in the *Los Angeles Times*, 8 September 1983.

20 – *Observer*, 11 September 1983.

21 – See C. A. Robinson, Jr, 'US Says Soviets Knew Korean Airlines 747 was Commercial Flight', *Aviation Week and Space Technology*, 12 September 1983.

22 – See above, p. 59.

23 – P. Taubman, 'US Security Agencies Said to have Spotted Soviet Jets on the Move', *International Herald Tribune*, 15 September 1983.

24 – *Washington Post*, 8 September 1983.

25 – *Los Angeles Times*, 19 September 1983.

26 – Sampson, 'Whatever Happened to 007?'

27 – *New York Times*, 2 September 1983.

28 – *Washington Post*, 2 September 1983.

29 – *New York Times*, 3 and 4 September 1983.

30 – *Mainichi Daily News*, 6 September 1983.

31 – *Washington Post*, 6 September 1983.

32 – *Washington Post*, 7 September 1983.

33 – *New York Times*, 8 September 1983.

34 – Ibid.

35 – Ibid.

36 – Ibid.

37 – *Mainichi Daily News*, 9 September 1983.

38 – *New York Times*, 10 and 12 September 1983.

39 – See above, p. 116.

40 – *New York Times*, 5 September 1983.

41 – Sampson and Bittorf, op. cit., 8 October 1983.

42 – *Washington Post*, 6 September 1983.

43 – Information in this paragraph is from D. van der Aart, *Aerial Espionage. Secret Intelligence Flights by East and West* (1985), pp. 88–95, and B. Gunston, *An Illustrated Guide to Spyplanes and Electronic Warfare Aircraft* (1983), pp. 70–77.

44 – van der Aart, op. cit., p. 90.

45 – *New York Times*, 6 September 1983.

46 – *New York Times*, 8 September 1983.

47 – *New York Times*, 11 September 1983.

48 – *New York Times*, 6 September 1983.

49 – *Washington Post*, 16 September 1983.

50 – Bamford, 'The Last Flight of KAL 007'.

51 – *Denver Post*, 13 September 1983.

52 – *New York Times*, 26 September 1983.

53 – D. McManus, 'US Softens its Stand on Soviet Downing of Jet', *Los Angeles Times*, 29 August 1984.

54 – *Observer*, 11 September 1983.

55 – McManus, op. cit.

56 – The following data on Japanese radar are drawn from 'Reply to the Interpellation Submitted by Mr Yutaka Hata, Member of the House of Councillors, Regarding the Subsequent Truth Finding of the KAL Downing Case', 14 May 1985 (Japanese Diet: Ref. Cabinet/House of Councillors, Question 102, No. 35).

57 – *New York Times*, 6 September 1983.

58 – ICAO, *Final Report*, p. 43. ICAO suggests that the steeper Russian curve could have been due to exaggeration by radar operators working from memory or to 'slant range effects' due to 007 passing directly over the Soviet radar antenna. Actually, of course, there should have been no need for ICAO to work from radar operators' memories: at least on the Japanese side there were radar tapes which they could have seen – had they been allowed to.

59 – T. Mangold, 'To Justify his Crusade, did Reagan Play with the Truth?', *Listener*, 10 November 1983.

60 – Ibid.

61 – *Washington Post*, 10 September 1983.

62 – Mangold, op. cit. Other quotes here from Mrs Kirkpatrick are from this same source.

63 – *Los Angeles Times*, 15 September 1983.

64 – Mangold, op. cit.

65 – *New York Times*, 3 September 1983.

66 – *New York Times*, 4 September 1983.

67 – *New York Times*, 5 September 1983.

68 – Ibid.

69 – Ibid.

70 – *New York Times*, 5 September 1983.

71 – *New York Times*, 6 September 1983.

72 – Ibid.

73 – *New York Times*, 5 September 1983.

74 – *New York Times*, 8 September 1983. For photographs of RC-135s showing a hump configuration see M. de Arcangelis, *Electronic Warfare. From the Battle of Tsushima to the Falklands and Lebanon Conflicts* (1985), facing p. 129; and R. L. Lawson (ed.), *The History of US Naval Air Power* (1985), p. 249. In addition, of course, a military version of the 747 exists – the E4-B. Some newspapers suggested that the Russians might have thought 007 was an E4-B, but this is implausible. To date the only use of the E4-B is as an airborne command post (in case of nuclear war). The Russians are aware of this – and the last place in the world they would have expected to see such a command post was near Soviet airspace.

75 – *Los Angeles Times*, 15 September 1983.

76 – See above, pp. 24–6.

77 – ICAO, *Final Report*, pp. 16–17.

78 – G. Takeda, 'Keeping the Russians Out of Japan's Air Space', *Gendai*, November 1983.

79 – *Los Angeles Times*, 15 September 1983.

80 – *New York Times*, 26 September 1983.

81 – *New York Times*, 7 October 1983.

82 – Ibid.

83 – *Washington Post*, 8 October 1983; *Mainichi Daily News*, 9 October 1983.
84 – *New York Times*, 25 October 1983.
85 – *Washington Post*, 21 October 1983.
86 – McManus, op. cit.
87 – *New York Times*, 25 September 1983.
88 – *New York Times*, 26 September 1983.
89 – See C. Robbins, *Air America* (1979).
90 – *Washington Post*, 3 September 1983.
91 – *Washington Post*, 7 October 1983.

CHAPTER NINE

1 – See above, pp. 27–30.
2 – *Los Angeles Times*, 15 September 1983.
3 – *Sunday Times*, 30 June 1985.
4 – Ibid.
5 – Robinson, 'US Says Soviets Knew'.
6 – *Washington Post*, 2 September 1983.
7 – *Japan Times*, 10 September 1983.
8 – *Guardian*, 13 September 1983.
9 – *Mainichi Daily News*, 2 September 1983.
10 – *Mainichi Daily News*, 3 September 1983.
11 – *New York Times*, 3 September 1983.
12 – Ibid.
13 – *Mainichi Daily News*, 3 September 1983.
14 – *New York Times*, 9 September 1983.
15 – *New York Times*, 15 September 1983.
16 – Ibid.
17 – This account of Wakkanai relies on the *New York Times*, 21 September 1983.
18 – *New York Times*, 8 September 1983.
19 – *New York Times*, 11 September 1983.
20 – *Washington Post*, 15 and 18 September 1983.
21 – Few could doubt, after all, that there *was* a close liaison between the US and South African governments; or that it would have been very surprising if Israel had invaded Lebanon without giving advance notice to the US, on whom it was so utterly dependent financially and militarily. Similarly, the US Deputy Assistant Secretary in Intelligence, Dennis Kux, toured Europe in September 1983, giving 'briefing sessions' on Soviet disinformation. The example of Soviet disinformation he chose was the allegation that the CIA had deeply penetrated the Ghanaian government. In July 1985, however, the arrest of the former CIA agent, Sharon Scranage, 'exposed many links in a CIA operation against the government of Flight-Lieutenant Jerry Rawlings (of Ghana)'. *Guardian*, 15 July 1985.
   If, in fact, all these things were true, citing them as 'Soviet disinformation' would have been a good way to ensure that minimal attention was paid to such charges when they did arise.
22 – *Mainichi Daily News*, 18 September 1983; *New York Times*, 17 September 1983.
23 – C. W. Burleson, *The Jennifer Project* (1979), p. 19.
24 – See de Arcangelis, op. cit., p. 289 for a map of the SOSUS network in this area.
25 – Lieutenant-Colonel D. Miller, 'Intelligence and the War at Sea', in Colonel W. V. Kennedy (ed.), *The Intelligence War. Penetrating the Secret World of Today's Advanced Technology Conflict* (1983), p. 190.
26 – Miller, op. cit., pp. 184–6.
27 – Miller, op. cit., p. 186.
28 – Ibid.
29 – Burleson, op. cit., pp. 28–33.
30 – Ibid.

31 – Burleson (op. cit) argues persuasively that the whole submarine was probably retrieved, and that the story that it was lost was a CIA cover story designed to conceal just how significant US intelligence gains from the operation had been. On the Jennifer Project, see also R. Varner and W. Collier, *A Matter of Risk. The Incredible Inside Story of the Mission to Raise a Russian Submarine* (1978).

32 – Miller, op. cit., pp. 184–5.

33 – Burleson, op. cit., p. 51.

34 – *New York Times*, 20 September 1983.

35 – *New York Times*, 15 September 1983.

36 – *Washington Post*, 21 September 1983.

37 – These, at least, were the figures constantly used by Administration spokesmen. But John Wheeler, the spokesman for Boeing, gave the range of the pinger in the digital flight recorder as 5 miles at depths up to 20,000 feet. *Los Angeles Times*, 10 September 1983.

38 – *Washington Post*, 20 September 1983.

39 – Ibid.

40 – *Washington Post*, 21 September 1983.

41 – *Mainichi Daily News*, 22 September 1983.

42 – *Los Angeles Times*, 21 September 1983.

43 – *International Herald Tribune*, 22 September 1983.

44 – *New York Times*, 23 September 1983.

45 – *New York Times*, 28 September 1983.

46 – *Washington Post*, 27 September 1983.

47 – *New York Times*, 28 September 1983.

48 – Ibid.

49 – *Mainichi Daily News*, 28 September 1983.

50 – Ibid.

51 – Ibid.

52 – *Mainichi Daily News*, 29 September 1983.

53 – *Washington Post*, 27 September 1983.

54 – Ibid.

55 – *New York Times*, 29 September 1983.

56 – *Mainichi Daily News*, 1 October 1983.

57 – *Mainichi Daily News*, 30 September 1983.

58 – *Mainichi Daily News*, 2 October 1983.

59 – *Mainichi Daily News*, 6 October 1983.

60 – *Washington Post*, 13 October 1983.

61 – *Mainichi Daily News*, 16 October 1983.

62 – *Washington Post*, 28 October 1983; *Mainichi Daily News*, 29 October 1983.

63 – *Washington Post*, 28 October 1983.

64 – See above, note 37.

65 – *New York Times*, 6 October 1983.

66 – ICAO, *Final Report*, p. 28.

67 – *Daily Telegraph*, 5 July 1985.

68 – These were the words of Mr D. Englington, chief air-traffic controller at Shannon airport, at the coroner's inquest. Cited in *The Times*, 18 September 1985.

69 – See above, p. 22.

70 – *Los Angeles Times*, 4 September 1983.

71 – John Keppel (whose career before retirement was as a State Department liaison officer with the CIA) has raised this as a (slight) possibility. The Russians naturally seized on such an explanation – omitting all of Keppel's reservations and qualifications. *International Herald Tribune*, 27 August 1984.

CHAPTER TEN

1 – *Los Angeles Times*, 22 September 1983.

2 – *Washington Post*, 10 October 1983.

3 – *Los Angeles Times*, 23 September 1983.

4 – *Washington Post*, 10 October 1983.

5 – *Los Angeles Times*, 28 September 1983.

6 – *Washington Post*, 12 October 1983.

7 – *Washington Post*, 13 October 1983.

8 – Ibid.

9 – *New York Times*, 14 October 1983.

10 – C. H. Farnsworth, 'Clark Endorses Tightening the Sale of Equipment to Russia', *International Herald Tribune*, 23 September 1983; K. Noble, 'US Panel Opposes Sale of Equipment to Russia', *International Herald Tribune*, 21 September 1983.

11 – *New York Times*, 26 September 1983.

12 – C. H. Farnsworth, 'US Rejects New Soviet Trade Ban', *International Herald Tribune*, 6 October 1983.

13 – Ibid.

14 – *International Herald Tribune*, 21 September 1983.

15 – Farnsworth, 'US Rejects New Soviet Trade Ban'.

16 – Ibid.

17 – *Washington Post*, 14 October 1983.

18 – *New York Times*, 15 October 1983.

19 – *New York Times*, 17 October 1983.

20 – J. B. Oakes, 'Clark's Low Wattage', *New York Times*, 18 October 1983.

21 – *Washington Post*, 13 October 1983.

22 – Ibid.

23 – Ibid.

24 – *Washington Post*, 15 October 1983.

25 – Ibid.

26 – Ibid.

27 – Ibid.

28 – Ibid.

29 – *New York Times*, 15 October 1983.

30 – *New York Times*, 14 October 1983.

31 – *Washington Post*, 23 October 1983.

32 – Ibid.

33 – *New York Times*, 14 October 1983.

34 – Ibid.

35 – Ibid.

36 – *Washington Post*, 23 October 1983.

37 – *New York Times*, 14 October 1983.

38 – Ibid.

39 – Ibid.

40 – *Washington Post*, 16 October 1983.

41 – *Washington Post*, 15 October 1983.

42 – *Washington Post*, 14 October 1983.

43 – *New York Times*, 18 October 1983.

44 – *Washington Post*, 23 October 1983.

45 – L. Cannon, 'McFarlane in the White House: A Modest Conciliator Comes of Age', *International Herald Tribune*, 27 February 1985.

46 – Ibid.

47 – Ibid.

48 – Ibid.

49 – *New York Times*, 15 October 1983.

50 – Cannon, op. cit.; *Washington Post*, 14 October 1983.

51 – *Los Angeles Times*, 16 October 1983.

52 – *Washington Post*, 16 October 1983.

53 – See above, p. 92.

54 – *Washington Post*, 22 October 1983.

55 – See B. Gwertzman, 'A White House Center of Influence', *International Herald Tribune*, 1 April 1985.

56 – Cannon, op. cit.

57 – *Washington Post*, 17 October 1983.

58 – *Washington Post*, 22 October 1983.

59 – *Washington Post*, 16 October 1983.

60 – *New York Times*, 18 October 1983.

61 – *Washington Post*, 23 October 1983.

62 – Ibid.

63 – Ibid.

64 – *Washington Post*, 16 October 1983.

65 – Ibid.

66 – *New York Times*, 30 September 1983.

67 – See above, p. 196.

68 – *New York Times*, 23 October 1983.


CHAPTER ELEVEN

1 – See above, p. 130.

2 – *New York Times*, 12 September 1983.

3 – ICAO, *Convention on International Civil Aviation* (6th edn, 1980), Article 50 (b), p. 21. The article does, however, urge that the principle of geographical balance be given weight too.

4 – This picture of ICAO relies on private interview material.

5 – *New York Times*, 14 September 1983.

6 – Ibid.

7 – *Boston Globe*, 19 September 1983.

8 – See below, p. 287.

9 – ICAO, *Convention*, Article 26, p. 10.

10 – See ICAO, *Minutes of the Extraordinary Session of the Council, 15 September 1983* (Doc.9416-C/1077).

11 – ICAO, *The Convention on International Civil Aviation . . . the First 35 Years* (undated), pp. 24–6.

12 – ICAO, *Minutes of the Extraordinary Session*, p. 35.

13 – *Los Angeles Times*, 16 September 1983.

14 – ICAO, *Minutes of the Extraordinary Session*, Annexe A.

15 – *Los Angeles Times*, 17 September 1983.

16 – ICAO, *Final Report*, p. 2.

17 – D. Corn, 'Fear and Obstruction on the KAL Trail', *Nation*, 17–24 August 1985.

18 – ICAO, *Final Report*, p. 36.

19 – See below, pp. 243–9 for a more detailed examination of these scenarios.

20 – ICAO, *Final Report*, p. 56.

21 – Press release by R. F. Tweedy, President, IFALPA, of 16 December 1983.

22 – *New York Times*, 13 December 1983.

23 – Ibid.

24 – 'The Reagan 45', *New Republic*, 16 April 1984, p. 6; *Aviation Week and Space Technology*, 2 January 1984.

25 – ICAO, *1818th Report to Council by the President of the Air Navigation Commission. Final Report of Investigation as Required by Council Resolution of 16 September 1983* (C-WP/7809), 16 February 1984. (Hereafter: *ANC Report*.)

26 – ICAO, *ANC Report*, p. 12.

27 – ICAO, *ANC Report*, p. 14.

28 – Ibid.

29 – ICAO, *ANC Report*, p. 13.

30 – See ICAO, Assembly 25th Session (Extraordinary), Montreal, 24 April–10 May 1984:
(i) *Plenary Meetings. Resolutions and Minutes* (Doc. 9437).
(ii) *Executive Committee. Report, Minutes and Documents* (Doc. 9438).

31 – ICAO, *Executive Committee*, p. 164.

32 – J. Ott, 'ICAO Stymied in Anti-Force Talks', *Aviation Week and Space Technology*, 30 April 1984.

33 – ICAO, *Plenary Meetings*, pp. 11–13.

34 – *New York Times*, 26 September 1983.

35 – See McConnell, 'The CIA and the Airlines'; V. Marchetti and J. Marks, *The CIA and the Cult of Intelligence* (1976), esp. pp. 166–82, 266–7.

36 – Robbins, *Air America*, p. 16.

37 – See McConnell, op. cit.

38 – R. Braunburg, 'Die Toten und die Vermarktung der Trauer', *Deutsches Allgemeines Sontagsblatt*, 11 September 1983.

39 – CAA, *World Airline Accident Summary*, cited in *Flight International*, 17 September 1983, p. 732.

40 – *Mainichi Daily News*, 3 October 1983.

41 – See Talbott, op. cit., pp. 253–5.

42 – R. J. Smith, 'Air Force Takes Aim at a Big Bird', *Science*, vol. 216, 16 April 1982.

43 – See, for example, *New York Times*, 6 October 1983.

44 – *Sunday Times*, 21 July 1985.

45 – *Guardian*, 22 July 1985.

46 – *Sunday Times*, 21 July 1985.

47 – Ibid.

48 – *Guardian*, 22 July 1985.

49 – See above, pp. 24–6.

50 – ICAO, *Final Report*, p. 43.

51 – Corn, 'Fear and Obstruction on the KAL Trail'.

52 – See above, pp. 30–31.

CHAPTER TWELVE

1 – ICAO, *Final Report*, pp. 45–52.

2 – ICAO, *Final Report*, p. 52.

3 – Ibid.

4 – ICAO, *ANC Report*, p. 14.

5 – M. Sayle, 'Flightpath to Disaster', 'The Inevitable Shootdown'; 'KE 007. A Conspiracy of Circumstance', *New York Review of Books*, 25 April 1984; 'The Sakhalin Crisis'; and see also his controversy with Pearson in *New York Review of Books*, 26 September 1985.

6 – ICAO, *Final Report*, p. 47.

7 – See Sayle, 'KE 007'; and the controversy with Pearson.

8 – Sayle attributes his map to a conversation with an official in the UK Civil Aviation Authority. Be that as it may, this hardly carries much authority (the official concerned has ceased to deal with matters relating to the 007 affair). The CAA has not published any map itself and it has not challenged the version of the relevant map produced by ICAO.

9 – Sayle may, though, be on stronger ground here than he realises. Robert Allardyce has carried out tests on Delco INS equipment which show that there is actually no known limit in distance 'abeam' at which the alert light will fail to illuminate. This may, of course, not be true of the Litton INS carried by 007 – but it quite probably is. (This finding has not, though, altered Allardyce's view that the Sayle version is wholly implausible.) (Private communication from R. W. Allardyce.)

10 – K. J. Stein, 'Human Factors Analyzed in 007 Navigation Error', *Aviation Week and Space Technology*, 3 October 1983.

11 – ICAO, *ANC Report*, p. 16.

12 – Takeda, 'Keeping the Russians out'.

13 – ICAO, *Final Report*, p. 43.

14 – See above, pp. 24–6.

15 – See above, pp. 30–31.

16 – ICAO, *ANC Report*, p. 14.

17 – Rohmer, op. cit., p. 63.

18 – Sayle, 'KE 007', p. 52.

19 – The 1 in 20,000 figure is that cited by Sayle in 'Flightpath to Disaster'.

20 – *New York Times*, 20 September 1983.

21 – M. Sayle, 'Reply to Pearson', *New York of Review of Books*, 26 September 1985.

22 – *New York Times*, 9 September 1983.

23 – *Newsweek*, 19 September 1983.

24 – Ibid.

25 – Kim's evasive tactics were mentioned by the former NSA Director, Admiral Bobby Inman, interviewed on ABC News, *Nightline*, 'Korean Air Tragedy'. Broadcast 1 September 1983. (Transcript.)

26 – Sampson and Bittorf, op. cit., 1 October 1984.

27 – *Newsweek*, 12 September 1983.

28 – Ibid. See also *New York Times*, 2 September 1983.

29 – *Le Monde*, 11–12 September 1983.

30 – *New York Times*, 11 September 1983.

31 – Sayle gives the £2000 figure in 'Shooting Down the Myths', *Spectator*, 8 October 1983; the dollar figure is from A. Dallin, *Black Box. KAL 007 and the Superpowers* (1985).

32 – *Le Monde*, 4 October 1983.

33 – Rohmer, op. cit., pp. 67, 207–13.

34 – ICAO, *Final Report*, p. 35.

35 – Sampson, *Empires of the Sky*, pp. 203–4; Sayle, 'Shooting Down the Myths'.

36 – *Atlanta Journal*, December 1984.

37 – H du B Reports, *Why the Russians Killed Larry McDonald*, vol. XXVI, letter 5, September 1983.

38 – Letter from M. du Berrier, 20 March 1984.

39 – Mrs K. McDonald interviewed on ABC News, *Nightline*, 'Korean Air Tragedy', broadcast 1 September 1983. (Transcript.) Mrs McDonald's willingness to appear on a panel discussion of the tragedy within hours of her husband's death was doubtless very brave, but excited inevitable criticism.

40 – I am grateful to Philip J. Klass for kindly sending me photographs to illustrate this point.

41 – See Powers, op. cit.; D. Wise and T. Ross, *The U-2 Affair* (1962).

42 – The US has, however, devised a programme designed to overcome this difficulty, using a Lockheed TR-1 plane equipped with an atomic clock in order to achieve an instantaneous 'fix'. See P. J. Klass, 'Air Force to Test Enemy Radar Locator', *Aviation Week and Space Technology*, 23 July 1984.

43 – See above, pp. 69–76.

44 – See above, pp. 73, 89.

45 – See above, p. 96.

46 – *Guardian*, 12 June 1984.

47 – 'Ex-CIA Chief Criticizes White House for Aid to Nicaraguan Rebels', *International Herald Tribune*, 10–11 August 1985.

48 – *Guardian*, 30 September 1984.

49 – Sampson, *Empires of the Sky*, p. 196.

50 – *Time*, 12 September 1983.

51 – General George Keegan interviewed on ABC News, *20/20*, 30 August 1984.

52 – *Keesings' Contemporary Archives*, 5 December 1980, p. 30607.

53 – *Keesings'*, 15 April 1980, p. 30217; 31 July 1981, p. 30999.

54 – *Keesings'*, 31 July 1981, p. 30999.

55 – *Keesings'*, 24 August 1979, pp. 29795–6; 15 April 1980, p. 30217; 5 December 1980, p. 30607.

56 – *Keesings'*, 5 November 1976, p. 28036; 13 April 1979, p. 29555; 15 April 1980, p. 30217. On South Korean lobbying in Washington, see also R. W. Howe and S. H. Trott, *The Power Peddlers. How Lobbyists Mold America's Foreign Policy* (1977), pp. 61–74.

57 – *Keesings'*, 13 April 1979, p. 29555.

58 – *Keesings'*, 25 April 1980, pp. 30216–7.

59 – *Keesings'*, 25 April 1980, pp. 30216–20.

60 – *Keesings'*, 25 April 1980, p. 30218.

61 – *Keesings'*, 5 November 1976, p. 28036.

62 – See above, p. 93.

63 – See above, p. 96.

64 – See above, pp. 6–7.

65 – See above, pp. 11, 14–15.

66 – E. Volkman, interviewed on Thames TV, *TV Eye*, 19 July 1984.

67 – See above, pp. 97–103.

68 – See Clark's 'Summit' speech, p. 196.

69 – Cited in Sampson, 'Whatever Happened to 007?'

70 – Gordon, 'CIA is Skeptical', pp. 525–6.

71 – Gordon, op. cit., p. 526.

72 – See Gordon, op. cit.; M. Westlake, 'On Course for Disaster', *Far Eastern Economic Review*, 13 October 1983, also says that 'there is a large gap in Soviet radar coverage of its northern airspace in East Asia'. Cited in Dallin, op. cit., p. 87.

73 – See above, p. 76.

74 – See above, p. 70.

75 – *New York Times*, 5 October 1983.

76 – See above, pp. 73–4.

77 – Gordon, op. cit., p. 525.

78 – Ibid.

79 – *Guardian*, 13 September 1984.

80 – *International Herald Tribune*, 13–14 October 1984. See also the similar criticisms made by a whole group of former US arms-control negotiators in C. Mohr, 'US Charges on Arms Pact Criticized', *International Herald Tribune*, 20 January 1984.

81 – W. Pincus, 'US, Soviet Easing Dispute over Siberian Radar', *International Herald Tribune*, 17 April 1985.

82 – S. Turner, *Secrecy and Democracy. The CIA in Transition* (1985), p. 88.

83 – Sampson, *Empires of the Sky*, p. 196.

84 – Bamford, *The Puzzle Palace*, pp. 137–8, 184–6. Bamford gives a figure of 33 such incidents up to 1959.

85 – Bamford, op. cit., pp. 133–46, 178–84.

86 – Bamford, op. cit., p. 145.

87 – Ibid.

88 – Ibid.

89 – C. Hitchens, 'The Crippling of Reagan', *Spectator*, 20 July 1985.

90 – *New York Times*, 6 September 1983.

CHAPTER THIRTEEN

1 – *Aviation Week and Space Technology*, 12 September 1983, p. 25.

2 – *Aviation Week and Space Technology*, 26 September 1983, p. 43.

3 – *Aviation Week and Space Technology*, 15 April 1984, p. 17.

4 – *Aviation Week and Space Technology*, 3 October 1983; *International Herald Tribune*, 3 January 1984.

5 – See above, pp. 81–2.

6 – *Guardian*, 30 August 1984. It is not known, though, whether these 'wanderers' were using the same, modern version of the INS as 007 – many older planes still lack such sophistication.

7 – *The Times*, 12 April 1985.

8 – *International Herald Tribune*, 6–7 October 1984.

9 – *The Times*, 12 April 1985.

10 – *Los Angeles Times*, 10 September 1983.

11 – C. Haberman, 'Korean Airlines Acts to Improve Image', *International Herald Tribune*, 27 March 1984.

12 – Ibid.

13 – *Asahi Evening News*, 3 December 1983.

14 – Haberman, op. cit.

15 – *New York Times*, 3 September 1983.

16 – *The Times*, 3 December 1983.

17 – *International Herald Tribune*, 3–4 September 1983.

18 – *Le Monde*, 15 September 1983.

19 – *The Times*, 3 December 1983.

20 – *International Herald Tribune*, 3–4 September 1983.

21 – *The Times*, 3 December 1983.

22 – *The Times*, 4 May 1985.

23 – S. Jameson, 'South Korea's President Chun Faces Problems on the Domestic Front Too', *Los Angeles Times*, 16 September 1983.

24 – Ibid.

25 – The following account of Reagan's tour rests heavily on the excellent accounts in *Le Monde*, 10, 13–14, and 15 November 1983.

26 – *Flight International*, 17 September 1983.

27 – S. J. Hoon, 'Slaughter of the Innocent', *Far Eastern Economic Review*, 15 September 1983.

28 – *Guardian*, 28 December 1983.

29 – *Guardian*, 18 August 1984.

30 – *Guardian*, 5 October 1984.

31 – *Guardian*, 28 June 1984.

32 – *International Herald Tribune*, 17 September 1984.

33 – *Guardian*, 28 June 1984.

34 – This paragraph is drawn from R. Owen, 'An Air of Guilt Around Moscow', *The Times*, 9 February 1984.

35 – R. Owen, 'Korean Airliner Crash Apologist Killed', *The Times*, 23 May 1984.

36 – Sampson and Bittorf, op. cit., 8 October 1984.

37 – Sampson and Bittorf, op. cit., 1 October 1984.

38 – *New York Times*, 31 August 1984.

39 – Owen, 'An Air of Guilt'.

40 – This paragraph is drawn from R. Gillette, 'Russian Pilots Urged to Ram Intruders', *Guardian*, 14 January 1984.

41 – See *Le Monde*, 11 January 1984; S. Schmemann, 'Soviet is Pressing its Case on KAL 007', *New York Times*, 31 August 1984.

42 – *The Times*, 9 April 1984.

43 – J. F. Burns, 'A Top Officer in Kremlin Dies Suddenly', *International Herald Tribune*, 23 May 1984.

44 – *The Times*, 9 April 1984.

45 – Owen, 'An Air of Guilt'.

46 – *International Herald Tribune*, 9 April 1984.

47 – Owen, 'Korean Airliner Apologist'.

48 – B. Gwertzman, 'Ogarkov's Views on Defense Seen as Clue in Soviet Shake-Up', *International Herald Tribune*, 18 September 1984.

49 – B. Gwertzman, 'KAL Flight 007: A Year Later', *International Herald Tribune*, 1–2 September 1984.

50 – R. Burt, 'The Year-Long Shadow of KAL Flight 007', *New York Times*, 31 August 1984.

51 – A. Clymer, 'US Public Holds Camp David Pact in High Regard, Poll Says', *International Herald Tribune*, 2 April 1985.

52 – M. Linton, 'US Blocking Inquiry into Jet Disaster', *Guardian*, 28 July 1984.

53 – See Chapter 5, footnote 72.

54 – For details see Sampson and Bittorf op. cit., 24 September 1984.

55 – G. Lardner, Jr, 'Authors of KAL Article Say Agent Warned of Espionage Law Violations', *Washington Post*, 3 February 1984.

56 – C. Haberman, 'KAL Victims' Families See US Holding Back', *International Herald Tribune*, 3 September 1984.

57 – Linton, 'US Blocking Inquiry'.

58 – ICAO, *Final Report*, p. 25.

59 – Ibid.

60 – ICAO, *Final Report*, p. 26.

61 – Linton, 'US Blocking Inquiry'.

62 – *International Herald Tribune*, 30 August 1984.

63 – G. C. Wilson, 'Air Force Destroyed Jet Radar Tape', *Washington Post*, 5 March 1985. The tape covered the Cape Newenham to Cape Romanzof section of the route.

64 – Ibid.

65 – Ibid.

66 – R. Chesshyre, 'Humbug and the Meese Sleaze Factor', *Observer*, 3 February 1985.

67 – See above, p. 103.

68 – M. White, 'Lawyers Raise Doubts on KAL Jet', *Guardian*, 4 September 1985.

69 – P. Shenon, 'US Denies Controllers Knew KAL Jet Had Strayed', *International Herald Tribune*, 12 September 1985.

70 – This paragraph is drawn from R. Witkin, 'Pilot Declines to Testify on Flight 007', *New York Times*, 1 November 1984.

71 – Cited by Corn, 'Fear and Obstruction on the KAL Trail'.

72 – The above paragraph relies on Corn, op. cit.

73 – Ibid.

74 – Ibid.

75 – Information gained in private interview.

76 – Ibid.

77 – Corn, op. cit.

78 – *Mainichi Daily News*, 27 November 1983.

79 – Ibid.

80 – See Allardyce and Gollin, 'The Final Moments of KAL 007'.

81 – See above, pp. 190–2.

POSTSCRIPT

1 – S.M. Hersh, 'The Target is Destroyed'. What Really Happened to Flight 007 And What America Really Knew About It, (1986) p.263.
2 – International Herald Tribune, 27 May 1985; The Guardian, 16 August 1986.
3 – Financial Times, 15 August 1986.
4 – ibid.
5 – Interestingly, the payoffs to KAL officials were much higher than those made to officials of other airlines. Thus $500,000 per aircraft bought was offered in the case of Pakistan International Airlines; $600,000 in the case of Air Zaire; $2 million in the case of Linea Aeropostal Venzolana; but $3.25 million in the case of KAL officials. These latter payments were concealed through Sampaquito Investments Ltd (Bahamas) and Jetaire Ltd (Guernsey). I. Walter, Secret Money. The Shadowy World of Tax Evasion, Capital Flight and Fraud (1985), p.28.
6 – Financial Times, 15 August 1986.
7 – Some of the following comments on Hersh are adapted from my review of his book in The London Review of Books, 23 October 1986.
8 – Indeed, Hersh was given airtime on one BBC TV programme – Newsnight – which had, at very short notice, cancelled my own appearance to discuss the KAL 007 affair just five months previously. A similar discrimination was exercised by BBC Radio 4 news programmes.
9 – Oddly, Hersh himself undermines – perhaps unconsciously – the likelihood of such a catalogue of errors being committed by a major civil airline, referring to a 1985 ICAO study of 48 accidental deviations from course in one six month period, which found that 43 were committed by private or military planes, only five by major civil airlines. Hersh, op. cit., p.183.
10 – Chatting in the studio prior to our radio debate, Mr. Hersh accepted my suggestion that we meet for a fuller discussion after the broadcast. (I was careful to ask whether his appointments schedule allowed time for this. He assured me he was free.) During the broadcast I put to him my question about his omission of the Japanese radar data. Immediately thereafter Mr. Hersh discovered that his schedule was too full to allow of any further discussion.
11 – See, for example, the interesting article by Tony Devereux, 'Taken By Stealth', Defence Attaché, no.3, 1986, pp.39-43. Thanks to atmospheric refraction even optical waves travel some 8% further than a purely geometric line-of-sight calculation would suggest, while radio waves go some 8% further still. Even without allowing for the (occasional) phenomenon of ducting, which sometimes permits radar to see many times beyond its normal range, the key development of recent years has been the computerised analysis of radar 'chaff' far beyond a strict line-of-sight horizon.
12 – Hersh reports that the US Electronic Security Command was actually able to monitor Soviet radar – to see what the Russians were seeing on their radar screens. Hersh, op. cit., pp.227-8. This would indeed be possible provided that Soviet radar data was digitally conveyed (and not by land line). It is also the key point about any 'passive probe' exercise: as Soviet radar operators radio their findings back to HQ, it is merely necessary to capture their radio transmissions to discover the complex pattern of reactions occasioned by the probe all the way back up the line to Moscow. Thus, for example, a passive probe over a quite peripheral part of the USSR could, thanks to radio and satellite monitoring, reveal a great deal about the whole Soviet air defence/communications network in the hinterland region between the periphery and Moscow. Hence a plane which 'strays' from a base in Turkey over Azerbaijan or Georgia can reveal a great deal of the southern USSR radar system to a radio operator sitting far away to the west in Cyprus. Many years ago, indeed, Cyprus operators were monitoring the effects mounted by US probes launched from

Afghanistan. (Information derived from a private communication from a former Cyprus radio monitor.)

13 – 'They bragged about it – how much they knew', reports one of Hersh's sources. Interestingly, Hersh makes no bones about the fact that the US gained 'minute-by-minute' information of Soviet responses to the 1978 KAL incursion, while apparently discounting that the same might have been true of the 1983 incursion. See Hersh, *op. cit.*, pp.13-15.

14 – Excerpts of which had already appeared in *Atlantic Monthly*.

15 – *Daily Telegraph*, 16 August 1986.

16 – Takemoto Shozo (Secretary, Association of KAL Incident Victims) 'Why The Bereaved Families Accuse the U.S.' Cyclostyled, 1986.

17 – It is perhaps worth noting that the Japanese government loyally supported the Reagan Administration. It was the SDA which retained its reservations about the incident – and which released the tell-tale radar data.

18 – As at 1.11.1986 $1 (US) = 873 won. It should be remembered that these sums are far larger than they might seem to western eyes given South Korea's far lower per capita income levels.

19 – See C. Simpson, *Lusitania* (1972).

# Bibliography

Below are listed the main sources consulted. For references to individual articles from newspapers and periodicals, readers should use the footnotes.

NEWSPAPERS
Boston Globe
Daily Telegraph
Guardian
International Herald Tribune
Japan Times Weekly
Le Monde
Los Angeles Times
Los Angeles Weekly
Mainichi Daily News
New York Times
Observer
Seattle Weekly
Sunday Telegraph
Sunday Times
The Times
Toronto Globe and Mail
Washington Post

PERIODICALS
Aerospace America
Asian Defence Journal
Aviation Week and Space Technology
Business Week (International edition)
Counterspy
Covert Action Information Bulletin
Defence Attaché
Der Spiegel
Far Eastern Economic Review
Flight International
Gendai
H du B Reports (Geneva)
The KAL 007 Information Bulletin and Newsletter
Keesings' Contemporary Archives
Le Monde Diplomatique
Listener
Nation
National Journal
New Republic

New Scientist
New Statesman
Newsweek
New York Review of Books
Nouvel Observateur
Science
Scientific American
Sekai
Spectator
South
The Economist
Time
US News and World Report

TRANSCRIPTS OF BROADCASTS

*National Radio Report*, Radio Station CKO-FM (Toronto, Ontario, Canada), broadcast at 11.30 am EDT, 5 September 1983. Tape.

*Panorama*, BBC 1 (UK), 'The Stopping of 007', broadcast at 8.00 pm, 7 November 1983. (Reprinted as T. Mangold, 'St. Reagan v. the "Empire of Evil"', *Listener*, 10 November 1983.)

ABC News, *20/20*, 'Cold War, Cold Blood' (US), broadcast 30 August 1984, show No. 432. Transcript.

ABC News, *Nightline*, 'Korean Air Tragedy' (US), broadcast on 1 September 1983, show No. 604. Transcript.

Thames Television, *TV Eye*, '007 – Licensed to Spy?' (UK), broadcast on 19 July 1984. Transcript.

BOOKS

R. C. Aldridge, *First Strike! The Pentagon's Strategy for Nuclear War* (1983)

D. Baker, *The Shape of Wars to Come* (1982)

J. Bamford, *The Puzzle Palace. America's National Security Agency and its Special Relationship with Britain's GCHQ* (1982)

R. Bonds (ed.), *Soviet War Power* (1982)

P. Bracken, *The Command and Control of Nuclear Forces* (1983)

C. W. Burleson, *The Jennifer Project* (1979)

D. Campbell, *The Unsinkable Aircraft Carrier. American Military Power in Britain* (1984)

A. Dallin, *Black Box. KAL 007 and the Superpowers* (1985)

M. de Arcangelis, *Electronic Warfare. From the Battle of Tsushima to the Falklands and Lebanon Conflicts* (1985)

J. Erickson, *The Road to Berlin* (1983)

J. Erickson, *The Road to Stalingrad* (1983)

S. Fay, *The Great Silver Bubble* (1982)

D. Ford, *The Button: The Pentagon's Strategic Command and Control System* (1985)

L. Freedman, *US Intelligence and the Soviet Strategic Threat* (1977)

T. Gervasi, *America's War Machine* (1985)

W. Green and G. Swanborough, *An Illustrated Guide to the World's Civil Airliners* (1982)

B. Gunston, *An Illustrated Guide to Military Helicopters* (1981)

B. Gunston, *An Illustrated Guide to Modern Fighters and Attack Aircraft* (1980)

B. Gunston, *An Illustrated Guide to USAF. The Modern US Air Force* (1982)

B. Gunston, *An Illustrated Guide to Spy Planes and Electronic Warfare Aircraft* (1983)

A. M. Haig, *Caveat: Realism, Reagan and Foreign Policy* (1984)

F. Halliday, *The Making of the Second Cold War* (1983)

J. Halliday, *A Political History of Japanese Capitalism* (1975)

S. M. Hersh, *The Price of Power. Kissinger in the Nixon White House* (1983)

R. W. Howe and S. H. Trott, *The Power Peddlers* (1977)

R. and L. Hurst, *Pilot Error. The Human Factors* (2nd edn, 1983)

F. Jones, *Air Crash. The Clues in the Wreckage* (1985)

J. Jordan, *An Illustrated Guide to the Modern US Navy. The World's Most Advanced Naval Power* (1982)

J. Jordan, *An Illustrated Guide to the Modern Soviet Navy* (1982)

W. V. Kennedy (ed.), *The Intelligence War. Penetrating the Secret World of Today's Advanced Technology Conflict* (1983)

R. L. Lawson, *The History of US Naval Air Power* (1985)

V. Marchetti and J. D. Marks, *The CIA and the Cult of Intelligence* (1976)

J. McMahan, *Reagan and the World. Imperial Policy in the New Cold War* (1984)

D. Miller, *An Illustrated Guide to Modern Sub-Hunters* (1984)

L. Mosley, *Dulles: A Biography of Eleanor, Alan, and John Foster Dulles and Their Family Network* (1978)

A. Pearson, *Conspiracy of Silence* (1978)

C. Peebles, *Battle for Space* (1983)

F. G. Powers, *Operation Overflight. The U-2 Spy Pilot Tells his Story for the First Time* (1970)

P. Pringle and W. Arkin, *SIOP: the West's Single Integrated Operational Plan for Waging Nuclear War against the Soviet Union* (1983)

C. Robbins, *Air America* (1979)

R. Rohmer, *Massacre 007. The Story of the Korean Air Lines Flight 007* (1984)

A. Sampson, *Empires of the Sky. The Politics, Contests and Cartels of World Airlines* (1984)

G. Segal (ed.), *The Soviet Union in East Asia. Predicaments of Power* (1983)

H. Seton-Watson, *The Russian Empire 1801–1917* (1967)

W. Shawcross, *Sideshow. Kissinger, Nixon and the Destruction of Cambodia* (1979)

SIPRI (Stockholm International Peace Research Institute), *World Armaments and Disarmament. SIPRI Yearbook 1985* (1985)

H. Smith, A. Clymer, L. Silk, R. Lindsey and R. Burt, *Reagan. The Man, The President* (1980)

J. St. John, *Day of the Cobra. The True Story of KAL Flight 007* (1984)

S. Talbott, *Deadly Gambits. The Reagan Administration and the Stalemate in Nuclear Arms Control* (1984)

S. Turner, *Secrecy and Democracy. The CIA in Transition* (1985)

US Department of Defense, *Soviet Military Power* (1983)

D. van der Aart, *Aerial Espionage. Secret Intelligence Flights by East and West* (1985)

R. Varner and W. Collier, *A Matter of Risk. The Incredible Inside Story of the Mission to Raise a Russian Submarine* (1978)

D. Wise and T. B. Ross, *The U-2 Affair* (1962)

D. Wood, *Jane's World Aircraft Recognition Handbook* (1984)

D. S. Zagoria (ed.), *Soviet Policy in East Asia* (1982)

Two other books have been published on the KAL 007 affair. One, *KAL Flight 007: The Hidden Story* (1985) by Oliver Clubb, arrived too late for me to use it in this study. There is also Kunio Yanagida's *Shoot-down* (1984), though I have been unable to ascertain that this has (yet) been translated from the Japanese.

## DOCUMENTS

ICAO, *The Convention on International Civil Aviation . . . the First 35 Years* (1979)

ICAO, *Council – 110th Session. Subject No. 14: Subjects Relating to Air Navigation. Final Report of Investigation as Required in the Council Resolution of 16 September 1983* (C-WP/7764, 2.12.83)

ICAO, *Council – 111th Session. 1818th Report to Council by the President of the Air Navigation Commission. Subject No. 14: Subjects relating to Air Navigation. Final Report of Investigation as Required by Council Resolution of 16 September 1983* (C-WP/7809, 16/2/84)

ICAO, *News Release. ICAO Council Receives Report on KAL 007* (PIO 24/83)

ICAO, *Convention on International Civil Aviation* (6th edn, 1980. Doc. 7300/6)

ICAO, *Council – Extraordinary Session. Minutes.* (Doc. 9416-c/1077. C-Min. EXTRAORDINARY (1983))

ICAO, *Assembly. 25th Session (Extraordinary). Plenary Meetings. Resolutions and Minutes.* Montreal, 24 April–10 May 1984 (Doc. 9437. A25-Res., P-Min.)

ICAO, *Assembly. 25th Session (Extraordinary). Executive Committee. Report, Minutes and Documents.* Montreal, 24 April–10 May 1984. (Doc. 9438, A25-EX)

ICAO, *The International Civil Aviation Organisation* (1983)

IFALPA, *Press Statement, 16th December, 1983. Korean Airlines Flight 007 on 1st September, 1983* (SEC/1/1-KAL RFT/NMM)

IFALPA, *To: Presidents of Member Associations. 16th December, 1983. Destruction of Korean Airlines Flight 007* (SEC/1/1-KAL LT/NMM)

# Index